# The Irish Constitutional Tradition

# The Irish Constitutional Tradition

*Responsible Government and Modern Ireland, 1782-1992*

## Alan J. Ward

*The College of William and Mary*

*The Catholic University of America Press*
*Washington, D.C.*

The paper used in this publication meets the minimum requirements of American National Standards for Information Science—
Permanence of Paper for Printed Library materials, ANSI Z39.48-
1984.
∞

This edition is not for sale in Europe, where the book is published
by Irish Academic Press, Dublin.

**Library of Congress Cataloging-in-Publication Data**
Ward, Alan J.
    The Irish constitutional tradition : responsible government
and modern Ireland, 1782–1992 / by Alan J. Ward.
        p.   cm.
    Includes bibliographical references and index.
        1. Ireland—Constitutional history. 2. Ireland—Politics and
government. I. Title.
JN1411.W37 1994
320.9415—dc20
93-16843
ISBN 0-8132-0784-3
ISBN 0-8132-0793-2 (pbk.)

# Contents

vi    Contents

# *Preface*

Although Irish nationalists engaged in abortive rebellions in 1798, 1803, 1848, and 1867, the dominant tradition in modern Irish nationalism has been constitutionalist, the attempt to solve Ireland's many problems by peaceful, constitutional means. Only for a brief period between 1916 and 1921 did revolutionary nationalism gain the support of a majority of the Irish people, and even the revolutionaries turned to constitutional nationalism when creating the first Dáil Éireann in 1919. This book is about the constitutional tradition in modern Irish political history. It concentrates on two subjects: first, the search for a constitutional relationship between Ireland and Britain, and second, the role that a particular model of government, responsible government, played in that search, and has played in independent Ireland and Northern Ireland since 1922. The two subjects are linked in significant ways and that linkage provides an important theme of the book.

I have tried to write a book that surveys Irish political history in a theoretical way useful to students, but I have also tried to make a scholarly contribution to the study of Irish history and politics. I should say at the outset, however, that there are two things this book is not. First, it is not a comprehensive political history of Ireland. By concentrating on the constitutional tradition I have necessarily excluded many of the customary cast of characters one finds in general political histories, particularly those from the revolutionary and cultural nationalist traditions. I have not considered what Emmet Larkin calls the Irish political tradition, by which he means the blending of personal, civil, political, and religious liberty in a uniquely Irish "communitarian ethos."[1] Second, the book does not contain a comprehensive account of contemporary Irish government and politics. Because it focuses on constitutions and the two central institutions of responsible government, the Cabinet and Parliament, it says very little about political parties, electoral politics, public administration, and the judicial system. What remains, therefore, is a selective interpretation of Irish political history that explores the Irish constitutional tradition by concentrating on Irish constitutional arrangements, actual and proposed. The book is rather old-fashioned in its concern for constitutions, but that is a way of saying that they have been neglected of late by political scientists.

I conducted much of my research in archives and specialized collections in Ireland and Britain. For their assistance I am grateful to the National Archives, Dublin; the National Library, Dublin; the libraries of University College and Trinity College; the Institute of Public Administration, Dublin; and the Franciscan Archives, Killiney, County Dublin. I am also grateful to the library of the Queen's University, Belfast; the Public Records Office, London; the British Library manuscripts room; and the British Library of Economics and Political Science. The book was conceived during my residency as a fellow at the Institute of Irish Studies, Queen's University, Belfast, in the academic year 1985–86, and I am particularly grateful to its then-director, Ronald Buchanan, O.B.E., for his support and friendship. I am also grateful to the College of William and Mary for providing me with the research leave that enabled me to finish the task.

In addition to these facilitators, I want to thank the many authors whose work supports portions of the book but who may be inadequately recognized in footnotes. Some are friends, but I regret that some are strangers. An incomplete list must include Derek Birrell and Alan Murie, Patrick Buckland, Basil Chubb, Joseph Curran, Ronan Fanning, Brian Farrell, Brigid Hadfield, David Harkness, John Kendle, Lawrence McBride, Lawrence McCaffrey, Oliver MacDonagh, R. B. McDowell, David Gwynn Morgan, and Catherine Shannon. Finally, I want to thank my many friends in Irish studies whose writings may not be cited often in this book but whose influence I have felt in many ways over many years, particularly Emmet Larkin and Tom Hachey, and other historians in the American Conference for Irish Studies, including James Donnelly, David Miller, and Maryann Gialanella Valiulis. In Dublin I particularly want to thank three good friends, Brian Farrell, Maurice Manning, and Ronan Fanning, who have always found time in their busy schedules to give me expert advice and information that has saved me countless hours of research.

# Responsible Government

Constitutions vary enormously in content, but at the very least each one identifies a model of government with major institutions, and rules that distribute powers between these institutions and regulate their relationships with each other and with citizens. Constitutions may also recognize certain fundamental rights of citizens and certain beliefs or principles of social policy that the state must uphold. All these elements can be found in the 1937 Irish constitution.

In 1987 the Irish Republic celebrated the fiftieth anniversary of the constitution; simultaneously, some of the personal papers of Eamon de Valera, those dealing with the constitution, were opened to the public at the Franciscan Archives, Killiney, County Dublin. These two events prompted scholars and journalists to offer their evaluations of the constitution, but the role of the Roman Catholic church in the drafting process and the principles of social policy in the document, particularly those dealing with divorce and the family, dominated the discussion. Largely overlooked was the question of whether the basic model of government provided in the Irish constitution has served the country well.

This book seeks to remedy that neglect. It concentrates on the model of parliamentary, or responsible, government currently practiced in Ireland and sets that model in a historical context. We should begin, therefore, by asking what the model is and where it comes from.

Responsible government was born in the United Kingdom. Its central characteristic is an executive drawn from members of the legislature. They retain their seats and are said to be "responsible" to the legislature. The model is variously known as Cabinet government, parliamentary government, and the Westminster model of government. The term used here is "responsible government," by which it was first known. To date, over thirty countries have secured their independence from the British Empire, and a great many of them adopted, even if some have since abandoned, responsible government. One of these was the Irish Free State, in 1922, which has the distinction of being the first state to incorporate the model into its constitutional law.

## Constitutional Rules and Responsible Government

The model of government practiced in the United States is laid out clearly in a formal document, "the Constitution," but such constitutional formality was unique in the eighteenth century. Britain, for example, had a constitution in the sense of a set of constitutional rules, but not one in the sense of a formal document, and that remains the case today.

Some British constitutional rules are defined in statutes—for example, the Parliament Acts of 1911, 1949, and 1963, which define the powers and composition of the House of Lords—but many of the most important rules have no legal standing at all. In A. V. Dicey's lectures on the constitution, published in 1885, these rules are termed *conventions of the constitution* which he described as "understandings, habits, or practices which, though they may regulate the conduct of the several members of the sovereign power, or Ministry, or of other officials, are not in reality laws at all since they are not enforced by the Courts." He illustrated their nonlegal character by referring to them as "constitutional morality." Dicey contrasted *conventions of the constitution* with *laws of the constitution* which are, he writes, "in the strictest sense 'laws,' since they are rules which (whether written or unwritten, whether enacted by statute or derived from the mass of custom, tradition or judge-made maxims known as the Common Law) are enforced by the courts."[1]

Two constitutional conventions provide the primary rules of responsible government in the United Kingdom. First, the Sovereign must appoint ministers to the government who have the support of a majority in the House of Commons. Second, while the Sovereign still controls the royal prerogatives, he or she must accept the advice of his or her ministers in exercising them.

What is true of the British constitution is also true of the constitutions of the British colonies that achieved self-government between

1852 and 1910: Australia, Canada, New Zealand, and South Africa.[2] Their constitutions from the outset were mixtures of law and convention, with convention determining the character of the executive. For example, the New Zealand constitution of 1852 assigned executive powers to the Governor, but it was the Prime Minister and Cabinet who were actually in control of the executive by 1856, although neither was mentioned in the constitution. Notwithstanding a revision of New Zealand's constitution in 1986, the rules of responsible government are still not written into constitutional law and the executive is still defined in terms of an eighteenth-century British monarchy.[3] This is true too of the Dominion of Canada, which achieved self-government in 1867, and of the Commonwealth of Australia, which achieved self-government in 1901. In both, British constitutional conventions rather than constitutional law still support the offices of Prime Minister and Cabinet.

In 1922 the Irish Free State broke from this pattern by adopting a constitution that described, for the first time in constitutional law, the British model of the executive as it actually functions. In the words of Leo Kohn, a distinguished German commentator, the Free State constitution "reduced to precise terms the conventional rules of the British Constitution."[4]

## Responsible Government

Responsible government is a model of government comprising certain constitutional rules, whether laws or conventions, and certain behaviors that follow from those rules. Broadly speaking, it has eight characteristics:

1. *Fusion of Power.* The executive, known in the Irish constitution as "the Government," is composed of members of the legislature and there is, through them, what Walter Bagehot described in 1867 as "the nearly complete fusion of the executive and legislative powers."[5] Members appointed to a government are people who already have or who must quickly find seats in the legislature.

2. *Majority Government.* The fusion of the executive and the legislature conditions what follows, because if members of the executive must be drawn from the legislature, it is natural that a majority in that body will insist on determining who exactly will form the government. It was

the recognition of this fact that marked the emergence of responsible government in Britain in 1841; once recognized, the principle quickly spread to the colonies. Responsible government therefore means that the government must be selected from the leaders of the party or coalition of parties capable of winning the support of a majority in the legislature. Furthermore, the government may continue in office only so long as it retains the support of the majority.

Majority government can only function if a government is able to leave office on losing the support of the majority. It must be replaced immediately by another drawn from the legislature, or the legislature must be dissolved to give the electorate an opportunity to select a new majority, and hence a new government. Responsible government is therefore incompatible with a fixed-term legislature. In practice, few governments resign because they lose the confidence of the legislature. They generally dissolve parliament at a time calculated to give them maximum electoral advantage.

3. *The Primacy of the Lower House.* In a bicameral legislature, which is the most common form of parliament, one of the two houses must always have primacy because a government can only be responsible to one majority, and hence to one house. The government's existence cannot depend on the support of both houses if there is any possibility that they will be controlled by different parties. At a minimum, primacy requires that a majority of government ministers, including the most important, must sit in one house, that the government must retain the confidence of a majority in that house to remain in office, and that financial legislation must originate there.

Early in Britain's constitutional history it was established that the House of Commons, the so-called lower house, which most directly represents the people and controls the supply of money, would have primacy over the House of Lords, the "upper house." In Ireland, the primacy of Dáil Éireann, the lower house, was clearly stated in the constitutions of 1922 and 1937.

4. *Party Government.* Majority government has led to the evolution of highly disciplined political parties in countries that have responsible government. If a government must resign on losing the support of a majority in the legislature, members of similar views have a powerful incentive to organize themselves into political parties and to accept party discipline in order to secure and hold power. Without the support of disciplined parliamentary parties, governments would have to de-

pend on the fluctuating whims of individual members of parliament, able to withdraw their support from day to day, and majority government would be impossible. Disciplined parties therefore developed in all responsible government legislatures before the end of the nineteenth century, and it was for this reason that attempts to diminish the importance of parties in the early Irish Free State Dáil were abandoned as impractical.[6]

A government built upon party discipline can only be defeated by an equally disciplined opposition, which must be constantly alert because an election might be called at any time. Furthermore, because the government must have the confidence of the lower house of the legislature, every vote taken there becomes a test of its right to govern. What results is a particularly competitive, and often acrimonious, style of parliamentary behavior. Instead of the continuous process of consensus building across party lines and from issue to issue, which is the American style in a loosely disciplined Congress where majority government is not at issue, we find battle lines drawn by disciplined parties treating each other as enemies.

Parties are almost never recognized in constitutions,[7] but they are certainly recognized in parliamentary practice. Opposition parties are generally consulted by governments concerning the parliamentary timetable, for example, and the leaders of major opposition parties typically receive additional salaries and allowances to aid them in performing for party business. "The Opposition" therefore has official recognition appropriate to a body of people who might be called upon to form a government at short notice.

The need for organized parties inside the legislature explains the need for organized parties outside too. National party organizations are vital for winning the elections that produce majorities in the legislature. To the interests, ideologies, and programs that draw people into parties in all democracies, therefore, we must add the organizational imperative that flows from the fusion of power and majority government in responsible government.

5. *Cabinet Government.* Governments are composed of ministers drawn from the leadership of the majority party or a coalition of parties in the lower house of the legislature. Within this governing group is a committee of senior ministers who dominate the government as a whole. Since the eighteenth century this committee has been known as "the Cabinet," a term frequently used in Ireland, although the constitu-

tion itself uses the word "Government." In contemporary Britain, where governments number almost one hundred, the Cabinet has only twenty to twenty-five members, and only in the smallest political systems, some Australian states, for example, can all the members of a government sit in the Cabinet. Responsible government is often known as Cabinet government in recognition of the role this committee plays in the management of the state. Its members sit in the legislature where their positions as leaders of a disciplined majority enable them to dominate the agenda and all major policy decisions.

Cabinet control is facilitated by two doctrines of responsibility. First, the members of the government are held to share *collective responsibility* for government policy, which is to say, *no government member may publicly dissent from a Cabinet decision.* In the eighteenth century this rule was used to prevent members of the government from being divided against each other by the King, but now it is used to augment party discipline and protect the confidentiality of government business in a very competitive political environment.

A companion doctrine is *ministerial responsibility*, which derives from the fact that ministers, as individual servants of the Sovereign, predate the Cabinet. Although members of the Cabinet are collectively responsible for overall government policy, ministers once held responsible by the Sovereign are now held responsible by Parliament for the management of their departments. Over time, however, the meaning of this doctrine has changed. Party discipline now ensures that no minister will be censured individually, and in an age of giant bureaucracies no minister can reasonably be held personally liable for every act of a subordinate. But ministerial responsibility still means that the minister speaks for the department in the legislature and is able to shield the department from parliamentary scrutiny.

6. *A Strong Prime Minister.* Someone has to lead the government and this person is the Prime Minister, known as "the Taoiseach" in Ireland. So powerful is this office in Britain that Richard Crossman, a Cabinet member himself, wrote in 1963, "The post-war epoch has seen the final transformation of Cabinet Government into Prime Ministerial Government."[8] One can argue that he was exaggerating but one cannot deny that the Prime Minister is the most important member of the government, if only because someone has to chair the committee which is the Cabinet and assign ministers to departments. The Prime Minister's power also derives from his or her role as leader of the majority in the

lower house and leader of a national political party. How the Prime Minister uses the position will vary, and no two behave exactly alike, but they are all extraordinarily powerful.

7. *A Weak Head of State.* The dominant position of the Prime Minister leaves no room for a powerful head of state. By a process of constitutional evolution the British Monarch had ceased to exercise significant independent powers by 1841, a process marked by the progressive transfer of his or her powers to a government drawn from Parliament. It is now clear everywhere that the head of state must appoint ministers who have the support of a majority in the lower house and must accept their advice in all normal circumstances.

8. *Concentration of Power.* The final characteristic of responsible government follows from all that has gone before. The model tends to concentrate political power. In the United States both Congress and the President are powerful. The precise balance between the two shifts from time to time, and from issue to issue, but in a very real sense they share power. In responsible government, power is highly concentrated in the hands of the Prime Minister and Cabinet.

There are a host of reasons for this high degree of concentration. First, the fusion of power permits the government to play a direct role in the management of the legislature. Second, the members of the Cabinet are the leaders of a disciplined majority in the legislature, a situation that allows them to insist on the passage of their programs. Third, collective responsibility produces a tightly knit executive. Fourth, responsibility allows ministers to dominate the expertise and information of the government departments they control and represent in Parliament. Fifth, power is further concentrated in the Prime Minister.

There are, of course, other centralizing forces at work in every modern society, for example, the demand for national programs of social welfare, health, employment, economic stability, and education. Furthermore, the cybernetic revolution has led to the centralization of data collection and analysis, and the modern mass media direct public attention to the leaders in our political systems. But responsible government is an independent source of political concentration, the result of the model of government itself rather than the pressures of modern life.

Such a high degree of concentration of power will strike those who think of government in terms of checks and balances, Americans particularly, as strange and threatening. However, as we shall see, it has been a characteristic of Irish constitutional thought since the nineteenth century that the state must be subject to certain constitutional restraints in its dealings with citizens. Specifically, the Irish home rule bill of 1886 would have denied Ireland the right to endow or restrict the practice of religion, a prohibition that was restated in subsequent home rule bills, the Government of Ireland Act of 1920, and the Irish constitutions of 1922 and 1937. Both constitutions also recognized certain fundamental rights of citizens and provided for judicial review of acts of the legislature. Irish courts have been particularly effective since the 1960s in protecting and extending the rights of citizens versus the rights of the state.

In time it might be necessary to add a ninth characteristic, "Legal Checks on Concentrated Government," to the generic model of responsible government presented above, but not until other countries that practice the model, particularly Britain and its former colonies, Australia, Canada, and New Zealand, have accepted Ireland's position concerning judicial review.

## The Evolution of Responsible Government

Responsible government did not appear overnight. It was the product of a long constitutional evolution in Britain and the colonies. Independent Ireland emerged only after the model had matured.

Dicey described constitutional conventions as "rules intended to regulate the exercise of the discretionary powers of the Crown" in Britain.[9] Whenever conventions failed to constrain the Monarch, Parliament was able to impose statutory constraints. In this process of constitution building, by conventions and statutes, the British constitution slowly moved through two transitions that culminated in responsible government. The first transition, which lasted from the first Parliaments in the late thirteenth century to the Glorious Revolution of 1688, was from monarchial to representative government, or limited monarchy. In this process the Sovereign was forced to share authority with Parliament. The critical event was the seventeenth-century battle for supremacy between the Stuart kings and Parliament which resulted, in 1689, in the accession of William and Mary and the adoption of the Bill of Rights which specified that the Crown might not suspend or dispense with laws, levy taxes, appropriate money, or maintain a standing army in peacetime without the consent of Parliament.

After 1689 many of the common law prerogatives of the Sovereign remained: to appoint ministers, summon and dissolve Parliament, create peers, conduct foreign relations, wage wars, give or withhold the royal assent to legislation, and so on. In the second transition, therefore, from representative to responsible government, effective control of these powers was transferred from the Sovereign to a government drawn from, and it was said responsible to, Parliament. It became clear that, by convention, the Sovereign could rule only "with the advice of," which meant "as directed by," ministers who had the confidence of a majority in the House of Commons. The Sovereign retained prerogative powers in constitutional law but they were strictly regulated by constitutional conventions. It was during this second transition that Ireland experienced the "Constitution of 1782."

John Manning Ward identifies the debate on Robert Peel's May 1841 motion of no confidence in the Whig government of Lord Melbourne as the moment when responsible government was unequivocally accepted into the United Kingdom constitution.[10] Before that time the relative powers of the Monarch and the Cabinet had fluctuated, depending on the degree to which the Monarch wanted, or was competent, to participate in the executive.[11] "[T]he development of the post of Prime Minister was hampered," John Mackintosh writes, "by the fact that in many ways the King was his own Prime Minister."[12] As late as the 1830s a determined Monarch could still prevail, within limits, on policy or the appointment of ministers, although his right to choose ministers had been challenged by the House of Commons as early as 1784.[13] The King still had the power to make a ministry, but not one that the House of Commons would not accept. That changed in 1841 when Queen Victoria lost all discretion in the matter of government formation. Parliament accepted the idea that a government that has lost the confidence of a majority in the House of Commons must resign, and that the Monarch must either appoint a ministry that does have such confidence, or dissolve Parliament to allow a general election to determine the issue of the majority.[14]

Three conditions had protected the powers of the Monarch until 1841. The first was the deference of his subjects. The second, until 1832, was an unreformed House of Commons in which a great many seats in "rotten boroughs" were controlled by the King and his aristocratic allies. The third was the very embryonic state of political parties. As late as 1830, Robert McKenzie notes, the House of Commons was so faction ridden "that it was impossible to get agreement between government and opposition as to which side had gained and which side had lost as a result of the [general] election. . . . Party organization . . . was of the most rudimentary; it consisted of a loose and sporadic cooperation between like minded people to achieve some common purpose."[15] In such a setting, the preferences of the King carried considerable weight.

The Reform Act of 1832 began to change the last two of these three conditions, and the first, deference, could not alone protect the Sovereign's powers. By eliminating rotten boroughs and enlarging the electorate the act destroyed the Sovereign's ability to determine the outcome of an election. Ward writes, "The Act left the King in command of only twenty or thirty seats at a general election. . . . The Commons took ten years to learn that it had gained the means of controlling the royal choice of Ministers."[16] By the time Walter Bagehot published *The English Constitution* in 1867 he was able to identify the central elements of responsible government, and he wrote of the Sovereign's powers: "To state the matter shortly, the sovereign has, under a constitutional monarchy such as ours, three rights—the right to be consulted, the right to encourage, the right to warn."[17] He had no doubt that the Sovereign no longer ruled. "She must sign her own death-warrant," he wrote, if the two houses of Parliament were to send it to her.[18]

The Reform Act also marked the beginning of the end of the House of Commons as, in Robert McKenzie's words, "a closed arena in which cliques and factions within the ruling classes contended for power."[19] As the electorate expanded in successive waves, in 1832, 1867, and 1884, parliamentarians had to organize popular support in order to win elections, and modern parties emerged.

Within a very few years of its recognition at Westminster, responsible government had been conceded to the most advanced British colonies, but not by the enactment of formal constitutions that embodied the model. Instead, the government instructed colonial governors to appoint ministers who possessed the confidence of the legislatures, and to act on their advice in the internal affairs of each colony. The Canadian colonies were the first to be treated in this way in the 1840s, and the New Zealand and Australian colonies followed a few years later.[20] Once responsible government was conceded, independence could not be denied indefinitely, something we should not forget when we consider Irish home rule.

One cannot do justice to a model of government in a few pages but the eight characteristics of responsible government outlined in this chapter, and the brief discussion of the evolution of responsible government that followed, will provide a framework for the discussion of Ireland in this book. They will help us to understand why the first attempt to create an independent Irish Parliament in modern times, in 1782, failed, and why the administration of Ireland under the Union after 1801 was at such odds with evolving parliamentary democracy in Britain. They will help us to understand how Irish home rule was designed by Gladstone, and how it might have worked had it been implemented in the late nineteenth century. They will help us to understand the Northern Ireland constitution of 1920, and its failure, and the Irish Free State constitution of 1922. Finally, they will help us to understand the Irish constitution of 1937 and the present system of government in the Republic of Ireland.

Part I

# Constitutional Developments
# in Ireland, 1782–1914

# CHAPTER I

# The "Independent" Parliament, 1782–1800

Independent Ireland began its life in 1922 as the Irish Free State with a constitution that embodied two contradictory principles. The first was that sovereignty resides in the people and all powers of government are derived from that source. The second recognized a monarch, King George V, as head of the Irish executive, with substantial powers drawn not from the Irish people but from the royal prerogative in English Common Law. This constitutional contradiction was forced upon Irish republicans in 1922 as the price of a negotiated independence and an end to their war with Britain. It was an anomaly to be tolerated by Ireland in the short run. For the British, however, it represented a much more important issue. It was the dying gasp in a long, anguished, and ultimately futile attempt to devise a constitutional formula that would simultaneously permit Ireland a measure of independence and protect vital British interests in the island.

Much of this book is about the constitutional issues involved in the attempt to reconcile British and Irish interests, an issue not finally resolved in Northern Ireland even today. The attempt might reasonably be said to have begun in 1171 when the Norman-English King Henry II went to Ireland to forestall the establishment there of a rival Norman-Irish kingdom. But books have to begin somewhere, and this one will resist the, admittedly very slight, temptation to trace the history of British–Irish relationships back eight hundred years. It will begin instead with a consideration of the Irish Parliament in the years 1782 to 1800, the period when the issue of the British–Irish constitutional relationship came into sharp focus. The difficulty of defining an appropriate relationship was particularly acute during this period, and the notion of responsibility, though not yet of the still evolving concept of responsible government, was at the heart of the problem. Had Ireland progressed as far toward responsible government as had Britain by 1782, its independence would have been assured. Instead, it found itself absorbed into the United Kingdom in 1801.

## Background to the "Constitution of 1782"

Henry II did not absorb Ireland into England in the twelfth century as Wales was to be formally annexed in 1536. In fact, the island was not fully conquered until 1603, and by then an Irish Parliament had existed for more than three hundred years, symbolizing the fact that Ireland was a discrete political community, a separate kingdom under the Crown and not simply an English colony.[1]

From very early times the autonomy of the Irish Parliament was undermined by attempts from Britain to dominate Ireland as a colony de facto. Britain could never accept the principle of the constitutional co-equality of two Parliaments, in large part because it was aware that a hostile Ireland would jeopardize its security, and it used three devices to manage Irish politics in the years before 1782.

The first device was the royal prerogative, the common law powers of the Crown, exercised by agents of the Sovereign. Henry II had claimed the Lordship of Ireland, and the Irish Parliament itself bestowed the title of King on Henry VIII in 1541, but the country was remote, and difficult to rule from England. It had no royal residence because the Sovereign rarely visited. Instead he or she appointed representatives, known at first as the King's Justiciar, then as his Deputy, and more recently as the Lord Lieutenant or Viceroy.

The second device used to manage Ireland was the manipulation of the Irish political class, using the influence and patronage of the Crown to reward Irish politicians for their support of British policies, particularly the Crown's requests for money. The historian W. E. H. Lecky wrote, "The lavish distribution of peerages had proved the cheapest and most efficacious means of governing Parliament."[2] Peerages were supplemented by offices and pensions; about a third of the members of the House of Commons held office with incomes from the state.[3]

After Catholics were denied seats in the Irish Parliament in 1691 the Irish political class was exclusively Protestant and rather small. The Irish House of Lords had 247 members in 1800, but about one-third rarely visited Ireland and took little interest in its affairs, and most of the rest identified with British interests, or could be "encouraged" to.[4] The Irish House of Commons had 300 members, two-thirds of whom held borough seats controlled by wealthy patrons, who traded them as property. In 1784 it was estimated that 52 peers controlled 126 seats and 61 commoners controlled a further 96.[5] A. P. W. Malcomson argues that while the British political class was too large to be manipulated as a whole, patronage and jobbery were effective in Ireland because the Irish political class was small enough to be parasitical.[6]

Edith Johnston adds that government influence in Parliament rested partly on the Irish Treasury group of M.P.'s, who held administrative or legal posts in the government, partly on members seeking legal or military advancement, partly on social climbers and peerage hunters, and largely on bribery in the form of sinecures, pensions, or local patronage.[7] But government influence also rested on a mutuality of interests. Johnston writes: "The Irish ascendancy could not maintain their position without the political and military shadow of England in the background: England, on the other hand, was faced with Ireland's strategic position and needed the tranquillity and loyalty of the neighbouring kingdom."[8] From 1691 to the Union in 1801, therefore, the relationship between the Irish Parliament and the British government, represented by the Lord Lieutenant, was one of barter: "Government . . . was not to be shared, but to be bargained with; consequently the situation between the Lord Lieutenant and the Irish politicians resembled a duel, the viceroy *versus* parliament."[9]

The third device used to manage Ireland was legislative. Two important statutes permitted Britain to control Irish legislation. The first was Poynings' Law of 1494, an act of the Irish Parliament named after the King's Deputy during the reign of Henry VII.[10] This provided that the Irish Parliament might only be summoned to consider legislation that had been requested by the Lord Deputy and Privy Council in Ireland and approved by the King and Privy Council in England.[11] Poynings' Law was supplemented by the Declaratory Act of 1719, "An act for the better securing the dependency of the Kingdom of Ireland upon the Crown of Great Britain." In it the British Parliament declared its right to legislate for Ireland, which "is and of right ought to be subordinate unto and dependent upon the imperial crown of Great Britain, as being inseparably united and annexed thereunto."[12] Britain's claim to legislate for Ireland had been asserted many times before but was challenged in Ireland, by Molyneux, for example, in 1698. The Declaratory

Act settled the matter as far as Britain was concerned. It also abolished the right of the Irish House of Lords to hear legal cases on appeal. Henceforward they would have to be appealed to the British House of Lords.

Neither Poynings' Law nor the Declaratory Act were as inhibiting as might be supposed. The impact of Poynings' Law was limited from the seventeenth century by the Irish Parliament's practice of passing "heads of bills," which Thomas Bartlett describes as "basically legislative suggestions."[13] Under this procedure, either Irish house could present a draft bill to the Irish Privy Council, but only after the Council had submitted it to London for approval could it be returned to Ireland for formal consideration. The Irish Council could amend the proposal or suppress it, as could the Privy Council in England, but this cumbersome and circular procedure did provide the Irish Parliament with a degree of legislative initiative.[14] The Declaratory Act was rarely used as the basis for Irish legislation: its power lay in its potential. Britain used parliamentary management in Ireland much more often than British legislation to effect its will.[15]

In practice, these three techniques of political management meant that Ireland, though a separate kingdom, had less political autonomy than many British colonies during the century or so before 1782.[16] Attempts to introduce a version of Poynings' Law into Virginia and Jamaica failed, for example, in the late seventeenth century,[17] and eighteenth-century colonial Americans controlled their own assemblies to a greater degree than did the Irish. "The constitutional history of the provinces in the eighteenth century," Leonard Larabee writes, "is fundamentally the history of a series of controversies between the assemblies and the prerogative in which the former won victory after victory."[18] This was much less true of Ireland until the American Revolution encouraged members of the Irish Parliament to demand their own liberation from British control.[19]

## The Constitution of 1782

The Irish Parliament had opposed Britain from time to time in the eighteenth century, particularly on requests for money, and in the second half of the century it became particularly sensitive to Irish public opinion, increasingly aroused by Britain's restrictions on Irish trade

and frequent demands for monetary contributions for military and imperial purposes. A "Patriot party" emerged in Ireland that agitated for
trade rights and government reform. It was supported in these demands
by the Irish Volunteers, a militia formed by Anglo-Irish gentry in 1778
to defend Ireland from a French invasion during the American war.
The Volunteers were effectively beyond the control of the government.[20]

In February 1782 delegates of 143 Ulster corps of Irish Volunteers,
representing perhaps twenty thousand men, met at Dungannon,
County Tyrone, to endorse an independent Irish Parliament, an independent judiciary, and religious toleration.[21] The following month the
British Tory government of Lord North was replaced for a short period
by a government led by the Earl of Rockingham, a Whig with sympa-
thies for Irish reform. In April Henry Grattan, the Patriots' leader,
moved an amendment to the Address to the King in the Irish House of
Commons in which he asserted Ireland's right to full legislative independence. He also called for the restoration of appellate jurisdiction to
the Irish House of Lords, and for the repeal of the Perpetual Mutiny
Act of 1780, by which Britain claimed permanent control of the army
in Ireland. As always in his reform speeches, Grattan was effusive in
his declaration of Ireland's complete loyalty to the British connection
through a shared Crown.[22] He rejected the American view that independence should be pressed to the point of complete separation from
the Crown.

Grattan's amendment, backed as it was by the intimidating presence
of the Volunteers, was carried without opposition. The British response was swift. In May 1782 the British Parliament repealed the Declaratory Act, with only one dissenting vote. The bill received the royal
assent in June, and in July the royal assent was given to an Irish bill
introduced by Barry Yelverton, M.P. This bill amended Poynings' Law
by removing the requirement that Irish bills must first be submitted to
the King in Council in Britain before their formal passage in Ireland.[23]
The practice of passing "heads of bills" now ceased and the Irish Parliament regained full authority to legislate for Ireland, subject only to the
royal assent. The Irish House of Lords also resumed its appellate jurisdiction and the duration of the Mutiny Act in Ireland was limited.[24]

Henry Flood, a Patriot leader, argued that the repeal of the Declaratory Act did not preclude Britain from reasserting the right to legislate

for Ireland at some future time.[25] Supported by the Volunteers, he demanded that the British Parliament renounce forever the right to legislate for Ireland. This it did in the Renunciation Act of January 1783, an act which Lecky described as "the coping-stone of the Constitution of 1782."[26]

## British-Irish Relations after 1782

With the constitution of 1782 in place, Britain now faced the same problem in Ireland that it had recently failed to solve in the American colonies: how to reconcile self-government for a dependency with the protection of British interests.[27] As a mercantilist power, Britain was determined to incorporate Ireland into its imperial economic design and to ensure that it not follow the secessionist example of the American colonies, which would have led to the piecemeal disintegration of the British Empire.[28] Britain also felt obliged to protect the Church of Ireland and the vast Irish holdings of British landowners, who were very well represented in the British Parliament. Finally, the government could not ignore the threat to Britain's physical security posed by an island that stood astride the Atlantic trade routes and had long-standing ties to hostile powers in Europe. When the British Parliament agreed to reform the constitutional relationship with Ireland, it also resolved that an agreement should be negotiated with Ireland, "establishing on a firm and solid basis the future connection of the two kingdoms."[29] It was understood in London that the British Parliament should be the only source of law on the Crown, and that the Empire should speak with one voice on defense, foreign relations, and commerce. The difficulty was to find a constitutional framework within which these objectives might be realized.

Britain had failed to solve this problem in America, but as Vincent Harlow points out, "British statesmanship in the last decades of the 18th Century was not so bankrupt in the sphere of colonial affairs as is usually depicted."[30] Harlow notes that by 1778 British advocates of conciliation with America had already "probed their way step by step towards the idea of Britain as the superintendent of a group of subordinate commonwealths."[31] Britain was prepared to negotiate a peace based on complete domestic legislative autonomy for the American colonies provided that they would accept a general superintending authority for the British Parliament in imperial matters, together with a formal agreement on trade preferences and an American contribution to imperial defense.[32]

The Americans rejected this formula, but Britain next tried to apply it to Ireland, after agreeing to Ireland's legislative independence in 1782. The Earl of Shelburne, who succeeded Rockingham as Prime Minister in July 1782, insisted that Britain should have "a superintending power . . . for all purposes of common concern whether in matters of state or general commerce."[33] The Irish would not yield on this point. Though prepared to pledge their loyalty to the British connection, they opposed any formal definition of the relationship. Grattan, for example, insisted that a shared Crown would provide a perfectly adequate bond between Britain and Ireland, and the fact that the Irish Parliament itself had voted that Irish legislation would be enacted under the great seal of Britain rather than the great seal of Ireland symbolized this connection.[34] Grattan never denied the right of the King to veto Irish legislation, only the right of the Irish and British Privy Councils to alter or suppress an act of the Irish Parliament.

In 1784 the new British Prime Minister, William Pitt, sought to use a commercial treaty with Ireland to secure the relationship that the Irish had already rejected.[35] Specifically, Pitt wanted to make British commercial concessions to Ireland conditional on an annual Irish contribution to Britain's imperial costs, a position later narrowed to a contribution to Britain's naval charges.[36] But even the Irish Chancellor of the Exchequer, John Foster, the appointee of a British Lord Lieutenant, rejected the proposition that commerce and defense should be linked. He wrote in 1785: "My opinion always was that it was the best policy to keep the commercial subject by itself, and to leave the Imperial concerns to the general unexplained but well-understood situation in which they are."[37]

Britain next sought to have an agreement emerge de facto from separate but similar pieces of legislation in the British and Irish Parliaments. This tactic failed too. Malcomson contrasts the opposing positions as follows:

The difference between the eleven Irish propositions and the twenty resolutions which emerged from the British Parliament was, in essence, that the former extended no further than the commercial relations between Great Britain and Ireland, whereas the latter extended to the commercial interrelationship of the whole British Empire—an interrelationship over which Great Britain, the constitutional sensitivities of the Irish Parliament notwithstanding, had of necessity to be the superintending power.[38]

By applying great pressure the Lord Lieutenant was able to win a narrow majority for the British position in the Irish House of Commons in 1785, but so narrowly, by 127 votes to 108, and in such a highly charged atmosphere, that Britain decided not to proceed.[39]

Britain continued to find the situation intolerable. The American colonies had been able to assert their independence, but it was inconceivable that Ireland would be allowed this choice. Lacking formal agreements on issues such as defense and commerce, and unwilling to trust to the constitutional instrument of a dual monarchy, Britain looked for other ways to control Ireland. There were some things, of course, that it could not or would not do. The British Parliament, for example, could no longer legislate for Ireland and the government chose not to advise the King to veto Irish legislation. The royal assent was only denied three times after 1782, always on minor matters.[40] Any other course would have provoked outrage in Ireland.

There were, however, things Britain could do, and the result is that in practical terms the British–Irish relationship changed very little after the constitution of 1782. The key to Britain's continuing control of Ireland was the Lord Lieutenant, who was still, R. B. McDowell reminds us, "the nominee of the British cabinet," not an official responsible to the Irish Parliament.[41] He controlled the Crown prerogative in Ireland, which extended to foreign relations and defense. In November 1783, for example, Lord North, the Home Secretary, who was responsible for Irish affairs, instructed the Lord Lieutenant, Lord Northington, not to lay peace treaties before the Irish Parliament. "If the King is to take the advice of the Irish Parliament in matters relating to war and peace, and foreign states," he wrote, "the utmost confusion must be the consequence."[42]

The Lord Lieutenant presided over every aspect of the executive in Ireland. He was assisted by the Chief Secretary. Until the appointment of Lord Castlereagh in 1798 the Chief Secretary was always English, and from 1784 he was the choice of the British government, rather than of the Lord Lieutenant himself.[43] He held a seat in the Irish House of Commons to manage government business but had no need of a majority to sustain himself in office.[44] In other words, he was not responsible to the House, and in Lecky's view, the fact that there was no ministry in Ireland responsible to the Irish Parliament was the "fatal fault in the Constitution of 1782." Of the two senior members of the Irish administration, he wrote, "They were Englishmen, strangers to Ireland, appointed and instructed by English ministers, and changed with each succeeding Administration."[45]

Above all, therefore, Ireland's subordination to Britain in the period of formal legislative independence from 1782 to 1800 was ensured by the role of the Crown and the absence of any sense of executive responsibility to the Irish Parliament. There was an enormous difference between the Crown's role in the two countries in the late eighteenth century. In Britain, the separation of powers had virtually disappeared. King George III, though still, when sane, a working chief executive, might pick his own ministers but they had to have the support of Parliament in order to ensure the passage of government legislation. In Ireland the situation was completely different. There the government did not have the support of a majority in the House of Commons. It owed its existence to the British government, and it secured votes of money and support for British policies from the Irish Parliament by using the techniques of manipulation it had practiced before the constitution of 1782. The Crown was therefore a more powerful institution in Ireland than in Britain, although it owed its power to constitutional practices that were becoming obsolete in Britain.

Britain's power was far from absolute, however. There were matters that the Irish insisted on deciding for themselves in the period after 1782. Catholic relief, for example, which Britain favored, was opposed by both the Irish Parliament and senior members of the Irish Privy Council. As a compromise, the Catholic Relief Act of 1793 admitted Catholics to the franchise but denied them the right to hold public office.[46] Britain was also opposed on the very important issues of British–Irish commercial relations in 1784–85 and the regency for the Prince of Wales in 1788–89.

On these matters, even members of the Irish Privy Council broke ranks with the Lord Lieutenant and supported what they deemed to be Irish rather than British interests. The Lord Lieutenant and the Chief Secretary came from Britain, but the remaining members of the Irish administration, the small Cabinet of "King's Servants," who included the Irish Chancellor of the Exchequer and the Lord Chancellor, were seasoned Irish politicians with an Irish agenda.[47] There were even times when their positions in the Irish Parliament, from which they challenged the Lord Lieutenant, gave them the appearance of responsible ministers. When John Foster was appointed Chancellor of the Exchequer in 1784, the Lord Lieutenant, the Earl of Northington, wrote that his was to be "a responsible office," something which Foster's biographer, Malcomson, regards as "an important constitutional and political development."[48] It was from this office, in fact, that Foster led the Irish opposition to the Anglo-Irish commercial proposals in 1784–85.

## Responsibility and the Irish Parliament, 1782–1800

Of course, Foster was not a responsible minister in the modern sense. He was selected by the Lord Lieutenant, not by a majority in the Commons, and this distinction was well understood at the time. In March 1784 Charles Sheridan, the Under-Secretary for Ireland, wrote to his brother, Richard Brinsley Sheridan, the playwright: "We have in fact no Irish governance; all power here being lodged in a branch of the English government, we have no cabinet, no administration of our own; no great offices of state, every office we have is merely ministerial, it confers no power but that of giving advice, which may or may not be followed by the Chief Governor."[49] One critic of this form of government is thought by Harlow to have been Richard Wellesley, Lord Mornington, an Irish member of the British Treasury Board who became Lord Lieutenant of Ireland from 1821 to 1827, as Marquis Wellesley. In late 1791 or early 1792 he proposed to the Home Secretary that management of the Irish Parliament should be placed in the hands of people responsible to that body.[50]

The principle of responsible ministers was also endorsed by Irish reformers such as Grattan. To make reform effective, they argued that it should be coupled with franchise reform and a substantial reduction in government patronage.[51] They proposed that the Lord Lieutenant would remain the chief executive in Ireland, as was the King in Britain, in no way dependent on a parliamentary majority for his own authority, but his ministers would be accountable to Parliament.

British governments were not convinced by such arguments, in large part because Tories believed that a responsible Irish ministry would pose a great danger to Tory interests.[52] The Regency Crisis of 1788–89 reinforced their suspicions. It arose when George III suffered a bout of insanity in November 1788 which caused the government to consider an unprecedented Regency for the Prince of Wales. There was no provision in constitutional law for such an appointment and the terms proposed for the Regency divided Parliament. The Prince was known to favor the Whigs, who argued that he should be invited by an address from Parliament to assume an unconditional regency. The Tory government proposed to appoint the Prince by identical parliamentary bills in Britain and Ireland that would contain conditions. Commissioners would be appointed to share his powers and he would be denied major patronage powers. Both houses of the Irish Parliament sided with the Whigs and on 17 February invited the Prince Regent to assume full royal powers in Ireland.[53] There was the very strong suspicion that Grattan had secured a commitment from the Whig leader, Fox, that Britain would abandon the management of the Irish Parliament by bribery and would agree to a ministry supported by Parliament. The Lord Lieutenant, Buckingham, wrote, "Grattan's language (but he is very silent) leans to the creation of an Irish responsibility."[54]

The degree of cohesion in the Irish Parliament on the regency issue was made possible by an odd alliance of members of the Irish administration, who feared that the denial of patronage to the Prince of Wales would undermine their ability to manipulate the Irish political class, and Patriots, who believed that the Whigs would support political and economic reforms in Ireland should they be returned to power with the Prince of Wales's support in Britain.

The crisis ended before either regency plan could be implemented. Buckingham refused to forward the Irish Parliament's address to the Prince of Wales in Britain, and was censured by the Irish House of Commons for his inaction, but on 20 February the news reached Ireland that George III had recovered his sanity.[55] The crisis passed, and Buckingham's successor from 1790 to 1792, the Earl of Westmorland, divided the Irish by a policy of selective amnesty while he appointed a new administration of determined antireformers.[56] Nonetheless, this crisis, which saw the British and Irish Parliaments taking quite different positions on the Crown, clearly exposed the weakness of a connection between the two countries that depended solely on a shared Sovereign, and it reinforced Tory resistance to responsible ministers in Ireland.

One of the Patriots' highest priorities was a reform of the Irish Parliament. There would have been an irresistible demand for a degree of responsibility in Ireland had the ownership of boroughs been eliminated and genuine elections been introduced, but this was something the Irish oligarchy refused to entertain. John Foster, for example, who served as the very powerful Speaker of the House of Commons from 1785 to 1800 after leaving the Irish Exchequer, controlled three seats in the House, his own for County Louth and two in the borough of Dunleer,[57] and he opposed every attack on the constitutional status quo after 1782, whether reform of patronage, representation, Catholic relief, or responsible ministers.[58] Indeed, the absence of responsibility enhanced his own power as Speaker because he, rather than a responsible Irish Prime Minister, could represent the House of Commons to the executive on those occasions when it opposed British policy.[59] But he also served as a member of the Lord Lieutenant's informal Cabinet of Irish advisers, working closely with the administration on economic policy,[60] and on the suppression of the United Irishmen in the 1790s.[61]

A party system, even if only very primitive, as in Britain, would also have strengthened the case for responsibility in Ireland. British Whigs encouraged their Irish counterparts to organize an antigovernment party after 1782, but this was never done, even in the aftermath of the Regency Crisis.[62] Indeed, Denis Kennedy argues that the Lord Lieutenant was able to exclude British party rivalries from Ireland by conciliating both Irish Whigs and Tories.[63]

In an unreformed Parliament, Grattan, who adopted a policy of consistent separation from the administration, usually found himself outvoted by more than two to one on reform, notwithstanding the name popularly attached to Parliament in the period 1782 to 1800, "Grattan's Parliament."[64] His Patriot party was never a permanent threat to the administration and its support fluctuated enormously. For example, a bill providing that treaties be laid before the Irish House of Commons was defeated by a vote of 9 to 128 in 1794.[65] A "responsibility bill," introduced in 1790 with the aim, its proposer said, "effectually to secure the responsibility of the servants of the crown in different departments of the executive government of Ireland to the parliament thereof," was defeated by a vote of 86 to 147.[66] The Treasury, or Responsibility, Act of 1795 was intended to bring the issuance and expenditure of public money under a Treasury Board responsible to Parliament, but it fell far short of parliamentary control. Parliament acquired some superintending power, but the appointment of Treasury officers remained with the Lord Lieutenant, who alone had the means to discipline them.[67]

The truth is that the reform movement was never strong enough to win parliamentary reform. Parliamentary independence was won in 1782 because of the intimidating support of the Irish Volunteers, but Parliament itself always rejected the Volunteers' demands for parliamentary reform. There were also divisions among the Patriot leaders themselves that made it difficult for them to maintain consistent positions, or to cooperate with the British Whigs, from whom they might have secured greater self-government.[68] They were divided on the wisdom of the Renunciation Act of 1783, for example, with Flood proposing and Grattan opposing the bill.[69] And while Grattan supported Catholic relief, Flood opposed it.[70] Some of the Patriots also accepted public office. Barry Yelverton, for example, who moved the amendment of Poynings' Law in 1782, became Irish Attorney General later that year and was raised to the peerage in 1800 for his support of the Union.[71]

For a number of reasons, therefore, it proved impossible to reform the Irish House of Commons by abolishing the system of owned seats, extending the franchise, or eliminating office and pension holders from Parliament. Such reforms would certainly have generated pressure for a new kind of Irish executive, with ministers supported by a parliamentary majority, as in Britain. In the absence of reform, the Irish Parliament was, in Johnston's phrase, "an uneasy, separate and irresponsible partner in the administration of the country."[72]

In Britain, William Pitt, the Prime Minister, favored a moderate measure of reform for Ireland; the extension of the franchise to Catholics in 1793, to conciliate Irish Catholics during the French war, passed at his urging, but he would not push reform very far. Indeed, he moved quickly to stop it when Whigs, led by the Duke of Portland, joined him in a coalition government and insisted that one of their number, Lord Fitzwilliam, should be sent to Ireland as Lord Lieutenant. Fitzwilliam arrived in Dublin in January 1795, determined to bring a "purified administration" to Ireland. He ignored Pitt's instructions by soliciting support from Grattan, dismissing most senior office holders, and supporting Catholic emancipation. He was peremptorily dismissed in February, when Pitt insisted: "All idea of a new system of measures, or of new principles of government in Ireland, as well as of any separate and exclusive right to conduct the department of Ireland separately from any other in the King's service is disclaimed and relinquished."[73]

## The Union

Britain's fears for its ability to control Ireland grew in the 1790s as agrarian violence spread; the United Irishmen, an organization founded in 1791, turned from radicalism to revolution; and the French sent a large invasion fleet to Ireland in 1796. This invasion failed, but a smaller attempt succeeded for a short while in 1798. Policymaking necessarily gravitated to London in these circumstances because of Ireland's need for arms and money. In 1797 the British had to loan Ireland £150,000[74] and by 1800 the army in Ireland had grown to sixty thousand men.[75] But by 1798 Britain's policy appeared to be failing, and its interests in Ireland had not been secured. Pitt therefore decided to use the Crown's patronage to secure the Irish Parliament's approval for a union that would give Britain the security it sought.[76] With the possibility of two Parliaments exercising separate powers on war and peace, he asked, "Can we really think that the interests of the empire, or of its different branches, rest upon a safe and solid basis at present?"[77]

It took Pitt two attempts to achieve his end. When the bill to establish the Union was defeated by 109 votes to 104 in the Irish House of Commons in 1799, he raised the reward. The gentlemen of Ireland accepted his new terms the following year, by a vote of 158 to 115.[78] However, it was not bribery alone that brought about the Union. As Bolton argues, after defeating Pitt's Union bill in 1799, the Irish anti-unionists had no agreed-upon alternative solutions for Ireland's plight. Those who were committed to parliamentary reform and Catholic emancipation, for example, were a minority. The majority retained the ascendancy values that had provoked the United Irish rebellion in 1798 and had opened Ireland up to the French. Pitt knew that the Protestant oligarchy's position was untenable in the long run but he recognized that restricting their powers by parliamentary reform would make the Irish Parliament unmanageable from Britain.[79] In the British House of Lords a former Chief Secretary, Lord Grenville, warned that a genuinely independent Irish Parliament might refuse to vote supplies for war, and might apply pressure on the King in his choice of ministers, a reference to responsibility in the British sense.[80] In the circumstances, Bolton concludes, Union was "the sole adequate solution of the dilemma."[81]

On 1 January 1801 the Union of Great Britain and Ireland began, but it is tantalizing to recall two cases of "what might have been." First, had the Irish Parliament accepted the conditions on its independence that Britain wanted to impose by treaty after 1782, Ireland would have taken on the character of a self-governing British colony. In that case, responsible government, and its corollary, independence, would surely have come to Ireland, as it came to other self-governing colonies, Australia, Canada, and New Zealand, in the mid-nineteenth century. Whether a self-governing Ireland, governed initially at least by Ascendancy Protestants, could have addressed its many problems any better than did the Union is something we can never know.

Second, for a short while during the drafting of the Act of Union the British government entertained the possibility of creating a subordinate assembly in Dublin that would elect Irish members of the Union Parliament and serve "for the purpose of all Irish business, canals, roads, etc."[82] Had that concept been pursued, Ireland would have had a kind of home rule parliament in 1801.

# CHAPTER 2

# The Incomplete Union and the Repeal Movement, 1801–1847

The Act of Union should have simplified the constitutional relationship between Britain and Ireland because the two countries were now governed under a single Crown by a single Parliament. The reality is that the Union failed abysmally as a constitutional device because it was approached in a strange way that did little to eradicate the sense that Ireland was a separate political community. From 1801 to 1921 Ireland was governed by a mixture of colonial and parliamentary government that was at odds with the concept of responsible government as it had finally emerged by midcentury. In this chapter I will consider the governmental structures established by the Union, their failure, and the reform movement for Irish self-government led by Daniel O'Connell in the nineteenth century.

## The Irish Executive under the Union

The British government paid very little attention to the future character of Irish administration when it drafted the Act of Union. It was much more concerned with the financial terms of the Union and the composition of the Union Parliament.[1] As a result, the pre-Union Irish administration continued intact after 1800, including the offices of Lord Lieutenant and Chief Secretary. McDowell records that they presided over twenty-two Irish departments in the early years of the Union, and that there were also several branches of United Kingdom departments in Ireland.[2]

Three officials competed for executive powers in Ireland in the early years of the Union: the Home Secretary, who was already responsible

for Scotland and Wales, the Irish Chief Secretary, and the Lord Lieutenant. Since 1782 the Home Department had been the principal office in
London for Irish affairs;[3] after the Union the incumbent Home Secretary, Pelham, anticipated that he would assume even more responsibility.[4] He believed that the Chief Secretaryship was redundant and that
the Lord Lieutenancy in Ireland could be reduced to the very minor
role it played in the English counties.[5] But the new Lord Lieutenant,
Hardwicke, had other ideas: he insisted that the unsettled state of Ireland called for a Viceroy with substantial discretionary powers and the
right of direct access to the Cabinet.[6] Pelham resigned in 1803 and
Hardwicke's interpretation appeared to prevail for a time, but eventually it was the Chief Secretary rather than the Lord Lieutenant who
became the most important Irish minister.

Before the Union the Chief Secretary was appointed by and was subordinate to the Lord Lieutenant.[7] He lived in Dublin and managed the
government's business as a member of the Irish Parliament. After the
Union his role was not immediately clear, and the fact that nine Chief
Secretaries were appointed between 1801 and 1812 did nothing to sta-
bilize the office.[8] Edward Brynn describes the quandary: "Was the
Chief Secretary henceforth to be the 'efficient' minister for Ireland or
merely an assistant to the Home Secretary? Was he responsible to the
Home Secretary or to the viceroy? Should he reside in London or in
Dublin?"[9] The answers to these questions evolved in practice. Because
the Chief Secretary was appointed by the United Kingdom government,
lived for much of the year in London, and was entrusted with the management of Irish affairs in the House of Commons, his power grew at
the expense of the power of his competitors,[10] particularly after the
young Robert Peel was appointed Chief Secretary in 1812. With the
support of the Prime Minister, Lord Liverpool, Peel was able to assert
himself in the administration.[11] Shipkey writes, "His greatest achieve-
ment as Chief Secretary was to ally his office with the Lord Lieutenancy
in a coordinated partnership, investing the latter with the pomp and
ceremony while delegating to his own office much of the exacting, routine work of administration which betokened the actuality of power in
Irish politics."[12]

By 1831, when the Chief Secretary entered the Cabinet for the first
time,[13] it was clear that he was a very important member of the government, and his deputy in Dublin, the Under-Secretary, had also gained
in importance,[14] but there was as yet no rule or convention that the

Chief Secretary would always prevail over his formal superior, the Lord Lieutenant. It was never clear, for example, which one would sit in Cabinet: it depended on the status of the individual and the temper of the government. The Conservative Prime Minister Arthur Balfour appeared to settle the matter finally in 1905, after a new Chief Secretary, Walter Long, insisted that the minister responsible to Parliament should be the effective head of the government in Ireland. Long expected the Lord Lieutenant, Lord Dudley, to act on his advice. Balfour agreed, and told Dudley that he would have the social and legal status of a constitutional monarch. He explained: "The 'tightening up' of the doctrine of Cabinet responsibility, the Union, and finally, the telegraph, have now transferred the real headship of the Irish government to the Minister who happens to be in the Cabinet and in the House of Commons."[15] Balfour's decision appeared to be definitive, but in the troubled year 1919 Prime Minister Lloyd George appointed Lord French to the Lord Lieutenancy, giving him enormous powers as military governor of Ireland, and he and the Chief Secretary, Edward Shortt, sat alternately in the Cabinet.[16] Thus ambiguity existed throughout the period of the Union.

The Lord Lieutenant, always a peer, occasionally spoke for the government in the House of Lords,[17] but spent most of his time in Ireland where he performed many executive functions that the representative of the Crown had performed before 1801. The Act of Union made no mention of his role, and he continued as before to be appointed by Letters Patent from the Crown in the style of a Governor-General, with important statutory and prerogative powers, including control of the instruments of law and order.[18] The Irish Privy Council similarly continued in being until 1922 as an administrative body because the Lord Lieutenant operated in many matters by Order in Council, an order issued by the Sovereign on the advice of the Privy Council. The Council also retained a judicial function.[19]

Several circumstances conspired to prolong the Lord Lieutenancy and the autonomous Irish administration. One was the continued separation of the British and Irish exchequers after 1800. For some time the two countries were left to service their own debts and maintain separate currencies and duties on trade.[20] Their exchequers were not combined until 1816.[21] It took thirty years to settle jurisdictional disputes concerning other departments of government that had been left unresolved by the Act of Union.[22] Nonetheless, by the early 1820s Ireland could have been administered by the Home Secretary or a new Secretary of State for Ireland had the country not been continuously threatened by disorder. This, above all, protected the Lord Lieutenancy.

Until 1815 the United Kingdom was at war with France, a country that had encouraged the Irish to rebel in 1798. Ireland also experienced serious agrarian violence, the work of secret societies such as the Ribbonmen and the Whiteboys. As Jenkins notes, "In contrast to those in Great Britain, the rural disturbances in Ireland were persistent, extensive, destructive, and savage. The smaller island seemed to be forever teetering on the brink of anarchy."[23] In the early years of the Union Britain believed that a Lord Lieutenant with broad discretionary powers, including control of the army, could better police Ireland than a secretary of state operating from London. As Lord Lieutenant Whitworth commented in 1814:

The great object is not to lose sight of the Distinction to be made between England and this part of Her majesty's Dominions. . . . The character and spirit of the governed are completely different. . . . It is only by a protecting force that the magistrates can be encouraged to do their Duty, and by an imposing one that the lower orders can be kept down.[24]

Whitworth's argument could have been repeated for most of the period of the Union because violence, or the threat of violence, was a preoccupation of every politician charged with Ireland until 1921.

If it could be argued seriously that the Lord Lieutenant had special, burdensome responsibilities, particularly in regard to maintaining law and order, then it followed that he should have considerable status, and this status added to the difficulties of abolishing the office. He was, after all, the representative of the Crown. He was invariably an aristocrat with a distinguished record of public service, and because his position had not been redefined in 1801, he continued to preside over an elaborate vice-regal court in Dublin.[25] Many of the Lords Lieutenant who served between 1801 and 1921 had also held Cabinet positions before their appointments to Ireland.[26] Such men could not be treated as ceremonial figureheads.

We must also remember that the members of the Irish Protestant ruling class quickly moved from opposing the Union in 1800 to supporting it. The quasi-colonial form of government was very much to their liking because it allowed them to continue to dominate Irish public offices. In 1823 Joseph Hume, M.P. for Aberdeen, who introduced bills in Parliament to abolish the Irish executive in 1823, 1830, and 1844, protested that "Protestant Ascendancy-men . . . absorbed nearly the whole patronage of the [Irish] government."[27] One of the reasons often cited in Parliament for retaining a separate Irish administration was that it enabled the Irish gentry to place their sons in public employment in Ireland;[28] this was the argument of a class long conditioned to patronage as a *right*. This Protestant dominance continued well after Catholic emancipation had destroyed its legal basis in 1829, so that for most of the period of the Union the senior levels of the Irish executive were the near-monopoly of Protestants. Even Peel was embarrassed by the Irish administration's failure to bring Catholics into its ranks in the 1840s,[29] but there was a pronounced fear of admitting them to power in a country almost continuously ravaged by violent protest from the Catholic community.

The continuance of the Irish executive was a serious defect in the system of responsible government that emerged in the United Kingdom in the 1840s. To the extent that authority and responsibility are not coterminous, responsible government is denied, a truth frequently noted by opponents of the Irish executive. In an 1850 parliamentary debate, for example, Bernal Osborne, M.P., complained that it was often unclear who was the responsible minister for Ireland: "Sometimes the Lord Lieutenant controlled the Chief Secretary. Occasionally the Chief Secretary controlled the Lord Lieutenant. Sometimes the Under-Secretary controlled both."[30] In 1857 J. A. Roebuck, M.P. who had moved the abolition of the Lord Lieutenancy, pleaded with the House of Commons, "Do away with the Lord Lieutenant; appoint, if you please, a real Governor for Ireland, and, above all, make him responsible to this House."[31] And in 1860 Edward Cardwell, M.P., said that an Irish administration in which the Lord Lieutenant had the powers, effectively, of a Secretary of State, was "not so constituted as to meet the requirements of the parliamentary system."[32]

Motions were introduced to abolish the Irish executive in 1823, 1830, 1844, 1850, 1857, and 1858,[33] but only in 1850, when it was introduced by the Prime Minister himself, Lord John Russell, did the measure pass the House of Commons. Russell had written in 1847:

A separate government—a separate court—and an administration of a mixed nature, partly English and partly Irish, is not of itself a convenient arrangement. The separate government within fifteen hours of London appears unnecessary—the separate court a mockery—the mixed administration the cause of confusion and delay.[34]

In 1850 Russell conceded that at the time of the Union there had been a need for an Irish executive who could "apply all the means of war against any enemy,"[35] but Ireland could now be controlled from London in any contingency. It was already only hours away by railway and steamship, and the electric telegraph was soon to reduce communications to a few minutes. Russell proposed that the powers normally exercised in Ireland by the Lord Lieutenant should be exercised directly by the Crown from London, and the powers of the Chief Secretary should be assigned to a new Secretary of State for Ireland sitting in the House of Commons.[36] He said, "I think no one will deny that, upon general principles, the two countries being united, there ought to be one single administration."[37] He found the relationship between the Irish and United Kingdom administrations clumsy, and even absurd, and he said that "to have the chief in Ireland, and his secretary in the Cabinet a concurrent party to giving orders to the Lord Lieutenant his own chief, is, in principle, most objectionable."[38]

Russell's motion was approved by 170 votes to 17 on its second reading[39] but was abandoned by the government because, McDowell writes, "the government's legislative programme was in a state of congested confusion."[40] However, the bill had also encountered strong opposition from Tories in the House of Lords, where the Duke of Wellington stressed the importance of having a Lord Lieutenant with command of the army in Ireland. "If we look at the history of the last fifty years, and more especially at the history of the last ten years," Wellington argued, "we shall find a continued series of military operations carried on at every period of that time."[41] Without a Lord Lieutenant the chief civil authority in Dublin would be the Lord Mayor, and Wellington asked if anyone in London would have tried to organize military operations in Dublin when Daniel O'Connell held that office. He added, "The Secretary of State conveys the commands of the Sovereign; but the Lord Lieutenant commands himself. He has that power by law, by patents, by usages and prescriptions."[42]

Given the Tories' permanent advantage in the House of Lords, Wellington's view prevailed; although new motions to abolish the Irish executive were introduced in the House of Commons in 1857 and 1858, they lacked government support and were defeated. It was invariably the case that there was almost no support for reform among the Irish members. Even those who supported the repeal of the Union wanted the Irish executive to continue because it distinguished the Irish political system from the British one. Daniel O'Connell, who criticized the influence of Irish Protestants in the Irish executive, nonetheless argued that the Lord Lieutenancy, if filled by a person of high rank, "would have an influence over factions which it would be in vain to expect from a government of clerks."[43]

Reform of the Irish executive was doomed in Parliament but it continued to be discussed inside the government into the early 1870s when it became temporarily enmeshed in the troubling issue, for both Queen Victoria and her government, of what to do with the Prince of Wales. When proposing the abolition of the Irish executive in 1850, Lord John Russell had said that the Queen would visit Ireland from time to time to provide the ceremony of royalty, and would maintain a residence in Phoenix Park.[44] A variant of this notion was revived during Gladstone's first administration (1868–74). In a memorandum to the Prime Minister dated 28 June 1871, Lord Kimberly, a former Lord Lieutenant, criticized the Lord Lieutenancy which, he said, "keeps up the notion that the Government of Ireland is separate from the Government of the rest of the Kingdom, and that Ireland is some sort of dependency upon Great Britain. It interferes with the unity of the Administration." As a substitute Kimberly suggested that a member of the royal family might live in Ireland for several months a year, but for ceremonial representation only because any role in government would undermine the "responsible advisers."[45] In October 1871 H. Y. Thompson, private secretary to the Lord Lieutenant, Lord Spencer, argued the same case. "The Lord Lieutenancy," he wrote, "ought to be abolished as a mark of national inferiority and colonial dependence." It simply reminded Irish nationalists that there once had been an Irish Parliament. Spencer called for regular visits to Ireland by members of the royal family. "For the Lord Lieutenant residing as the Queen's Representative in Dublin," he wrote, "I would substitute an Irish Balmoral, and nothing more."[46]

Gladstone put the case for combining the abolition of the Irish executive with periodic visits to Ireland by a member of the royal family to a very skeptical Queen Victoria in June 1871, and seems to have won her over, though not to the acquisition of a royal residence in Ireland or to visits by the Prince of Wales. Of the Prince, Gladstone wrote, "She mentioned considerations of health, of time, of character."[47] But nothing came of the idea in Gladstone's first ministry. Subsequent Conservative governments were unsympathetic to the idea and in the 1880s even Liberal party support disappeared because Gladstone invented a new role for the Lord Lieutenant. He would be the formal head of a responsible Irish executive under home rule.

## Failures of the Union

In a constitutional sense, then, the Union was incomplete. When combined with the appalling economic distress of Ireland, the perpetuation of the Irish executive helped create the irresistible impression that Ireland was not only badly governed from Britain, it was overgoverned too.

An argument made during the Union debates, by the Prime Minister, Pitt, among many others, was that the Union would lift Ireland out of poverty, ignorance, bigotry, and religious prejudice. Catholic emancipation, Pitt believed, could not be conceded in an independent Ireland without endangering the connection with Britain and the security of the Protestant minority, but within the United Kingdom it could proceed without risk.[48] Had Pitt's predictions been fulfilled, the history of Ireland would have been very different, but the reality, of course, is that the Union brought little relief to the Irish in any area of their lives, and particularly not to the rural poor, perhaps 75 percent of the Irish population.[49] Even Catholic emancipation, which Pitt had sought to tie to the Act of Union,[50] was delayed until 1829, and thereafter Catholics continued to be subject to substantial disabilities.[51]

The continued distress experienced by the Irish, and the almost continuous protests and violence it provoked, meant that the Union, which had been introduced to relieve Britain's insecurity, soon imposed enormous burdens on parliamentary government. Ireland received one hundred seats in the House of Commons and seats for thirty-two representative peers in the House of Lords, but it was never integrated into the British administrative or legal systems and it required special legislation on every conceivable issue throughout the period of the Union: rural distress, the poor law, local government, transport, land reform, the Church of Ireland, law and order, and much more. Ireland even had its own set of franchise reforms, six in all in the nineteenth century versus only three in Britain.[52] Parliament had no choice but to attend to these manifest problems. Toward the close of the 1823 parliamentary session Peel, then Home Secretary, informed the House of Commons that forty-nine of its eighty-four business days had been "appropriated" for Irish business.[53] Jenkins notes that in the first thirty years of Union, more than one hundred commissions and sixty-one committees investigated Ireland.[54] The United Kingdom found itself involved in every aspect of Irish life.

The heart of the problem was lack of agreement about the causes of Ireland's appalling predicament and what to do about it. Some argued that only reforms would produce domestic tranquillity, but others insisted that tranquillity must precede reform and would only be produced by firm repression. Some argued that rural violence was the result of economic distress, but others saw it as the product of political demagoguery or clerical agitation. There were disputes over whether the Catholic and Protestant secret societies should be suppressed equally. There were some who argued that Catholic emancipation would lead to demands for the repeal of the Union and the disestablishment of the Church of Ireland, and others who argued that only emancipation would produce a loyal Catholic population. Opinion in Britain was so divided on emancipation that governments were divided even among themselves. Tory Cabinets agreed, Jenkins writes, to "a collective neutrality [on Ireland] which permitted individuals to speak and vote their consciences in Parliament."[55] From 1818, the government deliberately appointed Lords Lieutenant and Chief Secretaries who disagreed with each other on the issue of Catholic emancipation. And lurking in the background of every debate on Ireland were the ghost of Adam Smith and the still living presence of Thomas Malthus. The provision of relief by the state, they taught, would create a dependent and indolent peasantry. The natural laws of the market and human reproduction should therefore be allowed to operate, free of state intervention.[56]

It is not surprising, therefore, that despite all the parliamentary and ministerial attention paid to Ireland no coherent Irish policy emerged apart from the almost continuous attention paid, of necessity, to curbing rural violence. The outcome was the growth of a Catholic nationalist movement based on massive disaffection, committed to the notion that the Irish should be allowed to govern themselves.

## Catholic Nationalism and the Repeal Movement

It was only with the emergence of Catholic nationalism that Irish representatives at Westminster began to organize coherently in support of Irish causes. In 1801 Ireland was assigned 100 seats in the United Kingdom House of Commons, a ratio of Irish to British seats of 1:5.5. The British thought this a reasonable compromise between the population ratio of the two islands, 1:2.5, and the ratio of Irish to British contributions to imperial expenditures, 1:7.5.[57] The number of Irish seats was raised marginally to 105 in 1832, in the face of Irish demands for a doubling of representation. It was reduced to 103 in 1870 only to be raised again to 105 in 1918. On a population basis Ireland was underrepresented in Parliament in 1801, but a hundred years later, after its population had been halved by death and emigration and Britain's population had grown, it was overrepresented. The transition to overrepresentation coincided with the expansion of the franchise, particularly in 1850 and 1884–85,[58] and the rise of Irish nationalist parliamentary politics. In the prereform years early in the century, before Catholic emancipation, Irish M.P.'s identified with Protestant ascendancy interests, but by the end of the century they were predominantly Catholic nationalists agitating for self-government.

Modern Irish nationalism has its origins in the Catholic Association, founded in 1823 by Daniel O'Connell to secure the right of Catholics to hold public office. The Association was a successful coalition of Catholic peasants and middle-class Catholic gentry. The latter had been able to vote since 1793, but could not hold office. From 1824 peasants were mobilized by the Catholic clergy to support the Catholic Association with penny-a-month "Catholic rents" collected after Sunday mass.[59] The substantial sums raised in this way and by subscriptions supported the costs of publications, legal defense, parliamentary lobbying, elections, and the Dublin headquarters. The association so mobilized Catholic voters that O'Connell himself won a by-election in County Clare in 1828 for a parliamentary seat that he, as a Catholic, could not take, and in 1829 the Tory government finally conceded Catholic emancipation.

Emancipation did not quell demands for political change from the Catholic community. Oliver MacDonagh describes the circumstances of the time in this way:

The constitutional implications of the Act of Union were by now fully apparent. On the one hand, the Protestant interest as a whole had moved on to support the Union; a quasi-colonial government for Ireland, in the form of a lord lieutenancy and its surrounding apparatus, had, contrary to the original expectations, been retained; and successive British cabinets had opted for a species of "indirect rule" based upon a privileged position for, and the near-monopoly of office and favors by, the loyalist minority. On the other hand, the Catholic Relief Act of 1829 had weakened and, in a limited sense, even broken into this redoubt.[60]

Roy Foster adds, "Protestants adhered to their monopoly of offices and influence. If the Union had been complete, Catholics would have been given access to the spoils system of the United Kingdom. As it was not, they could not; and they found another route."[61] That route was Irish nationalism and O'Connell's campaign for the repeal of the Union which he began on entering Parliament in 1830.

From the beginning of the repeal campaign there was confusion about what O'Connell meant by "repeal" and what constitutional relationship he envisaged for Ireland and Britain. "On constitutional issues," Kevin Nowlan writes, "such as the relations between Great Britain and Ireland in the fields of foreign and military policy and the degree of independence to be enjoyed by an Irish executive under the Crown, [O'Connell] was often vague."[62] Isaac Butt, a Conservative member of the Dublin Corporation in 1843, complained that O'Connell never described precisely what repeal meant, whether a return to the settlement of 1782, or something new.[63]

O'Connell's imprecision had several explanations. The most important, for a pragmatic politician, was probably the chronic lack of support he had to endure in the House of Commons, even from Irish members. The general elections of 1830 and 1831 ended the Tories' control of Ireland,[64] but O'Connell and the repeal movement were not the sole beneficiaries. Emancipation had been coupled with a punitive change in the franchise that reduced the Irish electorate from 216,000 to a mere 37,000. The Irish Reform Act of 1832 expanded the number of Irish seats to 105 and increased the Irish electorate, but only to 92,000—in a population of about 8 million. A property qualification ensured that M.P.'s would continue to be drawn from the landed gentry and aristocracy, whether Catholic or Protestant.[65] Tories continued to hold about one-third of the Irish seats after 1832, with strong representation in the northeast, while pro-Union Whigs and O'Connellite repealers shared the remaining seats. After the election of 1832 O'Connell led a group of 39 Irish members committed to repeal,[66] 13 of them Protestants,[67] but in 1835 his group won only 34 seats,[68] and in the 1841 general election, only 18 repealers were elected, as against 47 Whigs and 40 Conservatives.[69] When, with great reluctance, but under pressure from his supporters in Ireland, O'Connell moved in the House of Commons for a parliamentary committee to inquire into the effects of the Union in 1834, he lost the vote by a massive margin, 532 to 38, with only 1 English supporter.[70] Since repeal was clearly a nonstarter, O'Connell had little reason to formulate a precise repeal proposal.

O'Connell also knew that reform in Ireland would only emerge from negotiations with the British government, and it therefore had to be on Britain's terms. A specific proposal was unnecessary until there was some indication that the British were ready to deal. Furthermore, any proposal would have divided the repealers, many of whom were much more doctrinaire separatists than O'Connell himself. MacDonagh compares O'Connell in this sense to Charles Stewart Parnell, the next great Irish nationalist leader. "They were at one," he argues, "in being 'comparative separatists,' who recognized that the degree of separateness would be determined ultimately in Great Britain, and who committed themselves to no abstraction or ideal form of state."[71]

Pragmatism meant that O'Connell argued the case for repeal primarily in terms of the social and economic failures of the Union, not in terms of the romantic virtues of Irish nationality, a most important source of friction with the Young Ireland movement in the 1840s. It also explains why, in Nowlan's words, "The issue of the repeal of the Union seldom took on an absolute character in O'Connell's public speeches."[72] In an abstract sense, O'Connell believed that only an Irish Parliament could really be trusted to redress the injustices done to Ireland. In 1839, for example, he wrote, "It is my deep conviction that even if it were possible that Ireland could be well governed by an Imperial Parliament, it is to the last degree improbable that she should be so governed." Britain was so ignorant of Ireland, and its antipathy such a "powerful admixture of hatred and contempt," that reform at its hands was highly improbable.[73] But O'Connell also intimated many times that were Britain to undertake a genuine program of reform in Ireland—addressing tithes, the franchise, and local government, for example—repeal would become unnecessary and Ireland would be able to accept a place in the Union.[74] He was prepared to work with the

Whigs in this spirit, and he justified the "Lichfield House Compact" with them in this way in 1835: "I am as much a Repealer as ever I was but I see the absolute necessity of confronting those who say we prevented the Union from having a fair trial in the hands of a friendly Ministry, and also of giving a decisive check to Orangeism."[75] In 1836 he went so far as to say, "The people of Ireland are ready to become a portion of the Empire. . . . they are ready to become a kind of West Britons, if made so in benefits and justice, but if not, we are Irishmen again."[76] It was only when the Tories were returned to office in 1841, and all hope of reform had died for the moment, that O'Connell turned from parliamentary to popular agitation, and to a repeal campaign modeled on the great emancipation campaign of the 1820s. It culminated in the great "Repeal Year" of 1843[77] but was aborted when O'Connell was arrested for criminal conspiracy. He was subsequently convicted in 1844, but won on appeal to the House of Lords. But by then his campaign had lost its momentum.[78]

Even during his time on the hustings in 1843 O'Connell refused to commit himself to a detailed constitutional plan for Ireland, but this should not mislead us. One can detect, in his statements through the years, a pattern of support for a *limited* form of self-government. His position can be stated as follows: The Union had been procured by fraud. It had resulted in substantial underrepresentation for Ireland in the House of Commons. It had been accompanied by coercion and martial law, and had left the country destitute. Ireland could not expect reform from an unsympathetic Britain, and the Act of Union had therefore to be annulled so that Ireland might have, as O'Connell said in 1831, "a local legislature to attend to local interests."[79] "Self government," he wrote in 1832, "is necessary everywhere, but Ireland cannot subsist without a local and domestic legislature."[80] In 1839 he wrote, "I can entertain but little expectation of deriving any substantial benefits for Ireland, save by a Domestic Legislature."[81]

The key words are "local" and "domestic." O'Connell did not believe that an Irish legislature need mean Ireland's complete separation from Britain. Rather, permitting Ireland to address its own domestic problems would avert unrest and preserve the link with Britain.[82] "I will prevent the war and preserve the connection," he promised in 1831.[83] In Bath that year he said, "We only want a Parliament to do our private business, leaving the national business to a national assembly." He also added a federal dimension. Both Britain and Ireland should have local legislatures, which would leave the United Kingdom Parliament at Westminster free to deal with matters of concern to the Union as a whole, matters such as war, peace, imperial affairs, and foreign relations.[84] To emphasize Ireland's loyalty to the Crown in such an arrangement, the full title of the repeal organization that O'Connell launched in April 1840 was the Loyal National Repeal Association. No irony was intended.[85]

We still have to ask what O'Connell meant by "a local and domestic legislature." It certainly did not mean a return to the *status quo ante* 1801, which O'Connell dismissed as "simple repeal." As early as June 1813 he said, "I desire the restoration of our Irish parliament; I would sacrifice my existence to restore to Ireland her independent legislature; but I do not desire to restore precisely such a parliament as she had before. No: the act of restoration necessarily implies a reformation."[86] Simple repeal in 1813 would have restored the Ascendancy Parliament of 1782, something O'Connell clearly did not want, hence the necessity for a "reformation." By the repeal year of 1843, however, dramatic changes in the constitution had fundamentally changed what simple repeal might achieve. In 1782 a corrupt Protestant oligarchy controlled the Irish Parliament and the British government controlled the Irish executive, but the reform of Irish representation in 1801, which eliminated Ireland's rotten boroughs, together with Catholic emancipation in 1829 and the maturing of responsible government in Britain by 1841, meant that by 1843 repeal would have produced an independent Irish Parliament dominated by Liberals and repealers, many of them Catholics. More important, the Lord Lieutenant would have been obliged to accept the advice of Irish ministers responsible to the Irish Parliament, not to the British government. The only remaining constitutional link with Britain would have been a Crown that had lost its powers to command. Simple repeal of the Act of Union would therefore have produced an Ireland in 1843 with the status of an independent British dominion, a constitutional form the self-governing colonies were not to achieve until the next century.

It is inconceivable that O'Connell did not realize the significance of the constitutional changes wrought by emancipation, franchise reform, and responsible government. Richard Davis states, for example, that the decision to extend responsible government to Canada in 1842 had an electric effect in Ireland because of its implications for repeal.[87] Yet O'Connell persisted in rejecting simple repeal and endorsing the local and domestic Irish legislature he had supported in Parliament in 1831. His address, "To the People of Ireland," which the Repeal Association adopted on O'Connell's motion in June 1843, stated, for example:

Our objects . . . are these—the restoration of a separate and local parliament for Ireland—the restoration of the judicial independence of Ireland. The first would necessarily include the making of all laws that should be of force within the entire precincts of Ireland—by the Sovereign, the Lords, and the Commons of Ireland, and to the total exclusion of any other legislature from any interposition in affairs strictly Irish. The second would necessarily include the final decision of all questions in litigation by Irish tribunals seated in Ireland, to the total exclusion of any species of appeal to British tribunals.[88]

The precise relationship with Britain that would follow repeal was not treated in the address, but it is clear that the Irish Parliament which O'Connell envisaged would have had only domestic jurisdiction, "within the entire precincts of Ireland."

O'Connell's position, that Ireland should have limited self-government, not the substantial independence being given to the colonies, was perfectly consistent with his federalist plan of 1844, his most specific proposal for the future government of Ireland. It would be wrong to dismiss this plan as an aberration adopted for tactical reasons: it had too much in common with O'Connell's long-standing endorsement of a domestic legislature to support that conclusion. In an open letter to the Repeal Association in October 1844, O'Connell expressed "a preference for the Federative plan, as tending more to the utility of Ireland, and to the maintenance of the connection with England than the mode of simple Repeal." The letter argued that federalists and repealers shared a great deal. They were each determined "at all hazards, to preserve the connection between Great Britain and Ireland, through the means of a sole executive, and the golden link of the Crown." They were agreed on the need to repeal the Act of Union prior to the reconstitution of the United Kingdom. They were agreed that there should be a new Irish Parliament, which O'Connell proposed should have a House of Commons with three hundred members, elected on a household franchise. They were agreed that this parliament should have the power "to enact all laws to be of force in Ireland; in short, that it should be an efficient parliament for all legislative, financial, and judicial purposes, within Her Majesty's realm of Ireland." They were agreed that it should have no foreign policy, defense, or imperial powers. Indeed, federation would have, O'Connell insisted, the great advantage over repeal of providing "for questions of Imperial, colonial, military, naval, and of foreign alliance and policy, a congressional or federative Parliament, in which Ireland should have her fair share and proportion of representation and power."[89] Before 1800 Ireland had lacked a role in governing what one federalist now called the "Hiberno-British Empire."[90]

In the letter to the Repeal Association O'Connell continued his attack on simple repealers. He insisted that they would have Ireland return to a status that offered the country less, in the sense of less participation in United Kingdom affairs, than did federation. "The simple Repealers," he also wrote, "are of the opinion that the reconstructed Irish Parliament should have precisely the same power and authority which the former Irish Parliament had."[91] This was an unfair and disingenuous attack because by 1844 the reestablished Parliament of 1782 would have been a genuinely sovereign parliament, not the restored, discredited legislature of the years 1782 to 1800. The attack therefore confirms O'Connell's long-standing preference for some form of local assembly in Ireland rather than an independent Irish Parliament.

This is not quite what O'Connell always said in public, of course. He dissembled. In a statement to the Dublin Corporation in 1843 he said that he would never *ask* for anything less than a sovereign Irish legislature, "but if others offer me a subordinate parliament I will close with any such authorized offer and accept that offer."[92] In fact, the evidence of other public statements through the years suggests that he would have been delighted to settle for less than Irish sovereignty. The advantage of a federal plan is that it would have enabled Ireland to have a Parliament of its own, one that was neither sovereign nor subordinate because the essence of federalism is that the federal and provincial legislatures are coordinate. In his federalist letter O'Connell proposed that the Irish Parliament should have coordinate powers with the British Parliament in a new United Kingdom federation, the whole structure being sanctioned by a new constitution.

O'Connell's espousal of federalism did not win the support of Irish federalists, men such as Sharmon Crawford, an Ulster landlord, who distrusted his style of leadership and would have nothing to do with his proposals.[93] In fact, O'Connell found almost no support anywhere for his plan.[94] Most of his colleagues in the repeal movement were hostile to federalism, and his support of federalism led to the first clear, public criticism of O'Connell by the Young Irelanders.[95] Whig and Tory leaders were similarly unimpressed. Nowlan argues that they saw federation as a modest, more plausible, and therefore more dangerous plan than simple repeal.[96] With no allies, O'Connell quickly abandoned his new position, but he had no alternative to offer.

The federal controversy shows how fragile O'Connell's support really was, and how difficult it was to propose a clear program of reform that would have widespread appeal. The controversy also clarified a fundamental challenge to O'Connell's leadership in the repeal movement which might be dated to October 1842. In that month the *Nation* began publication as the literary vehicle of a significant splinter movement of young repealers, the Young Irelanders.[97] They attacked O'Connell for his willingness to compromise on repeal by entering a parliamentary alliance with the Whigs, and for his apparent indifference to Irish nationality, which they defined in Gaelic terms. Charles Gavan Duffy, the first editor of the *Nation*, rejected the federal plan because it unacceptably limited Ireland to local concerns and excluded many of the greatest concerns of any nation, including trade and defense. The *Nation* overcame an early willingness to share in "the common exigencies of the empire"[98] and by 1844 was arguing that "[a] share in the British Empire would be an insecure, mercenary, passionless and wicked partnership."[99] O'Connell was both a royalist and an imperialist but many in the Young Ireland movement were Anglophobic anti-imperialists who wanted no part of empire.

Despite a rhetoric of romantic and revolutionary nationalism, the Young Irelanders campaigned in practice for the simple repeal of the Act of Union by Parliament. Nowlan argues that they were no more successful than O'Connell in defining the connection that would exist between Britain and Ireland after repeal,[100] but in reality they needed no plan. They knew that the British constitution had changed dramatically since 1801 and that responsible government would soon give the Kingdom of Ireland the freedom to act independently. Nowlan himself quotes from an 1845 essay by the Young Irelander Michael Joseph Barry, which describes the implications for Ireland of the 1782 constitution if combined with responsible government:

Now, an Irish minister responsible to the Parliament of Ireland only would not advise the Sovereign to declare war, *on the part of Ireland*, except when sure of the approbation of the Irish Parliament; and, on the other hand, would advise such a step, when he was certain of its approval, notwithstanding, the British minister might oppose such a declaration, *on the part of England.*[101]

In the period 1782 to 1800 British governments had rejected the notion that Ireland and Britain, as separate kingdoms under the Crown, might be allowed to have different foreign and defense policies, and they rejected it again in the 1840s. "Interesting as an exercise in political speculation," Nowlan notes, "such an advanced theory was most unlikely to appeal to any section of Tory or Whig opinion in mid-nineteenth century England."[102]

Simple repeal was absolutely out of the question, therefore, but so too was what O'Connell preferred, his "local and domestic" legislature. It was less that the idea was consciously rejected by Britain than that it was not understood or considered in the 1840s. It was premature. Home rule had not yet been named and British politicians debated Irish self-government as if it necessarily meant the restoration of a dual monarchy that would threaten the integrity and security of the British Empire. What would happen, O'Connell's greatest parliamentary opponent, Sir Robert Peel, asked in 1834, if the British and Irish legislatures were to disagree on issues of war, foreign relations, commerce, the debt, or the Crown? Recalling the overthrow of James II in 1688 and the Regency Crisis of 1788, he said, "There have been only two occasions in modern times in which a difference between the two countries, as to the rights of Sovereignty could by possibility have occurred, and on both it did occur."[103] Without the Union, Peel argued, England would be reduced to the condition of a fourth-rate power in Europe. This was still his view in 1843 when he said he would rather face civil war in Ireland than imperial disintegration,[104] and in 1844, when he argued that the Union was necessary to "preserve the security of the Empire."[105] He refused to consider the possibility that O'Connell's plan for a domestic parliament might offer an alternative that could secure the Union.

Given his long-standing commitment to a limited form of self-government, why did O'Connell persist in using the deceptively simple language of "repeal of the Union"? MacDonagh suggests that repeal gave unity to O'Connell's career.[106] What he espoused in 1801 he still appeared to espouse in 1843, and repeal fitted comfortably in an age of single-issue, populist campaigns, whether opposing slavery and the corn laws or favoring Catholic emancipation and parliamentary reform. MacDonagh continues, "Repeal also lived on quite another plane; in fact its natural habitat was the ideal."[107] Ideals are rarely realized, of course, and O'Connell knew this truth perfectly well. Repeal was, therefore, less a specific proposition than an invitation to the British to negotiate.

But why should the British negotiate? The O'Connellites had very little support in Parliament and were never in a position to win a vote, or demand repeal as a condition for supporting a government. In these circumstances other impulses determined British policy, one of which was widespread suspicion of O'Connell in Britain. His demagoguery; his espousal of the adult, male franchise and the secret ballot; and his leadership of a mass movement tied, Britain insisted, to recurring violence—all threatened the stability of society in Ireland and the integrity of the Union. The Ascendancy's political monopoly had been broken in Ireland, but not its hold on the land, and O'Connell threatened this too because of his commitment to tenants' rights. Finally, O'Connell's campaign for Catholic emancipation had refocused the religious dimension of British–Irish relations in a threatening way. Roy Foster notes, "It is ironic that Catholic emancipation appears in British terms as an important step in secularizing the state, but in Ireland laid the foundation of politics as interpreted in terms of confessional identification."[108]

In the end the repeal movement was killed less by British repression than by its own contradictions, and by the overpowering influence of the Great Famine of 1845 to 1849, which disturbed every aspect of life in Ireland. In July 1846, after O'Connell had put his parliamentary party behind a successful Whig challenge to Peel's government,[109] the Young Irelanders seceded from the Repeal Association, wanting no further part in parliamentary politics. They formed the Irish Confederation in January 1847.[110] A few months later, in May, O'Connell, whose health had been failing for several years, died in Genoa, on his way to Rome. His son John succeeded him as leader of the thirty-nine repealers elected to Parliament in August 1847,[111] but the party disintegrated in 1848. That year the Irish Confederation itself split[112] and a faction, led by William Smith O'Brien, prematurely, and with deplorably little aptitude, staged a rebellion that was easily suppressed.[113]

Popular history is always selective, in Ireland as elsewhere, and this is particularly true regarding Irish nationalism. The Young Irelanders entered the pantheon of Irish patriot heroes with their rising in 1848, but the commitment they and the United Irishmen of 1798 had to a nonsectarian Ireland is largely ignored. O'Connell also entered the pantheon as "the Great Liberator" of Irish Catholics, but his commitment to a constitutional link with Britain and his belief in parliamentary politics is similarly neglected in the popular mind. His attempt to combine mass organization with parliamentary politics inspired his successors in the constitutional tradition, as did his belief that Irish nationalism might be accommodated within a constitutional framework that included Britain, but as Trench points out, "To the vast majority of those who thronged his mass meetings, repeal meant driving the Saxon into the sea and taking back the lands the Saxon had usurped."[114] It was this revolutionary misrepresentation of O'Connell's position that successive British governments feared in every Irish nationalist movement.

# CHAPTER 3

# Home Rule, 1870–1914: The Legislation

The small size of O'Connell's parliamentary party, never more than 39 in an Irish delegation of 105, its lack of party discipline in Parliament, and the overwhelming rejection of repeal by British politicians meant that repeal was always doomed. However, when O'Connell turned to an alliance with Whig governments in order to secure at least some improvements for Ireland, he opened himself to the Young Irelanders' charge that his nationalism was conditional. Similar weaknesses were apparent in the Independent Irish party, the parliamentary wing of the Irish Tenants' League, in the 1850s. Forty-eight of the Irish M.P.'s elected in 1852 pledged themselves to support no government that would not commit itself to the reform of tenants' rights, but they lacked strong leadership, party discipline, and support in Britain. The party was also undermined by the opposition of Paul Cullen, Archbishop of Dublin, who feared that any form of Irish nationalism would provoke British repression.[1] It was not until the 1870s, under the leadership of Isaac Butt, that constitutional nationalists were able to assemble the elements of a campaign that could no longer be ignored in Britain. It included a powerful mass organization, which was reorganized in 1882 as the Irish National League, a highly disciplined Irish Parliamentary party, with strong leadership and the support of the Roman Catholic clergy. It was known as the home rule movement, a term that requires some elaboration.

## Devolution and Home Rule

John Kendle has pointed out that the terms "home rule," "federalism," "federal home rule," "home rule all round," and "federal devolution" were used interchangeably during the home rule debates, but they have discrete meanings that should not be confused.[2] Irish *home rule* was an example of *devolution*, a system of government in which a central legislature creates *subordinate* regional assemblies to which it devolves responsibility for regional affairs. The central legislature retains responsibility for matters of concern to the state as a whole, such as defense and foreign relations, and it can withdraw or redefine the powers of the regional assemblies at any time. In the nineteenth century devolution was practiced by Britain in its relations with its self-governing colonies. The term "home rule" was primarily identified with devolution to Ireland, but several Scottish home rule bills were also introduced in Parliament during the Irish home rule campaign years, from 1886 to 1914, and again in 1978. The phrase "home rule all round" was used to describe a comprehensive plan of devolution to regional legislatures in England, Ireland, Scotland, and Wales. *Federalism* refers to a constitutional system in which a central legislature and regional legislatures exercise *coordinate* powers, the two levels of authority being defined in a constitution that can only be revoked or amended by extraordinary means, not by ordinary legislation. As in home rule, the regional legislatures have responsibility for regional affairs and the federal or central legislature for foreign affairs, defense, and the Crown, but the regional legislatures are not subordinate. During the home rule debates federalism was associated with the United States and Canada, and from 1901 with Australia. The terms "federal home rule" and "federal devolution," each of which combined the incompatible concepts of federalism and devolution, were oxymorons.

Most proposals for Irish self-government after 1870 were devolutionary, no matter that some were called "federal." They included Gladstone's minimalist proposal in 1880 that regional legislation should be considered in parliamentary committees composed of members of Parliament from the region,[3] his 1882 proposal for purely administrative devolution to four provincial councils,[4] and Irish nationalists' demands for full domestic self-government.

It is ironic, given their dissatisfaction with every home rule bill, that home rule was devised by Irish nationalists themselves, most of whom would have preferred something more ambitious than devolved power. They recognized, however, as did O'Connell, that independence was out of the question and that a local or domestic Parliament was the most they could reasonably hope to secure from the United Kingdom.

They were able to convince Gladstone of home rule's merits by the end of 1885, and since then it has been the preferred strategy of all United Kingdom governments faced with the disintegrative threat of regional nationalism. It was the constitutional basis for the home rule bills of 1886 and 1893, the Government of Ireland Acts of 1914 and 1920, and the Scotland and Wales Acts of 1978.

Home rule has been popular through the years because of its supposed advantages over its competitors: secession, federation, or an unsatisfactory status quo. Home rule permits the population of a region to make policies for itself that are appropriate to the region. It brings government closer to the people and diminishes the sense of alienation from government produced by distance. It relieves the United Kingdom Parliament of an enormous burden of regional legislation, but reserves sovereignty to that body, thereby averting the possibility that the United Kingdom and its regions might adopt conflicting policies on important matters. Finally, because Parliament devolves power by ordinary law, home rule avoids the major reconstruction of the constitution that federation requires.

Despite these apparent advantages, the devolution bills introduced in the United Kingdom Parliament all had serious flaws. These were apparent as early as 1886, and were still apparent in 1978, when the Scotland and Wales Acts were rejected by referenda in those regions.[5] Governments have always resorted to devolution to escape from political problems and their proposals have invariably had the character of compromises forced by political pressures. For example, Irish home rule was introduced in 1886, 1893, and 1912 to forestall Irish separatism and placate the Irish Parliamentary party, on which the Liberal party depended for a majority in the House of Commons. John Vincent writes that, to Gladstone, "Home Rule was an expedient to adopt lest worse befell."[6] The Government of Ireland Act of 1920, with its provision for two Irish Parliaments, north and south, was designed to solve the Irish problem without provoking Ulster into civil war. The Scotland and Wales Acts of 1978 were designed by the Labour government to thwart the growth of nationalist parties in two regions the Labour party must dominate if it is to form a government. Thus home rule has always been proposed as a solution to a particular political problem, not as a reasoned and comprehensive plan to refashion the British constitution in a way deemed worthy in itself. Furthermore, home rule has always been addressed to problem regions and never, in a parliamentary bill at least, to the United Kingdom as a whole. "Home rule is not a constitutional remedy," Arthur Balfour rightly argued in 1914, "it is a parliamentary device."[7] It is not surprising, therefore, that nationalists have always disputed home rule bills as inadequate.

Of all the devolution bills between 1886 and 1978, only the Government of Ireland Act of 1920 went into effect, and that only partially, in Northern Ireland. I will discuss that act separately because of its importance to Northern Ireland. In this chapter I will consider only the first three Irish bills, those introduced in 1886, 1893, and 1912. The 1886 bill was defeated by 311 votes to 341 after the defection of 93 Liberal unionists in the House of Commons. Gladstone resigned following the defeat and in the subsequent general election the Conservatives were returned to power with a majority of 118, including the support of the Liberal unionists. Gladstone returned to office in June 1892, once again with the support of the Irish party that by this time had been split into Parnellite and anti-Parnellite factions by the O'Shea divorce scandal, in which Charles Stewart Parnell, the party leader, was cited as a corespondent. The second home rule bill was introduced in February 1893. It passed the House of Commons by a vote of 307 to 267, but was soundly defeated in the House of Lords by a vote of 419 to 41. In 1894 Gladstone resigned in favor of his Liberal colleague, Lord Rosebery. In 1895 the Tories assumed power and led Britain for ten years. The Liberals returned to power in 1905 and were confirmed with a clear majority in the general election of January 1906. They had temporarily set home rule aside in 1900 and their overall majority in the House of Commons from 1906 to 1910 enabled them to govern without Irish support.[8] There was no reason, therefore, to bring the issue forward until the general election of January 1910, when Prime Minister Asquith unequivocally committed his next government to home rule. The election on January 1910 put the parliamentary balance decidedly in Irish hands. The Liberals returned 275 members, the Conservatives 273, Irish nationalists 82, and Labour 40. A second general election in 1910 confirmed the Liberals' dependence on Irish votes in the House of Commons. The Liberals and Conservatives each won 272 seats, Irish nationalists won 84, and Labour 42.[9]

Asquith introduced the third home rule bill in 1912, after the passage of the Parliament Act of 1911. The act eliminated the House of Lords' veto by providing that a bill that passed the House of Commons three times in successive sessions would become law over the opposition of the House of Lords. Home rule passed this test between 1912 and 1914 but then met with enormous resistance from Ulster unionists. Just as World War I was looming in Europe, the unionists threatened civil war in Ireland. The Government of Ireland Act, 1914, received the royal assent but was immediately suspended for the duration of the war, and was subsequently abandoned.

The fact that home rule reached the statute book in 1914 but was stolen by the unionists' threat of civil war has led historians to concentrate on the act of theft, rather than on the quality of the property that was stolen. The questions with which this chapter and the next deal, therefore, are the following: were the home rule bills introduced in 1886, 1893, and 1912 good or bad, and were they capable of solving the Irish problem within a constitutional framework acceptable to Britain and both communities in Ireland? In the remainder of this chapter I will consider the evolution of the home rule movement between 1870 and 1914, and the provisions of the three home rule bills introduced in those years. In chapter 5 I will evaluate home rule by considering the home rule debates.

## Isaac Butt and the Rebirth of Constitutional Nationalism

Daniel O'Connell and the Irish federalists had come very close to defining home rule for Ireland in the 1840s, but it was left to Isaac Butt and his successors to clarify and promote the concept. Butt was a Conservative member of the Dublin Corporation in the 1840s. As a barrister he defended Young Irelanders changed with sedition, and as a member of Parliament supported tenants' rights between 1852 and 1865.[10] In May 1870 he formed the Home Government Association for "the restoration to Ireland of that right of domestic legislation, without which Ireland can never enjoy real prosperity or peace."[11] Although he had been very critical of Daniel O'Connell thirty years earlier, Butt now echoed O'Connell's arguments. Irish radicalism, he insisted, was the product of British misgovernment, and only a domestic Irish Parliament would have the competence to legislate for Ireland. By resolving Ireland's grievances with home rule, self-government would protect the Union and the British Empire.[12]

Butt was still a conservative, and most of the founding members of the Home Government Association were Protestants who shared his view that the Protestant gentry should participate fully in Irish self-government. In November 1873, after a national conference attended by nine hundred delegates in Dublin, the Home Government Association became the Home Rule League, with the support of more than twenty Irish members of Parliament. It quickly presented a constitutional plan for Ireland that recommended that "domestic legislation" should be devolved to an Irish Parliament. The Imperial Parliament would retain responsibility for matters affecting the Crown, foreign relations, defense, and the empire.[13]

In 1874 fifty-nine homerulers were elected to Parliament and an Irish Parliamentary party was formed by Butt with members pledged to support home rule.[14] The party specifically avoided a commitment to tenants' rights because it wanted the support of the conservative Protestant gentry,[15] but it failed to win them over. The strength of the new party came largely at the expense of the Liberal party, which began its slide to extinction in Ireland with only twelve victories in the 1874 election. The Conservatives won thirty-two seats, twenty of them safe seats in Ulster. The electorate was dividing itself into Irish nationalists and Conservative Ulster unionists. The 1874 election provided the Conservatives with a strong majority in the House of Commons and they remained in government until 1881, but during that time the Irish party gained the support in Ireland and the discipline in Parliament that enabled it to demand Irish self-government as the price of its cooperation with a Liberal government a few years later.

In 1870 the Home Government Association proposed what it called "a Federal Union for England, Scotland and Ireland," but it refrained from offering a complete plan. "That must come," it declared, "with the authority of a United Ireland."[16] Butt was less wary than his colleagues in the association and published his own federal plan in 1870. It was very much like O'Connell's plan of 1844 and was justified in much the same way.[17] Federation, Butt argued, would enable Britain to recognize Ireland's separate existence within the general framework of the Union, would relieve the United Kingdom Parliament of much work, and would permit Ireland to participate in imperial affairs. Butt recommended the establishment of domestic Parliaments for England, Ireland, and Scotland. The Irish Parliament, for example, would consist of the Queen, the Irish House of Lords, and a 250-to-300 member elected House of Commons. It would have "supreme control in Ireland except in those matters which the Federal Constitution might specifically reserve to the Imperial Assembly."[18] Butt wrote, "The Imperial Parliament ought plainly to be the great Council of the Empire, with which should rest the constitutional right of advising the sovereign on all questions of peace and war, and of the foreign relations of the country."[19] He proposed that the Queen should be represented in Ireland by the Lord Lieutenant, who would act on the advice of Irish ministers on all Irish matters, as was the practice, he suggested, in Australia or Canada.[20] This was an authentic federal proposal and Butt preferred that it should result from a new United Kingdom constitution. However, he was prepared to accept devolution, with a subordinate Irish Parliament, should that be the decision of the United Kingdom Parliament.[21]

Butt never introduced his comprehensive scheme to Parliament and only discussed devolution in general terms when moving three motions in the House of Commons. The first was an amendment to the Address on the Queen's speech, in March 1874, which he lost by 50 votes to 314.[22] The second was a resolution put forward in June 1874 to establish a committee of the whole house to consider relations between Britain and Ireland.[23] If established, Butt proposed that the committee examine the following resolution:

That it is expedient and just to restore to the Irish Nation the right and power of managing all exclusively Irish affairs in an Irish Parliament; and that provision should be made at the same time for maintaining the integrity of the Empire and the connection between the Countries by reserving to this Imperial Parliament full and exclusive control over all Imperial affairs.[24]

Prime Minister Gladstone attacked Butt's proposals as premature, and the Attorney General for Ireland, Dr. Ball, presented a list of specific criticisms of points that Butt himself had not made.[25] Ball argued that Ireland could not be permitted to control the law of property, the police, or commercial relations with Britain. He insisted that Protestants in the north of Ireland would never agree to the Catholic majority controlling education in the island,[26] and he concluded with what would be the central argument against home rule in later years, that once in existence the Irish Parliament would want to expand its powers. In other words, home rule would lead to Irish independence. Butt certainly did not support an independent Ireland. However, in his 1870 essay on federalism he had opened himself to the charge of fomenting separatism by suggesting that devolution would provide a framework within which Ireland could evolve peacefully. "No-one could guarantee an eternal Union of two countries," he wrote in 1870, and "the hour of separation might come."[27]

In June 1874 Conservatives and Liberals joined in voting down Butt's motion to create a parliamentary committee, by 61 votes to 458. Two years later to the day, he introduced a resolution for a select committee to consider self-government for Ireland, and lost again, this time by a vote of 61 to 291.[28] By then, however, he was about to face a fundamental challenge to his leadership.

## Parnell, Gladstone, and Home Rule

Many members of the Irish party wanted a much more aggressive campaign for Irish self-government than Butt was waging. Charles Stewart Parnell and Joseph Biggar were prominent in the use of parliamentary rules to obstruct the governments' business in the House of Commons, much to Butt's annoyance.[29] When he died in 1879 Butt had already been eclipsed by Parnell as the effective leader of the Irish party, although Parnell was not elected to the leadership until after the general election of March 1881. Meanwhile, in October 1879 Parnell helped Michael Davitt launch the Irish National Land League, a mass organization dedicated to the reform of tenants' rights. The League practiced civil disobedience in the middle ground between constitutional and revolutionary nationalism. In 1880 Parnell traveled to the United States where he cooperated with the revolutionary Clan na Gael to raise money. Irish-Americans soon became the major source of funds to pay election expenses and subsistence allowances to Irish members of Parliament, and there was a steady stream of fundraising trips to North America by the leaders of the Irish party.[30] Although no revolutionary himself, Parnell was prepared to court the support of men more violent than he, and like O'Connell he became associated in the British public mind with violence in Ireland.

Sixty-one homerulers were elected in 1881, and as their new leader Parnell substituted strong party discipline and parliamentary obstruction for Butt's more gentle persuasion. He abandoned Butt's policy of trying to conciliate Ireland's Protestant gentry and set out to woo the Catholic middle class. The Catholic church also came to his support because of his agreement to allow clerical control of all levels of education.[31] Parnell's relations with the Land League also identified the Irish party firmly with the interests of tenant farmers; in 1881 he was imprisoned for eight months for his part in the land movement. The League was banned but its successor, the Irish National League, founded in 1882, became the popular arm of Irish constitutional nationalism.[32]

The decisive parliamentary breakthrough for Parnell and his party came after the 1884–85 Irish Reform Act, which increased the Irish electorate by half a million, from 4.4 percent to 16 percent of the population. In June 1885 the Irish party voted with the Conservatives in Parliament to force Gladstone to resign, and in the subsequent general election, held in December, eighty-six homerulers were elected, eighty-five from Ireland and one, T. P. O'Connor, from Liverpool. Though a Protestant himself, Parnell now controlled a Catholic-based party, the first modern, mass, disciplined, political party in parliamentary history. Furthermore, the party held the balance in the House of Commons. There were 249 Conservatives, 86 homerulers, and 335 Liberals. Parnell held the key to whether Gladstone and the Liberals would replace the Conservative caretaker government of Lord Salisbury, which had held office since June 1885.[33] As Roy Foster puts it, "The Parliamentary Party could now deliver,"[34] but they bided their time.

Parnell and Gladstone began to discuss a plan of home rule some time before the Liberals took power in 1886. In September 1885, for example, Gladstone agreed to support "every grant to portions of the country of enlarged powers for the government of their affairs,"[35] but he was in no hurry to embrace home rule specifically or publicly. He did not want to be seen to be bribing the Irish, and rather hoped that the Conservatives would devise a home rule plan that the Irish nationalists could accept, and which would relieve him of an issue that threatened to divide his own party.[36] As late as August 1889 Gladstone was still advising Parnell that "the Irish party ought to hold itself independent of British Liberalism, in order to be in a condition to accept Home Rule for Ireland from the Tories ... without our consent or even knowledge."[37]

Gladstone's public neutrality was strained in December 1885 when his son, Herbert, disclosed that the Liberal leader was prepared to endorse home rule,[38] but it was not until late January 1886, after the Conservatives had decided to suppress the Irish National League, that Parnell threw his support to the Liberals. The caretaker government of Lord Salisbury fell on 27 January and Gladstone's second ministry took office on 3 February, without yet formally committing itself to home rule.[39] On 8 April, however, the Prime Minister introduced his first Government of Ireland bill in the House of Commons. "Our inefficient and spurious coercion is morally worn out," he said. It was time to discuss "how to reconcile Imperial unity with diversity of legislation." It was also time, he said, to "stand face to face with what is termed Irish Nationalism. . . . I hold that there is such a thing as local patriotism, which, in itself, is not bad, but good."[40]

## The Unionist Response

Home rule posed the most significant challenge to date to the Act of Union although the terms of the Union had already been fundamentally altered. In 1800 the Union was a bargain struck between the Irish Protestant oligarchy and Britain which the Protestants anticipated would preserve their religion, property, and status, in return for their assent to the Union. By 1886, however, there had been a steady erosion of their position. Parliament had legislated Catholic emancipation, enlargement of the franchise, disestablishment of the Church of Ireland, and land reform. More reform was to come during the years of the home rule controversy, much of it passed under Conservative governments that held power between 1895 and 1905. Local government reform in 1898 and the 1903 land act, which enabled Irish tenant farmers to purchase their land, were two important examples, and in 1908 the Liberals established the National University of Ireland, a Catholic institution.

These enormous changes in Irish life led the unionists to cling more firmly to what was left: the Union itself. Given the reforms, they could see no material reason for the continuance of Irish nationalism in anything but a benign cultural form. Arthur Balfour, for example, the Conservative Prime Minister from 1902 to 1905, believed that economic and social grievances, not political ones, were at the heart of the home rule agitation; Catherine Shannon notes that his "belief in the 'elevating' effects of land ownership carried with it the firm expectation that eventually most Irishmen would recognize and admire British institutions and values and cherish the British connection."[41] Unionists also saw something very menacing in an Irish nationalism that defined the nation in exclusivist Catholic and Gaelic terms.[42] They began to argue that there were two nations in Ireland, both deserving of consideration.

Because unionists were heavily concentrated in the northeast part of the island, the Irish question came to be debated as "the Ulster question," the right of the Protestants of Ulster to block home rule or exclude themselves from its operation.[43] It was going to be extraordinarily difficult to design a constitution for Irish self-government that would quell their fears.

One of the effects of the unionists' hostility to home rule was their resistance to any attempt to reorganize the system of administration in Ireland, for fear that it would fall into the hands of homerulers.[44] The pre-Union system of Dublin Castle administration had barely been altered since the Union, and Liberals and nationalists could be excused for thinking the system incoherent, and even out of control, but any attempt at general reform of the system, for example, what O'Halpin calls the "apolitical vision of rational Public organization" devised by the Irish Under-Secretary, Sir Anthony MacDonnell, in 1904, was blocked by unionists and their allies in the Irish administration.[45] It was not until 1920 that the government was prepared to challenge this obstruction.[46] Until then, O'Halpin writes, "Irish Unionists were prepared to tolerate the existing structure, though they complained of its inefficiency, because they could see no alternative to it which did not lead towards home rule."[47]

## The Home Rule Bills

The first home rule bill was drafted by Gladstone himself because of opposition to home rule in his Cabinet and the Liberal party.[48] His major advisers were two civil servants, Sir Edward Hamilton and Sir Reginald Welby.[49] O'Day suggests that many of the flaws of the bill were a direct consequence of Gladstone's failure to thrash out contentious issues with his Cabinet before the legislation was introduced.[50] It was generally assumed at the time that the Irish had not been consulted either. Gavan Duffy described the 1886 bill as the work of "eminent Englishmen, sitting sublimely apart from the people whose destiny was in question, like a congress of the Great Powers delivering orders to Bulgaria."[51] As a member of the Victorian state government, in Australia, Duffy had chaired a royal commission on the Australian constitution,[52] but there had been no such commission or parliamentary select committee on Ireland before Gladstone introduced his bill. "Is there anybody in England," Duffy asked in amazement in 1891, "who would venture to present the Australians with a scheme framed by a Cabinet at Westminster in which not a single Australian had a seat or was in any way taken into counsel?"[53]

Duffy did not know that Parnell and Gladstone had discussed home rule quite frequently, though secretly because the terms were an extremely sensitive issue in Ireland. Parnell's mistress, Kitty O'Shea, and her husband, Captain William O'Shea, were used as confidential intermediaries.[54] Parnell's "A Rough Sketch of the Proposed Constitution for Ireland," which reached Gladstone on 30 October 1885, actually bore a very close relationship to the bill Gladstone introduced the following April.[55] On 22 December 1885, Gladstone welcomed Parnell's contributions and wrote that "for years I have publicly expressed my inability to pronounce upon Home Rule until it was explained to me. In this matter great progress has now been made."[56]

What exactly did Parnell propose? In a speech at Cork in January 1885 he said, "We cannot ask for less than restitution of Grattan's parliament, with its important privileges and wide and far-reaching constitution,"[57] but his "Rough Sketch" asked for very much less than the independent Parliament of 1782. He proposed, instead, a single Irish chamber of 300 members, 206 elected and 94 nominated, which would be a subordinate assembly to legislate for Irish domestic purposes only. It would have the power to raise taxes for Irish purposes, including customs duties, and would control the police and the judiciary. It would also make a payment to the imperial treasury to cover the costs of United Kingdom military forces in Ireland, but it would take no part in the foreign and defense policies of the United Kingdom. Parnell left open the question of whether the Irish would sit at Westminster, but he recognized that the United Kingdom Parliament would have the power to override Irish self-government at any time for "weighty and urgent cause." In a letter to Captain O'Shea on 14 December 1885, intended for Gladstone's eyes, Parnell argued that home rule would protect, not threaten, the Union. He wrote, "It did not involve the repeal of the Act of Union, an irrevocable step, and the Imperial Parliament, having conferred the privilege [of home rule] by Statute, would thus always be in a position to recall it by a similar method, if the privilege were abused."[58] Parnell also suggested that there might be provision for "a special proportionate representation for the large Protestant minority of Ireland" in the Irish Parliament. He made no explicit reference to responsible government but this model was implied in his proposal that the Irish legislature might be dissolved short of its full three-year term, presumably if a government were to lose the confidence of the legislature. He also proposed to abolish the office of Lord Lieutenant, preferring, as he confirmed in a letter to J. J. O'Neill Daunt in July 1885, that Irish ministers should advise the Crown directly.[59] Parnell's influence on Gladstone was substantial, therefore, but the first home rule bill was in no sense negotiated between them. Parnell did not see the bill before its introduction[60] and others in the Irish leadership knew almost nothing about it.[61]

For the constitutional language of home rule, Gladstone turned to the 1840 constitution of the colony of Canada and to the Canadian federal constitution of 1867.[62] He had been Colonial Secretary for a short time in 1845 and 1846, when the debate on responsible government was raging in the colonies,[63] and he had actually drafted a constitution for the "Middle Island of New Zealand," though it was not adopted.[64] In a memorandum, probably authored in 1850, he wrote, "The test of a good colonial policy is, that it shall prepare colonies for independence and self-government," but he viewed a successful policy as one that would "generate a sentiment of grateful attachment" to the United Kingdom, not prompt complete separation.[65] There is no evidence that he imagined in 1850 that the system of colonial self-government might be extended to Ireland,[66] but when it came to drafting a home rule bill in 1886 he looked for precedents in the colonies, and to Canada particularly.[67] He even denied that home rule laid down new constitutional principles because it had already been applied in the colonies.[68] It is no surprise, therefore, that the first home rule bill was in many ways the constitution of a self-governing colony.

Gladstone did not want the colonial analogy pressed too far, however. He insisted that his first home rule bill was "not parallel" but "strictly and substantially analogous" to the Canadian constitution.[69] "More restrictions, not found in the Canadian Act of 1867, would it is believed be cheerfully accepted in Ireland," he wrote. He noted, for example, "As regards defence, [Ireland] could not raise even a Volunteer or a militia force except through and under Imperial authority."[70] Nonetheless, three characteristics of colonial government were present in the first home rule bill. First, the Irish Parliament was clearly subordinate to the United Kingdom Parliament. Second, in the 1886 bill, though not in subsequent bills, Irish representatives were denied seats in the United Kingdom Parliament, except to vote on amendments to the home rule bill itself, an exception denied their colonial counter-parts. Third, executive authority was vested in the Queen and her representative, the Lord Lieutenant, who had the powers of a colonial governor: to appoint ministers; to summon, prorogue, and dissolve Parliament; and to give the royal assent, "subject to instructions from Her Majesty."

The 1886 bill was the model for the home rule bills of 1893 and 1912, and all were known as Government of Ireland Bills. We can therefore usefully consider them together.[71]

## The Irish Executive

Home rule defined the Irish executive in very traditional terms as the Lord Lieutenant, acting for the Sovereign, and advised by ministers of his choice. He would conduct all the functions of the Crown in Ireland, with the power to appoint ministers; summon, prorogue, and dissolve the legislature; and give or withhold the royal assent to bills "subject to instructions from His Majesty."[72] In the 1912 bill reservation was added to the Lord Lieutenant's powers, a power present in all the colonial constitutions but long obsolete. That is to say, before signing or rejecting a bill the Lord Lieutenant might "reserve" it for the Sovereign's further consideration. Finally, home rule provided that money bills might only be introduced into the legislature on the recommendation of the Lord Lieutenant. The language of home rule thus provided many opportunities for the British government to interfere in the Irish legislative process through its advice to the Crown, and through the Lord Lieutenant, who was a member of the government. This is why Parnell had argued in 1885 that there should be no Lord Lieutenant. He wrote, "On the whole . . . I am at present inclined to think that when the Irish Parliament is restored, it will be better for us to deal directly with the Crown rather than with a nominee in Ireland of the English Government of the day."[73]

Whatever its constitution might say about the royal assent and reservation, Gladstone always intended that Ireland should practice responsible government, with an Irish Cabinet controlling the executive through its advice to the Lord Lieutenant.[74] Indeed, Parnell saw responsible government as one of home rule's great advantages over the constitution of 1782.[75] The question facing Gladstone was whether responsible government should be mentioned in the home rule bill in some way, or whether it should be left to the operation of constitutional conventions. Several of the Australian colonial constitutions adopted after 1850 had alluded to responsible government by requiring ministers to find seats in the legislature within three months of their appointment, although there was no requirement that they have the support of a majority.[76] The 1886 home rule bill said nothing of this kind, nor did it include the even more oblique way of identifying responsible government which Gladstone included in an early draft: "It shall be understood that the Royal Veto shall be exercised upon the same principles as in the Dominion of Canada and other great legislative dependencies of the Crown."[77] In Canada, Governors-General had already been instructed to accept the advice of their ministers in all ordinary circumstances. Gladstone abandoned this approach, which defined Ireland's powers by analogy with Canada, but it was revived in the Irish constitution of 1922.[78]

The leaders of the Irish party were not satisfied with Gladstone's provisions on the executive in 1886. Parnell had argued in 1885 that there should be no Lord Lieutenant, but if there had to be one the Irish preferred that he have as little discretion as possible. That is to say, he should act only on the advice of Irish ministers in Irish matters. For example, the British government should never give instructions to the Lord Lieutenant, and the disallowance of an Irish act by the Crown after the Lord Lieutenant had already given his assent should be the only form of United Kingdom intervention, to be used only in very exceptional circumstances. The 1886 home rule bill did not meet this standard. In 1892 the leaders of the anti-Parnellite Irish party argued their case in secret meetings held in Dublin, the minutes of which were sent to Gladstone. The leaders were particularly concerned to exclude from the 1893 bill the power of *reservation*, which is to say, the power of the Lord Lieutenant to reserve a bill to London before giving his assent. The minutes of the 18 November meeting record the following: "The Lord Lieutenant should not have the power of reserving a Bill for reference home, before consenting or vetoing, but should transmit home a completed Act, which the Crown might disallow. Disallowance, in short, to be the only form of veto."[79] A minute of the 1 December meeting, based on a strict interpretation of what responsible government should mean in Ireland, adds:

The reservation must be made on the advice of an Irish Minister. But it is ridiculous to suppose that an Irish Minister will advise the reservation of his own Bill. . . . The only tolerable check in this region is the power of

disallowance for cause stated viz that the bill is seriously injurious to imperial interests. Unlimited disallowance ostentatiously places the Irish Parliament at the mercy of Imperial Executive. . . . If veto and reservation must
positively be retained, then it must equally positively on the other side be
stated expressly that both powers are to be exercised on Irish advice.[80]

The 1893 bill gave the Irish some of what they wanted in the executive. The Lord Lieutenant was to be the formal executive, as before,
but he was not empowered to reserve a bill. There was also, in Clause
5.2 of the bill, a clear break from past British and colonial practice:
"There shall be an Executive Committee of the Privy Council of Ireland
to aid and advise in the government of Ireland being of such numbers,
and comprising persons holding such offices as Her Majesty may think
fit, or as may directed by Irish Act." Clause 5.3 required the Lord Lieutenant to give or withhold the royal assent to Irish bills on the advice
of the Executive Committee, although this was "subject nevertheless to
any instructions given by Her Majesty in respect of any such Bill."
There was no requirement that the Executive Committee have the support of a parliamentary majority, or even sit in Parliament; but it was
clearly to be a responsible Cabinet, and the bill required the Lord Lieutenant, in ordinary circumstances, to accept its advice on Irish matters.
Finally, his term of office was set at six years,[81] meaning that he would
not have to resign with each change of government in Britain, the practice hitherto for Irish Viceroys.

The home rule bill of 1893 came very close to defining responsible
government in constitutional law, but Gladstone refused to go the ex-
tra mile by recognizing, in the bill, that the Lord Lieutenant would only
appoint ministers who had the support of a majority in Parliament. His
reasoning was that Ireland should be treated no better than Canada,
where constitutional law still recognized the royal prerogatives and responsible government was regulated by conventions. "The Canadian
system has been at work for a quarter of a century," Gladstone wrote,
"and has proved itself compatible with perfect autonomy."[82]

The 1893 home rule bill had gone far toward recognizing responsible
government, but the 1912 home rule bill moved one step forward and
two steps back. It retained the Executive Committee of the Privy Council, the Irish Cabinet, from the 1893 bill and added the Australian rule
that ministers must secure seats in Parliament, in the Irish case within
six months of their appointment.[83] Simultaneously, however, it withdrew the obligation of the Lord Lieutenant to give or withhold the

royal assent on the advice of the Irish Executive Committee.[84] It also added the power of reservation for the first time. The royal assent to an Irish bill might be postponed indefinitely, therefore, on instructions from the Sovereign.[85]

Why, long after responsible government had matured as a system of government in Britain and the dominions, were United Kingdom governments so reluctant to define it in constitutional law in Ireland, and so equivocal about recognizing it even obliquely? One can conjecture that there were three major reasons. First, most politicians were royalists with a natural diffidence about passing laws to limit the discretionary powers of the Crown, even if these powers had long been limited in practice in Britain. It was a case of not pointing out that the emperor had no clothes. No one would demean the Sovereign by revealing the truth that she no longer controlled the prerogative. But deference to royalty does not explain everything. Second, therefore, governments did not wish to open the question of constitutional conventions to discussion. The exercise of the royal prerogative was regulated in the United Kingdom and the British Empire by constitutional conventions that gave, and still give, governments enormous powers through their advice to the Sovereign. Any attempt to identify the prerogative in law in Ireland threatened to open the question of the role of conventions everywhere in the empire. Third, the Crown played a very important role as the formal instrument of imperial unity at a time of substantial constitutional transition. In the colonies, for example, Governors were instructed on the subjects the colonial legislatures might not handle, and therefore on which bills to veto, but in extreme cases the royal prerogative could be used to overrule an act of a colonial legislature. It was this power that ultimately guaranteed that the empire would act as one in imperial affairs. There was no longer any serious expectation that the prerogative would be used, in Ireland or elsewhere, but as Gavan Duffy, a former Premier of the colony of Victoria, Australia, advised in 1886: "In Ireland, till experience has taught us the precise lines within which lie questions of national interest, and outside which lie Imperial interests, it is a just precaution to retain a veto. . . . After a few Parliaments, it could be dispensed with, as in time it will be dispensed with in the colonies."[86]

As we shall see, in 1922 the founders of the Irish Free State challenged all three of these reasons for not defining responsible government in law, and the response of the United Kingdom then was precisely what Gladstone's response was in 1886: "It would not I imagine be possible to devise a formula for limiting the action of the veto."[87]

## The Irish Legislature

In 1886 Gladstone proposed a unicameral Irish legislature modeled, it appears, on the Synod of the Church of Ireland. It would have two "orders" that would debate together but might vote separately. Parnell preferred this system to a bicameral Parliament with an Irish House of Lords.[88] The First Order was to have 103 members elected on a very restrictive property franchise, serving fixed ten-year terms with 20 percent of the membership being rotated every two years. For a transitional period, twenty-eight of these seats were to be reserved to representative Irish peers, serving for thirty years or life. The Second Order, with 206 members, was to be elected by means of a popular franchise. Its members would serve for ten years or until the order was dissolved and a general election was held.

The 1893 and 1912 bills abandoned the two "orders" and proposed instead conventional bicameral legislatures, although the leaders of the Irish party had expressed a preference that the issue of a second chamber be left to the Irish Parliament to decide. They confessed to being divided between a "democratic inclination for one chamber, and the feeling that two chambers would look more like a parliament."[89] The 1893 bill used the nomenclature of the colonies and proposed a popularly elected Legislative Assembly with 103 members, its members serving for five years or until a dissolution, and a Legislative Council elected on a restrictive franchise, with 48 members serving fixed eight-year terms. The 1912 bill described the lower house as the Irish House of Commons for the first time, and assigned it a membership of 164, serving for five years or until a dissolution. The upper house was to be a 40-person Senate nominated by the Lord Lieutenant. This was amended in committee so that the Senate would become an elected chamber after a five-year transition period. Its members would then be elected to fixed five-year terms by the four Irish provinces acting as separate constituencies.

By 1886 it was established that in responsible government the popularly elected chamber should have priority, so each of the home rule bills sought to limit the powers of the First Order or upper house. The

1886 bill provided that the First Order could only delay a bill for three years,[90] a period shortened to two years for the Legislative Council of 1893[91] and the Senate of 1914.[92] All three bills borrowed a provision from Australian colonial constitutions to resolve disputes. A measure on which the two orders or houses disagreed would be resolved, at the end of a maximum period of delay, by a vote of the two sitting together. This formula gave the Second Order or lower house a numerical advantage in the resolution sessions. The 1914 act, which followed the rejection of the Liberals' budget by the House of Lords in 1909, also provided that a money bill had to originate in the House of Commons and might not be rejected by the Senate.[93]

The fact that there were three quite different plans for the upper house, or First Order, in the three home rule bills—four, if we include the nominated chamber that was proposed in 1912 and amended in committee—illustrates that Gladstone and Asquith were both struggling with the major problem posed by second chambers in responsible government, how to devise a representation formula that does not produce two chambers that are mirror images of each other, and therefore redundant. In 1886 and 1893 they proposed the conservative device of a property qualification to produce an independent chamber, but the 1912 bill used instead the principle of the geographic representation of Ireland's four provinces.

## Irish Powers

Under each home rule bill the supremacy of the United Kingdom Parliament was assured. It was implicit in the 1886 bill, because Parliament is supreme in the United Kingdom, but to reassure unionists the 1893 bill and the 1914 act stated, in an example of legislative overkill, that "the supreme power and authority of the Parliament of the United Kingdom shall remain unaffected and undiminished over all persons, matters, and things in Ireland, and every part thereof."[94]

All three home rule bills assigned essentially the same powers to the Irish Parliament. It would "make laws for the peace, order and good government of Ireland," subject to certain matters being reserved to the United Kingdom Parliament to protect the interests of the United Kingdom as a whole, and subject also to certain restrictions on Irish powers to protect the Protestant community in Ireland. In most of the self-governing colonies reserved subjects were identified in instructions from the Sovereign to the colonial Governor, and were amendable at will by the Crown. Ireland was accorded considerably more respect. The reserved matters were stated in the act, and Gladstone used the enumeration of specific powers in articles 91 and 92 of the Canadian dominion constitution of 1867 as his model.

Which matters were reserved to the United Kingdom? To protect the interests of the United Kingdom as a whole, Ireland was not to be allowed to legislate regarding the Crown, peace and war, military forces, honors and titles, foreign and colonial relations, trade and navigation, customs, excise, legal tender and coinage, copyright and patents, and the home rule act itself. The 1914 act extended the list to include subjects developed since 1893, including the management of the 1903 Land Act and the Liberals' programs of old age pensions and national insurance. The right of legal appeal to the United Kingdom was also reserved to the United Kingdom in the legislation. In the 1886 bill the House of Lords was specified as the Court of Appeal for Ireland, but the 1893 bill and 1914 act assigned the task to the Judicial Committee of the Privy Council, which was also to determine *vires* under home rule.

Few areas of Irish power were specifically identified in the legislation. They included the Post Office, the judiciary, and the police, with the latter to be transferred over a period of time. For the most part, Irish powers were residuary, which is to say, they were all those not specifically reserved to the United Kingdom.

Finally, the home rule legislation identified certain restrictions on the Irish Parliament. It would not be permitted to legislate to establish or endow religion, restrict the free exercise of religion, set religious tests for office, require a child to attend religious instruction in a public school, or restrict the equal protection and due process of law. The restrictions were clearly designed to protect the Protestant minority but they were challenged by unionists for not recognizing the rights of the Protestants explicitly. In debate, the Liberals insisted that a number of provisions in their bills protected the minority perfectly well. First, the restrictions concerning religion were clearly targeted at the minority denominations. Second, all three bills provided a right of legal appeal to the United Kingdom. Third, the First Order of 1886 and the Senate of 1893 and 1912 were conservative bodies likely to protect the minority. Fourth, the three bills gave the First Order and the Senate powers to delay legislation.

This brief description provides a bare outline of the origin and content of the three home rule bills. What is missing, of course, is a discussion of the very heated debate that home rule provoked. As the bills were very similar, so too were the debates. They will be discussed in the next chapter.

# CHAPTER 4

# Home Rule, 1870–1914: The Debates

When considering the home rule debates, we have to bear in mind that any reform of Irish government had to satisfy both Ireland *and* Britain if it was to be the outcome of a constitutional process. For the Irish it had to provide a substantial measure of self-government. For the British, whether members of the Liberal or Conservative parties, it had to satisfy three conditions: preserving the Union, recognizing the supremacy of the United Kingdom Parliament, and protecting the rights of the Protestant minority in Ireland. The dispute between the two major British parties was not about these conditions in principle, but about whether home rule could meet them. The Liberals insisted that it could. The unionists, whether Conservative or Liberal unionist, disagreed.

The home rule debates of 1886, 1893, and 1912–14 turned primarily on two related questions. First, would the Irish accept the subordinate status assigned to their Parliament and the restrictions on its powers spelled out in the home rule bills? Second, if the Irish chose to violate those restrictions, would it be possible for the United Kingdom's government and Parliament to bring Ireland into compliance with the law? Liberals answered yes to both questions. Conservatives and unionists answered no. At one level the argument was about constitutional details, but at another it was about human nature. Those supporting home rule professed to trust the Irish, and those opposing it did not.

Conservatives and unionists would have opposed any home rule bill for Ireland, no matter how flawless, but we cannot dismiss their criticisms of all these bills as merely the defensive posturings of a privileged class. They used sophisticated reasoning as well as appeals to irrational emotion, sometimes combining both in one statement. Goldwin Smith, for example, a former Regius Professor of History at Oxford University, mounted a powerful critique of the constitutional assumptions of home rule while simultaneously arguing that the "Celts of Ireland are as yet unfit for parliamentary government."[1] The more sophisticated part of the anti–home rule attack, maintained over a period of thirty years, exposed a number of flaws in home rule that suggest that it would not have created a relationship between Britain and Ireland that would have survived in the long term. These flaws included the formula for representing Ireland in the United Kingdom Parliament, Ireland's financial relationship with the United Kingdom, and the formal constitutional relationship between the two countries.[2]

## Flaws in the Home Rule Plan

### The Representation Formula

The first flaw, the representation formula, was recognized by the historian E. A. Freeman as early as 1874, when Isaac Butt introduced his first home rule motion into Parliament.[3] Gladstone called it "The Double Dilemma"[4] and "the most difficult of all" issues.[5] It followed from the fact that whereas Ireland would be self-governing under home rule, Britain and the United Kingdom would be governed by the one government and one Parliament. This raised the question of whether the Irish should sit in that Parliament, and with what powers. If they were to sit with full powers, they would be able to vote on domestic British legislation, and in a closely divided Parliament their support might determine which party would form the government for the United Kingdom, and hence for Britain too. On the other hand, if the Irish were to be excluded from sitting at Westminster, ostensibly to prevent them from participating in British affairs, Ireland would be reduced to the status of a self-governing colony, with no participation in United Kingdom or imperial affairs. Various formulae were offered to solve this dilemma, none of them theoretically elegant. They ranged from no Irish representation in the United Kingdom Parliament, to full Irish representation but with very limited voting rights, to full representation with full voting rights, to partial representation with full voting rights. The latter was the formula adopted in the 1914 and 1920 Government of Ireland Acts.

Gladstone began the discussion of representation in 1886 by proposing to exclude the Irish from Westminster altogether.[6] In doing so he first rejected a proposal that Isaac Butt had made in 1874, that Irish members of Parliament should have partial representation at Westminster, with the right to participate only in United Kingdom business. Gladstone insisted that in practice no clear line could be drawn between United Kingdom and Irish matters, and that the proposal also ignored the problem of government formation. How might a majority government be formed in a Parliament containing two majorities, he asked, one for British affairs and one for United Kingdom affairs? A government enjoying the support of a British majority on British issues might find itself voted out of office by the addition of Irish votes on United Kingdom issues. The arrangement was inherently unworkable.

Thus Gladstone concluded, with little enthusiasm, that the Irish would have to be excluded from Parliament.[7] "There cannot be," he argued, "a domestic Legislature in Ireland dealing with Irish affairs, and Irish Peers and Irish Representatives sitting in Parliament at Westminster to take part in English and Scottish affairs."[8] His one concession was that the Irish might sit in Parliament to debate changes in the home rule legislation itself, something he described as the "Magna Charta for Ireland."[9] He also left open the possibility that the Irish Parliament might vote its assent to an amendment to home rule by an address to the United Kingdom Parliament, in which case Irish M.P.'s need never come to Westminster.

By deciding to exclude the Irish from the United Kingdom Parliament, Gladstone opened himself to two unionist charges. First, home rule would violate the principle of "no taxation without representation." Second, it would effectively repeal Article III of the Act of Union, which provided for a single Parliament for Ireland and Britain.[10] In 1893, therefore, Gladstone changed his mind. On the first reading of the 1893 bill he rejected his own arguments of seven years earlier and adopted Butt's scheme. He now proposed that eighty Irish M.P.'s, his estimate of Ireland's share of representation by population, together with a number of representative Irish peers, should sit in the United Kingdom Parliament, but they would not be permitted to vote on legislation that was *expressly* or *exclusively* British.[11] He regarded confidence motions as United Kingdom matters, which meant that the Irish would be permitted to participate in government formation.

The impracticality of separating British from United Kingdom matters was quickly recognized in Parliament and the 1893 bill was amended, with Gladstone's approval, to permit the Irish to vote on all matters.[12] But having attacked Gladstone for violating the principle of "no taxation without representation" in 1886, unionists now accused him of undermining responsible government at Westminster by proposing to allow Irish members to participate in British affairs. A. V. Dicey wrote, "Great Britain is, under the new constitution, not allowed to appoint the British Cabinet."[13] In the House of Commons Arthur Balfour attacked the proposition that the choice of a government for Britain, a choice that had become critical with the development of responsible government, might be decided by eighty Irish M.P.'s. As he pointed out:

[The] whole tendency of Constitutional change during the last one hundred and fifty years, almost the last two hundred years, in this country has been to throw more and more into the Cabinet of the day—a Body not recognized by our Constitution—the whole control not merely of our foreign affairs, but of the program of legislation which is to be laid before this House.[14]

It was clear that allowing the Irish to be represented at Westminster would give Ireland too much power in British affairs, but denying them representation would give them no power in United Kingdom affairs. There was no satisfactory solution to this dilemma, short of a comprehensive plan involving devolution to Scotland, Wales, England, and Ireland that would have allowed all regional matters to be removed from the United Kingdom Parliament. This plan came to be known as "home rule all round" and it foundered because there was no widespread demand for home rule outside Ireland. Few English, Scottish, or Welsh politicians wanted home rule for themselves, or were prepared to reconstruct the constitution for the sake of Ireland. "Federalism," as A. V. Dicey erroneously called this plan, "offers to England, not a compromise but a constitutional revolution."[15] Nor were Irish nationalists themselves willing to wait for home rule until a comprehensive plan might be devised for the United Kingdom, or even for the whole British Empire, as some suggested. Tim Healy, M.P. for Londonderry South, said in 1886, "Henry II is dead 700 years, and it is time we were getting something done for Ireland. Ireland, in any case, should not have to wait until the Colonies—Victoria, South Africa, Nova Zembla, and Heaven knows where else the British Empire ranges—consent to federate in an

Imperial Senate."[16] The government recognized the point. "Ireland will not wait, the state of Ireland will not wait, till a scheme of federation is adjusted and framed," John Morley said in 1886.[17]

In the end the British compromised on representation, pushing principle aside. The 1914 home rule act called for 42 Irish M.P.'s in the United Kingdom Parliament with full powers after home rule, not the 105 members Ireland had at the time, nor the 80 members its population might have justified.[18] To put this more cynically, the act mandated Irish overrepresentation on British matters and underrepresentation on United Kingdom matters.[19]

The debates on Irish representation were largely ignored by the leaders of the Irish party themselves, who preferred that Ireland have no representation at all at Westminster. Parnell, for example, thought that it would detract from the significance of the Irish Parliament in Dublin,[20] an argument Gladstone endorsed in 1886,[21] and Timothy Healy, M.P., thought it would place too much strain on Ireland to have to supply representatives to two Parliaments.[22] In 1893 John Redmond, M.P., now leader of the Parnellite faction of the Irish party, argued that disaffected Irishmen might try to use the United Kingdom Parliament as a court of appeal from decisions already made in the Irish Parliament. He accepted Irish representation at Westminster only as a temporary expedient, until issues such as the control of the Irish police and the administration of the Irish Land Act of 1881 could be resolved.[23] The preference of these Irish nationalist leaders, therefore, was for a subordinate Irish Parliament and no Irish participation in United Kingdom decisions. This was the definition of a self-governing British colony in the second half of the nineteenth century and it confirmed many unionists in their belief that home rule would be used as a stepping-stone to Irish independence. Why else, they asked, would the Irish want no role at all in United Kingdom affairs?

## The Financial Relationship

The second flaw in home rule was the proposed financial relationship between the United Kingdom and Ireland. Every home rule bill reserved the major taxing powers to the United Kingdom, something the Irish party consistently opposed. The most controversial financial issue in 1886 was control of customs and excise because no matter what constitutional provision might be made to safeguard the supremacy of the United Kingdom, it would have little practical effect if Ireland were free to treat commerce with Britain as "foreign trade." The concern with customs and excise in 1886 was broadened later, as new taxes and government spending programs were introduced, to encompass budgetary policy in general.

Gladstone originally planned to cede customs and excises to Ireland, as Parnell wanted, but he backed off in the face of opposition from the Chancellor of the Exchequer, Hugh Childers, and others. They argued that experience elsewhere, in the United States, Germany, and Australia, for example, had demonstrated that a Union would not survive if its parts were free to create tariff barriers against each other.[24] Gladstone conceded the point and thereafter identified customs and excises as the "battle line" for home rule.[25]

The 1886 bill proposed that the Irish Parliament might impose direct taxes, but the United Kingdom would collect customs and excises, which represented more than three-quarters of Ireland's revenues at the time.[26] From this sum would be paid Ireland's imperial contribution, an amount fixed for thirty years at £4,242,000 per annum, which was one-fifteenth of United Kingdom expenditures in 1886, together with a payment of £360,000 per annum to a fund to service the national debt. The balance of the Irish customs and excise revenues would be returned to Ireland, where they would be joined with locally raised revenues to pay for expenditures authorized by the Irish Parliament. The formula shielded Ireland from having to contribute to any increases in imperial expenses for thirty years, but its income was at the mercy of the United Kingdom Parliament, which could raise or lower customs and excise duties, and hence Irish revenues, at any time.

Parnell accepted the 1886 home rule bill in principle on its second reading but vowed to try to secure control of customs and excise at the committee stage of the bill. He saw these taxes not only as Ireland's major sources of income, but as ways of sheltering certain Irish industries from competition, if only temporarily.[27] Parnell even argued that a customhouse was more important to Ireland than a Parliament.[28] To provide the country with an acceptable financial cushion for self-government, he also wanted a reduction in Ireland's imperial contribution from one-fifteenth to one-twentieth of 1886 imperial expenditures.[29] In the event, of course, there was no opportunity to amend the bill in committee because it was defeated on its second reading, in June 1886.

The 1893 bill continued to deny Ireland control of customs and excise.[30] It provided that the United Kingdom would return to Ireland a variable sum amounting to two-thirds of all taxes collected in Ireland, estimated at about £2,000,000 in 1893. Ireland's income would depend, again, on decisions about customs and excise made for the United Kingdom as a whole.[31] Furthermore, a provision that the financial terms would be reviewed after six years removed the long-term guarantee against an increase in the imperial contribution that had been built into the 1886 formula.

The Irish objected again. John Redmond accepted the bill in general but added, "[Nationalists] believe it is impossible to govern Ireland successfully under these financial clauses."[32] But Gladstone would not yield. He wrote to Sir William Harcourt in January 1893, "My opinion is that detailed negotiation on particulars of Finance between the Cabinet and the Irish is impossible and that the Cabinet should at once present to them not quite but something like an ultimatum."[33]

By 1912, when the third home rule bill was introduced, the relative condition of the Irish economy had worsened and financial relations were complicated by the costs of the Liberals' new social programs, particularly the old age pension, which accounted for one-third of all government spending in Ireland. Ireland went from a £2,000,000 surplus in tax collections over spending in 1886 to an estimated deficit of £1,500,000 in 1912–13. It was even asked if Ireland could ever anticipate financial independence. Surprisingly, in these circumstances, a government committee on Irish finance chaired by Sir Henry Primrose reported in favor of "an autonomous Ireland, self-sufficing so far as its own local administration and finances are concerned,"[34] subject only to the United Kingdom continuing to pay the cost of old age pensions granted before home rule.

The Liberal Chief Secretary, Augustine Birrell, was alone in the Cabinet in supporting the Primrose plan.[35] He told John Redmond that it was rejected in Cabinet for "public considerations outside the purely financial aspect of the Irish problem."[36] By that he meant that the Cabinet's commitment to introduce a plan of "home rule all round" at some future date had caused the rejection. Members of the Cabinet believed that if Ireland were to be financially independent, as Primrose recommended, it ought not to be represented at Westminster. But this principle could not be applied to Scotland, Wales, and England too, at some future time, without producing a constitutional absurdity, an arrangement in which there would be no United Kingdom Parliament because no region would be represented in it.

The Prime Minister, Herbert Asquith, assigned the task of preparing new financial terms to the Postmaster General, Herbert Samuel, and the bill that emerged was dramatically different from the Primrose plan. It proposed that all Irish taxes, except post office receipts, would be paid to the United Kingdom. Ireland would receive in return a grant for Irish expenditures and the United Kingdom would pay for certain "reserved services," including old age pensions, national insurance, land purchase, and tax collection. Should Irish taxes produce a surplus over Irish expenditures for a three-year period, the terms would be renegotiated to provide for an imperial contribution.

John Redmond, by now the leader of a united Irish Parliamentary party, accepted these terms rather than risk losing home rule altogether, but he preferred that Ireland should be financially autonomous, even if it would be poorer.[37] "Admittedly, it is a provisional settlement," he insisted. "When the time for revision does come . . . we will be entitled to complete power for Ireland over the whole of our financial system."[38]

The final versions of all three home rule bills provided, therefore, that the United Kingdom would collect the bulk of Ireland's taxes and return some proportion of them to Ireland, but the level of Irish revenues would depend primarily on fiscal policy made in London and the Irish Cabinet would find itself primarily accountable to the Treasury in London, not to the Irish Parliament in Dublin, for Irish expenditures. The situation was ripe for conflict, as R. J. Lawrence explains:

Unable to inaugurate with confidence those social reforms on which Irishmen set great store, forbidden to protect local industries, and in general constrained from trying to evade the repercussions of policies shaped mainly by England and directed mainly to her interest—in these conditions Irish politicians, though formally in possession of political authority, would be reduced to near impotence. They, their opponents in other parties, the press and the electorate would soon realize that the Chancellor of the Exchequer in effect dominated their Parliament, and political pressures would inevitably find their chief outlet in renewed protests against British ascendancy.[39]

A. V. Dicey had recognized the same danger in 1882, when he warned, "Semi-independence makes it easy for men to attribute every mishap to the absence of absolute freedom."[40]

## The Constitutional Relationship

The third flaw in home rule was the ambiguity of the proposed constitutional relationship between Britain and Ireland, which attracted the most criticism because it went so clearly to the heart of the Union. Gladstone believed that home rule did represent "a most important modification" of the Act of Union,[41] but the Union itself would remain intact because the supremacy of the United Kingdom Parliament and the royal prerogative would both be unaffected in Ireland. In a March 1886 memorandum he wrote:

The means available in this country for maintaining the unity of the Empire are superior to those which exist in most if not all other countries; because the Imperial Legislature is by the unwritten constitution not only above all other powers, but is strictly supreme and of unlimited power; neither fettered by written constitutions, nor by co-existing, co-ordinate Legislatures.[42]

Constitutional lawyers such as A. V. Dicey and Sir William Anson were less sanguine. They argued that by reserving only certain matters to the United Kingdom, and specifying that a court, the Privy Council, would determine *vires*, home rule would actually diminish the supremacy of the United Kingdom Parliament. It could only assert itself in matters transferred to the Irish Parliament by amending or abolishing the home rule statute, a controversial process, not by acting within the framework of home rule.[43]

When it became known that Gladstone was prepared to recognize the supremacy of the United Kingdom Parliament explicitly in the second home rule bill, he provoked, in their own words, the "vehement, unanimous, and decisive" opposition of the Irish leaders, who charged unionists with agitating "for barren gratification of asserting power."[44] As a compromise, the Irish nationalists suggested that "the parenthetic recital of [supremacy] in the preamble is the least injurious" to them,[45] and this is what the government proposed in the draft presented to Parliament in 1893. But in committee it accepted amendments that recognized supremacy not only in the preamble but also in the bill itself. Section 2 stated that, notwithstanding anything in the act, the supreme power and authority of Parliament within the Queen's dominions would remain unaffected. Section 33 used the language of the Colonial Laws Validity Act of 1865 to recognize the supremacy of United Kingdom law over Irish law in cases of "repugnancy," that is to say, in cases of conflict between the two. The 1912 bill similarly recognized the supremacy of Parliament, mentioning Ireland specifically this time, in Section 1.2, and it reproduced the repugnancy clause in Section 41.2.[46]

Appeasing the unionists in this rather gratuitous way did nothing to clarify what United Kingdom supremacy actually meant in practice. In 1893 the Liberal Chancellor of the Duchy of Lancaster, James Bryce, stated that the final judges of whether the United Kingdom should intervene in Ireland would always be "the regular advisers to the Crown—that is to say, the British Cabinet," but the right of the Crown to intervene would be "a power to be kept in reserve, only to be used if the gravest case should arise—and in particular if the restrictive provisions of the Bill should be transgressed." He believed that a constitutional convention would emerge to guarantee this interpretation.[47] John Redmond thought it inconceivable that the United Kingdom would overrule an act of the Irish Parliament, or that it would violate a moral obligation to respect home rule. Instead, he argued, "The supremacy of Parliament would be as a sword which often is most powerful while sheathed."[48]

Bryce and Redmond clearly did not believe that either parliamentary supremacy or the royal prerogative would ever be invoked against Ireland in normal circumstances. As Bogdanor puts it, "For as long as Home Rule worked normally, the Irish legislature would be a coordinate and not a subordinate body."[49] But unionists fully anticipated that abnormal circumstances would arise in Ireland. They believed that Irish nationalists would use their Parliament, their responsible government, their judiciary, and their police to pursue independence, and if that were to happen no government in London would be able to enforce the supremacy of the United Kingdom without the use of military force. In 1886 George Trevelyan, the Scottish Secretary, who resigned from Gladstone's Cabinet because of its support of home rule, asked, "[H]ow can you limit any Parliament in the subjects it will discuss, let alone a Parliament in a country which had produced such men as Wolfe Tone, O'Connell, Shiel and John Mitchell?"[50] In 1893 Joseph Chamberlain said in the House of Commons, "It would be to accuse [the Irish] of want of patriotism from their own standpoint if they do not use every weapon which you place in their hands in order to establish the full rights of the nation whose independence you are acknowledging."[51] And in 1910 Arthur Balfour wrote to J. L. Garvin, the federalist editor of the *Observer*, "Have you any means, short of two Army Corps, or a Naval Blockade, which can prevent an Irish Parliament and an Irish Executive from defying you? They will have money, police and organization: In Ireland the Imperial Parliament will have none of these things."[52] The threat, the unionists argued, was not simply to Britain's position in Ireland, but to the integrity of the empire as a whole, because Ireland would set a precedent for the colonies. Indeed, Lord Salisbury, who became Conservative Prime Minister in 1887, made opposition to home rule the cornerstone of his imperial policy.[53]

In 1912 Balfour went to the heart of the matter by distinguishing between constitutional fact and constitutional fiction in the matter of supremacy:

There were some centuries in which our British Sovereigns described themselves as Kings of France. It appeared on all their coins, it appeared in all their formal State documents, but it did not make them Kings of France. . . . and the power of our Sovereigns as Kings of France is exactly on a parallel with that supremacy of the British Parliament about which you talk so much . . . and which you know as well as I do as practical politicians can never be exercised in any critical moment when its exercise might be necessary.[54]

Balfour pointed out that the hypothetical problem of how to constrain Ireland was compounded in the 1893 and 1912 bills by the provision that Irish members would sit at Westminster. How, Balfour asked rhetorically, would they vote on a motion to suspend home rule or overrule the Irish Parliament? And how might a Liberal government deal with a crisis in Ireland if it depended on Irish votes for its survival?

## Colonial Analogies

Each side in the home rule debate used colonial analogies to make its case about the constitutional relationship that could develop between Britain and Ireland under home rule. There were some very strong resemblances between Ireland and the colonies, and Gladstone himself wrote of them in 1893:

The disease—disaffection.
The medicine—self-government.
The result—Harmony, strength, honor.[55]

It is legitimate, therefore, to ask if the colonies had been bound more closely to Britain by self-government. Or had colonial self-government set in motion the disintegration of the empire?

Gladstone himself had no doubts. Colonial self-government had cemented the empire by removing the only source of friction between the United Kingdom and the colonies. This imperial harmony was described most effusively in 1887, by Lord Thring, the chief parliamentary draftsman at the time of the first home rule bill:

An Anglo-Saxon colony, no less than a human being, has its infancy under the maternal care of the governor, its boyhood subject to the government of a representative council and an Executive appointed by the Crown, its manhood under Home Rule and responsible government, in which the Executive are bound to vacate their office whenever they are outvoted in the Legislature. Changes are ever taking place in the growth, so to speak, of the several British possessions, but what is the result? Nobody ever dreams of these changes injuring the imperial tie or the supremacy of the British Parliament, that alone towers above all unchangeable and unimpaired.[56]

G. Gavan Duffy, a Young Irelander who emigrated to Australia in 1856 and rose to be Premier of the colony of Victoria before returning to Europe and active involvement in the home rule debate, agreed that the colonial model of home rule had brought the parts of the empire closer together, but he added a rider. Imperial unity could only be maintained if burdens were shared in an imperial federation. Duffy did not believe the colonies would accept indefinitely a system in which they were "liable in life and property for wars over which they have no more control than over the wind and waves." Nor did he think the United Kingdom would continue to defend prosperous colonies at the expense of its own taxpayers.[57]

Unionists forcefully challenged the case being made for Irish home rule by colonial analogy. It was already clear, they argued, that the colonies were perceptibly evolving toward independence. They also argued that the colonies' continued attachment to Britain was the result of a natural affection that did not exist in the case of Ireland and Britain. Indeed, the absence of affection for Britain would encourage Ireland on the path to independence. George Trevelyan said in 1886 that "the colonies liked us better when the colonial system was set up than the Irish do now, and . . . the colonies do not have to pay over £4,500,000 a year to this country."[58]

Unionists also pointed out that there were two particular lessons for home rule to be drawn from Canada. Goldwin Smith explained that the constitutional relationship between the Canadian provinces and the Dominion of Canada was stable because it was fixed in place by a federal constitution, but the constitutional relationship between Canada and Britain, ostensibly maintained by means of the royal prerogative and the legislative supremacy of the United Kingdom Parliament, was plainly growing weaker as Canada matured. Smith wrote, "Externally, the relationship of Canada to England is not, as is always assumed, stationary—so that it could be reproduced as a permanent institution—but shifting. It is that of a dependency which is in progress towards independence, and has now almost reached the goal."[59] Responsible government, about which the Canadian constitution of 1867 said absolutely nothing, had given control of the executive to the Canadian Cabinet, and the United Kingdom's formal supremacy had become largely irrelevant because there was no practical way of enforcing it. Smith concluded, "If the bond thus reduced to a thread is not snapped, and is even cherished, it is because Canada enjoys, or believes that she enjoys, free of cost, the protection of British armaments, and because the feeling of British Canadians towards the mother country is exactly the opposite of that of the Irish."[60]

The lessons for Ireland were clear. If Ireland were to be another Ontario, a reliable province, the United Kingdom would have to be reconstituted as a federation, on the Canadian model. But if Ireland were to be another Canada, it would necessarily evolve toward independence. To the unionists, this was an unacceptable risk: whereas Canada's permanent separation would pose no threat to Britain's safety, "the separation from Ireland," Smith argued, "would be the abandonment of part of the citadel, with the moral certainty that France or some other enemy would march in."[61]

One of the most influential opponents of the Liberals' use of the colonial analogy was A. V. Dicey, Vinerian Professor of Law at Oxford University. His opposition to home rule, expressed in three books and a number of journal articles, was influenced by a passionate unionism, but he was nonetheless the most sophisticated constitutional commentator of his day and his writings on home rule were integrated into his impressive scholarship on the constitution. He too argued that responsible government had transformed the self-governing colonies, and that Britain's relationship with each self-governing colony was kept in "tol-

erable working order by a series of understandings and of mutual concessions," not by parliamentary supremacy and the royal prerogative.
He warned:

If either England or Victoria were not willing to give and take, the connection between England and the colony would not last a month. The policy,
in short, of colonial independence is, like most of our constitutional arrangements, based on the assumption that the parties to it are willing to
act towards one another in a spirit of compromise and goodwill.[62]

Dicey recognized, but discounted, an argument Gladstone had made
in an 1893 memorandum entitled "The Colonies No Parallel." The argument held that there were major differences between the colonies
and a home rule Ireland. Most notably, the colonies had their own military forces, controlled their own commercial policies, and made no imperial contributions, none of which would apply to a home rule Ireland.[63] To Dicey, however, it was much more significant that Ireland
would have responsible government than that it would have no army.
An Irish ministry, he insisted, "must in ordinary matters be at least as
free as the Ministry of a self-governing colony."[64]

Colonial precedents suggest, therefore, that Irish self-government
could well have been a step toward Irish independence. In 1886 John
Morley argued in Parliament that the royal prerogative would be intact
in Ireland, as it was in the self-governing colonies,[65] and Gladstone was
advised by the Colonial Office that Canada was still bound by the Colonial Laws Validity Act of 1865, by which United Kingdom law prevailed over colonial law in cases of conflict. But Gladstone knew that
the Canadians disputed this interpretation,[66] and unionists could see
perfectly well for themselves that the authority of the United Kingdom
was already nearly defunct in New Zealand, Australia, and Canada.

## Nationalist Obfuscation

In their attempts to put a benign face on home rule, the Liberals
found their arguments undercut by their Irish allies. In part the problem was Parnell's association with men of violence. In 1879 he helped
Michael Davit, a former revolutionary, to found the National Land
League, an organization dedicated to land reform, and in 1880 he became its President. The Land League operated in the middle ground
between constitutional and revolutionary nationalism during the "land

war" of 1879 to 1882. It was, McCaffrey writes, "an agrarian movement bordering on insurrection,"[67] and was banned in 1881 for its use of boycotts and violent intimidation directed at landlords and collaborating tenant farmers. Parnell himself was imprisoned in 1881 for his role in the movement. Unionists insisted that he was a willing partner in the violence that had persisted in the countryside throughout the nineteenth century. The threat of force therefore lurked in the background of constitutional nationalism in the 1880s, but successive land reforms, including Gladstone's Land Act of 1881, the Conservative's Ashbourne Act of 1885, and Wyndham's Land Act of 1903, ended the land agitation. Furthermore, as Oliver MacDonagh argues, "Redmond was inhibited by his own beliefs from enlisting Irish militancy as an ally."[68] After Parnell's withdrawal from the movement, the charge that revolutionary and constitutional nationalism were linked was spurious, although the suspicion lingered.

A second problem for the Liberals was that the Irish nationalist leaders never disguised their feeling that each home rule bill was imperfect. Before British audiences they accepted home rule and were conciliatory. In the *Contemporary Review*, in 1893, for example, John Redmond wrote:

These, then, are the safeguards against any rash, violent, or oppressive proceedings by the Irish Legislature. The physical force of England, undiminished and reinforced by a moral force she never had on her side before, the continued and unimpaired supremacy of Parliament, the Veto of the Crown, the constitutional tribunal to decide questions of *ultra vires*, and the existence of the Second Chamber, to which may also be added the express reservation from the Irish Legislature of power to deal with certain questions affecting religion and kindred matters.[69]

However, the statements Redmond and other Irish leaders made to non-British audiences were much more ambiguous than those they made in Parliament or to the British press, and at times they flirted with the rhetoric of independence. I could cite many examples, but three will suffice. The most famous is this extract from Parnell's speech of 21 January 1885, in Cork: "No man has the right to fix the boundary to the march of a nation. No man has a right to say to his country: 'thus far shalt thou go and no further,' and we have never attempted to fix the *ne plus ultra* to the progress of Ireland's nationhood and we never shall."[70] In 1909 T. P. O'Connor, a veteran nationalist M.P. for Liverpool, told a Massachusetts audience: "Give to us as you gave to Parnell and I'll promise you that within a few years the land of Ireland will belong to Ireland, her universities will be her own, and her liberty will be won so that her emblem will take its place along with the other flags of the world's nations."[71] The following year John Redmond told a convention of the United Irish League in Buffalo, New York, "[Home rule] concessions are only valuable because they strengthen the arm of the Irish people to push on to the great goal of national independence."[72]

These statements surely involved more than simple carelessness. Nationalist leaders were always searching for phrases that would have meaning for their listeners, and O'Connor and Redmond often addressed anglophobic Irish-Americans, the paymasters of Irish nationalism, who wanted to hear about an independent Irish republic, but before less-committed audiences they compared Irish home rule to the limited autonomy of an American state or a Canadian province. In October 1910 Redmond told the New York Press Club, "By home rule we mean something like you have here, where Federal affairs are governed by the Federal Government and State affairs by the State Government."[73] At other times the analogue was a self-governing Crown dominion, such as New Zealand or Canada. In Montreal in 1901, for example, John Redmond claimed that Ireland wanted only what Canada already had. He said, "It was only by the concession of home rule that the rebellious Canadians were turned into loyal, prosperous and contented citizens."[74]

These speeches complicated the Liberals' task in Parliament. Unionists asked what it was the Irish nationalists really wanted: an independent republic; a self-governing dominion under the Crown, like Canada; or a province, like Ontario. A former Chief Secretary, Walter Long, said in the House of Commons in 1911, "I confess I am unable to understand whether [Redmond], in taking the case of Canada as a precedent, puts Ireland in the position of the Dominion, or in the position of one of the provinces of Canada."[75] Redmond's reply was categorical: "Ireland's demand is for full legislative and executive control of all purely Irish affairs subject to the supreme authority of the Imperial Parliament. . . . I deny I am a Separatist."[76] But why should unionists have believed him?

In one important sense it did not matter what Irish nationalist politicians actually said because their audiences heard what they wanted to hear. On the one hundredth anniversary of the first home rule bill, John A. Murphy reminded us of this: "In the popular perception . . . concepts like Emancipation, Repeal and Home Rule transcended specific legal and political categories and denoted, quite simply, Irish control and Irish power. Home rule was freely interpreted as the ending of the Union, the undoing of the conquest and the panacea for Irish problems."[77] The problem for Liberal politicians was that unionists chose to interpret home rule in exactly this way, and it terrified them.

## Alternatives to Home Rule

### Chamberlain's Central Board and the Irish Council

There were two major sets of proposals for securing Irish self-government by agreement that would have avoided the constitutional problems of home rule. One was Joseph Chamberlain's "Central Board" scheme, and others like it, which would have given the Irish less than home rule. The other was federalism, which would have given them more. Neither plan was acceptable to Parliament, although each had powerful supporters.

In 1886 Joseph Chamberlain led the Liberal unionists out of the Liberal party in opposition to Gladstone's home rule bill, but a year earlier, as President of the Board of Trade, he had been a forceful supporter of a devolution plan that secured considerable support in the Cabinet. His approach was based upon a number of assumptions. First, the system of Irish government, with its almost continuous resort to coercion, was a failure. "It is nonsense," Chamberlain said in June 1885, "to talk of a constitutional system and constitutional government if the constitution is always being suspended."[78] Second, the issue of Irish nationality had to be addressed. "We have to recognize and to satisfy the national sentiment," he said, "which is in itself a praiseworthy and a patriotic and an inspiring feeling."[79] Third, it would be injurious to Britain and fatal to Ireland to concede to Ireland, or to any other part of the United Kingdom, the right to live as "an absolutely independent community" or to withdraw its representatives from Westminster.[80] The key to the Union, Chamberlain insisted, was "the maintenance of the full representation of Ireland in the Imperial Parliament."[81] Fourth, governing Ireland placed unnecessary burdens on the United Kingdom. There should be, therefore, a substantial devolution of responsibilities so that Ireland might itself deal with those matters that it could handle best.[82] The problem for the United Kingdom, as Chamberlain said, was to find a constitutional formula that could accommodate these assumptions:

While we have to conciliate the national sentiment of Ireland, we have to find a safe mean between separation on the one hand, which would be disastrous to Ireland and dangerous to England, and on the other hand that excessive centralization which throws upon the English Parliament and upon English officials the duty and burden of supervising every petty detail of Irish local affairs, which stifles the national life, which destroys the sense of responsibility, which keeps the people in ignorance of their duties and functions of government, and which produces a perpetual feeling of irritation while it obstructs all necessary legislation.[83]

C. H. D. Howard identifies five principle phases in Chamberlain's thinking about devolution,[84] but the proposal that came closest to adoption by the Cabinet, in April and May 1885, provided for the "the practical disappearance of what is known as Castle Administration," including the Lord Lieutenancy. In their place it proposed a system of elected County Boards, and an elected Central Board, with powers to legislate and administer certain all-Ireland affairs. Both levels of government would have the power to tax and borrow for their own purposes. Ireland would retain its representation in the United Kingdom Parliament, but "every purely Irish question would be dealt with by an exclusively Irish authority without reference or responsibility to any external body."[85]

Of course, Chamberlain's notion of a "purely Irish question" did not include general finance, or control of the judiciary, the police, and the military,[86] and Parnell viewed the plan not "as a substitute for the restitution of our Irish Parliament but solely as an improvement of the present system of local government in Ireland."[87] He wanted the Central Board to have no legislative powers so that it would pose no threat to the establishment of an Irish Parliament.[88]

Chamberlain was very concerned with nomenclature, and the word "Parliament" was unacceptable to him. Instead, he wrote:

I would give . . . the widest possible interpretation to the word Local Government, and would include in it not merely local and municipal affairs but also questions which may be described as national, although they do not concern Imperial interests. A Central Board should have if possible some distinctive title as, for instance, the National Board of Ireland.[89]

In 1887 Chamberlain accepted the idea that the Central Board might imitate "the cumbrous forms of our parliamentary government,"[90] but he did not really want Ireland to have responsible government. His proposal that members of the Central Board should serve fixed terms, with one-third elected annually, would have made it impossible to adopt responsible government because it precluded a dissolution of the legislature on the fall of a government.[91] It was the absence of responsible government, combined with more limited powers for Ireland and a less-grandiose conception of a legislature and an executive, which gave Chamberlain's scheme its advantages over home rule as a form of devolution. Under his plan Ireland would never have been in a position to challenge the supremacy of the United Kingdom.

On 9 May 1885 the Cabinet rejected Chamberlain's scheme. He had the support of Gladstone and all but one of the commoners in the Cabinet, but was opposed by all but one of the peers, Lord Granville.[92] The plan would probably have passed the House of Commons, with the support of many of the Liberal unionists who later voted with Chamberlain against home rule in 1886, but the opposition of so many peers in the Cabinet, including the Lord Lieutenant, Spencer, suggests that the motion would have lost in the House of Lords. Spencer believed that the Central Board could not be limited in practice to the matters reserved to it by law because the members of the Irish party, the "Healy's, and O'Briens, and T. P. O'Connors," were unfit for government![93]

The Liberal government of Campbell-Bannerman (1905–8) returned to the concept of limited devolution with its Irish Council bill in 1907.[94] This was largely the work of the Under-Secretary for Ireland from 1902 to 1907, Sir Anthony MacDonnell.[95] The bill proposed the creation of an Irish Council with eighty-two members elected on the local government franchise and twenty-four nominated by the Crown. The Under-Secretary for Ireland would serve as a member ex officio and the President of the Irish Council would be appointed by the Lord Lieutenant from among its number. Instead of a responsible executive, the plan called for administration by committees, with the chairmen appointed by the Lord Lieutenant. The Council would have administrative powers over the departments of government, but no legislative powers, and even its decisions on administrative matters might be reserved by the Lord Lieutenant. Funds would be transferred to the Council from the Treasury in an annual grant.[96]

The Irish Council plan offered Ireland far less than home rule, and less even than Chamberlain's plan, and when the Irish party rejected it unanimously, the bill was withdrawn.[97] But like Chamberlain's Central Board, it made more constitutional sense than home rule because it clarified Ireland's subordination to the United Kingdom. There was no provision for an Irish Parliament, the supremacy of the United Kingdom Parliament was absolutely unquestioned, the powers of the Irish body were strictly limited, and responsible government, the instrument of independence in the colonies, was precluded. The fatal flaw, of course, was that the proposal was unacceptable to Irish nationalists who insisted on an Irish Parliament and responsible government.

## Federalism and Home Rule All Round

There was another route to home rule, to which Chamberlain turned when he abandoned the Central Board plan in 1886.[98] It was federalism, or its close relative, "home rule all round." In the House of Commons in February 1893 Chamberlain said that there were only two ways to solve the Irish problem.

[Either] the Irish Government and the Irish Legislative Body should be a wholly subordinate body—something like an enlarged edition of the London County Council . . . [or] at the same time that you give a Parliament to Ireland you should give a Parliament to England, a Parliament to Scotland, and a Parliament to Wales, and . . . you should set up over these four Parliaments a fifth for the United Kingdom.[99]

Like most of the so-called federalists, Chamberlain was actually arguing for devolution, with subordinate, not coordinate, regional legislatures deriving their powers from the United Kingdom Parliament. He was proposing "home rule all round," but that clumsy appellation never quite displaced the less cumbersome word "federalism."

Chamberlain believed that home rule all round had three particular advantages over Gladstonian Irish home rule. First, it was easier to argue for all rather than for one that no region should control its own customs and excise. A Union in which the constituent units all had different customs duties would be a union in name only because there would be no financial management of the whole, trade would be inhibited, and friction would be certain. Second, home rule all round would solve the problem of Ireland's representation in the United Kingdom Parliament. Because the United Kingdom Parliament would not legislate for any of the regions, Gladstone's "double dilemma" would no longer exist. Third, it might be possible to satisfy Ulster by assigning it a legislature of its own.[100] Chamberlain alluded to this possible solution in 1886 when he said to a hostile chorus of Liberals and Irish nationalists in the House of Commons, "One of the great difficulties of this problem [is] that Ireland is not a homogeneous community. . . . it consists of two nations. . . . it is a nation which comprises two races and two religions."[101] He might not have known the difference between a nation and a race, but Chamberlain's meaning was perfectly clear.

Home rule all round received some support from Wales and Scotland, where home rule movements had been stimulated by Ireland's example. Indeed, Scotland's distinctive character was recognized by the creation of the Scottish Office and a Secretary of State for Scotland in 1885.[102] A number of Scottish home rule bills were introduced, all modeled on Irish home rule,[103] but the Welsh agitation was more modest, generally calling for administrative devolution.[104] Welsh and Scottish members combined in motions for home rule all round, in 1891, 1892, and 1898,[105] but Irish nationalists generally kept their distance from these activities, not wishing to complicate matters with further controversy.

Home rule all round never secured much support in Parliament, although it staged something of a revival in the period that began with the rejection of the Liberal's budget by the House of Lords in 1909 and ended with the outbreak of World War I in 1914. During this period a dramatic series of developments indicated that Ireland was approaching civil war. The Ulster unionists had begun to act relatively independently of the Conservative party since 1905,[106] and having recognized that the Parliament Act of 1911, which limited the Lords' veto to two years, meant that home rule would become law quite soon, they armed themselves for resistance. At Craigavon, County Down, on 25 September 1911 Sir Edward Carson, the Ulster unionist leader, declared, "We must be prepared. . . . the morning Home Rule is passed, ourselves to become responsible for the Protestant Province of Ulster."[107] A year later he led virtually the entire adult Protestant population of Ulster in signing the Ulster Covenant, which pledged them to resist home rule by force if necessary.[108] In January 1913 various Protestant drilling units in Ulster were combined into the 90,000-man Ulster Volunteer Force. In March 1914 British army officers at the Curragh barracks in County Kildare vowed to resign rather than enforce home rule, and in April 1914 the Ulster Volunteers acquired 35,000 rifles in a gun smuggling operation.[109]

The Irish nationalist response to this mounting unionist intimidation was to form the Irish Volunteer Force in October 1913, and 1,500 rifles were smuggled into the country in July 1914. The Ulster crisis had reached such a point by then that the Army Council warned that a civil war in Ireland, involving perhaps 200,000 volunteers from both sides, would tie down the entire British Expeditionary Force and would jeopardize the defense of the empire.[110]

Meanwhile, the Parliament Act of 1911 had left Conservatives with only one constitutional instrument with which to defeat the Liberals' plans for social reform and home rule, a general election that might bring the Conservatives back to power. The crisis in Ireland provided the best means, they thought, to force an election, and they played what Randolph Churchill many years before had called the "Orange card."[111] At Blenheim Palace in England, Bonar Law, the leader of the Conservative party from 1911 to 1921, offered his encouragement: "I can imagine no length of resistance to which Ulster can go in which I should not be prepared to support them, and in which, in my belief, they would not be supported by the overwhelming majority of the British people."[112] In 1912 the Conservative party was reconstituted as the National Union Association of Conservatives and Liberal Unionist Associations, popularly known as the Unionist party.[113]

Asquith refused to call a general election and King George was persuaded by the Prime Minister that it would be unconstitutional to dissolve Parliament against the advice of his ministers.[114] Asquith recognized the depth of feeling in northeast Ulster. "But we cannot admit," he said, "and we will not admit, the right of a minority of the people, and relatively a small minority . . . to veto the verdict of the vast body of their countrymen."[115]

During this period a number of influential Conservatives looked to what they called federalism as a way out of the dilemma.[116] One of them, F. S. Oliver, wrote that it provided "the only solution of the Irish question, because it is the only means which enables Nationalists to realize their ideal of Irish unity, while allowing Unionists to keep inviolate the Union of the Three Kingdoms."[117] Other supporters included the editor of the *Observer*, J. L. Garvin, and members of the Round Table, a movement founded in September 1909 by men who had worked with Lord Milner in South Africa.[118] They saw the issue as linked to a greater federation of the empire.

Arthur Balfour, who was the Conservative leader until November 1911, refused to accept federalism as anything but a device which might be used to unify previously independent units. In what had been a unitary state, he argued, it would simply encourage separatism.[119] Inside the Liberal Cabinet, however, several of Asquith's ministers became strong supporters of home rule all round. They included Winston Churchill, David Lloyd George, and Sir Edward Grey, the Foreign Secretary. Grey hoped for "a great Constitutional Reform; which will include Home Rule for the different parts of the United Kingdom, the reform of the Second Chamber, and a permanent adjustment of the relations between the two houses."[120]

In 1911 the Cabinet considered plans presented by both Churchill and Lloyd George. Churchill's plan was the more radical of the two because he proposed that England be divided into ten or twelve self-governing regions so that it would not dominate the United Kingdom Parliament.[121] Lloyd George's plan was more modest. He accepted the reality that Irish nationalists would not wait for a comprehensive plan of home rule all round to be worked out.[122] He recommended that home rule be granted to Ireland immediately, and only subsequently to England, Scotland, and Wales. In the interim, M.P.'s for England, Scotland, and Wales would sit in parliamentary grand committees to consider legislation for their regions.[123]

The Cabinet rejected both plans, although one draft of the third home rule bill did include Lloyd George's grand committees.[124] They were dropped because Birrell and the Irish party leaders feared that Scottish and Welsh M.P.'s would try to expand the provisions on Scotland and Wales during debate in the House of Commons, which might endanger Irish home rule.[125] When introducing the bill, Asquith would say no more than "I . . . have always presented the case for Irish Home Rule as the first step in a larger and more comprehensive policy,"[126] which was essentially Gladstone's position in 1886.[127]

In the end, home rule all round simply did not have enough support. Home rule M.P.'s were never a majority in Scotland or Wales. In Ireland only William O'Brien, an outcast from the Irish party and founder of the All for Ireland League, endorsed the plan, but he and his supporters won only eight seats in Parliament in the election of December

1910.[128] John Redmond consistently opposed home rule all round because it unnecessarily complicated home rule for Ireland. He would only agree that a bill for Irish home rule should be drafted so as not to preclude home rule all round.[129] In Ulster the unionists wanted no part of a settlement that left them in a Dublin Parliament, or even one that gave them their own Parliament in a new federation. They wanted the Union to continue, as before. Finally, there was no popular support for devolution in England.

## Partition

To avoid the ultimate showdown, civil war, attention turned to one final alternative to an all-Ireland form of home rule, the partition of Ireland. In 1886 Gladstone had said he would consider the exclusion of "Ulster itself, or, perhaps with more appearance of reason, a portion of Ulster,"[130] and the logic of the unionists' equal claim to self-determination was argued in every home rule debate, if only for argument's sake, because few unionists really wanted anything but the status quo. By 1912, however, Ulster's resistance had changed matters completely. As the home rule bill approached the end of its first passage through the House of Commons on 28 December, it was the Ulster unionist leader himself, Edward Carson, who moved that all nine counties of Ulster be excluded from home rule.[131] The government had already rejected an amendment moved by a Liberal backbencher, Thomas Agar-Robartes, in June to exclude Belfast and the four Protestant-majority counties of Antrim, Armagh, Down, and Londonderry,[132] and it argued again that Ulster's exclusion would make the very complex financial provisions of home rule unworkable.[133] The unamended third home rule bill therefore passed its third reading in the Commons on 16 January 1913 by a vote of 367 to 257 but was defeated by 69 votes to 326 in the Lords on 30 January. The process was repeated in July 1913.[134]

When the government itself began to move toward partition, it found that the first rejection of the third home rule bill by the House of Lords in January 1913 had given the unionists a substantial advantage. The Parliament Act of 1911 provided that for a bill to be enacted over the objections of the House of Lords, it had to pass the House of Commons three times in its original form. If the government wanted to change the bill now it had either to begin the whole process anew or come to an agreement with the House of Lords on an amendment.[135]

In the fall of 1913 there began, in secret, a determined effort by Asquith to negotiate a new agreement with the Conservative and unionist leaders Law and Carson and the Irish nationalist Redmond. Asquith had finally recognized the strength of Ulster's resistance, and the unionists had finally recognized the inevitability of a home rule act by the summer of 1914. A compromise was needed. The negotiations continued erratically into the Buckingham Palace Conference of July 1914, and the central issue was partition.

Two questions were central to these negotiations. First, should partition be temporary or permanent? Second, should the excluded area be nine, or six, or four Ulster counties? Traditional Ulster had nine counties, but three of these, Donegal, Monaghan, and Cavan, had large Catholic majorities, and two, Fermanagh and Tyrone, had small Catholic majorities. Only Armagh, Antrim, Down, and Londonderry had Protestant majorities. Unionists typically spoke of the rights of Ulster, but as a result of a by-election in 1913 nationalists held one more seat in Parliament for Ulster than did the unionists. A third question, whether Ulster should have home rule for itself, was not seriously considered. The partitioned area would have remained an integral part of the United Kingdom.

The Buckingham Palace Conference broke down after only three days because of apparently irreconcilable positions on the area to be excluded from home rule, but if one considers the negotiations as a whole, from October 1913 to July 1914, it is possible to see the outlines of a potential settlement.[136] Law and Carson began by insisting that all nine Ulster counties should be permanently excluded. Law later suggested the exclusion of four to six counties but noted that Carson would not accept fewer than six. The government, with Redmond's very reluctant acquiescence, countered that the three Ulster counties with the largest Catholic majorities should be included in home rule immediately and the remaining six counties should be temporarily excluded for six years. Implicit in this counterproposal was an important concession. The government knew that the six-year temporary exclusion period must include at least one general election, and that if a Conservative government were elected it would certainly move to make the exclusion permanent. But the unionists were not prepared to take this risk. They argued that it only provided a temporary stay of execution, and they offered instead a plan that each of the six counties should be given the option to vote for inclusion. This proposal also contained an important concession because presumably only the four counties with Protestant majorities would have opted for exclusion. The differences between the unionist and nationalist leaders had therefore narrowed considerably. By conceding a six-county temporary exclusion, Redmond had opened the door to permanent exclusion. By conceding county option, the unionists had reduced their claim from nine to four counties. But time ran out before the implications of these concessions could be explored.

The home rule bill had to pass the House of Commons for the third time before the end of the 1913–14 session, in the summer of 1914, if it was to meet the terms of the Parliament Act. It was passed by the Commons on 25 May and went to the House of Lords. There, on 23 June, the government introduced a separate amending bill to exclude six counties temporarily. The Lords, determined on a showdown, substituted an outrageous amendment that called for all nine Ulster counties to be permanently excluded, a position from which Carson and Law had already retreated. The government rejected the amendment and the bill, as originally introduced in April 1912, was approved over the objections of the Lords. Civil war in Ulster now appeared certain.

At this eleventh hour, with the encouragement of the King, the abortive Buckingham Palace Conference was convened on 21 July.[137] It broke down on 24 July, and when the Cabinet assembled later that day the news from the Palace was eclipsed by the news from Europe. Sir Edward Grey, the Foreign Secretary, read to his colleagues the terms of the Austro-Hungarian ultimatum to Serbia.[138]

The third home rule bill received the royal assent on 14 September 1914, but by then the war in Europe had started. Home rule for a united Ireland went onto the statute books but was immediately followed by a Suspensory Act that delayed its introduction until the end of the war, that is to say, until the postwar peace treaty. The nationalists believed they had won the long campaign, and Redmond threw himself into a recruiting campaign for the army in Ireland, but unionists had no intention of accepting the matter as finally settled. They knew that the Suspensory Act had provided Parliament with an opportunity to pass an amending bill at some stage that would make special provision for Ulster.[139]

The breakdown of the negotiations on exclusion leaves us with many unanswered questions about partition. We do not know, for example, if Redmond and Dillon, the nationalist representatives to the Bucking-ham Palace Conference, could have carried their supporters with them, even on a plan of temporary exclusion. It would have entailed ac-cepting the existence of two kinds of Irishmen, or two nations, a notion Redmond dismissed as "revolting and hateful,"[140] and "an abomina-tion and a blasphemy."[141] It would have denied, even if only temporar-ily, the principle of majority rule in the island as a whole, and it would have risked the permanent exclusion of some Ulster counties. Nor do we know if Law and Carson could have carried their supporters with them in a program of permanent exclusion of some part of Ulster. It involved the sacrifice of southern unionists to the home rule state, and it still posed a threat to the integrity of the British Empire. Bonar Law had justified the county option plan by saying, "A Parliament for the whole of Ireland would be practically independent, but a Parliament from which Ulster is excluded would in the nature of the case be subor-dinate, and [would] really be in the same relative position to the Impe-rial Parliament that one of the Provinces of Canada is to the Canadian Parliament."[142] But this was disingenuous. An Irish home rule Parlia-ment, embittered by the loss of Belfast and the north, might well have set its sights on early independence, as Carson and Law must have known when they recommended partition.

Hindsight suggests that the best solution to the Irish problem in 1914 would have been the permanent exclusion of four Ulster coun-ties, with some additional border adjustments such as the assignment of the city of Londonderry to the home rule state. George Dangerfield insists that forcing permanent exclusion on the nationalists in this way would have been unheroic and perfidious,[143] but this assumes that the unionists had no case for special consideration and that their orga-nized resistance posed no threat of civil war. Dangerfield was wrong on both counts. The exclusion of the four Protestant-majority counties would have been eminently sensible, might have minimally satisfied both sides, and might have averted a civil war. But there was no time to negotiate a settlement in the spring of 1914, and have it accepted by the rival communities before the deadline for enacting home rule ran out in the summer of 1914. To have delayed home rule pending a negotiated partition settlement would have required the government to abandon the 1912 home rule bill and start again. It would have alienated the nationalists and removed any immediate incentive for the unionists to cooperate.

## The "Greening of Dublin Castle"

Home rule was not achieved in 1914, but in an important sense the nationalists were already taking control of Ireland and the support structures for a home rule state were nearly in place. In a process that Lawrence McBride describes as "the greening of Dublin Castle," radical transformations of the Irish civil service and judiciary were well underway.[144] At the beginning of Gladstone's third ministry in 1892 both services were dominated by Protestant unionists. For example, forty-five of the top forty-eight civil service positions in Ireland were held by Protestants. By 1914 their number was down to twenty-eight, three of whom were Liberal homerulers. In 1892 there were eighteen Protestants and three Catholics on the Supreme Court bench. By 1914 there were an equal number of each. Even more substantial changes were occurring at lower levels of the bureaucracy and the judiciary, the result of competitive examinations and the appointment policies of governments, particularly the Liberals from 1906 to 1914. The process of change slowed when unionists entered the coalition government in December 1915, but it could not be reversed.

In 1915 John Redmond and the Under-Secretary, Sir Matthew Nathan, began to plan a completely new and compact structure of government for the new home rule state to replace the sprawling and unwieldy Dublin Castle administration. They proposed a small responsible executive, drawn from the Irish Parliament, with a Prime Minister and seven department ministers.[145] This planning process stopped when the war continued, but the model that Redmond and Nathan planned, of a small ministry into which were folded all the departments of the old Dublin Castle administration, was adopted in both Northern Ireland in 1921 and the Irish Free State in 1922.

## Would Home Rule Have Worked?

The Irish party won an empty victory in 1914 because the terms of the Suspensory Act were not honored at the end of the war. The Ulster unionists' long resistance to home rule, their evident willingness to prepare for civil war, and their powerful friends in government after Lloyd George formed his coalition ministry in December 1916 all conspired to destroy the dream of Gladstonian home rule for a united Ireland. But had home rule gone into effect, would it really have provided a permanent solution to the Irish problem? Probably not, at least as Gladstone conceived it.

Between 1886 and 1914, after hundreds of years of bitter conflict between Britain and Ireland, the Liberals attempted to solve the Irish problem with a scheme of devolution based on a quasi-colonial constitution which rested, in large part, on constitutional conventions to regulate the relationship between the two. That model had proven successful in the colonies because it was flexible. Indeed, it was handling the transition from colonial self-government to dominion independence with remarkable ease during the period that Irish home rule was being debated. But dominion independence is not what Liberal governments wanted from home rule. They insisted that Ireland was too close to Britain, too important to British security, and too integrated into British political and economic life to follow, or be allowed to follow, the colonies into independence. As Lord Spencer, twice Lord Lieutenant of Ireland, said in 1887, "The geographical position of Ireland, the social and commercial connections between the two peoples renders such a thing impossible."[146] It could equally be argued, however, that Ireland had a more intense nationalism, and grievances that were more deeply rooted, than could be found in any of the colonies. Even the most magnanimous of Irish nationalists saw themselves not as expatriate Englishmen but as members of an oppressed Irish race. As Nicholas Mansergh concluded, "While the Irish enjoyed less freedom [than the self-governing colonies] they were likely, despite the modesty of their immediate claims, in the long run to demand more than their colonial counterparts. Even their constitutional leaders talked not of concessions to be granted but of rights to be acknowledged."[147]

Gladstone's solution to the Irish problem was therefore extremely problematical. Whether it could have provided a final solution would have depended not on the provisions of the home rule statute, but on trust. Gladstone himself recognized this in 1886: "I ask that we should learn to rely less upon merely written stipulations and more upon those better stipulations which are written on the heart and mind of man."[148] The Liberals asked Parliament to give home rule, and the Irish, a chance. In 1893 James Bryce, for example, told the House of Commons: "I must . . . observe that it is easy to conjure up difficulties with all new schemes. Why, if any philosophic visitor were to come down here from some other planet and ask someone to explain the British Constitution to him, would he not say, 'Such a scheme cannot work; it is too full of complications and contradictions.' "[149] And in 1913 Asquith added, "Given perversity on the one hand and pedantry on the other, there is not a Constitution in the world which could not be wrecked in a week."[150] But what were the chances of the home rule constitution avoiding wreckage? Given that the unionists always anticipated the worst from home rule, which they insisted went too far, and that Irish nationalists were always dissatisfied with home rule, which they insisted did not go far enough, the chances were not good. Parnell's acceptance of home rule as "a fair offer" which "would lead to a final settlement" was probably disingenuous.[151] He knew that the 1886 bill would fail and lost nothing by endorsing it. "Indeed," writes O'Day, "the more sure the bill was to fail, the more fully it could be supported."[152]

The probability is that rather than creating a permanent framework for British–Irish relations, home rule would have been a decisive step toward Irish independence. In an essay in *Albion* I concluded,

Rather than settling the problem of the British–Irish relationship . . . home rule might have been the focus of powerful centrifugal forces as Parnell and his successors demanded greater autonomy for Ireland. Talented Irish politicians would have looked for their political fortunes to Dublin, not to Westminster, because no Irishman would have been allowed to govern Britain. In Dublin they would have operated within the flexible framework of colonial home rule and responsible government which had already brought the self-governing colonies to the brink of independence by 1886. And had Parnell become Prime Minister of Ireland, with the backing of three quarters of the Irish Parliament and the support of what was, organizationally, probably the most advanced political party in the world, it is difficult to imagine a list of reserved matters in a British statute restraining him for very long.[153]

Independence is not a bad thing, and it would have been much better for Ireland had it emerged via quasi-colonial home rule rather than a bloody war of independence, but that is the wisdom of hindsight. At the time of the first three home rule debates no British political party wanted Irish independence.

In the end, home rule was not defeated because of its constitutional imperfections. Rather, Gladstone and Asquith grossly underestimated the determination of the Protestants in Ulster to resist the establishment of a Dublin Parliament, no matter how limited its powers. It is a great irony, therefore, that when home rule was finally adopted in Ireland, it was in a unionist-controlled Northern Ireland that had never wanted it.

Part II

# Home Rule and Northern Ireland

# CHAPTER 5

# The Government of Ireland Act and Home Rule in Northern Ireland, 1921–1972

By November 1918, when a truce was declared in Europe, two redistributions of political power, one in the United Kingdom and one in Ireland, had changed everything for Ireland and set the stage for an inevitable conflict there. In the United Kingdom as a whole World War I saw the decline of the Liberals, the party of home rule. In December 1916 a new government came to power, and although it was led by a Liberal, David Lloyd George, it was actually a Conservative-dominated coalition, and remained so until October 1922. It was inconceivable that such a government would ever surrender the Ulster unionists to a Dublin Parliament. Simultaneously, in Ireland, the Irish Parliamentary party of Parnell and Redmond died and constitutional nationalism was temporarily eclipsed by revolutionary nationalism in the aftermath of the Easter Rising, which began on 24 April 1916.

## The Easter Rising

The Easter Rising was a rebellion led by members of the Irish Republican Brotherhood. The rebels were known to the government and the general public as Sinn Féin, the name of a political organization founded by Arthur Griffith in 1905. Griffith's original program called for a dual monarchy for Britain and Ireland, on the Austro-Hungarian model, but by 1916 Sinn Féin was republican. Signs of mounting dissatisfaction with the Irish Parliamentary party were already evident in 1913, when John Redmond had to struggle to take control of the National Volunteers, a militia organized in response to the Ulster Volunteers. As World War I began it became clear that he and his colleagues were insensitive to the changing mood of Ireland. F. S. L. Lyons argues, "Part of this rigidity was the natural conservatism of old age and middle class, but part sprang from an attachment to the parliamentary game as played by British rules which was to render [the Irish party] dangerously vulnerable."[1] The challenge to the party came in 1916.

The official chronology of independent Ireland dates from the proclamation of the Irish Republic by Patrick Pearse on the steps of the General Post Office in the first minutes of the Easter Rising, on 24 April 1916. The Rising found no immediate popular support and ended in total military defeat; it might well have meant comparatively little to the future of Ireland had it been suppressed with less severity. Pearse and fourteen other leaders were executed by firing squad after military trials in May, and Sir Roger Casement, who had actually come from Germany by submarine to stop the Rising because of inadequate German support, was hung in London on 3 August after a civil trial for treason. The leaders of the Irish party begged the government not to martyr the rebels by executing them, but the sentences were carried out.[2] As a result, it mattered little that the government had acted with comparative restraint to suppress what was, after all, a wartime rebellion with proven collusion by Germany, or that seventy-five death sentences were commuted, or that most of the 1800 rebels interned without trial were released before the end of 1916. What mattered was that Irishmen had shed their blood for Irish freedom and sixteen men had joined Wolfe Tone and Robert Emmet in the pantheon of Irish martyrs.

Nationalist opinion now turned in favor of Sinn Féin, which was formally reorganized in October 1917 as a political organization. Having failed as military planners in 1916, Sinn Féin leaders now proved to be very adept politicians. Republicans began to win parliamentary by-elections in January 1917, but Sinn Féin's policy was to refuse to take seats at Westminster, where Arthur Griffith had always argued the Irish could not win, and to create instead an Irish Parliament.[3] The opportunity to implement this program came in the general election of December 1918 when, despite having forty-seven of its candidates in prison, Sinn Féin won seventy-three Irish seats. The Irish party was reduced to a mere seven, one of which was in England. Unionist strength grew from nineteen to twenty-six seats, largely in the northeast of Ireland. Most Irish seats in the House of Commons were held, therefore, by republicans who refused to take their seats. Instead, on 21 January 1919, the twenty-seven Sinn Féiners who were still at liberty and in

Ireland met at the Mansion House, Dublin, in the first public session of Dáil Éireann, the Parliament of the Irish Republic. On the following day they formed a government. Their intention, quite simply, was to govern Ireland de facto. Even more ominous for the United Kingdom was the fact that on 21 January the first shots were fired in Solohead-beg, County Tipperary, in the Irish War of Independence.

## Last-Minute Attempts to Find a Solution to the Irish Problem

The Easter Rising and its aftermath had a very adverse effect on public opinion in the United States and Australia, with consequent repercussions on Britain's conduct of the war in Europe, and it was this, as much as the deteriorating situation in Ireland, which led to several last-minute attempts between 1916 and 1920 to solve the Irish problem within a Gladstonian home rule framework.[4] These efforts began just a few weeks after the Rising when Prime Minister Asquith told the House of Commons that Dublin Castle administration had broken down.[5] He asked David Lloyd George, the Minister for Munitions, to recommend a plan to settle the Irish problem and to accept office as Minister for Ireland, replacing both the Lord Lieutenant and the Chief Secretary. Lloyd George accepted the task but refused the office.

For the framework of his 1916 Irish proposal, Lloyd George returned to the government's partition proposal of mid-1914, which is to say, the immediate introduction of home rule, subject to the temporary exclusion of six Ulster counties and their administration by a Secretary of State. If no final plan for the excluded area were agreed upon within one year of the end of the war, it would continue to be governed by a Secretary of State.[6] Lloyd George appears to have convinced the leaders of the Irish party that the exclusion of six Ulster counties would be temporary, and the leaders of the Ulster unionists that it would be permanent. In the event, the Irish party could only have been saved from extinction by the immediate and unqualified introduction of the 1914 home rule act, so it rejected the Lloyd George plan which effectively gave the Ulster unionists, acting through the pro-unionist majority in the Cabinet, a veto over a united Ireland. The negotiations collapsed in July 1916.

When Lloyd George himself became Prime Minister in December 1916 he passed the task of finding an Irish solution to an assembly of

Irishmen, the Irish Convention, which he convened in July 1917. The report, which the Convention chairman, Sir Horace Plunkett, presented to the Prime Minister on 4 April 1918 had been approved by a vote of forty-four to twenty-nine, but it was of very little use. It recommended a settlement modeled on the Government of Ireland Act of 1914, with essentially the same form of executive, the same reservations to the United Kingdom Parliament, the same restrictions on the Irish legislature concerning religion, and the same Irish representation at Westminster. The critical question of control of customs and excise was deferred, at the government's suggestion, until some future date.[7]

The chairman of the Irish Convention, Sir Horace Plunkett, was surprisingly optimistic about the report, and therefore appallingly naive. "The Convention has," he wrote, "laid a foundation of Irish agreement unprecedented in history."[8] Lloyd George's enthusiastic reception of the report demonstrates that he too was badly out of touch with Ireland. "The Sinn Féin demand is for the control of Customs," he wrote, "otherwise they would have agreed with the majority."[9] In truth, Sinn Féin had boycotted the entire proceedings, the Ulster unionists rejected the report because it proposed a united Ireland, and eleven of the Irish party representatives rejected it because it proposed to defer a decision on the question of control of customs and excise. The fact that the Southern unionists had joined with a majority of the Irish party and five Labour representatives to form a majority for the report meant almost nothing in the face of this opposition.

The convention report was also received by the government at a particularly inappropriate time. It came just days before the government announced, on 9 April, that military conscription would be extended from Britain to Ireland. The decision, which caused John Dillon, the new leader of the Irish party, to lead his members out of the House of Commons, unified nationalist opinion as never before by bringing Sinn Féin into a temporary alliance with the Irish party, the Catholic bishops, and the trades unions, a combination that prevented conscription in Ireland that spring. Conscription actually destroyed the Irish party, a judgment confirmed by the December 1918 general elections.[10]

Notwithstanding the rejection of the Irish Convention report by the most powerful forces in Ireland in 1918, the government persisted in arguing that a solution to the Irish problem could still be found somewhere within the framework of Gladstonian home rule.

## The Government of Ireland Act, 1920

World War I ended in November 1918, and by that time unionists in Britain had finally been forced to face up to the imperative need to solve the Irish question, which had seriously endangered the United Kingdom during the war and continued to disturb relations with important allies, particularly the United States. The government was also faced with the need to do something about the 1914 Government of Ireland Act, which had only been suspended pending the formal end of the war, not abandoned. The coalition's election manifesto in 1918 called for Irish self-government, but rejected Ireland's severance from the British Empire and the forcible inclusion of six Ulster counties in a Dublin Parliament.[11] The way out of the dilemma was suggested by wartime discussions of partition and the conversion of some unionists in the Cabinet to home rule all round, or federalism, as they insisted on calling it. The solution lay in the creation of two subordinate Parliaments in Ireland, one in Belfast and one in Dublin, the two to be compatible with a future scheme of home rule all round. Walter Long, the unionist chairman of the Cabinet committee on Ireland, which was created in April 1918, wanted to implement this plan even before the war ended.[12]

On 7 October 1919 Long was again appointed to chair a Cabinet Irish committee, and on 4 November he presented a report that contained the framework of what became the Government of Ireland Act the following year.[13] His committee ruled out a single Irish Parliament, albeit with special protections for Ulster, because this would have permitted Ulster unionists to impede Irish self-government. It also rejected the position Law and Carson had adopted in 1913, that certain Ulster counties should remain wholly governed from Westminster. This proposal had the disadvantage of leaving Britain in control of a part of Ireland, something public opinion in the United States and the dominions would condemn as a violation of Irish self-determination. A divided Cabinet therefore accepted the idea that home rule should be given to both parts of Ireland.[14]

There was certainly no thundering demand for self-determination in the north of Ireland, but the Ulster unionists accepted the plan as the lesser evil. They were, Buckland says, "suspicious of the good faith of their British allies and less certain about their willingness to protect Ulster unionist interests."[15] The unionists also feared that the British Parliament would soon be controlled by Liberals and Socialists known to be unfavorable to Ulster unionism.[16] The unionists were divided, however, on the area to be partitioned, some believing that there would be a comfortable Protestant majority of about 56 percent in a nine-county Northern Ireland, and others arguing that this was highly problematic. In the event, they had to accept the Cabinet's decision for a six-county partition, with a 66 percent Protestant majority overall but Protestant majorities in only four counties.[17] The first Prime Minister of Northern Ireland, Sir James Craig, accepted this as a supportable area.[18] On 25 February 1920 the government presented the final Government of Ireland Bill, the fourth, to Parliament. It was approved by both houses and received the royal assent on 23 December 1920. The act came into force on 3 May 1921; Section 76.2 repealed the Government of Ireland Act of 1914.

The act created two home rule Parliaments in Ireland, one for six counties in the northeast and the parliamentary boroughs of Londonderry and Belfast, and another for the remaining twenty-six counties. It created essentially the same constitutional systems for the two parts of Ireland as the predecessor home rule bills had proposed for Ireland as a whole, with the exception of elections by proportional representation, the composition of the two Senates, and the Council of Ireland.

The system of elections to the two Houses of Commons was proportional representation in multimember constituencies.[19] This plan was borrowed from the Irish Convention report to ensure parliamentary representation for the Protestant community in the south, approximately 10 percent of the population. The system was applied to the north too, although the Catholic population there, about 35 percent of the total, was sufficiently concentrated to have ensured fair representation under the British system of election in single-member constituencies.

The desire to protect the minority also influenced the composition of the Southern Senate. The original government bill proposed that two unicameral Parliaments should be established in Ireland but this proposal was amended in the House of Lords to provide for two bicameral legislatures. All but two seats in the Northern Senate, those reserved for the Lord Mayors of Belfast and Londonderry, were filled by an election in the House of Commons using proportional representation, a system that gave Catholics substantial representation in the upper house.[20] In the South, however, the Senate was based on the model recommended by the Irish Convention in 1918, which is to say, a nominated house representing a variety of interests.[21] The British government assumed that this procedure would permit substantial representation of Protestants, although a memorandum prepared for the Cabinet committee on Ireland by Sir F. Greer, the Parliamentary Counsel to the Irish Office, argued that the representation of interests was a more important factor in deciding the composition of the Senate than the protection of the minority.[22]

The Council of Ireland was an important element in the 1920 act because it provided a mechanism for the unification of Ireland.[23] Composed of twenty representatives each from the Northern and Southern Parliaments, it was provided with limited powers to recommend legislation for the whole of Ireland by Order in Council.[24] It was also empowered to exercise powers that might be delegated to it in identical terms by the two Irish Parliaments,[25] and to administer matters concerning railways, fisheries, and contagious diseases for the whole of Ireland.[26] The act provided that the two Irish Houses of Commons might vote to create a single home rule Parliament to replace the Council,[27] and that the United Kingdom Parliament might transfer customs and excise to the new body.[28] However, there was also a provision in the act that if half the members of either the Northern or Southern Parliaments failed to take their seats, it could be adjourned by the Lord Lieutenant without prejudice to the other.[29] This procedure was used very quickly.

Elections were held in May 1921, and unionists won 40 of the 52 seats in the Northern House of Commons. The Northern Parliament first met on 7 June 1921 and was formally opened by King George V on 22 June 1921. As the government had anticipated,[30] Sinn Féin was unopposed for all but 4 of the 128 seats in the Southern House of Commons, the 4 being the seats for the Protestant Dublin University. When the Parliament assembled for the first time on 28 June 1921, only 19 members of both houses attended, the 4 Dublin University members and 15 senators nominated by the Lieutenant Governor. The number dropped to 14 at the next sitting, and pursuant to Section 72 of the act, the Southern Parliament was adjourned by the Lieutenant Governor on 13 July. It was subsequently abolished by the Irish Free State (Agreement) Act of 1922.[31]

Two days before the Southern Parliament was adjourned, a truce was declared in the War of Independence which opened the way for the negotiations that would lead to the Anglo-Irish Treaty of 6 December 1921 and an independent Irish state.

The Anglo-Irish Treaty envisaged the establishment of an independent dominion in Ireland and was drafted as if for the whole island, but Article 12 gave the north the right to opt out, by an Address to the King from the Northern Parliament. It exercised that right on 7 December 1922[32] and the Irish Free State (Consequential Provisions) Act amended the 1920 Government of Ireland Act to apply only to the north. Specifically, the financial provisions were rewritten, Irish representation at Westminster was limited to thirteen representatives from Northern Ireland, and the title of Lord Lieutenant was changed to Governor of Northern Ireland. A Privy Council for Northern Ireland was created to replace the Privy Council for Ireland. The Lord Chief Justice of Northern Ireland was assigned judicial functions originally to have been carried out by the Lord Chancellor for Ireland, and the Court of Appeal in Northern Ireland became the High Court of Appeal.[33] The Council of Ireland was abolished in 1925.[34]

In this bizarre conclusion to a long struggle, only that part of Ireland that had opposed home rule now had the opportunity to practice it. Northern Ireland offers us, therefore, the only example we have of Gladstonian home rule in operation, albeit in the inhospitable milieu of a divided society. As J. J. Lee writes, "Partition . . . saved the South from the most explosive internal problems affecting new states, race and religion, by the simple device of exporting them to the North."[35] Those problems would destroy home rule in Northern Ireland.

## The Constitution of Northern Ireland

From 1921 to 1972 Northern Ireland had a constitution, the Government of Ireland Act of 1920, as amended by the Irish Free State (Consequential Provisions) Act of 1922 and subsequent amendments.[36] We can most usefully consider this constitution by reviewing its provisions on the executive and the legislature, the powers assigned to Northern Ireland, and the system of responsible government that it established. The chapter will end by evaluating home rule in Northern Ireland.

### The Northern Ireland Executive

Like its colonial and home rule antecedents, the Northern Ireland constitution only partially identified the model of government that was to be used in Northern Ireland.[37] There was no explicit reference to the rules of responsible government and executive powers were assigned to the Governor, acting for the Sovereign.[38] The Governor had the power in law to create departments and appoint ministers; to summon, prorogue, and dissolve Parliament; to give or withhold the royal assent to legislation; to recommend appropriations of public money; and to convene a joint sitting of both houses of Parliament. He was empowered to appoint a Comptroller and Auditor-General, appoint county court judges, and refer questions on the validity of Northern Ireland laws to the Judicial Committee of the Privy Council. The act also empowered the Sovereign to delegate prerogative and other executive powers to the Governor, including the powers of pardon, reprieve, and remission of sentences. Finally, the Governor was empowered to reserve a bill to the Sovereign for further consideration before giving the assent. A reserved bill would lapse if the royal assent were not forthcoming within a year.[39]

Despite assigning these enormous executive powers to the Crown, the constitution implied that responsible government would be practiced and that the Governor would only act on the advice of his ministers. First, borrowing from the language of the 1893 home rule bill and the 1914 Government of Ireland Act, an Executive Committee of the Privy Council, composed of ministers, was created to aid and advise the Governor.[40] The word "Cabinet" was not mentioned but that is exactly what the Executive Committee was. Second, borrowing from the 1914 act and Australian precedents, the constitution required ministers who were not already sitting in Parliament to secure seats within six months of their appointment.[41] These were significant provisions, but for the most part responsible government was left to conventions because the formal constitution itself did not require the Executive Committee to advise the Governor on the royal assent,[42] did not make any reference to the appointment of a Prime Minister, and did not require the Governor to appoint ministers who had the support of a majority in the House of Commons.

## The Northern Ireland Legislature

Northern Ireland was provided with a bicameral Parliament containing a Senate and a House of Commons.[43] The Senate was composed of the Lord Mayors of Belfast and Londonderry and twenty-four members elected to eight-year terms by the Northern House of Commons using proportional representation, with one-half elected at four-year intervals.[44] The House of Commons had fifty-two members, forty-eight representing constituencies and four representing the graduates of Queen's University.[45] University seats were abolished in Britain in 1948 but survived in Northern Ireland until 1969 when they were replaced by an additional four constituency seats.[46] The first constituencies were multimembered, with four to eight members each, and elections were by the single-transferable vote system of proportional representation. This system was replaced in 1929 by elections in single-member constituencies by simple majority vote. The length of a Parliament was set at five years "unless sooner dissolved,"[47] itself an oblique reference to responsible government.

The constitution used the Australian procedure for resolving deadlocks between the two chambers which had been included in the home rule bill of 1893 and the act of 1914, which is to say, a joint sitting in which a two-thirds majority would decide the issue.[48] In practice, the selection system for the Senate produced an upper house that was a mirror image of the lower, and the deadlock provision was never used. On the rare occasions of disagreement, one house would yield to the other.[49]

## Northern Ireland Powers

The Northern Ireland Parliament was empowered to make laws for the "peace, order and good government" of Northern Ireland, subject to certain matters of concern to the United Kingdom as a whole that were assigned permanently to the United Kingdom Parliament. These were very much the same as in earlier home rule bills, with the addition of new technologies such as wireless telegraphy and aerial navigation. They included the Crown, peace and war, military forces, treaties and foreign relations, dignities and titles of honor, treason, alienage and naturalization, foreign trade, submarine cables, lighthouses, buoys and beacons, coinage, legal tender and negotiable instruments, trade marks, copyrights, and patents.[50] Northern Ireland was authorized to impose taxes,[51] but all the most important ones—on customs and excise, excess profits, corporation profits, and personal incomes—were assigned to the United Kingdom.[52]

A small group of limitations, termed "reserved matters," was assigned to the United Kingdom for the moment, but the constitution provided that they might be transferred to a united Ireland at some future date.[53] They included the Post Office, the Post Office and Trustee Savings Banks, stamp designs, registration of deeds, and the Public Records Office of Ireland. When the south rejected home rule, these matters were retained permanently by the United Kingdom, although Northern Ireland established its own Records Office.

Residuary powers, all those not specifically assigned or reserved to the United Kingdom, were transferred to Northern Ireland, subject to the same prohibitions concerning religion that had been included in all the previous home rule bills. That is to say, Northern Ireland was prohibited from legislating to establish, endow, or prohibit the free exercise of religion, to discriminate on account of religion, to require a child to attend religious instruction in a school receiving public money, or to make a religious ceremony a condition of marriage.[54]

The Northern Ireland constitution provided that *vires* for Northern Ireland bills would be determined by the Judicial Committee of the Privy Council, in practice on a reference by the Governor, a United Kingdom Secretary of State, or the Joint Exchequer Board, the body charged with coordinating the financial provisions of the act.[55]

## Responsible Government in Northern Ireland

Since Gladstone's time there had been no doubt that responsible government would be adopted in Ireland, although it was only implied in the provisions on the executive in the Northern Ireland constitution. In practice, it was understood that the Governor would accept certain British conventions concerning majority rule and ministerial advice, and that Britain would respect the convention of nonintervention that had evolved in its relations with the self-governing colonies in the second half of the nineteenth century. That is to say, responsible Northern Irish ministers would govern what has come to be known as "the province."

Exactly how was responsible government expressed in the Northern Ireland?

FUSION.   The fusion of the executive and the legislature was identified in Section 8.4 of the constitution, which required ministers to obtain seats in Parliament within six months of their appointments, and Section 8.5, which required them to sit in the Executive Committee of the Privy Council, in effect the Cabinet. Before 1971 every minister already had a seat at the time of appointment, but that year, shortly before home rule was abolished, in an attempt to broaden the ministry during a time of great community tension, two ministers were appointed from outside: David Bleakley, formerly a Northern Ireland Labour party M.P., was appointed Minister of Community Relations, and Gerald Newe, a Roman Catholic, was appointed Minister of State in the Prime Minister's Office.[56]

MAJORITY GOVERNMENT.    Government by ministers having the support of the majority in the House of Commons was not required by the Northern Ireland constitution, but the Governor accepted this British convention when he appointed Sir James Craig as the first Prime Minister. Craig was leader of the Unionist party, which had won forty of the fifty-two seats in the first general election to the House of Commons in May 1921. The Irish party and Sinn Féin each won six seats. In the history of the Northern Ireland Parliament, no unionist government ever lost a vote of confidence or a major vote in the House of Commons.

THE PRIMACY OF THE LOWER HOUSE.    The Northern Ireland constitution did not identify the primacy of the House of Commons but several provisions ensured that it would be the responsible chamber. First, whereas senators served fixed eight-year terms,[57] members of the House of Commons served for the length of a Parliament, which was five years "unless sooner dissolved."[58] This meant that a general election could be called at any time to find a new government from the House of Commons, not the Senate. Second, the Senate was not permitted to initiate or amend financial legislation.[59] Third, the provision for resolving a deadlock between the two houses, a vote by members of both houses in a joint sitting, gave the House a majority of fifty-two to twenty-six.[60] Fourth, the constituency for the twenty-four elected senators was the House of Commons itself, which therefore controlled the composition of the upper chamber.[61]

These constitutional provisions favoring the House of Commons were reinforced by a number of practices. First, although there was no restriction in law on the number of senators who might serve in the Cabinet, there was a powerful belief that ministers should sit in the responsible chamber, although they were permitted to attend and address either chamber.[62] For most of the period from 1921 to 1972 only one senator sat in the Cabinet, and there were never more than two.[63] Second, the constitution required financial measures to be introduced in the House of Commons, but even nonmoney legislation was dominated by the Commons. Only noncontroversial bills were introduced in the Senate.[64] It also sat for fewer days each year, between twenty-five and thirty days a year, as against eighty-six to eighty-eight days in the House of Commons in the period 1966–71. Membership in the House naturally carried greater responsibility and much higher status than membership in the Senate. The most important role of the upper house was to provide members for parliamentary joint committees.[65]

PARTY GOVERNMENT.    Party government was particularly strong in Northern Ireland where the party system reflected deeply entrenched sectarian divisions and the Unionist party was the highly organized political voice of the majority Protestant community. The number of Unionist party M.P.'s reached a high of forty in the House of Commons in 1921 and a low of thirty-two in 1925, but with the support of other unionists, the unionist bloc never fell below thirty-five in a chamber of fifty-two. Even the Northern Ireland Labour party, which won four seats in 1962 and 1965, could be counted on to support the Union. The anti-unionist opposition never approached a majority. The largest opposition group through the years was the Catholic-based Nationalist party, which ranged from a high of eleven M.P.'s in 1929 to lows of six in 1921 and 1969.[66] So anxious was Sir James Craig to focus political debate in Northern Ireland into a clear choice between unionists and nationalists that the electoral law was amended to abolish proportional representation for local elections in 1922, and for Northern Ireland parliamentary elections in 1929.[67] The effect was to hinder the development of any party, such as the Northern Ireland Labour party, which might have weakened fortress unionism.[68] Indeed, so polarized and uncompetitive did Northern Ireland elections become that whereas only one parliamentary seat was uncontested in 1921, and twelve in 1925, thirty-three were uncontested in 1933, 63 percent of the total.[69]

Party government was built upon a well-organized Unionist party in the constituencies, based on Orange lodges, and on a disciplined party in Parliament. Buckland found Unionist M.P.'s voting against the government on only 95 of 771 divisions between 1921 and 1938, and then only in very small numbers.[70] Only three people who were not members of the Unionist party ever sat in a northern government.[71]

CABINET GOVERNMENT.    In law the Cabinet was the Executive Committee of the Northern Ireland Privy Council, composed of those holding full ministerial office. The constitution authorized the Lord Lieutenant, the governor's title until 1922, to appoint ministers and create departments.[72] Acting on Craig's advice he created departments, including the Department of the Prime Minister, and announced the names of the Executive Committee on 31 May 1921, before Parliament assembled for the first time.[73]

Northern Ireland began with only six, largely part-time, Cabinet ministers and seven departments serving the Prime Minister, Finance, Home Affairs, Education, Labour, Agriculture, and Commerce. The last two were administered by a single minister until 1925.[74] By 1971 the government as a whole had grown to twenty members, with fifteen full-time Cabinet ministers, four non-Cabinet Parliamentary Secretaries, and a non-Cabinet Attorney General. There were more members of the Unionist party in the government than sitting on the back benches in the House of Commons, which ensured the government's absolute control of Parliament.[75]

By law, money bills could only be introduced into the House of Commons on the recommendation of the Governor,[76] and this gave the Cabinet a monopoly on financial measures through its advice to the Crown. The Cabinet also dominated almost all the remaining parliamentary time through its control of the majority party. There were never more than two private members' bills introduced each year until 1965–66, when the number increased a little. Only four such bills became law in the fifty-year history of the Northern Parliament, and they passed with Cabinet support or on free votes it had approved.[77] Only a small number of amendments to government bills were accepted from the opposition or government backbenchers.[78]

The Northern Ireland Parliament was not organized to challenge the Cabinet's dominance in any way. There was no effective committee system, for example. British parliamentary practice was followed and each bill received three readings and a committee stage in each house, but the practice was to conduct the committee stage in a committee of the whole house, and only occasionally to establish an ad hoc select committee for a particular bill. Furthermore, there were no committees appointed for full parliamentary sessions, other than those dealing with administration, such as the Public Accounts Committee and the Committee on Statutory Rules, Orders, and Regulations.[79] Not until 1971, with the Northern Ireland political system on its last legs and the government looking for ways to involve the opposition in solving the political crisis, did Prime Minister Faulkner propose the creation of three substantive sessional committees to deal with social affairs, the environment, and industry, but this gesture came too late.[80]

The Cabinet, though clearly dominating the political system, was not insensitive to back-bench and Senate opinion, particularly unionist opinion, or to interest groups outside Parliament. It often dropped or amended measures that were opposed, and it experienced substantial unionist opposition to accommodationist policies with the United Kingdom in the period 1969–72,[81] but Parliament was never an independent actor.

Given that the Unionist party was in office from 1921 to 1972, that ministers were very rarely defeated in elections, and that there was a very small pool of potential ministers in the House of Commons, it is not surprising that the circulation in office that one would customarily anticipate in a competitive party system was absent in Northern Ireland. Indeed, the government had the character of an oligarchy. Only sixty M.P.'s served in the government from 1921 to 1972.[82] Early ministers often served extraordinarily long terms, including one, Sir R. D. Bates, who served as Minister of Home Affairs for twenty-two years. J. M. Andrews served in the Cabinet for twenty-two years as Minister of Labour, Minister of Finance (1937–41), and Prime Minister (1940–43). The first Prime Minister, Sir James Craig, served from 1921 to 1940, and the third, Sir Basil Brookeborough, from 1943 to 1963.

Within the Cabinet the convention of collective responsibility applied, although commentators note that it became difficult to maintain in the turbulent last three or so years of the Northern Parliament.[83] The convention that collective responsibility would apply to government members outside the Cabinet, that is to say, to Parliamentary Secretaries, was less strictly observed in Northern Ireland than at Westminster. When not acting as spokesmen for the government, they could express disagreement with government policy on matters outside their own departments' concerns. This was a measure of the government's security in office, but it could not be carried too far.[84]

Inside the Northern Ireland political system, then, the Cabinet was extraordinarily powerful, but it also derived power from Northern Ireland's constitutional relationship with the United Kingdom. The Treasury in London and the Ministry of Finance in Belfast negotiated Northern Ireland's annual budget, which was largely made up of transfers from the United Kingdom, and Northern Ireland ministers served

as agents for United Kingdom departments in Northern Ireland, negotiating with counterparts at Westminster on financial matters and services.[85] These relationships were quasi-diplomatic; indeed, Buckland
describes Craig as acting at times "less as Northern Ireland's Prime
Minister than as its ambassador in Britain."[86] The effect, of course, is
that both Northern Ireland and United Kingdom Parliaments were effectively locked out of this critically important process.[87]

A STRONG PRIME MINISTER.   The Northern Ireland constitution
made no provision for the office of Prime Minister. It was created by
the then Lord Lieutenant pursuant to his general power to create departments and appoint ministers.[88] In May 1921 he invited Sir James
Craig, the leader of the Unionist party, to take the post following the
Unionists' victory in the first Northern Ireland parliamentary elections,[89] and Craig nominated the rest of the ministry. Until 1969 there
was no prescribed procedure within the Unionist party for selecting the
Prime Minister. Instead, the Governor consulted with the outgoing
Prime Minister and party whips, who themselves conducted "soundings" in the party. In 1963 controversy broke out when the outgoing
Prime Minister, Lord Brookeborough, chose not to offer advice on his
successor. Terence O'Neill was selected over two other candidates after
soundings conducted by William Craig, the Chief Whip. A formal procedure was subsequently instituted and in 1969 and 1971 James
Chichester-Clark and Brian Faulkner were appointed by the Governor
after party ballots.[90]

The Prime Minister's power came from his role as leader of the Unionist party in Parliament and the province, his role as adviser to the
Governor, and his responsibilities for forming and directing the government. The peculiar circumstances of Northern Ireland also helped
to establish his supremacy. The first Prime Minister, Sir James Craig,
was Edward Carson's chief lieutenant and had personally planned Ulster's militant resistance to home rule in 1914. He was an authentic
leader, and very much more than a Cabinet "chairman." Craig set a
pattern of strong Prime Ministerial leadership and Northern Ireland
Prime Ministers often acted on important matters without consulting
the Cabinet. O'Neill, for example, consulted none of his colleagues
when he invited the Prime Minister of the Irish Republic, Seán Lemass,
to meet him in Belfast in 1965, and Faulkner alone made the decision to
intern suspects without trial in August 1971.[91] However, all the Prime

Ministers came under attack within the Unionist party from time to time. Indeed, Andrews (1940–43), Brookeborough (1943–63), O'Neill (1963–69), and Chichester-Clark (1969–71) all resigned under pressure from members of the party, and even Craig came under considerable pressure in his final years.[92] Faulkner (1971–72) also faced bitter criticism but managed to survive until his government resigned to protest the decision by the British government of Prime Minister Edward Heath to assume responsibility for law and order in Northern Ireland in 1972.

A WEAK HEAD OF STATE. The Northern Ireland Governor had enormous powers in law but the conventions of responsible government ensured that they were very limited in practice. In normal circumstances he was expected to accept the advice of his ministers, and as we shall see, when he was instructed from London in 1922 to reserve a bill to the Crown, the United Kingdom was forced to back down in the face of the threatened resignation of Craig's government. From that point on, any independent role for the Governor was nullified, and he was left to provide the constitutional facade for responsible government in Northern Ireland. The office was abolished in July 1973, sixteen months after the suspension of the Northern Ireland Parliament.[93]

CONCENTRATION OF POWER. The concentration of power was particularly evident in Northern Ireland, in part because of the unionist monopoly on power. The Cabinet dominated both the executive and Parliament, and its role in conducting relations between Northern Ireland and the United Kingdom further concentrated power in ministers' hands.

## Did Home Rule Work in Northern Ireland?

Having discussed the constitutional framework of Northern Ireland I am in a position to ask if home rule worked effectively. I can most conveniently do this by asking if the flaws in home rule that were recognized in 1886, 1893, and 1914 were evident in Northern Ireland during the period of home rule from 1921 to 1972. These flaws were the representation formula for Irish representation at Westminster, the financial provisions of home rule, and the constitutional relationship between Ireland and the United Kingdom.

## The Representation Formula

The problem which Gladstone described as "the most difficult of all,"[94] the representation dilemma, existed after the creation of Northern Ireland, but to a negligible degree that enabled it to be swept under the rug. In 1886 Gladstone's problem was what to do with 80 Irish M.P.'s at Westminster, but in the 1920 Government of Ireland Act, Ireland as a whole was assigned 46 seats, of which Northern Ireland had only 13, including 1 for Queen's University.[95] Only the northern members took their seats at Westminster, and their number was reduced to a negligible 12 in a chamber of 650 by the abolition of university seats in 1948.[96] Northern Ireland representation was not raised to a more proportional 17 seats until 1979, but that was seven years after the abolition of the Northern Ireland Parliament had eliminated the representation dilemma altogether.[97]

The majority of Northern Ireland members, the Ulster unionists, voted with the Conservative party at Westminster during most of the period of devolved government, although they were organized independently. Their numbers were too few to be decisive in government formation or policymaking until the period 1974 to 1979, when they helped to sustain, and then defeat, the minority Labour party government of James Callaghan after the Conservative government of Edward Heath had abolished the Northern Parliament in 1972.[98]

The Government of Ireland Act made no provision for continued Irish representation in the House of Lords. The Act of Union had provided that twenty-eight representative Irish peers would sit in the House of Lords, but this number steadily declined to zero after 1921. Those Irish peers already in the House continued to sit until their deaths, but they were never replaced by the Governor after 1921, and the last one died in 1961. In 1965 twelve Irish peers petitioned the House of Lords to be allowed to sit, but the Committee of Privileges found against them because the "Ireland" they claimed to represent had ceased to exist in 1922.[99]

One need not mourn the political demise of the Irish hereditary peerage to recognize that the effective elimination of a proportional number of Northern Ireland peers, together with the underrepresentation of the province in the United Kingdom House of Commons by four or five seats until 1979, was a handicap for Northern Ireland, but it was never deemed significant. The financial and constitutional relationships raised much more serious problems.

## The Financial Relationship

R. J. Lawrence writes, "A fundamental object of the Home Rule Bills was to create a distinct and self-sufficient fiscal unit that would both pay for its own services and help to pay for imperial services."[100] Given this objective, the financial provisions of the Government of Ireland Act failed utterly. Indeed, they were already obsolete as they were being written and they were subject thereafter to frequent ad hoc adjustments.[101] Northern Ireland was expected to pay the costs of both its own services and United Kingdom services in the province, and to make an imperial contribution, a sum fixed at £7,920,000 per annum.[102] It had two sources of income, "transferred" taxes, on minor items such as motor vehicles, stamps, and betting, which were raised by Northern Ireland itself, and "reserved" taxes, amounting to 80 percent or more of the province's revenues, which were collected by the United Kingdom in Northern Ireland and returned to Northern Ireland after deductions for United Kingdom services in the province and the imperial contribution. Reserved taxes included all the major taxes: customs, excise, incomes, corporation profits, excess profits, and purchases.

From the beginning, therefore, Northern Ireland was at the mercy of tax rates set in London. When those rates were cut in the 1920s, its income dropped. Furthermore, its own economic difficulties, including an unemployment rate that reached 24 percent in 1925, more than twice the British rate, meant that the yield per head on taxes in Northern Ireland was always lower than in the more prosperous Britain.

The biggest drain on the Northern Ireland Treasury was the National Insurance program, which had been uniform throughout the United Kingdom since 1911. In 1922 the Northern Ireland government decided that all its social services would, broadly speaking, be kept in step with those in Britain and that it would pass parity legislation to implement its own versions of British programs.[103] In effect, this allowed the British government to set priorities and spending levels for Northern Ireland's social services indirectly through the level of the equivalent services in Britain. Because Northern Ireland was unable to support these social programs from taxes generated in the province, whether reserved or transferred, the United Kingdom began to pay a

subsidy. By 1968–69 it had reached £72,000,000 per annum.[104] Northern Ireland was also unable to pay its full imperial contribution, which
fell by agreement to a derisory £10,000 in 1934–35 and 1935–36.[105]
It is clear, therefore, that Northern Ireland had very much less freedom
to shape its domestic policies than was ever anticipated by the supporters of Irish home rule. The United Kingdom essentially determined
Northern Ireland's revenues and its major spending programs. It also
determined the province's foreign trade policy, including north–south
economic relations.

There were areas of difference between British and Northern Irish
policies. For example, Northern Ireland chose not to keep in step with
British housing policy, and even in areas that the two governments accepted as appropriate for parity, Northern Ireland had some freedom
to design its own responses. In some services parity meant virtual uni-
formity, for example, in cash benefits. In some it meant similarity, as
in the provision of personal social services. In other areas parity meant
a remote similarity, as in education. In agriculture, Northern Ireland
showed considerable marketing initiatives.[106] In general, however, initiative was not a marked feature of Northern Ireland's public life until
1962.[107] Late that year the Minister of Finance, Terence O'Neill, who
was to become Prime Minister in 1963, launched what he called a
"three-pronged attack upon our problems, relying largely upon our
own skill, determination and enterprise."[108] What followed were programs of regional economic growth, incentives for industrial development and diversification, improvements in roads and other economic
infrastructure, housing, job training, and so on. The Royal Commission on the Constitution reported in 1973 that between 1965 and
1970, only 32 percent of Northern Ireland bills were reenactments of
Westminster legislation to produce parity. Of the remainder, 30 percent were peculiar to Northern Ireland and 38 percent fell between the
two categories.[109]

That O'Neill failed to transform Ireland was not due to his lack of
initiative but to the intensity of Northern Ireland's problems as one of
the United Kingdom's distressed regions, and to the sectarian violence
that he innocently helped to renew. It was not President Gorbachev
alone who discovered that *perestroika*, the social and political reconstruction that must accompany economic modernization, causes social
disruption that can bring the whole experiment tumbling down.
O'Neill's willingness, albeit from his own staunchly Protestant per-

spective, to attack sectarianism as both unfair and inefficient proved unacceptable to many in his own party, and he resigned in April 1969.[110]

## The Constitutional Relationship

The financial relationship meant that Northern Ireland was always subordinate to economic decisions made in Britain, but it was the constitutional relationship that actually caused the breakdown of home rule. The relationship raised anew several questions that had been anticipated in the home rule debates as early as 1886: Would the two levels of government trespass upon each other's jurisdiction? How and when might the general supremacy of the United Kingdom Parliament be asserted? And would Northern Ireland violate the prohibitions against legislating on religious matters contained in Section 5 of the constitution?

Four legal provisions made it clear, in law, that the Northern Ireland Parliament was subordinate to the United Kingdom Parliament in all matters, even those transferred to Northern Ireland in the constitution. First, the general principle of parliamentary supremacy applied. In a great crisis the United Kingdom Parliament could amend or suspend the Government of Ireland Act itself, as it finally did in the Northern Ireland (Temporary Provisions) Act of 1972, which suspended the Northern Ireland Parliament and vested powers in a new Secretary of State for Northern Ireland.[111] Second, Section 6.2 of the Government of Ireland Act, which had its origins in the Colonial Laws Validity Act of 1865, provided that in any case of "repugnancy," or conflict, between Northern Ireland and United Kingdom laws, the latter would prevail. Third, a general statement inserted in the home rule bills of 1893 and 1914, and again in Section 75 of the 1920 act, asserted a blanket supremacy for the United Kingdom in the following words: "Notwithstanding the establishment of the Parliament of . . . Northern Ireland . . . or anything contained in this Act, the supreme authority of the Parliament of the United Kingdom shall remain unaffected and undiminished over all persons, matters, and things in Ireland." Fourth, the Governor had the power to give or withhold the royal assent to Northern Ireland bills, or reserve them to the Sovereign.[112]

Given this evidence, there should have been no doubt that the United Kingdom was supreme in law, but when and how its supremacy would be enforced was as unclear after 1921 as it had been to the unionist opponents of home rule in the 1880s and 1890s. The unionists had always complained that home rule contained no clear statement of when supremacy would be invoked, or how, short of an act of war.

At one level, the constitutional relationship between the United Kingdom and Northern Ireland was very smooth. They did not often conflict over Northern Ireland statutes because Northern Ireland bills were circulated to the United Kingdom government for comment before their introduction in Belfast,[113] and each act was certified by the Attorney General as dealing with a transferred matter.[114] The United Kingdom also limited friction by increasing the scope of Northern Ireland's powers from time to time.[115] Few Northern Ireland statutes were challenged in the courts and fewer still were found to be unconstitutional,[116] in large part because Northern Ireland courts applied a generous "pith and substance" doctrine, drawn from Canadian practice. In the words of Lord Atkin, in *Gallagher v. Lynn* (1937), "If, on the view of the statute as a whole, you find that the substance of the legislation is within the express powers, then it is not invalidated if incidentally it affects matters which are outside the authorized field."[117]

No Northern Ireland bill was denied the royal assent, for *vires* or any other reason, and only one was reserved to the Sovereign, in 1922, with repercussions that precluded the use of reservation ever again. The occasion was the reservation of the Local Government Bill (N.I.), by the Lord Lieutenant, the Duke of Abercorn, after its approval by the Northern Ireland Parliament on 5 July 1922. The bill proposed to abolish proportional representation in local council elections.[118] Local electoral law was within the transferred authority of the Northern Ireland Parliament, but the Irish Free State Provisional government protested to London that the bill was an attack on the minority in the North and would prejudice the work of the Boundary Commission, which had yet to adjudicate the Northern Ireland border under the terms of the Anglo-Irish Treaty. When the Governor reserved the bill, on instructions from London, the Northern Ireland government, already upset by his use of clemency in several cases of Irish nationalists arrested in the North,[119] threatened to resign. "No government could carry on in Northern Ireland," the Prime Minister, Sir James Craig, insisted, "if it knew that the powers of the Parliament . . . were to be abrogated."[120] His resignation would have forced the United Kingdom to assume responsibility for governing Northern Ireland because there was simply no alternative, under responsible government, to his Unionist party government.

The United Kingdom government thought the legislation unwise but succumbed to Craig's pressure and agreed to the royal assent. Winston Churchill, the Colonial Secretary, cited the convention of nonintervention as justification. He told the Provisional government that if the Crown were to withhold its assent in this case it would create "a precedent limiting for the future the powers of Dominion Parliaments," including, by implication, the Irish Free State itself.[121] The Free State Provisional government challenged this interpretation because Northern Ireland was not a dominion, by then a term denoting a coequal member of the British Commonwealth. Hugh Kennedy, the legal adviser to the Provisional government, insisted that it had been agreed during the Anglo-Irish Treaty negotiations of 1921 that there would be only one dominion in Ireland, the Irish Free State, and "therefore no arguments with reference to Dominion legislation can affect this question."[122] Churchill would not change his mind. He concluded that the bill could not be vetoed because it was clearly within the powers of the Northern Ireland Parliament and its rejection in London would establish an unacceptable precedent for the dominions.[123] The bill received the royal assent on 11 September 1922, and henceforward the Governor acted only on the advice of Northern ministers on matters reserved to Northern Ireland.

Britain was tempted to intervene again in 1925 and in 1930, to prevent the passage of two Northern Ireland education bills. The bills appeared to violate Section 5 of the 1920 act, which prohibited the establishment or restriction of religion. The 1925 bill permitted local school management committees to require teachers to give nondenominational Bible instruction in state schools, and the 1930 bill required state-supported schools to provide religious education at the request of the parents of not fewer than ten students. Because the Catholic church accepts only one true church, recognizes the Bible as only one source of doctrine, and attaches much less significance to it in the education of children than do Protestants, the effect of the acts was to preclude Catholics from attending state schools or transferring their schools to the state system. In effect, it also permitted management committees to set religious tests for employment by requiring teachers to give instruction in the Bible. The result is that the great majority of Protestant children attended fully supported state schools, while the great majority of Catholics attended partially state-supported private Catholic schools.[124]

The United Kingdom government considered denying the royal assent to these education bills on the ground that they were *ultra vires*. It backed off in 1925 because of an impending general election in Northern Ireland, where the veto would have become a campaign issue, and backed away again in 1930 because there was no substantial opposition to the legislation in Northern Ireland. The Roman Catholic church found it difficult to attack the bills because its preference was not to ban religious education in schools, or to have Catholic state schools, but to have full state funding for independent church schools, something Protestants had not sought. In 1945, however, the British Home Secretary finally advised Northern Ireland that the provisions on religious education in the 1930 act were, in his view, *ultra vires*. In 1947, in the face of fierce opposition from its supporters, and without a court test of *vires*, the Northern Ireland Parliament decided that religious instruction would no longer be compulsory in state schools.[125]

This successful attempt by Britain to intervene in Northern Ireland in a religious matter did not lead it to attack other examples of what have been termed religious discrimination there. The reason is that the alleged acts of discrimination were against Catholics, not against the Catholic religion per se. Furthermore, the grievances that led to the current round of sectarian conflict, beginning in the mid-1960s, were in areas that were indisputably within the powers transferred to Northern Ireland in 1920 in the Government of Ireland Act: local government, public housing, employment, and the police. Until 1968 the local government franchise was limited to property owners, who were disproportionately Protestant and Unionist, and there was some manipulation of electoral boundaries to maintain unionist control, particularly in Londonderry. Public housing and local government employment, both areas of substantial discrimination, were responsibilities of local government. In the Northern Ireland civil service, Catholics were underrepresented at every level, as they were in the police forces, particularly the armed reserve police, the "B" Specials, who were despised in Catholic areas and were exclusively Protestant.[126]

Section 5 of the Government of Ireland Act applied to none of these matters. They were all within the jurisdiction of Northern Ireland. Nonetheless, the grievances of the minority community called for some kind of remedy that was clearly not available in Northern Ireland. Why, therefore, did the United Kingdom Parliament not call upon its acknowledged supremacy under Sections 6.2 and 75 of the constitution to legislate in these matters? One answer is that a convention of nonintervention was assumed to exist. Ivor Jennings, the distinguished British constitutional scholar, argued in 1959, "It would be unconstitutional for [the United Kingdom] parliament to exercise its legal power of legislation in the matters delegated to the parliament of Northern Ireland, except with the consent of that parliament."[127] Jennings was applying a convention drawn from Britain's relations with the dominions, and Churchill's remarks in 1922, when reservation was attempted, confirm that he too was thinking of Northern Ireland as if it were a dominion. But it is clear from each of the home rule debates, and from the language of the home rule bills themselves since 1893, that Northern Ireland was not a dominion and that the United Kingdom Parliament intended its supremacy to be real, not formal. Nothing less could have placated Ulster unionists during the debates on the first three home rule bills. They feared for their lives, religion, and property in a home rule Ireland.

Nonetheless, a convention of nonintervention was asserted by Churchill in 1922 and was supported by a 1923 ruling by the Speaker of the United Kingdom House of Commons which prohibited parliamentary questions on Northern Ireland: "With regard to those subjects which have been delegated to the Government of Northern Ireland, questions must be asked of Ministers in Northern Ireland, and not in this House."[128] A succession of British governments, anxious to avoid reinvolvement in Ireland even as the situation there worsened in the 1960s, agreed with the Speaker, and backbenchers were prevented by the ruling from asking questions about internal conditions in Northern Ireland. They were also denied the right to raise Northern Ireland subjects in special motions, such as adjournment debates, or from introducing legislation of their own.[129] M.P.'s were permitted to discuss the vote of money for Northern Ireland services but not the closely related matter of the administration of those services.[130]

A reciprocal convention was respected in Northern Ireland where the Speaker of the House of Commons ruled that matters reserved to the United Kingdom in the constitution were not proper subjects for discussion, "except possibly by certain forms of Resolution, such as an Address to the Crown . . . [or] where the Government of Northern Ireland had themselves undertaken any action or proceeding in respect of a reserved matter."[131] Nationalists withdrew from Parliament in 1926 when the Speaker refused to allow a discussion of the Post Office in Northern Ireland, a matter reserved to the United Kingdom in 1920.[132]

Calvert insists that the constitutional relationship between the United Kingdom and Northern Ireland need not have been viewed in this noninterventionist way. Northern Ireland was not a dominion and did not have to be treated as such. The dominions were completely self-governing, they had never been part of the Union, they enjoyed no representation at Westminster or any financial integration with the United Kingdom, and in none of their constitutions was there anything comparable to Section 75 of the Government of Ireland Act, which asserted the supremacy of the United Kingdom unequivocally. Furthermore, Northern Ireland was not covered by the terms of the Statute of Westminster (1931), which recognized the sovereignty of the dominions. Calvert also notes, "A convention of the constitution requires a consistent practice coupled with a recognition of the obligatory character of the practice by those who are affected by it." The United Kingdom failed the test of obligatoriness because although it never legislated on a transferred matter, it sometimes used intimidation to get its way in Northern Ireland. As Calvert writes, "There have . . . been occasions when interference was threatened failing the taking of legislative action on the part of Northern Ireland by its Parliament, and legislative action has consequently been taken, even with great reluctance." No dominion received such treatment.[133]

Why did Britain opt for Jennings's interpretation of the constitution, rather than Calvert's? There are four possible explanations, which are all interconnected—or tangled. First, there were the circumstances of the early years of Northern Ireland. Having "rescued" itself from Catholic domination only to come under siege by the Irish Republican Army (I.R.A.) in its early years, Northern Ireland was obdurate in defense of its formal powers, and it was encouraged in this course by almost all right-wing British politicians. British policy was to support the status quo, and it remained so, under Conservative and Labour governments, until the 1960s.[134] Furthermore, given the unionist majority in Northern Ireland, Britain had either to capitulate to Northern Ireland, or govern the province itself, something it certainly did not want to do.

The second explanation for Britain's reluctance to intervene is that many United Kingdom politicians were genuinely convinced, as was

Professor Jennings, that a constitutional convention of nonintervention existed, notwithstanding Sections 6.2 and 75 of the constitution. The third explanation is simple ignorance. Most people in Britain did not know enough, or want to know enough, about Northern Ireland to think that intervention was necessary. Ireland, having once obsessed Parliament, was now thankfully forgotten. Fourth, it is likely that politicians accepted the assurances of Northern Ireland politicians and civil servants that intervention was unnecessary because complaints of discrimination were grossly exaggerated.[135]

The full explanation for nonintervention probably lies in a combination of all four explanations, with different people and governments responding in different ways, but the practice ended in the late 1960s. The violent Ulster unionist response to the civil rights movement of the 1960s finally brought intervention.

In the House of Commons on 25 October 1967, Labour Home Secretary Roy Jenkins gave a strong public warning to Northern Ireland, albeit couched in parliamentary language:

Under the Northern Ireland constitution, certain powers and responsibilities are vested in the Parliament and Government of Northern Ireland. Successive Governments here have refused to take steps which would inevitably cut away not only the authority of the Northern Ireland Government but also the constitution of the province. . . . Nevertheless, [the Prime Minister] and I have not concealed from the Prime Minister of Northern Ireland, with whom we have had continuing discussions, the concern felt here.[136]

The pressure from London was maintained. In a radio broadcast on 9 December 1968 the Prime Minister of Northern Ireland, Terence O'Neill, spoke of the United Kingdom's rights under Section 75 of the constitution:

Because Westminster has trusted us over the years to use the powers of Stormont for the good of all the people of Ulster, a sound custom has grown up that Westminster does not use its supreme authority in fields where we are normally responsible. But Mr. Wilson made it absolutely clear to us that if we did not face up to our problems the Westminster Parliament might well decide to act over our heads.[137]

At a unionist rally on 10 December O'Neill's Minister of Home Affairs, William Craig, challenged O'Neill's interpretation of the constitution:

I would resist any effort by any government in Great Britain, whatever its complexion might be, to exercise that power in any way to interfere with the proper jurisdiction of the Government of Northern Ireland. It is merely a reserve of power to deal with an emergency situation. It is difficult to envisage any situation in which it could be exercised without the consent of the Government of Northern Ireland.[138]

Craig was dismissed on 11 December because, O'Neill wrote, "you chose to dispute my views on Section 75 of the Government of Ireland Act and to say that any use of Westminster's sovereign powers under that Section should be 'resisted.' "[139]

Northern Ireland underwent substantial reforms between 1968 and 1972. They were begun by O'Neill and continued by his successors, James Chichester-Clark from 1969 to 1971, and Brian Faulkner from 1971 to 1972, but each leader was brought down by unionist opposition to change. The reforms included reorganization of the police and the replacement of the "B Specials," a new system of public prosecutions, a new Northern Ireland Housing Executive that took control of all public housing, the appointment of a Minister for Community Relations, and the enactment of antidiscrimination legislation, including the Community Relations Act (1969) and the Prevention of Incitement to Hatred Act (1970). Reforms also included the reorganization of local government, the abolition of plural voting in local elections, the suspension of the Londonderry City Council, the appointment of ombudsmen at both provincial and local levels, reform of public employment, and the appointment of the first Catholic to the Cabinet as Minister of State in the Prime Minister's Office.[140]

This rush of reforms was too late. They were never quite enough, or soon enough, for the civil rights advocates, and they aroused unionists to a frenzy of resistance. New public order legislation was widely resented, and with the province on the brink of civil war in August 1969, the Northern Ireland government requested that the army move into the streets of Londonderry and Belfast to maintain order. A wing of the I.R.A. took advantage of the presence of British troops to reorganize itself into a fighting unit as the Provisional I.R.A.

The reforms were put in place without destroying the fiction that Northern Ireland was responsible for its own affairs. No attempt was made by the United Kingdom to legislate for the province, but its presence was felt in various ways: in advisory committees, such as the Hunt Committee on the Police (1969); in commissions of inquiry, such as the Cameron report on civil rights protests (1969) and the Compton report on physical brutality (1971); in joint working parties of civil servants from both governments; and in the attachment of senior United Kingdom civil servants to the Northern Ireland Cabinet Office and Home Office to serve as watchdogs.[141]

In March 1972, however, home rule in Northern Ireland was destroyed by the forces that had brought it to life fifty years earlier. Faced with the news that the United Kingdom would assume responsibility for law and order, Brian Faulkner resigned. The Northern Ireland Parliament was prorogued by the Northern Ireland (Temporary Provisions) Act, 1972, and the supremacy of the United Kingdom Parliament was finally asserted, not to override the authority of the Northern Parliament but to extinguish it. The act vested all government powers in the newly created office of Secretary of State for Northern Ireland, to be held by William Whitelaw. Lacking a legislature to make laws, the province was to be governed by Orders in Council having "the same validity and effect." Direct rule had begun.[142]

In some ways, Northern Ireland was overgoverned during the life of the Northern Ireland Parliament. A small territory with only one and a half million people found itself governed by a Parliament installed in great splendor in a building rising over Belfast at Stormont, to the east of the city. It was a majestic building that would have done credit to a medium-sized sovereign state, and its architecture made a statement. So too did the language of British institutions that was adopted for the Northern Ireland constitution. A discussion document prepared by the United Kingdom government in 1973 recognized the dangers of this arrangement:

There is a view that any new legislature should not be called a Parliament. It is argued that the title and the adoption of elaborate Westminster procedures have not only been out of proportion to the real functions independently performed and to the size of the population covered by them, so that these arrangements have led to what may be described as "over-government," but also have promoted a false view of "Stormont sovereignty" which has been positively harmful.[143]

This was exactly Joseph Chamberlain's criticism of home rule in 1885, and why he argued for a more modest plan of devolution to a Central Board. "Stormont sovereignty" was certainly not written into the Northern Ireland constitution, but before the end of 1922 the six counties were being treated by the United Kingdom, in residuary matters at least, as if they were an independent dominion. Birrell and Murie note that Northern Ireland ministers "travelled abroad and were received by foreign governments as having the status of government Ministers of a sovereign state."[144]

The architecture at Stormont was inappropriate for Northern Ireland, but so too was responsible government, the model of government practiced in the building. Responsible government, with fusion of powers, majority government, and party government, encourages a particularly confrontational style of politics. It is acceptable in a homogeneous society, or in a balanced pluralist society where no group is predominant, but it could do nothing but exacerbate conflict in Northern Ireland, a society divided by sectarianism into two hostile communities. Responsible government guaranteed that the majority unionist community would control Northern Ireland indefinitely. Every attempt at a Northern Ireland settlement since 1972 has tried, therefore, to find a substitute for responsible government that will substitute cooperation for confrontation, so far with no success.

During the home rule debates Conservatives always insisted that a Dublin Parliament and government would behave in unacceptable ways, particularly in their treatment of the Protestant minority, and that if this happened, the United Kingdom would not be able to exercise its formal supremacy to protect its citizens in Ireland. Ironically, as Lawrence points out, it was these same Conservatives who "in 1920 imposed on Northern Ireland the very predicament which they and their predecessors had analyzed."[145] As we have seen, all the issues that led to the civil rights movement in the 1960s fell within the statutory authority of Northern Ireland, and until 1968 no United Kingdom government was willing to intervene.

In one important respect, however, the Conservatives' foreboding about home rule proved false. The home rule debates raised the probability that financial disputes would cause a rupture between the two levels of government. This might have happened, had there been a nationalist home rule government in Dublin. Nationalists always insisted that home rule gave them inadequate financial powers, and they were even prepared to forego supposed economic benefits for the sake of greater self-government. For a number of reasons, however, the financial relationship did not destroy home rule in Northern Ireland. Its financial plight was so awful that independence was inconceivable, and it continues to preclude a secessionist solution today. Very soon after the installation of self-government, Northern Ireland found itself bankrupt and dependent on financial aid from Britain. Its governments therefore had no choice but to comply with British policies on general finance and to provide essentially the same social services as in Britain.

Overriding even these economic imperatives for continued Union, however, was what the Union meant to unionists. They accepted home rule in 1920 not because they wanted it for itself but because it was their best means of remaining in the Union. And this remained their position until home rule was abandoned in 1972.

One should not conclude from this chapter that devolution was a disaster. Northern Ireland was able to chart its own course in many areas of life, even those invaded by British economic and social priorities. Even within the constraints of Treasury control, Prime Minister O'Neill was able to demonstrate that the province could develop its own industrial, health, and agricultural policies. Its educational system has always been different from those of England, Wales, and Scotland, resolutely oldfashioned in many ways, and it maintained a distinctively conservative morality when British law was becoming more permissive in the 1960s. The Royal Commission on the Constitution concluded in 1973 that while home rule did not cure the political and community problem of Northern Ireland, it had "considerable success as an experiment in devolved government, which was presumably not uppermost in the minds of its authors."[146] The experience of Northern Ireland makes a good case for administrative devolution, at the very least, and for some legislative devolution too. The tragedy, given the unique character of its population, is not that Northern Ireland was given devolution but that Gladstonian home rule, with majoritarian responsible government, was an inappropriate model of devolved government.

# CHAPTER 6

# Northern Ireland: A Constitutional Postscript, 1972–1992

In no period of United Kingdom history has there been more constitutional controversy and innovation than in the years since 1969, when the Royal Commission on the Constitution began to sit under the chairmanship of Lord Kilbrandon. Since then a bewildering number of commissions, reports, white papers, discussion documents, bills, and acts of Parliament dealing with the constitutional structures of the United Kingdom have been produced. Much of this activity has been directed at Northern Ireland, but between 1969 and 1978 the country was also exploring devolved assemblies for Scotland and Wales, and since the 1960s the constitutional terms of Great Britain's relationship with the European Community have been the subject of almost continuous discussion and negotiation.

In Northern Ireland the search for a successor to the Parliament of 1921 began almost immediately after its suspension by the United Kingdom Parliament in March 1972. A commitment to respect the wishes of the majority has precluded the transfer of Northern Ireland to the Irish Republic, but no United Kingdom government has yet been willing to integrate the province into the British political system. Advocates of integration argue that the extension of British party politics into Northern Ireland would calm the province by diluting its sectarian politics in the broader ideological currents of Westminster, but British politicians fear being drawn into an Irish quagmire. Furthermore, the government's own *Northern Ireland Constitutional Proposals* observed in March 1973:

In considering the possibility of "total integration" account must . . . be taken of the fact that the majority of parties in Northern Ireland are opposed to it, that it would represent a complete reversal of the traditions of half a century, that it would impose a substantial new legislative burden on the Westminster Parliament, and that it would be unacceptable to the Republic of Ireland and would make cooperation with the Republic more difficult.[1]

Integration has been ruled out, therefore, but so too has the restoration of majoritarian responsible government, the model used in home rule. Responsible government creates winners, who form governments, and losers, who sit in opposition. It works best when there is some expectation that political parties will share power by alternating in government at irregular intervals. It worked extremely badly in Northern Ireland where Ulster unionists formed a permanent majority and nationalists never accepted the system as legitimate. Responsible government exacerbated the problems of sectarian politics by providing a prize, a highly centralized political system that the unionists could permanently dominate.

Northern Ireland is a segmented society, which McGarry and O'Leary define as follows:

Segmented societies are divided into separate subcultures which possess radically different identities and values. The subcultures frequently have their own network of separate and exclusive voluntary associations, such as political parties. They enjoy different leisure activities, read separate newspapers, attend separate educational institutions, and live in segregated neighborhoods.[2]

Such societies are extremely difficult to govern, as can be seen in India, Cyprus, and Lebanon, to name only three examples, because stable government requires the consent of large minority groups. If minorities feel they have no stake in the political system they can undermine it, perhaps fatally. This happened in Northern Ireland after the nationalist population, recognizing that it was shut out of decision making at the provincial level, began to campaign for civil rights in the 1960s.

## Power Sharing

Where democratic government has succeeded in segmented societies—in Belgium, for example—it has been the result of one form or another of power sharing, what Arend Lijphart calls "consociationalism."[3] In such a polity an agreement is reached that the fundamental values of each major community will be respected by the state and that no single community will monopolize political power.

As soon as the Northern Ireland Parliament was abandoned in 1972, the United Kingdom decided that a consociational framework had to be devised that would allow the alienated nationalist minority to participate in government. The Parliament of 1921 had failed and the government's *Northern Ireland Constitutional Proposals* of 1973 strongly opposed the use in Northern Ireland of either the word "Parliament" or the Westminster model of majoritarian, responsible government.[4] The alternative proposed in 1973 was "power sharing," which would require the cooperation of both communities. The language of responsible government was ostentatiously avoided and the proposals used the words "assembly" and "executive," rather than "parliament" and "cabinet."

The Northern Ireland Assembly Act of May 1973 created a seventy-eight-member unicameral Assembly elected by proportional representation. Its powers, and those of the new Northern Ireland Executive, were defined in the Northern Ireland Constitution Act of July 1973 which abolished the office of Governor and provided that legislation by the Assembly, termed *measures* rather than *acts*, would receive the royal assent from the Queen in Council. A United Kingdom minister, William Whitelaw, the Secretary of State for Northern Ireland, replaced the Governor as the formal link between the province and the United Kingdom, and it was he who appointed the Northern Ireland Executive, from members of the Assembly. The Executive included a "chief executive member," who replaced the Prime Minister. Power sharing was not mentioned in the act, per se, but the Secretary of State was required to see that the Executive, having regard to its support in the Assembly and the electorate, was "likely to be widely accepted throughout the community."[5] This was understood to mean that it must include representatives from both the unionist and nationalist communities.

The rejection of majority government was a significant challenge to responsible government in the 1973 constitution. Another was the role assigned to the Executive. It was not a traditional Cabinet and was not given control of the royal prerogative, which Northern Ireland governments had controlled from 1921 to 1972 through their advice to the Governor. The role of the Governor was taken by the Secretary of State and his three Ministers of State, and there was no room in such a system for a convention of nonintervention by the United Kingdom. Members of the Executive were the heads of Northern Ireland departments, but they were also, more significantly, chairmen of consultative committees of the Assembly which were established to supervise the work of each department. Section 7.4 of the Constitution Act required that the head of each department "shall, in formulating policy with respect to matters within the responsibility of that department, consult so far as practicable with the consultative committee . . . and where such policy is to be implemented by a proposed measure, he shall consult as aforesaid before the proposed measure is introduced." The intention was clearly to share power by breaking the virtual monopoly on legislation that Northern Ireland Cabinets had exercised under responsible government. The new model was based on the system of government by committees used in United Kingdom local government.

The allocation of powers between the United Kingdom Parliament and the Northern Ireland Assembly was very similar to the traditional division in home rule. Matters of concern to the United Kingdom as a whole were *excepted* to Parliament, including the Crown, the armed forces, foreign relations, and major taxing powers. Some powers formerly transferred to Northern Ireland that had proven controversial, such as the election franchise, were also excepted. Other matters, notably law and order, were *reserved* to the United Kingdom temporarily, pending the establishment of stable government in Northern Ireland. All other matters were immediately *transferred* to Northern Ireland, including health, social services, education, the environment, employment, training, and agriculture. Finally, Section 17.1, which was much broader than Section 5 of the 1920 Government of Ireland Act, prohibited Northern Ireland from adopting any measure that "discriminates against any person or class of persons on the ground of religious belief or political opinion."[6]

Assembly elections were held in June 1973 and the first power-sharing Executive was formed in November. Brian Faulkner, the former Unionist Prime Minister and now leader of the Ulster Unionist party, was appointed Chief Executive, and Gerry Fitt, a member of the new nationalist party, the Social and Democratic Labour party (SDLP), was his deputy. The Executive numbered fifteen members, seven from the Ulster Unionist party, which had won twenty-four Assembly seats, six from the Social and Democratic Labour party, which had won nineteen seats, and two from the centrist Alliance party, which had won eight seats. The Social and Democratic Labour party had dominated the vote in nationalist districts, but it was ominous that the unionists had split into six groups, five of which opposed Faulkner. In aggregate they out-polled Faulkner's party by 235,873 votes to 211,362, and four of them were represented in the Assembly, by a total of twenty-six seats to twenty-four for the Ulster Unionist party. Had the anti-Assembly un-ionists been organized as one party, the power-sharing experiment would have been stillborn.[7]

The Executive was sworn in on 31 December 1973 and powers were transferred to the Assembly on 1 January 1974, but early in December 1973 a highly controversial meeting was held in Sunningdale, England, which was to destroy the Assembly a few months later. The meeting, which was attended by representatives of the United Kingdom, the Irish Republic, and the newly designated Northern Ireland Executive, agreed to the creation of two new all-Ireland institutions. The first, a Council of Ministers, was to be composed of six members each from the government of the Irish Republic and the Northern Executive and was to have "executive and harmonizing functions." The second, a Consultative Assembly, was to be composed of thirty members each from the Assembly and Dáil Éireann with "advisory and review func-tions." The decision to create all-Ireland political institutions was greeted with outrage in the unionist community, and the fact that the Irish Republic had agreed at Sunningdale that there should be no change in the constitutional status of Northern Ireland without the consent of a majority of its people did not placate them. Unionists be-lieved that the door had been opened to a united Ireland.[8]

The Sunningdale Agreement was rejected by the governing council of Faulkner's own party on 4 January and he resigned from it three days later to form the pro-agreement Unionist party of Northern Ire-land.[9] However, unionist opposition groups now combined their forces in the United Ulster Unionist Council. In the United Kingdom general election of February 1974 the Council polled 50.8 percent of the vote and won eleven of Northern Ireland's twelve seats at Westminster. Faulkner's new party could win only 13.1 percent of the votes and no seats. The Social and Democratic Labour party won 22.2 percent of the votes and one seat.[10]

Faulkner's weakened Executive still had enough cross-party support in the Assembly, which was unaffected by the United Kingdom elec-tion, to survive in office, and even to win a vote on the Sunningdale

Agreement on 14 May, but it had serious internal disputes, particularly over security issues, and it was soon brought down by extraparliamentary action. A fourteen-day general strike, organized by the Ulster Workers' Council, led to the resignations of Faulkner and the remaining unionist members of the Executive on 28 May. By then there was absolutely no possibility of forming a new, broad-based, Executive within the terms of the 1973 Constitution Act, and on 29 May the Assembly was prorogued.[11]

The fury directed by a majority of unionists against the all-Ireland institutions devised at Sunningdale had destroyed the power-sharing system in Northern Ireland, but it really stood no chance of surviving for much longer in the highly charged political atmosphere of the time. The Executive and the Assembly had been called upon to function with the cooperation of unionist and nationalist parties which agreed in condemning revolutionary violence but disagreed fundamentally on the future of Northern Ireland and its relations with the Irish Republic. Furthermore, constitutional politicians were challenged by militants in their own communities and had to assert sectional interests in order to retain credibility with their own followers. A sectarian political system that had killed Gladstonian home rule was not, or was not yet, up to the delicate task of consociational coalition building that power sharing required. The controversy over whether the Labour government of Harold Wilson might have saved power sharing had it acted decisively to suppress the general strike in May is really an irrelevancy because the February general election results for the Northern Ireland seats in the United Kingdom Parliament had already demonstrated that the experiment was opposed by a majority in Northern Ireland.

## Direct Rule

The collapse of the Assembly did not mean that Northern Ireland reverted to the *status quo ante* 1921. The United Kingdom still had no desire to absorb the province into the Westminster system. Instead, the Secretary of State and four Ministers of State took control of the Northern Ireland government departments and direct rule was reestablished. Almost all new law in areas transferred to Northern Ireland in 1973 would henceforward be made by Order in Council, a form of delegated legislation whereby a minister, through his or her advice to the Sovereign and Privy Council, makes law under a broad authority from

Parliament, in this case, the Northern Ireland Act of 1974.[12] Orders must be approved by Parliament but they do not receive the three readings and committee stage of normal legislation. They may be considered by Standing Committees on Statutory Instruments, or by the Northern Ireland Committee in the House of Commons, or by the House as a whole, but debate is limited to a few hours and no amendments are permitted. Some orders simply extend to Northern Ireland legislation that has already been approved for Britain. They perform the function of what was known as "parity legislation" before 1972. Other orders are designed specifically for Northern Ireland. They are usually generated by Northern Ireland departments and discussed with interested parties before being introduced. From 1975 to 1988 the number of orders each year varied from fifteen to twenty-eight, the average being twenty-three,[13] which was well below the Northern Ireland Parliament's average of about thirty-five acts each year.[14] Parliament can legislate directly for Northern Ireland in what were once transferred matters—the Fair Employment (Northern Ireland) Act of 1976, for example—and did so three times in 1992.[15] Because there have been no Northern Ireland M.P.'s on the government benches since direct rule, the Secretary of State and the Ministers of State necessarily sit for British constituencies; this places a special responsibility on the senior members of the Northern Ireland civil service who advise them.

## The Northern Ireland Constitutional Convention

Direct rule has been in operation continuously since 1974 but has always been thought of as temporary. The attempt to find an acceptable form of devolution has continued almost without a break, with a series of government white papers, and formal and informal negotiations.

In May 1975 the Northern Ireland Constitutional Convention was convened by the Labour government of Harold Wilson to allow the Northern Irish themselves to solve their problem, but it was reminiscent of the Irish Convention of 1917–18, with equally lamentable results. Seventy-eight delegates were elected from Assembly constituencies, but the United Ulster Unionist Council, which polled 54.8 percent of the vote and won forty-seven seats, dominated the proceedings. The parties that supported power sharing polled only 42.6 percent of the vote and won only thirty-one seats. The majority wanted a return to majoritarian responsible government but the United Kingdom was committed to "partnership and participation on a basis which commands the most widespread acceptance,"[16] which is to say, power sharing, although the term was studiously avoided. The convention majority report of 10 November 1975, which opposed power sharing, was rejected in London because it did not "command sufficiently widespread acceptance throughout the community to provide stable and effective government."[17] Furthermore, it ignored the all-Ireland dimension of the Northern Ireland problem, which had been addressed at Sunningdale. As Hadfield argues:

To put matters starkly, the Unionists dislike power-sharing and are opposed to an institutionalized Irish dimension; the SDLP rejects majority rule and is (increasingly) insistent upon a formal Irish dimension in any constitutional settlement. It is hard to see how there can be any compromise between these views without massive concession on, or indeed surrender of, a fundamental aspect of [each party's] policy, and further this scenario takes no account of the rise of political support for Provisional Sinn Fein (the political wing of the Provisional IRA), which advocates a total and immediate withdrawal of the British presence in Ireland, which, it believes, should be undivided.[18]

## "Rolling Devolution"

Another attempt to replace direct rule was "rolling devolution," introduced by a Conservative Secretary of State, James Prior.[19] The Northern Ireland Act of 1982 which he piloted through Parliament provided for yet another seventy-eight-member unicameral Assembly, with six statutory committees. This time the Assembly had only "scrutinising, deliberative and consultative" powers in matters transferred to the Northern Ireland Assembly in 1973, or matters referred to it by the Secretary of State. It had no legislative power and executive power remained in the hands of the Secretary of State, but the act provided that there would be, as it were, a "rolling devolution" of legislative and executive functions to Northern Ireland as and when a degree of cross-community consensus emerged in the province. As the political system stabilized it would receive progressively more and more powers.[20]

Progress toward devolution became impossible because the new Assembly was boycotted throughout its life by the parties of the nationalist community: the SDLP, with fourteen seats, and Sinn Féin, with five seats. The SDLP, fearful of losing ground to Sinn Féin in nationalist areas of Northern Ireland, and determined that executive power sharing should be restored, refused to participate in such a weak measure of devolution. Fifty-nine members of other parties did take seats, including assorted unionists and members of the Alliance party. The Assembly was elaborately organized to permit an impressive amount of scrutiny, deliberation, and consultation, which were its only powers under the act.[21] It usefully reviewed draft Orders in Council before their submission to Parliament at Westminster, and a great many of its recommendations were accepted by the United Kingdom government. It certainly helped to make the government accountable, to a degree, to the people of Northern Ireland, but it never represented the nationalists directly and in November 1985 the unionists voted to adjourn in protest against the Anglo-Irish Agreement.

## The Anglo-Irish Agreement

The Anglo-Irish Agreement was negotiated for the United Kingdom by the Conservative government of Margaret Thatcher, and for the Irish Republic by the Fine Gael–Labour coalition of Garret FitzGerald.[22] The groundwork for the agreement was laid by the New Ireland Forum, a conference involving all the constitutional nationalist parties in Ireland, north and south, which was convened by the coalition in Dublin in 1983 and 1984.[23] The agreement affirmed that "any change in the status of Northern Ireland would only come about with the consent of a majority of the people of Northern Ireland." It recognized that no majority yet exists for such a change, but it also declared that if a majority does so consent, both the United Kingdom and the Irish Republic will support the establishment of a united Ireland.[24] Direct rule continues in Northern Ireland, but an Intergovernmental Conference was created through which the government of the Irish Republic is given a formal consultative role in Northern Irish affairs.[25] The Intergovernmental Conference is also the framework within which the United Kingdom and the Irish Republic work "for the accommodation of the rights and identities of the two traditions which exist in Northern Ireland," and "for peace, stability and prosperity throughout the island of Ireland by promoting reconciliation, respect for human rights, cooperation against terrorism and the development of economic, social and cultural cooperation."[26] Ironically, while the British and Irish governments represent themselves in the Intergovernmental Conference, and the Irish government represents the interests of the nationalists, no one from Northern Ireland represents the unionist majority. Furthermore, while the SDLP was consulted at every stage, unionists were completely shut out of negotiations. It is true that there would have been no agreement had they participated, but it was not only unionists who thought it odd that Britain and Ireland should seek to promote reconciliation in Northern Ireland by ignoring the representations of the majority community. Mary Robinson, for one, now President of Ireland, resigned from the Irish Labour party because of the agreement.

The Anglo-Irish Agreement explicitly affirmed Britain's long-term commitment to devolution in Northern Ireland. Article 4(b) stated that "responsibility in respect of certain matters within the powers of the Secretary of State for Northern Ireland should be devolved within Northern Ireland on a basis which would secure widespread acceptance throughout the community." That is to say, direct rule will continue until the Northern Irish themselves can agree otherwise, and once again, "widespread acceptance" is taken to mean that there must be cross-community support and power sharing. Should a devolved administration come into being, the Intergovernmental Conference will cease to consider matters that are transferred to Northern Ireland.

In July 1991 new negotiations began between the Secretary of State, Peter Brooke, and the leaders of the constitutional parties in Northern Ireland on a form of devolution. They failed in their early stages. The formal role of the Irish Republic in the Intergovernmental Conference was the major obstacle to unionist cooperation, and the meetings broke down because the United Kingdom government would not cancel a planned session of the conference. But the negotiations demonstrated that the unionists had moved, in some ways, toward the nationalist position by agreeing to a number of north–south arrangements: an Irish government office in Belfast; a standing British–Irish body, with Northern Ireland represented in the British team; and ad hoc meetings between Irish ministers and members of a Northern Ireland Assembly. The unionists also accepted the reality that majoritarian responsible government, the preferred executive model of most unionists, would not be reintroduced into the province. However, while denying Cabinet government to themselves they also insisted on blocking the strong, power-sharing executive that nationalists had sought since 1974.[27]

Negotiations resumed in 1992 in what were described as three "strands," with agreement on all three being necessary for a final settlement. Strand one, which began in Belfast on 9 March, included the British government and representatives of what are now the four constitutional parties in Northern Ireland, the Ulster Unionist party, the Democratic Unionist party, the Alliance party, and the Social and Democratic Labour party. It considered political arrangements within Northern Ireland itself. Strand two, which involved the United Kingdom and Irish governments and the four constitutional parties, under the chairmanship of Sir Ninian Stephen, a former Governor-General of Australia, considered relationships in Ireland as a whole. These talks began in London on 6 July. Strand three, which began in Dublin on 28 July, concerned future relationships between Britain and Ireland.

The strand two talks marked a particularly historic phase of the Northern Ireland problem because on 30 June 1992 all the constitutional parties of Northern Ireland met with representatives of both the British and Irish governments for the first time, in London, in preparatory talks. The Northern Ireland parties were invited as observers at what was formally an intergovernmental meeting, but each made a statement. The substantive strand two talks began on 6 July at Lancaster House, London, where Britain had resolved the Rhodesian problem in 1979.[28] To appease the unionists, the Irish Republic agreed publicly that the removal of Articles 2 and 3 of the Irish constitution, the contentious claim to Northern Ireland, might be considered in the talks. The Irish government had long been prepared to put these articles to a constitutional referendum in the Republic if a Northern Ireland settlement could be reached that would be sufficiently radical to win over a skeptical Irish electorate.[29]

The SDLP and the unionists were still far apart on a settlement as the delegates assembled in London. The SDLP proposed a Northern Ireland Assembly and an Executive Commission, with three members elected from Northern Ireland by proportional representation, and one each appointed by Britain, the Irish Republic, and the European Commission. The Ulster Unionist and Democratic Unionist parties, joined now by the Alliance party, proposed that an eighty-five member Northern Ireland Assembly be created, and that executive responsibilities be entrusted to government departments headed by nominees of the Assembly. There would be no Cabinet. Instead, the Assembly would act through committees whose members, chairmen, and vice-chairmen would reflect party strength in the Assembly. Finally, there would be separate elections to a three person "panel," which would have what the plan described as "significant consultative, monitoring, referral and representational functions." These functions and the panel's relationship to the Assembly were unclear as the talks began.[30] The panel and the Assembly committee system would both constitute power sharing of a kind, but not the strong power-sharing executive that the SDLP demands. The unionists were proposing a form of limited devolution modeled on local government in Britain, which James Molyneux, the Ulster Unionist party leader, had advocated in the 1970s. He argued on 13 December 1976, for example, that because the Northern Ireland Parliament had tended to duplicate legislation passed at Westminster, legislative devolution was a comparatively unimportant issue:

The devolution which matters and has always mattered in Ulster is not legislative but administrative devolution. . . . [It] is essentially legislative and not administrative devolution which raised the dilemma between the irreconcilable ultimate objectives in Ulster and rendered insistence upon majority rule as essential to one side as it was unacceptable to the other. . . . [Ulster] needs a regional government in which—as in the present government of metropolitan regions in England—all political parties would automatically participate in proportion to their elected representation.[31]

Molyneux did not press this approach in 1976 because of opposition from other unionists,[32] but sixteen years later it was on the table in London.

The optimism that greeted the three-strand talks in 1992 proved unfounded. They suffered a major setback when the Democratic Unionists dropped out of the process before strand two negotiations moved to Dublin on 21 September.[33] All three strands were suspended in November 1992 without prejudice to further talks at a later date. A joint declaration by Britain and Ireland on 15 December 1993 demonstrated their commitment to self-determination in Northern Ireland, but a new constitution is not in sight.[34]

## Constitutional Confusion

This brief description of developments in Northern Ireland gives some sense of the complex constitutional problems the United Kingdom has faced there since 1972, but they were not the total of its constitutional concerns in recent years. In 1973, for example, the Royal Commission on the Constitution recommended devolved government in Scotland and Wales.[35] Three white papers and five years later, Parliament approved bills to devolve powers to assemblies in each region, but the terms were rejected by referenda in both countries in March 1979.[36]

For much of this period the United Kingdom was also involved in negotiating its entry into the European Community. The Conservative government of Edward Heath finally led the country into membership on 1 January 1973, only to find the issue reopened by Harold Wilson's Labour government in 1974. The terms of entry were subsequently renegotiated with other Community members and put to a referendum in 1975. Only then was membership confirmed, but controversy has surrounded each step in the constitutional evolution of the Community since then, including the votes in Parliament on the Maastricht Treaty in November 1992 and May 1993.

During these years, therefore, the United Kingdom has been faced with constitutional challenges on two levels. On one level it has been involved in the supranational constitution of the European Community. On another, it has struggled to come to terms with regional nationalism in Northern Ireland, Scotland, and Wales. Neither challenge has been handled particularly well. The entry into Europe was a particularly graceless affair, and although it was finally achieved, the debate continues. The attempts to deal with regional nationalism, on the other hand, have completely failed to date. In large part this is because they have been political expedients to forestall challenges to the state or the government, not consistent and comprehensive constitutional reforms. This was always the case with home rule. As Arthur Balfour pointed out in 1914, "Home rule is not a constitutional remedy, it is a parliamentary device."[37] It is no surprise, therefore, that the flaws we found in Irish rule in 1886 were reproduced almost exactly in the Scottish home rule act of 1978.

The net result of all this constitutional activity has been constitutional incoherence on a grand scale. Imagine, if you can, what the constitutional structures of the United Kingdom would now be if the initiatives of the 1970s had all succeeded. Northern Ireland's internal affairs would be the responsibility of a subordinate Assembly and a power-sharing Executive that could accomplish nothing without cooperation between unionists and nationalists. Scotland would have classical, Gladstonian home rule, with legislative and administrative devolution, an Assembly, and a responsible Executive, very much like Northern

Ireland between 1921 and 1972. Wales would have only administrative devolution, its internal affairs managed by committees drawn from an Assembly with no legislative powers, very much like the Irish Council proposed in 1907. England would be the only part of the United Kingdom without devolved government. Whereas the Royal Commission on the Constitution concluded in 1973 that alienation from central government called for regional assemblies in Scotland and Wales, the alienation it identified in England called only for regional advisory and coordinating councils![38]

The Labour government's proposals for regional devolution would have reopened Gladstone's "double dilemma," because the government and Parliament of the United Kingdom, in which representatives of Northern Ireland, Scotland, and Wales would continue to sit, would be the government and Parliament of England too. But the Labour government was not worried about England. It was worried about Scotland's seventy-one seats and Wales's thirty-six seats in the House of Commons. The Labour party traditionally has a majority in both countries and can reasonably expect to govern only with their votes, and that, in a nutshell, is why Labour worked so hard on devolution in the 1970s. The party was threatened by the drift of voters to the Scottish Nationalist party and its Welsh counterpart, Plaid Cymru, which had been evident since the late 1960s. In the October 1974 general election the Scottish Nationalist party won eleven seats, forcing the Conservatives into third place in Scotland, and Plaid Cymru won three seats in Wales.[39]

The double dilemma and other flaws in home rule that were recognized in 1886 were perfectly well understood by many M.P.'s in the 1970s so that the House of Commons debates on the Scotland Bill were exercises in déjà vu. As Francis Pym, a Conservative, pointed out:

If the Bill for Wales is enacted, there will be in this House four different categories of Members, all with different roles and responsibilities. Indeed, in that event this House would have five different roles—one for Scotland, one for Wales, one for Northern Ireland, one for England, and one for the United Kingdom as a whole, and all different. Only the people of England will have the whole range of Government examined by Members from every part of the United Kingdom.[40]

The Labour member for West Lothian, Scotland, Tam Dalyell, a formidable opponent of his own party's policies on devolution, pointed out that under the Scotland Bill he, with a Scottish seat, would be able to vote on the affairs of English constituencies but not on the domestic affairs of his own constituency in Scotland.[41] And Enoch Powell, by then a unionist M.P. from Northern Ireland, echoed Joseph Chamberlain when he said, "It is not possible within a unitary parliamentary State to devolve widespread legislative authority to an elective Assembly in one part of that State unless the State itself is to be resolved into a federation."[42]

Finally, in addition to the House of Commons that Pym described, with its four types of members and five types of responsibilities, and the regional assemblies in Northern Ireland, Scotland, and Wales, there would have been the European Community, which has the power to make rules and regulations that are binding in each member state. All these institutions and levels of government would have been constitutionally discrete, and the United Kingdom would have owed this incredible constitutional complexity to the alleged genius of a "flexible constitution." The one certain outcome is that power would have moved to ministers and the army of civil servants and lawyers necessary to manage such exotic constitutional arrangements. The United Kingdom is blessed, perhaps, that so little came to pass.

## The Future?

Notwithstanding all the effort put into finding a solution, the United Kingdom is left with no answer to the long-standing constitutional problems posed by Northern Ireland. But some kind of resolution is inevitable because the status quo, direct rule by Order in Council from Britain, is intolerable in the long run. It deprives the people of Northern Ireland of the right to participate in any substantial way in legislating for the province, either at Westminster or at Stormont.

If there is to be a settlement of the Northern Ireland problem that can be implemented by consent, three options must be ruled out in the short run: an independent Northern Ireland, Gladstonian home rule with responsible government, and a united Ireland under the Irish Republic. The first two would perpetuate unionist control of the province, which is unacceptable to nationalists, and the third is unacceptable to unionists. Power sharing remains a viable option, and has been accepted by the unionists in muted form, but a formula for government has yet to be devised that is acceptable to all sides. As the Unionist Task

Force report of 1987 pointed out, unionists would be more positive about power sharing if the SDLP would agree that the government of the Irish Republic should no longer play a role in Northern Ireland as custodian of the nationalists' interests.[43]

One significant incentive for the constitutional parties of Northern Ireland to cooperate is that, in the absence of an agreed alternative, direct rule will surely evolve into Northern Ireland's complete integration into the British political system. Integration has been rejected by the United Kingdom, the Irish Republic, and most of the leading politicians in Northern Ireland, but for anti-integrationists there are some ominous signs at Westminster. Direct rule was designed to be temporary, and its imperfections are well understood. Slowly, therefore, changes are being made to bring Northern Ireland into line with Scotland and Wales as regions with administrative devolution under laws made at Westminster. Northern Ireland has lost its Governor and now has a Secretary of State, just like Scotland and Wales. The House of Commons has created a Northern Ireland Standing Committee,[44] and the Speaker now permits members of Parliament to question the government on the internal affairs of Northern Ireland. The Secretary of State for Northern Ireland now answers questions during question time and Parliament appears to be intruding itself inexorably into Northern Irish affairs through debates on Orders in Council and legislation.

There are some who welcome these developments, members of the Campaign for Equal Citizenship for Northern Ireland, for example. One of its founders, Hugh Roberts, argues that the present character of politics in the province is the consequence of its isolation from Britain, a choice made by British politicians in 1920. Even with devolved government in Belfast, he insists, there could have been considerable Irish integration into Britain's politics had British political parties been willing to contest elections in Northern Ireland, which they consistently refused to do. "In these ways," Roberts writes, "has it been made impossible for the people of Northern Ireland to engage in normal, purposeful, non-sectarian party politics."[45] Only in 1989 did the Conservative party decide to establish constituency associations in the province. It won only 5.7 percent of the vote there in the United Kingdom general election in 1992.[46]

The United Kingdom government does not want full integration, which would burden Parliament, and it knows that the plan does not yet have sufficient support in Northern Ireland to succeed. Furthermore, there is the possibility that were integration to occur, electoral exigencies might force the British parties to divide on Northern Ireland issues, with Labour becoming the party of Irish nationalists and the Conservatives, once again, the party of Ulster unionists. Nonetheless, integration must come in time if an acceptable alternative is not produced.

Part III

*Independent Ireland*

# CHAPTER 7

# From the Dáil Éireann Constitution to the Anglo-Irish Treaty, 1919–1921

Home rule was implemented in Northern Ireland in 1921 but the rest of Ireland took the course which was to lead to the Irish Republic of today. There were three major stages in the evolution of the present Irish constitution: the Dáil Éireann constitution of 1919, the Irish Free State constitution of 1922, and the constitution of 1937. There was essential continuity from stage to stage, and each was built firmly on British constitutional concepts that had evolved since the eighteenth century. In that sense, the Irish revolution was very conservative.

## Dáil Éireann

Irish nationalists had been practicing a form of parliamentary government for nearly two and a half years when they rejected the implementation of the Government of Ireland Act in June 1921. Sinn Féin had campaigned in the November 1918 United Kingdom general election with three objectives: to withdraw Irish members of Parliament from Westminster, to establish an Irish Parliament in Dublin, and to appeal to the Paris Peace Conference for recognition of Ireland's right to national self-determination. After its election success, the party quickly moved to implement all three goals.

Sixty-nine Sinn Féin candidates won a total of seventy-three seats in the 1919 election, twenty-six without a contest, although forty-seven candidates were in prison. The winners rejected their seats at Westminster and twenty-seven of them assembled at the Mansion House, Dublin, on 21 January 1919 as deputies in the first public session of Dáil Éireann, or Parliament, of the Irish Republic.[1] Of the forty-two who did not attend, thirty-four were still in prison, six were abroad, either on missions or as deportees, and two were ill.[2]

Members of the Sinn Féin Executive had worked assiduously since the election to ensure that Dáil Éireann would be impressively organized as a parliamentary assembly, although its procedures were simpler, and less formal, than those at Westminster, and its proceedings were not recorded to perfection.[3] It met a total of twelve times, six in 1919 and three each in 1920 and 1921. Meetings had to be conducted in secret after the Dáil was proscribed on 12 September 1919, two days after Sinn Féin, and the attendance, which reached fifty-two on 1 April 1919 after the release of Sinn Féin prisoners, dropped to a little over twenty in 1921 as deputies were arrested or went into hiding. Of those who were elected in 1918, only two had not been arrested or posted as wanted by the police by August 1920.

The Dáil's membership was 69 when it first sat in January 1919, but in May 1921 Sinn Féin used the elections for the two Irish Parliaments under the Government of Ireland Act to elect a much larger assembly. One hundred and twenty-five Sinn Féiners accepted membership in the new Dáil, 124 from the south and 1 from the north. In the south, only the 4 members representing Dublin University refused to take their seats, and they attended the Southern Parliament until it was adjourned.[4]

Dáil Éireann was an inexperienced body. Only two deputies, Laurence Ginnell and James O'Mara, had sat in the Westminster Parliament,[5] and only 10 percent had experience in government at any level.[6] Their inexperience was largely due to their youth. In 1919 33 percent of the deputies were under thirty-five years of age and 73 percent were under forty-five.[7] But the *London Times* was quite wrong to describe the first Dáil Éireann as "the stage play at the Mansion House."[8] In fact, it represented an extremely important milestone in Irish constitutional history. As Brian Farrell describes it, "[Dáil Éireann] appeared to many, including the British authorities who made no effort to interfere with its meeting, little more than a charade. Yet this was the constitutional cornerstone of the new Irish State; or origin of a cabinet system of government that has persisted to the present day."[9] At the first session, on 21 January, deputies elected Seán T. O'Kelly as Speaker, appointed four clerks, took a roll call, and adopted the Dáil constitution. They also approved a Declaration of Independence, appointed three delegates to the Paris Peace Conference,[10] approved a "Message to the

Free Nations of the World," and adopted a "Democratic Program" that embodied, in muted form, some of the goals of Socialists such as James Connolly who had participated in the Easter Rising.[11] The following day the Dáil adopted standing orders and elected Cathal Brugha as President, in effect Prime Minister, of the Dáil Éireann Cabinet, formally known as "the Ministry." It also approved his four nominees for the remaining positions in the Cabinet, Eoin MacNeill, Michael Collins, George Plunkett, and Richard Mulcahy.

Brugha was only the provisional President because Eamon de Valera, the senior survivor of the Easter Rising, and Chairman of Sinn Féin since October 1917, was in prison in England with many other party leaders. De Valera escaped from Lincoln Prison in February and the remaining Sinn Féin prisoners were released in March, so the Dáil was able to meet in April to elect de Valera President and approve his nominees for a larger Cabinet. These were Arthur Griffith for the Ministry of Home Affairs, George Plunkett for Foreign Affairs, Cathal Brugha for Defence, Constance Markievicz for Labour, Eoin MacNeill for Industry, William Cosgrave for Local Government, Michael Collins for Finance, Robert Barton for Agriculture, and Laurence Ginnell for Propaganda. Ernest Blythe was appointed Director of Trade and Commerce, with a seat in the Cabinet.[12] When de Valera left on an extended visit to the United States from June 1919 to December 1920, Griffith served as Acting President.[13] On his return to Ireland, de Valera found the Cabinet too large and reconstituted it as a body of seven, including Arthur Griffith for Foreign Affairs, Austin Stack for Home Affairs, Cathal Brugha for Defence, Michael Collins for Finance, W. T. Cosgrave for Local Government, and Robert Barton for Economic Affairs.[14]

Dáil Éireann was seriously handicapped by having to operate underground after it was banned in September 1919,[15] and in the circumstances it could have had only limited effectiveness. Indeed, McCracken describes its legislative output as negligible.[16] A heavy burden was carried by members of the Cabinet who were constantly harassed by British forces. They moved frequently but were able to assert varying degrees of control over important aspects of life in the nationalist parts of Ireland. The Minister for Finance, Michael Collins, for example, collected more than £370,000 for the Dáil Éireann National Loan. This made possible the employment of a number of experienced civil servants, supported a number of department activities, and paid for military operations. The Dáil itself had seven full-time officials by

June 1919. Ministers and ministry heads received salaries, and deputies drew expenses and allowances.[17]

In some areas of Irish life the Dáil had only limited success, in education, labor, fisheries, and trade and industry, for example, but the Minister for Agriculture, Robert Barton, was able to set up a land bank for land purchases in the west of Ireland, and the Department of Home Affairs established a comprehensive court system which, by the time of the truce in July 1921, operated nine hundred parish and seventy district courts. Sinn Féin victories in local elections in 1920 also led almost all the local councils outside the northeast to break off relations with the Local Government Board in Dublin, and de Valera found it necessary to appoint two ministers, William Cosgrave and a junior minister, Kevin O'Higgins, to deal with them. These were very limited successes, it is true, but Chubb may be too harsh in describing Dáil Éireann as "essentially a publicity exercise."[18]

The Cabinet was weakest, perhaps, in its direction of the military. The Minister of Defence, Cathal Brugha, never gained control of the Irish Republican Army from the Supreme Council of the Irish Republican Brotherhood. Michael Collins was in the anomalous position of serving in the Cabinet, as Minister of Finance, and in the Supreme Council of the I.R.B.[19]

## The Dáil Éireann Constitution

The framework for the system of government created by Dáil Éireann was the constitution of Dáil Éireann, adopted on 21 January. Hugh Kennedy, the legal adviser to the Irish Free State government, insisted in 1923 that there was no constitution for the Irish Republic per se between 1919 and 1921, only a constitution for the Dáil,[20] but Farrell argues that those who drafted the document intended it to provide a provisional constitutional framework for the Irish Republic.[21]

The constitution was a very short document of only five articles, all of which dealt with the legislature and the executive. Despite its brevity, it was a document of immense significance because it presented the most basic rules of the British model of government in a formal constitutional document for the first time.[22] Responsible government had been evolving in Britain since the eighteenth century but it was still regulated there primarily by constitutional conventions, not constitutional law. This was also true in the dominions, none of which identified the

Prime Minister or Cabinet in constitutional law.[23] Dáil Éireann very obviously broke from this tradition.

Article 1 of the Dáil constitution vested all legislative powers in a unicameral Dáil Éireann. Article 2 identified the essential elements of responsible government by assigning all executive powers to a Cabinet, the Ministry, consisting of a President elected by Dáil Éireann and four executive officers nominated by the President and approved by the Dáil. Ministers were individually dismissible by either the President or a vote of the Dáil, and the whole Cabinet could be dismissed collectively by the Dáil. Every member was required to have a seat in the Dáil at the time of appointment and to be "at all times . . . responsible to the Dáil."

On 1 April 1919 Article 2 was amended to provide for a Cabinet of ten, but when he returned from the United States in December 1920, de Valera found it unwieldy. He moved a further constitutional amendment on 25 August 1921 to reduce it to a President and six ministers. He also nominated what he called "extra-Cabinet" ministers, who were responsible to the Dáil and the Cabinet but did not themselves share in collective responsibility. Farrell does not see in this the seeds of the "external minister" concept of the Irish Free State constitution. Extra-Cabinet ministers appear to have been modeled on British junior ministers.[24]

The constitution was completed with three articles. Article 3 provided for the election by the Dáil of its Chairman (Speaker) and Deputy Chairman, and Article 4 provided that only the Dáil might authorize the supply of public monies. It also authorized the appointment of an Auditor. Article 5 stated that the constitution was provisional and might be amended on seven days' notice.

## Responsible Government

From the outset Dáil Éireann, the parliament of revolutionary nationalists, practiced British responsible government, and most of the model's eight characteristics were evident. There was (1) fusion of the executive and legislature, because ministers were required to sit in the Dáil, and (2) majority government, because the President was elected by the Dáil and his choice of ministers was subject to Dáil approval. (3) The primacy of the lower house was unquestioned because there was no second chamber. (4) Party government was not practiced in the normal way because only one party was represented in the Dáil, but (5) there was Cabinet government, and both collective and ministerial responsibility to the Dáil were recognized in the constitution. (6) There was a strong Prime Minister, the President, who was empowered to nominate and dismiss the rest of the Cabinet, and (7) the absence of a head of state meant that there was no one to challenge the President's predominance. Finally, (8) there was substantial concentration of power. This would have happened in the best of circumstances under responsible government, but it was inevitable in Ireland because the Dáil functioned underground for most of its life, and met infrequently.

Dorothy Macardle argues that the President "was, *ipso facto*, head of the State,"[25] and this was de Valera's view. In 1922, for example, he defended his use of the title "President of Ireland" during his American tour: "It is President of Dáil Éireann, which is written down as the Government of the Irish Republic. So I was President of the Republic of Ireland."[26] But this was reading too much into the constitution. Hugh Kennedy, the legal adviser to the Provisional government, argued in 1923 that de Valera used the title in America "without any authority whatever, for the purpose of impressing those he met,"[27] but when the Cabinet was reorganized in August 1921, de Valera was formally proposed to the Dáil for the office of President of the Republic.[28]

Responsible government was well suited to the circumstances of an underground parliament fighting a war of independence because it requires, at a minimum, only a small executive drawn from the members of a single legislative chamber. It was also the model with which the Irish republican leaders were most familiar, and they appear to have had no doubt at all that it was the one they should have. Not everyone was satisfied, however. There were, in particular, two attempts by Deputy J. J. Walsh to curb the executive. His challenge was insignificant in itself but is interesting because of the responses he provoked from members of the Cabinet.

In June 1919 Walsh sought to amend Article 2 to provide that executive powers would be vested in ministers assisted by committees of the Dáil, rather like the system established for the Northern Ireland Assembly in 1973. The motion was withdrawn when Arthur Griffith, the Acting President, promised to appoint "consultative committees."[29] These became quite active, and one might regret that a committee system that began so well was not reproduced in the Irish Free State and the Irish Republic.[30] Nonetheless, Walsh found the system unsatisfactory because ministers were under no obligation to accept committee decisions. Therefore, in September 1920, he moved the following motion:

Whereas Mr. de Valera has repeatedly publicly announced in America that the Constitution of the Irish Republic was based on the democratic foundations underlying the Constitution of the United States; and whereas the latter body provides for the consideration of all phases of legislative activity through the medium of Committees whose findings are subject only to the veto of the whole Parliament—a method already in vogue in County and Borough Councils in Ireland—and as no such machinery has yet been set up within the Irish Republican Government, with the consequent practically entire exclusion of three-fourths of the people's representatives from effective work on the nation's behalf, we now resolve to bring this Constitution into harmony with the American idea of Committees elected by the whole House, and clothed with similar powers.[31]

By a vote of thirty-three to one, the Dáil agreed to postpone Walsh's motion for a year, and the issue died, but the force of Walsh's objection to the dominant role of the executive in responsible government was clear. He resented the lack of influence of ordinary members of the legislature.[32]

Cabinet ministers could have countered Walsh by arguing that difficulties in summoning the Dáil made it impossible for them to consult with deputies more than minimally. Instead, they argued a distorted interpretation of responsible government that has been used by Cabinets elsewhere whenever they have been charged with accumulating too much power. Michael Collins, for example, argued that committees were unnecessary because ultimate power lay with the Dáil, not the ministry. He added that deputies were free to raise any matter in the Dáil, and that a minister or Cabinet whose policies were opposed could be voted out of office.[33] Collins certainly knew that this was a fiction. The legislature's control of the executive he described had essentially evaporated in Britain before the end of the nineteenth century, and comes into play very rarely. The Cabinet almost invariably dominates Parliament. Indeed, the Dáil standing orders adopted in January 1919 provided that ministerial motions would have precedence over other business, and spoke of the Cabinet's right to "arrange such business in such sequence as they think fit."[34]

More revealing, perhaps, than Collins's use of a fiction was Arthur Griffith's insistence that Walsh's proposal to take responsibility away from ministers and place it in the hands of committees amounted to a complete revolution in the constitution.[35] One might ask what was so revolutionary about changing the provisional constitution of a revolutionary state then only in its twentieth month? The answer, of course, is that Walsh's proposal was revolutionary in the context of the British model of government. Like the constitution makers of Australia, New Zealand, Canada, and South Africa, Griffith could conceive of no alternative to responsible government as it was practiced in Britain. The Dáil standing orders confirmed this. They provided rules for the order of business, questions to ministers, debates, divisions, supply, closure, the quorum, and other matters that had been copied from the British House of Commons.[36] They reveal, Farrell notes, "an almost total acceptance of the British pattern of legislative–executive relations,"[37] and he attributes much of the stability of postindependence Irish politics to the willingness of Dáil Éireann to endorse a model of government, with its accompanying political values, that was already well known and understood. The home rule agitation, he writes, had "created a considerable consensus in Ireland on what the process of representation and government was about. There was never any serious dispute; a familiar and acceptable model—the Westminster model—was available and was simply taken over."[38]

## The Anglo-Irish Treaty

Dáil Éireann was a provisional assembly, and its most important task was to secure recognition from Britain. The Northern Ireland home rule Parliament was opened in June 1921, and at that point, having secured self-government for the Protestant population of the north, Lloyd George and the Conservatives in his government were able to set aside the abortive Southern home rule Parliament in order to prepare a separate settlement with the Irish republicans. "By guaranteeing the permanent tie of Ulster with the United Kingdom," John Fair writes, "[the Government of Ireland Act] obviated the need for watchdog practices by the British Conservative Party."[39] A truce in the War of Independence began on 11 July, and between 14 July and 24 July Lloyd George and de Valera began the negotiations that were to lead, in December, to what were termed "Articles of Agreement for a Treaty between Great Britain and Ireland," and thereafter to the formation of the Irish Free State. At first the talks stalled on the issue of recognition. De Valera insisted that the United Kingdom must negotiate with the

Irish Republic that had been proclaimed in 1916.[40] Lloyd George disagreed, but did not set preconditions for negotiations. On 27 September he invited de Valera to resume the talks, and de Valera accepted the following day, saying, "[O]ur respective positions have been stated and are understood."[41]

Negotiations began in London in October 1921. The Irish delegation was led by Arthur Griffith and included Michael Collins, George Gavan Duffy, Robert Barton, and E. J. Duggan. Erskine Childers served as Chief Secretary and Hugh Kennedy as legal adviser.[42] Both sides proceeded as if the future of the whole island was open for discussion. The Irish position was that Ireland should be reunited, although the Northern Parliament might continue to exist in a subordinate relationship to the new Irish Parliament, but it was inconceivable that Lloyd George would agree to the Ulster unionists being included in an all-Ireland Parliament without their consent. The real issue for the negotiations was not the future of Ireland as a whole, therefore, but the constitutional relationship to be established between the twenty-six counties and the United Kingdom. On that question the two sides were far apart.[43]

Lloyd George offered Ireland the status of a dominion, a term used since 1907 for the self-governing colonies of Canada, Australia, New Zealand, and South Africa. More specifically, he wanted Ireland to recognize the Crown in its constitution and accept membership in the British Empire. He also insisted that Britain should retain naval bases in Ireland and other facilities for air defense and communications. The proposal represented very much less than unqualified Irish independence. The Irish countered that the United Kingdom must recognize Ireland as a republic, with no role for the Crown in its internal affairs. They rejected membership in the British Empire, proposing instead that Ireland should have what de Valera described as an "external association." King George V would be recognized as head of the association but Ireland would be free to pursue an independent foreign policy.

De Valera recognized that Griffith would be under such intense pressure in London that he might agree to a role for the Crown in the Irish Free State as the price of a settlement. By remaining in Dublin, he believed he would be able to prevent this capitulation. He wrote to Joseph McGarrity, a prominent Irish-American, "I felt convinced . . . that as matters came to a close we would be able to hold them from this side from crossing the line."[44] His plan went sadly awry. Griffith and his colleagues were accredited by Dáil Éireann with plenipotentiary powers to "negotiate and conclude" a treaty with Britain, and this is what they did, although de Valera had told them in October to await instructions from Dublin before finalizing the agreement.[45] On 6 December 1921, faced with Lloyd George's threat to resume the war in Ireland, they succumbed and all the delegates signed a treaty that accepted the essentials of the United Kingdom proposal, a twenty-six-county Ireland with dominion status under the Crown. They also agreed that the United Kingdom would retain naval bases and other military installations in Ireland. The only significant concession by Britain was an agreement that a boundary commission would be created to review the border with Northern Ireland. The Irish were informally encouraged to believe that this commission would lead to a united Ireland because border adjustments would leave Northern Ireland with only three or four counties, and pressure would be then be applied from London for these to merge voluntarily with the south.[46] The Irish were misled. The Boundary Commission was chaired by a South African judge, Richard Feetham, who interpreted his responsibility so narrowly that only minor territorial adjustments were recommended in 1925, and the Irish Free State withdrew from the process at the last minute.[47]

The British appeared to have won in 1921, and in the House of Commons Lloyd George praised the Anglo-Irish Treaty for providing "allegiance to the Crown, partnership in the Empire, security of our shores, non-coercion of Ulster."[48] But de Valera was appalled at what had been done and challenged the agreement when his Cabinet met in Dublin on 8 December 1921. His major objection was not to partition, but to the Crown and the continued British connection in the constitution. There was real substance, and real danger, he insisted, in the role the Crown would play in Ireland. "I say in a Treaty words do mean something," he argued, "else why should they be put down."[49] In the Cabinet he and two other uncompromising republicans, Cathal Brugha and Austin Stack, neither of whom had been with Griffith in London, insisted that Ireland should hold out for recognition of the Irish Republic. They lost by four votes to three. In the majority were three Cabinet ministers who had signed the treaty, Griffith, Collins, and Barton, together with William Cosgrave. Their view was that Griffith's delegation had secured all it reasonably could from Lloyd George. Given that the Irish Republican Army could not win a military victory, and that Lloyd George had convincingly threatened that the war would be resumed if his terms were rejected, the treaty was the best that could have been secured.[50]

The division in the Cabinet was reproduced in the Dáil debate on the treaty on 7 January 1922. Collins defended the settlement. It was not, he argued, "the ultimate freedom that all nations aspire and develop to, but the freedom to achieve it."[51] Arthur Griffith defended his own role: "I have some principles; the principle that I have stood on all my life is the principle of Ireland for the Irish people. If I can get that with a Republic I will have a Republic; if I can get that with a monarchy, I will not sacrifice my country for a form of government."[52] Not one member of the Dáil liked the treaty but it was approved, reluctantly, by 64 votes to 57.[53] It was approved with much greater enthusiasm in the British House of Commons, by 401 votes to 58, and in the House of Lords, by 166 votes to 47.[54]

What exactly had the Irish delegation agreed to?[55] The treaty did not contain a constitution for the new state, which was to be decided by the Irish themselves in 1922, but it set certain guidelines for that document. Article 1 assigned the Irish Free State the same constitutional status as the dominions, with a Parliament "and an Executive responsible to that Parliament." Article 2 provided that the relationship of the Free State to the United Kingdom would be that of Canada, "and the law, practice and constitutional usage governing the relationship of the Crown or the representative of the Crown and of the Imperial Parliament to the Dominion of Canada shall govern their relationship to the Irish Free State." Article 3 provided that the representative of the Crown in Ireland would be appointed in the same way as in Canada. Article 4 required the members of the Free State Parliament to swear allegiance to King George V, not as King of Ireland but "in virtue of the common citizenship of Ireland with Great Britain and her adherence to and membership of the group of nations forming the British Commonwealth of Nations." In the other dominions the oath was to the King personally.

The security concerns of the United Kingdom were addressed in Article 6, which entrusted the sea defense of Ireland to the Royal Navy; in Article 7, which gave Britain rights to harbors and other defensive installations in Ireland; and in Article 8, which allowed Ireland to maintain "a military defence force" not to exceed the ratio of forces to population in Britain. Articles 11 and 12 recognized and protected the status of Northern Ireland, but permitted the Parliament of Northern Ireland to request a change. Article 12 also provided that a boundary commission would "determine in accordance with economic and geographic conditions, the boundaries between Northern Ireland and the rest of Ireland." Article 16 of the treaty was designed to protect the Protestant minority by restating the prohibitions against endowing or restricting religion that had been contained in all the home rule bills and in Article 5 of the Government of Ireland Act of 1920.

From January to June 1922 the Irish and the British wrestled with the problem of how to translate the guidelines supplied by the Anglo-Irish Treaty into a constitution that both governments could accept. For the Irish the problem was compounded by the fact that they were also looking for a constitutional formula which would reconcile the pro- and antitreaty republicans. They failed, and by the second half of 1921 the Free State had slipped into civil war.

## The Transfer of Power

De Valera was culpable, and undemocratic, in pressing the antitreaty case to the point of civil war in 1922, against the wishes of majorities in his Cabinet, the Dáil, and the electorate. Before doing so, however, he was instrumental in the first peaceful transfer of power in modern Ireland, which occurred in January 1922.

On 6 January 1922, as the debate on the Anglo-Irish Treaty was drawing to a close, de Valera submitted his resignation to the Dáil, arguing that he could not serve as head of a government that was divided. Griffith and Collins prevailed on him to defer the resignation until after the treaty vote the next day, because a vote on the presidency would have unnecessarily complicated matters at that stage of the debate. The treaty was approved on the evening of 7 January, and when the Dáil reassembled on 9 January de Valera again submitted his resignation and that of his government because he had lost the confidence of the house. Collins suggested that he should remain as a member of the Cabinet, but de Valera would not accept "divided responsibility."[56] He was renominated for the presidency and defeated, by fifty-eight votes to sixty, having made it clear that if reelected he would fight on for the republic. On the following day, antitreaty deputies left the Dáil and Arthur Griffith was elected President by a unanimous vote of those remaining. The Dáil then approved his nominees for the Cabinet: Michael Collins for the Ministry of Finance, William Cosgrave for Local Government, G. Gavan Duffy for Foreign Affairs, Eamonn Duggan for Home Affairs, Kevin O'Higgins for Economic Affairs, and Richard

Mulcahy for Defence. Authority was therefore transferred in a very orderly way from a Cabinet led by de Valera to another, led by Griffith, which had the support of a majority of the Dáil. The rules of responsible government had been respected despite the highly charged atmosphere.[57]

This account actually oversimplifies what was happening in the Dáil in January 1922, because two new Cabinets came into being, not one. The United Kingdom government was prepared to enter into an agreement which was officially described as a "treaty between Great Britain and Ireland," but it stubbornly refused to recognize the authority of Dáil Éireann. Articles 17 and 18 of the Anglo-Irish Treaty therefore called for the establishment of a Free State Provisional government and for the M.P.'s elected for constituencies in southern Ireland under the terms of the Government of Ireland Act to meet to approve the treaty. Dáil Éireann was excluded from the process.

These petty requirements were not meant to force the Irish to comply with the Government of Ireland Act as a prerequisite to being granted independence because the meeting of southern M.P.'s was not a meeting of the Southern Parliament. It was convened by Griffith, as leader of the Irish delegation in London, not by the Lord Lieutenant, as would have been required by law, and it did not include the Southern Senate. The requirements were actually meant to challenge the legitimacy of Dáil Éireann.

On 14 January 22 sixty protreaty Sinn Féin members who had been elected to the Southern Parliament in May 1921, together with four members elected by Dublin University, responded to Griffith's summons. They approved the treaty and elected the Provisional government, both by unanimous vote, and adjourned, never to meet again. Michael Collins was elected Chairman of the Provisional Government. He kept the Ministry of Finance portfolio for himself, and nominated William Cosgrave for Local Government, Kevin O'Higgins for Economic Affairs, P. J. Hogan for Agriculture, and Joseph McGrath for Labour. Eoin MacNeill served as a member without portfolio. It was to this Provisional government that the United Kingdom formally transferred executive powers for the twenty-six counties on 16 January 1922. Arthur Griffith continued to preside over the Dáil Cabinet, and the fiction of two Cabinets was maintained although the Dáil Cabinet actually held its final recorded meeting in April 1922. In practice the two administrations were merged. As far as Britain was concerned, the formal head of the executive in Ireland was still the Lord Lieutenant, under the Government of Ireland Act, 1920, but he was expected to act on the advice of the Provisional government and wisely had very little contact with it.[58]

In August 1922 both Griffith and Collins died, Griffith on 12 August from natural causes and Collins on 22 August in an ambush by anti-treaty forces. William Cosgrave had already become Acting Chairman of the Provisional Government and Acting Minister for Finance on 12 July, to relieve Collins for the conduct of the civil war, and on 30 August he assumed both positions on a permanent basis. He also succeeded Griffith as President of the Dáil Ministry a few days later, so that the two Cabinets were now formally combined.[59] Cosgrave was to lead the Free State for its first ten years, but although experienced and capable, he did not have the popular standing of either Collins or Griffith. The fact that they were gone was an immense tragedy for the Irish Free State at this stage of its development, but their loss also led to a change in the direction of Ireland in later years. De Valera used his position as the senior survivor of the revolution to take control of the state in 1932 and this had consequences for constitutional government that will become evident in the following chapters.

# CHAPTER 8

# The Irish Free State Constitution of 1922

In December 1922 the Irish Free State constitution went into effect, the result of a year-long drafting process that began in January 1922 with the establishment of a constitution drafting committee. On 8 March the committee submitted three separate drafts to the Provisional government, one of which was used as the basis of the Irish draft constitution submitted to the British government on 27 May. After intense negotiations, a substantially amended draft was agreed to by the two governments on 15 June. It was submitted to Dáil Éireann on 22 September and underwent further amendment before being approved by the Dáil on 25 October. This draft was accepted by the British Parliament on 4 December and received the royal assent on 5 December, the expiration date of the transition period specified in the Anglo-Irish Treaty. The constitution went into effect the following day. The process was cumbersome and led to a legal controversy in later years over whether the constitution had been authorized by a vote of Dáil Éireann, as the Irish asserted, or by a British Act of Parliament, as Britain asserted.

## Drafting the Irish Free State Constitution

When de Valera went into opposition in January 1922 it fell to the Provisional government to draft the constitution for the new Irish Free State.[1] Michael Collins was chairman of the drafting committee, but he attended only two meetings and the effective chairmanship fell to his deputy, Darrell Figgis, a writer, who was Arthur Griffith's choice for the committee. Collins selected the rest of the committee himself. It included James Douglas, a Quaker businessman who subsequently became a Free State senator, C. J. France, an American lawyer, and James MacNeill, a former civil servant who was the brother of Eoin Mac-Neill. James MacNeill subsequently became the Free State High Commissioner in London and Governor-General. The committee also included James Murnaghan, professor of law at University College, Dublin, and three barristers: John O'Byrne, Hugh Kennedy, and Kevin O'Shiel. Murnaghan, O'Byrne, and Kennedy subsequently served as Supreme Court judges. Kennedy, who was an adviser to the Irish delegation during the Anglo-Irish Treaty negotiations in 1921, also served as legal adviser to the Provisional government and Attorney General to the Irish Free State. Alfred O'Rahilly, professor of mathematical physics at University College, Cork, joined the committee soon after it began its work. All the members of the committee had experience in public affairs, but only Collins had participated at the highest levels of Sinn Féin policymaking.[2]

The members of the constitution committee differed among themselves on three major issues: the proposed Senate, the executive, and the Supreme Court. On 8 March, therefore, they submitted three draft constitutions to the Provisional government. Draft A was signed by Figgis, MacNeill, and O'Byrne. The rather similar Draft B was signed by Douglas, Kennedy, and France. Draft C, the most radical and least influential, was signed by O'Rahilly and Murnaghan.[3] Draft B was adopted by the Provisional government as the basis for the document it submitted to the United Kingdom in May 1922.

In the drafting process the Provisional government was influenced by four considerations. The first was that the constitution should write responsible government and the evolving independence of the dominions unequivocally into Irish constitutional law. In one sense the drafters were conservative. As Brian Farrell writes, "They were not adventurers in setting up new structures nor in defining new rights. They adopted the model they knew best."[4] In another sense, however, they were radicals. Although it had been practiced for more than seventy years, responsible government had not yet been recognized in British or dominion law. Indeed, dominion government was still colonial in form. The Irish wanted a constitution that would contain no suggestion that Ireland was a colonial subordinate of the United Kingdom, and to this end they also wanted a constitution that would reflect a populist value which Emmet Larkin believes was already settled in the Irish mind by the 1840s: that sovereignty derives from the people.[5] The second consideration of the drafters was that the constitution should reconcile de Valera and the antitreaty republicans with the Free State. The third consideration, the obligation to implement the terms of the Anglo-Irish Treaty in the constitution, was very difficult to square with the first two because it was biased in favor of a conventional dominion constitution, which is to say, a constitutional monarchy. The fourth consideration was that certain promises made by Griffith to the southern unionists should be fulfilled as matters of honor.

The British government viewed the Anglo-Irish Treaty and the Irish Free State constitution as a single package. It represented the final attempt, in a series that had begun in 1782, to devise a constitutional relationship that would permit Ireland to have legislative independence while protecting vital British interests in the island. The key to the relationship was the role the British insisted the Crown would play in the Irish constitution. For the Provisional government, on the other hand, the Crown was an unwelcome imposition, a price to be paid for independence. It was, Kevin O'Higgins told the Dáil, one of "the penalties we are paying for our inability to achieve all the things we wrote on our battle standards."[6] The Provisional government was therefore determined to minimize the Crown's influence in every way possible.

As a result of these conflicting interests, the Irish Free State constitution embodied two contradictory principles. First, Britain insisted that Ireland must be a constitutional monarchy, and Article 51 recognized King George V as head of the Irish executive with formal powers, stated in Article 41, that were derived from English Common Law. Second, the Provisional government insisted that the constitution must recognize the sovereignty of the Irish people, and Article 2 declared that all powers of government were derived from the people. Such an odd combination of monarchy and popular sovereignty could only be the result of a compromise, and not every compromise in politics makes complete sense.

The Anglo-Irish Treaty laid the foundation for an Irish constitutional monarchy by stating, in Article 1, "Ireland shall have the same constitutional status in the Community of Nations known as the British Empire as the Dominion of Canada, the Commonwealth of Australia, the Dominion of New Zealand, and the Union of South Africa." The Free State was to be a *dominion*, a title used for the self-governing colonies since 1907, but it was difficult for the Irish drafting committee to know exactly what this meant in constitutional terms because Britain and the dominions appeared not to know themselves. The dominions had already used responsible government to establish their independence from Britain de facto during World War I, and their future relationship with Britain appeared to lie in what the Imperial Conference of 1917, inspired by General Smuts of South Africa, described as an "Imperial Commonwealth," or "British Commonwealth of Nations." He had in mind a body of coequal states sharing foreign and defense policies that would be determined by some process of consultation.[7] By 1922, however, no constitutional adjustments had been made in the dominion constitutions to implement this new Commonwealth. In each country a British Governor-General remained as the legal head of the executive, with power to withhold the royal assent or reserve bills on instructions from London. Responsible government was not yet recognized in law, and the dominions were still subject to the Colonial Laws Validity Act of 1865 that gave British law priority over colonial law in cases of conflict.

The "British Empire" was in the very early stages of the transition to the "Commonwealth" in 1922, its structures not yet defined in precise constitutional form, and there was resistance in the dominions to defining their new relationship with Britain very precisely. In June 1921, for example, Prime Minister Hughes of Australia, believing that Australian independence was best protected by leaving things as they were, opposed a British proposal that imperial foreign and defense policies should be decided at periodic meetings of an Imperial Cabinet. "The great merit of the constitutional relationship existing between Britain and the dominions," Hughes argued, "is and always has been its elasticity."[8]

In the absence of an imperial constitution or Cabinet, and given that the United Kingdom Parliament could no longer realistically legislate for the dominions, it was the Crown that tied the Commonwealth together. King George V, as the head of the executive in each member country, was both an honored symbol of the new Commonwealth and the legal instrument of its unity. In the words of the British government's law advisers, "The Throne is the bond which knits together the Commonwealth of Nations known as the British Empire. . . . No constitution which is in form or substance Republican can find a place in that community."[9]

This constitutional formulation posed particular problems for republicans in Ireland, who despised the Crown. They also questioned the authenticity of Britain's commitment to the Commonwealth. Prime Minister Lloyd George assured his Commonwealth counterparts that Britain and the dominions would be coequal, but this is not quite what he told the Irish during the Anglo-Irish Treaty negotiations. In October 1921 Lloyd George told the Irish delegation that in cases of disagreement between the two countries, the foreign policy of the United Kingdom must prevail. He insisted, for example, that no dominion might remain neutral in an imperial war.[10] In their response to the first draft of the Irish Free State constitution in May 1922, the British government's legal advisers made it clear that while the prerogative of the royal assent was obsolete in dominion domestic legislation, this was not the case in imperial matters.[11] Before the first Governor-General, Timothy Healy, was appointed in December 1922, the Colonial Secretary, the Duke of Devonshire, was instructed by the Cabinet to ascertain that Healy would not give the royal assent to any Free State bill without first consulting the Colonial Secretary should he have the slightest suspicion that the measure fell outside the constitutional powers of the Free State Parliament. Healy gave a written assurance to this effect on 2 December.[12]

Lloyd George's constitutional double-talk about dominion "independence" under the Crown raised anew a critical question of the home rule debates. If the royal prerogative was not obsolete in a dominion, when might it be used and on whose advice, that of Britain or the dominion government? Britain could not supply a definitive answer. Indeed, in the House of Commons in December 1921 Lloyd George said it would be "difficult and dangerous" to give a clear, legal definition to what constituted the independence of a dominion.[13] We can infer that definition was dangerous because it would have had to address the role of the royal prerogative in the dominions, which would have exposed the fragility of the dominion constitutions.

In order to evade this danger in Ireland, the future relationship between the Irish Free State and the United Kingdom was addressed by analogy in the Anglo-Irish Treaty. Article 2 of the treaty required the Free State to follow the "the law, practice and constitutional usage of Canada" in defining the relations of the Free State to the United Kingdom Parliament and Crown. Canada was the model to which Gladstone had also turned for guidance in 1886. By way of explanation, Lloyd George told the House of Commons, "All we can say is that whatever measure of freedom Dominion status gives to Canada, Australia, New Zealand, or South Africa, that will be extended to Ireland."[14]

The Irish constitution drafting committee now used the reference to Canada in Article 2 very cleverly to trap the British government. They saw that the reference was, on its face, contradictory, because Canadian constitutional *law* on the executive was totally different from Canadian constitutional *usage and practice*. In law, the Canadian Governor-General had enormous powers, but in reality the country was governed by a Prime Minister and Cabinet who were not even mentioned in the constitution. The Irish saw no reason to restate this contradiction in Irish law and opted to include Canadian usage and practice in the constitution rather than Canadian law. Michael Collins warned the British as early as November 1921 that this would be done. He wrote:

The only association which it will be satisfactory to Ireland to enter will be based not on the present technical, legal status of the Dominions, but on the real position they claim, and have in fact secured. . . . It is essential that the present *de facto* position should be recognized *de jure*, and that all its implications as regards sovereignty, allegiance, constitutional independence of the governments should be acknowledged.[15]

Collins outlined how he proposed to accomplish this when he chaired the first meeting of the constitution drafting committee on 24 January 1922.[16] He accepted the reality that the Anglo-Irish Treaty defined Ireland as a dominion within the British Empire, but he instructed the committee "not to be bound up by legal formalities," and "to define and produce a free democratic constitution." He particularly wanted Articles 3, 4, and 6 of the treaty to be excluded from the constitution so that Ireland might be seen to be independent of Britain.[17] Article 3 required the representative of the Crown in Ireland to be appointed as in Canada. Article 4 required an oath of allegiance to the Crown to be sworn by members of the Irish Parliament, and Article 6 stated that the Royal Navy would provide sea defense for the Irish Free State. Some notes Collins prepared on or before 20 January indicate that he thought at that time that the articles should be included in the constitution,[18] but by 24 January he was determined that as few treaty restrictions as possible should make their way into the document. Ireland could continue to be bound by the treaty without necessarily writing its terms into the constitution. Collins's objective was to draft the constitution in such a way that it would not, in itself, be a barrier to Ireland's further constitutional evolution. He also believed that if the Provisional government could exclude the Crown from the constitution it had every chance of winning de Valera's support for what would be essentially a republican document. Collins and de Valera agreed not to submit the Anglo-Irish Treaty to a vote of an extraordinary meeting of Sinn Féin on 21 February 1922 and to postpone a general election, in each case for fear of dividing the country, but they hoped that a constitution might be drafted that would reconcile the two sides in the treaty debate.[19]

The members of the drafting committee all understood Collins's tactical reasons for wanting to exclude the Crown, but they also approved the decision on its own merits. They found the monarchial form of government abhorrent because it suggested that Ireland was a colony, as the dominions had been, not an ancient nation. It presented an inaccurate image of Ireland, as a country constitutionally subordinate to Britain, and contradicted popular sovereignty. It also disguised the truth, which was that powers legally possessed by the King in Britain and the dominions were actually exercised by Cabinets. In articles written for the *Irish Independent* in 1922, Darrell Figgis explained why the new Irish constitution should not be modeled on dominion constitutions:

They were . . . but colonies on whom their mother-country was pleased to bestow constitutions. . . . It is clear from them that the mother did not propose to let the children wander far from her control, even though she permitted them to walk with their own feet. Not only in the actual provisions of these constitutions, but in their very conception and plan, drawn exactly according to English methods and from English experience, it is evident that a state of perpetual tutelage was imagined for the peoples to whom they were given.

That has now changed. The colonies have come to be nations, very jealous of their nationhood. . . . The consequence is that the provisions of these constitutions cannot be enforced since they do not square with experience. They encumber the documents which contain them as so much dead timber. They are sometimes carelessly, and more often dishonestly, described as legal fictions. They are dead letters—dead timber which a wise woodman would soon hew away.[20]

The Provisional government's draft constitution, presented to the British government on 27 May 1922, was based not on the "dead timber" of Canadian law, but on living Canadian practice.[21] It recognized the sovereignty of the people and contained no reference to a Governor-General. The only reference to the Sovereign came very late, in Article 75(a), which identified the King's representative as the "Commissioner of the British Commonwealth," in effect a Commonwealth ambassador to Ireland, with no powers in Irish affairs. The draft contained no oath of allegiance to the Crown and executive powers were assigned not to the Sovereign but to the Executive Council, a Cabinet elected by Dáil Éireann. The draft precluded the Commonwealth from any constitutional role in the Free State's foreign and defense policies by assigning the power to declare war and ratify treaties to Dáil Éireann. And to reinforce this point, the draft made no reference to British basing rights in Ireland, which had already been agreed to in Article 7 of the Anglo-Irish Treaty. Finally, the draft made no mention of the right of appeal from Irish courts to the Judicial Committee of the Privy Council in London. This was not specifically required by the Anglo-Irish Treaty but Lloyd George saw it as indispensable to the integrity of the Commonwealth. Indeed, he had described the Privy Council as "the Great Imperial Court of Appeal to decide questions of common interest to all the Dominions."[22]

In a memorandum to his colleagues on the drafting committee, Figgis wrote, "There may be some little difficulty with English law officers but I do not think that should deter us."[23] There was, in fact, much more than "some little difficulty." The British government rejected the Irish draft categorically. On a purely practical level, it objected that the document made no reference to British military rights in Ireland, pensions for departing civil servants, and an Irish contribution to the national debt. On a basic constitutional level, it objected because the document was essentially republican.[24] Lloyd George told Griffith and Collins on 27 May, "As far as the Treaty is concerned, the basis of your Constitution was to be the Constitution of Canada. That is specifically stated in the Treaty. . . . So far from being this, [the draft constitution] amounts to setting up what is really an independent republic in Ireland."[25] A memorandum from the Law Officers two days later advised that the Irish had submitted "a Republican constitution almost without disguise."[26]

In a strict constructionist sense both the Irish and British arguments had merit. Austen Chamberlain, one of the United Kingdom signatories to the treaty, believed that the draft was "flagrantly at issue with the Treaty in half a dozen vital points," but he conceded that the Irish "meant [the constitution] to be the Treaty—of course the Treaty stretched as far as it can go in their sense, but still the Treaty."[27] The problem was not really with the treaty or the proposed constitution but with the Canadian constitution on which it was supposed to be modeled. Britain insisted that the Free State must adopt Canadian legal forms but the Irish insisted on having Canada's usage and practice, what Darrell Figgis has described as "the living tissue of her constitutional experience."[28]

After the Irish draft had been rejected in London, Hugh Kennedy, legal adviser to the Irish delegation, sent a memorandum to the British government in which he explained rather patiently that Ireland was not obliged to use the language of the Canadian constitution because it was not a colony, as Canada had been. The Irish, he wrote, "cannot agree that they are bound to mould [the] constitution into forms of the English Common Law." Furthermore, it was inconceivable that Canada could be barred by Britain from adopting the language of the proposed Free State constitution should it now choose to do so.[29] Britain's response was visceral. The constitution had to contain the oath, the right of appeal to the Judicial Committee of the Privy Council, and British military bases in Ireland. Furthermore, in order to protect the integrity of the British Empire, the Crown had to be identified in the constitution, and the representative of the Crown, however named, had to control the royal assent to Irish bills.[30]

The British were particularly obdurate because of their suspicions about the purpose of an election pact Collins and de Valera had signed a short while before, on 20 May. The pact was designed to regulate the general election scheduled for 16 June, and to give the Provisional government time to prepare a constitution that would be acceptable to moderate antitreaty republicans.[31] The fact that in his famous "Document No. 2" de Valera had already allowed that "for purposes of common concern, Ireland shall be associated with the States of the British Commonwealth" marked him as moderate.[32] He was also prepared to swear an oath, in his words, "to the constitution of the Irish Free State, to the Treaty of Association and to recognize the King of Great Britain as Head of the Associated States."[33]

The election pact called for an uncontested election. Sinn Féin would present a "National Coalition Panel" to the country for approval, with the protreaty and antitreaty factions each having the same number of nominations as its current membership in the Dáil, sixty-six protreaty and fifty-eight antitreaty. After the election the Provisional government would be reorganized. The President would be elected by the Dáil as a whole, the Minister of Defence would represent the army, and there would be nine other ministers, five drawn from the majority and four from the minority. The government would therefore have a protreaty majority.

The long-term success of the plan depended on the Provisional government striking a deal on the constitution in London that de Valera would accept. Akenson and Fallin speculate that de Valera's participation in the pact signified that he approved the draft constitution that was submitted to the British a few days later.[34] However, Hugh Kennedy warned Collins that problems lay ahead because the executive identified in the pact, including as it did an antitreaty minority, would violate Article 17 of the treaty, which required members of the Provisional government to signify their acceptance of the treaty in writing.[35] De Valera would never accept this condition.

The British government's reaction to the pact was harsh. With Northern Ireland under severe attack from the I.R.A. at the time, the government was not about to condone the inclusion of antitreaty republicans in the Provisional government. Winston Churchill, the Colonial Secretary, who was responsible for relations with the Provisional government, questioned the pact in the House of Commons, and in a meeting of the British signatories to the treaty on 23 May he expressed his fear that the Provisional government would "slide into accommodation" with the antitreaty faction. Lloyd George refused to use the pact as a cause for breaking off negotiations on the constitution, but when Churchill met with Irish representatives on 26 May he asked them directly if the antitreaty members of the proposed executive would declare in writing their acceptance of the treaty. Griffith replied that Cabinet members would do so, but not *external ministers*, a formula which Churchill found unacceptable.[36]

External ministers will be discussed in chapter 10, but for the moment my readers should know that Article 48 of the Provisional government's draft provided that there would be an Irish executive with two kinds of ministers. Internal ministers, holding the key ministries, would be collectively responsible for the major policies of the government, but nonexecutive, or external, ministers, in lesser ministries, would not share in collective responsibility and would not necessarily sit in the Dáil. This executive was devised for reasons largely unconnected with accommodating de Valera and his supporters but it suggested a way to bring them back into government by appointing them as external ministers de facto before the formal introduction of the constitution later in the year. Collins proposed that only the protreaty internal ministers would have to sign their acceptance of the treaty. He believed that the plan would enable de Valera to cooperate in building the domestic structures of the new state while Collins himself and Griffith would concentrate on building a satisfactory relationship with Britain. With luck a civil war might be averted.

When the draft constitution was delivered to London on 27 May the Irish were told unequivocally that if the Provisional government were to include ministers who had not given their written assent to the treaty, Britain would resume some of the powers already transferred to the Free State.[37] Two days later the British government rejected the draft constitution. In doing so it blocked the reconciliation between Collins and de Valera that Churchill so feared, but it also unwittingly helped to bring on the civil war that Collins had tried so hard to avoid.[38]

It was back to the drawing board. Hugh Kennedy and the British Lord Chief Justice, Gordon Hewart, redrafted the constitution, and on 15 June the Provisional government agreed to a revised draft that complied with British demands concerning the Crown and other matters. It was approved by the British Cabinet the following day, election day in Ireland. It had been published that morning in Dublin, but too late to affect the election results.[39]

Collins had already rejected the election pact with de Valera on 14 June because he knew that its terms could not be honored within the framework of the new constitution. By then it was too late for the Provisional government to file protreaty candidates against the already nominated antitreaty candidates on the Sinn Féin National Coalition Panel, but many people had filed for election outside the panel process and all but 37 of 142 seats were contested.[40] The results showed that the protreaty faction returned 58 deputies, the antitreaty faction 36, Labour 17, Farmers 7, and Independents 6. Because of the confusion caused by the pact and its rejection, the election results are difficult to interpret, but O'Sullivan estimated that 78 percent of the poll and 72 percent of the newly elected Dáil supported the treaty.[41]

The antitreaty deputies boycotted the Dáil when it reassembled but when the draft constitution was submitted to the Dáil by William Cosgrave on 18 September 1922 it still met with strong opposition to the provisions on the Crown. Deputy Darrell Figgis, who had argued most strongly in the constitution committee that the constitution should reflect Canadian practice, not Canadian law, was particularly hostile to the changes imposed in London. He believed that the original draft would have been accepted by the British government but for the growth of antitreaty violence in Ireland, although this is highly unlikely.[42] Deputy George Gavan Duffy, who had signed the treaty in December 1921, also insisted that it imposed no obligation on the Free State to mimic Canadian constitutional law.[43]

When Cosgrave introduced the constitution in the Dáil he divided it into three parts: (1) those sections that the Dáil might amend, (2) those sections dealing with the Senate that should be accepted as matters of honor because they had been agreed upon with the southern unionists, and (3) fifteen articles dealing with the Crown and the British connection that were treaty obligations. The Dáil did amend the first category in significant ways, but it respected the Provisional government's commitments to the southern unionists and the treaty.[44]

The constitution was finally adopted by the Dáil on 25 October 1922. After passing both houses of the United Kingdom Parliament on 4 December it received the royal assent on 5 December and went into effect the following day. Article 44 of the constitution, which authorized the Free State to create subordinate legislatures, was designed to accommodate the Northern Ireland Parliament, but on 7 December that body used its authority under Article 12 of the Anglo-Irish Treaty to declare that the powers of the Free State should not extend to Northern Ireland. This meant that the constitutional structures of the two parts of Ireland, north and south, were complete, for the time being at least, by the end of 1922.[45]

The antitreaty "Irregulars" in the Irish Republican Army had already rejected this outcome in March 1922 when they repudiated the authority of the Dáil. On 13 April they occupied the Four Courts, the court building in central Dublin, and on 28 June, acting under pressure from Britain, the Provisional government ordered Free State forces to fire on the occupiers. The Irish Civil War had begun.[46] In October de Valera was elected "President and Chief Executive" of an Irish Republic by a rump Dáil convened by the antitreaty members of the I.R.A.[47]

The Civil War represented a clear clash of principles. On one side, the antitreaty forces claimed that the integrity of the existing Irish Republic, proclaimed in 1916 and affirmed in 1919, was the issue. On the other side, the Provisional government claimed that the real issue, as Collins put it, was "the right of the people to govern themselves. It is the principle of government by the consent of the governed."[48] The Anglo-Irish Treaty had been approved by the Dáil Executive in December 1921 and by Dáil Éireann in January 1922, albeit by narrow majorities; it had been endorsed by the Irish people in the June general election; and the new Dáil had approved the Free State constitution in October. The people of Ireland had spoken, and while it is true that both the Provisional government and the Dáil had acted under duress, because Britain had threatened to resume the war if its terms were not accepted, in a democratic sense this was not important. It was for the people and their elected representatives to decide whether to accept the unpleasant terms offered by Britain, not the I.R.A. As Collins said in the Dáil, "It is for the Irish people—who are our masters, not our servants, as some think—it is for the Irish people to say whether [the treaty] is good enough."[49] De Valera disagreed. He explained his position in a speech in Killarney on 18 March 1921: "The Majority have never a right to do wrong."[50] This was the voice of minority revolutionaries, and nascent dictators, through the ages.

## The Irish Free State Constitution

Having discussed in broad outline the clash of constitutional principle between the British government and the Irish Provisional government in 1922, we can consider the Irish Free State constitution in more detail.

In Irish law the constitution was authorized by Act Number 1 of 1922, the first act of the Free State Dáil. The act contained three clauses and two schedules. Clause 1 identified the constitution printed in Schedule 1 as the "Constitution of the Irish Free State." Clause 2 stated that the constitution would be "construed with reference to" the Anglo-Irish Treaty, which was printed as Schedule 2. Clause 3 stated that the act would be cited as the "Constitution of The Irish Free State (Saorstat Éireann) Act 1922."[51]

The constitution in Schedule 1 contained eighty-three articles. Those of major concern to this book will be discussed under five headings: the constitutional relationship with Britain, the executive, the legislature, the powers vested in Ireland, and responsible government. The remainder of this chapter will deal with the first four headings. Chapter 10 will consider responsible government.

## The Constitutional Relationship with Britain

Article 1 of the constitution recognized the Irish Free State as "a co-equal member of the Community of Nations forming the British Commonwealth of Nations." By recognizing the Free State in this way the constitution clarified the meaning of dominion status in law for all the dominions for the first time. They were each the constitutional equal of the United Kingdom.

The symbol of the Commonwealth, the Crown, was represented in several articles. Article 12 defined the Oireachtas, the Irish Parliament, in traditional British terms as the King, Dáil Éireann, and the Senate, known as Seanad Éireann. Article 60 provided that the Representative of the Crown, styled the Governor-General, would be appointed "in like manner as the Governor-General of Canada." In Canada it was the practice of the Sovereign to consult with the Canadian Prime Minister before making an appointment; in a letter of 13 December 1921 Lloyd George assured Arthur Griffith that the Free State government would be similarly consulted.[52] In fact, the Provisional government ignored the element of consultation implied in the Prime Minister's letter and simply nominated Timothy Healy, the idiosyncratic veteran of Irish nationalism, who became the first citizen of a dominion to be its Governor-General. For many years to come, the other dominions simply responded to Britain's nominees.[53]

Article 51 vested the executive authority of the Free State in the Governor-General, and Article 41 authorized him to give or withhold the royal assent to bills, or reserve them "for the signification of the King's pleasure." A reserved bill would fail unless approved by the King within one year. The constitution did not include the obsolete Canadian rule that the Crown might disallow a bill that had already received the royal assent from the Governor-General. The powers of the Governor-General were restricted by the important qualification that he would use his powers "in accordance with the law, practice and constitutional usage governing the like . . . in the Dominion of Canada." It was Canadian "practice and constitutional usage" for the Governor-General to accept the advice of his ministers on the royal assent.

In Britain and dominions, the authority to wage war and conduct foreign relations lay with the Crown, but the Provisional government's draft constitution of 1922 assigned both to the Oireachtas. The Free State constitution represented a compromise between these two positions. Article 49 provided that the Free State would not be committed to active participation in any war without the consent of the Oireachtas "save in case of actual invasion," but the constitution no longer contained Article 73 of the Provisional government's draft, which had reserved the ratification of agreements and treaties to the Oireachtas. Ratification was now vested in the Crown as a residuary power.

The Crown was also recognized in Articles 17 and 66. Article 17 restated Article 4 of the Anglo-Irish Treaty, which was the oath to be sworn by every member of the Oireachtas:

I ——— do solemnly swear true faith and allegiance to the Constitution of the Irish Free State as by law established, and that I will be faithful to H.M. King George V., his heirs and successors by law in virtue of the common citizenship of Ireland with Great Britain and her adherence to and membership of the group of nations forming the British Commonwealth of Nations.

Article 66 specified that the Judicial Committee of the Privy Council would be the final court of appeal for cases brought in the Free State, as it was for the other dominions.

As we can see, the Crown was featured very prominently in the constitution, but the Crown's prominence was an illusion. Leo Kohn wrote in 1932 that the constitution actually represented "the transformation of the new reality of Dominion autonomy into a framework of positive law."[54] It accomplished this by recognizing popular sovereignty and responsible government in such a way that the Crown was effectively neutralized.

Article 3 of constitution recognized popular sovereignty as follows: "All powers of government and all authority legislative, executive, and judicial in Ireland, are derived from the people of Ireland, and the same shall be exercised in the Irish Free State (Saorstat Éireann) through the organizations established by or under, and in accord with, this Constitution." The organizations referred to included the Governor-General, and it therefore appeared that powers derived from the people were to be exercised by the Crown, a very strange notion in a monarchy. Articles 41 and 51 also required the Governor-General to act "in accordance with the law, practice and constitutional usage" of Canada, which is to say, on the advice of his ministers, the practice in Canada.

More important, however, was the fact that the constitution wrote into constitutional law certain rules of responsible government that are conventions elsewhere. On 29 May 1922 the British government agreed that it was acceptable, at last, for a constitution to recognize, as Dicey had observed in 1887, that the prerogatives of the Crown had become privileges of the people, exercised by the Cabinet in the King's name.[55] Specifically, as I shall discuss in greater detail below, Britain agreed that the Governor-General would appoint the Dáil's nominee as President of the Executive Council, or Prime Minister.

If so much was conceded to Free State republicanism in the 1922 constitution, why did Lloyd George and his colleagues insist that the Governor-General must retain the formal powers of the royal assent, reservation of bills, and ratification of agreements with foreign states? The answer lies in part in the influence of die-hard Tories in the government, and their emotional commitment to the Crown, but more than this was involved. The Irish Free State constitution was actually caught up in the dying gasp of the imperial paramountcy which Britain had been attempting to combine with Irish self-government since 1782. That paramountcy was now subsumed in a new Commonwealth of Nations being constructed upon the constitutional structures of the old empire. The Commonwealth was expected to adopt foreign and defense policies at periodic conferences of Prime Ministers, and the Crown was to be the formal instrument of these policies. But to protect this instrument, one law had to prevail in cases of intra-Commonwealth constitutional disagreements—for example, on the law of the royal succession. The royal prerogative was therefore retained in each dominion for use in remote contingencies involving the Crown or some completely unforeseen crisis of intra-Commonwealth relations. As the United Kingdom legal advisers, Sir Edward Grigg and Lionel Curtis, argued, "It is true that this supremacy is a power in reserve, which would be used only on the advice of the Imperial Conference; but it is an existing and necessary power nevertheless."[56] It was inconceivable to the British negotiators that the Commonwealth could survive without the Crown, but as Ernest Blythe reminded his colleagues during the Dáil debate on the constitution:

Nothing that we can state in the constitution . . . will alter the reality in the least. The reality in regard to the doing of acts of State, and the taking of Executive action will depend upon the fact that an Irish Army will hold this country and the armed force of the country will be an Irish force. . . .

and these trappings [of monarchy], which are of much importance to the British, are of little or no importance to us.[57]

## The Irish Free State Executive

Article 51 of the Irish Free State constitution vested the executive authority of the Free State in the King, acting through his representative, the Governor-General who was obliged to act "in accordance with the law, practice and constitutional usage" of Canada. That is to say, he was obliged to accept the advice of the Cabinet. The obligation to take advice was made explicit in certain cases. For example, the Governor-General was authorized to recommend money bills to the legislature[58] and dissolve Dáil Éireann[59] on the advice of the Executive Council, the Cabinet. Most importantly, of course, he was required to appoint as President of the Executive Council, or Prime Minister, a person nominated by Dáil Éireann, and appoint as members of the Council persons nominated by the President and confirmed by the Dáil.[60]

## The Irish Free State Legislature

The Irish Free State Parliament, known in the English-language version of the constitution by its Irish name, Oireachtas, took up quarters in the same building it now occupies, Leinster House, the Dublin mansion of the Dukes of Leinster, which it purchased from the Royal Dublin Society.[61] It was required to sit at least once a year.[62]

The lower house used the name Dáil Éireann, in English, Chamber of Deputies, which it adopted from its predecessor of 1919. Each member was customarily known in Irish as *Teachta Dála*, member of the Dáil, a designation abbreviated to TD which is still in use. The number of members was set not by the constitution per se but by the rule stated in Article 26, that the ratio of electors to deputies should be not less than one per thirty thousand nor more than one per twenty thousand. The Dáil elected in June 1922 was permitted to sit with full powers for up to one year,[63] and it was responsible for drawing the constituencies for the first Free State general election, in August 1922. It set the number of constituency seats at 147; the University of Dublin and the National University of Ireland also received three seats each.[64] The first Dáil elected under the new constitution therefore had 153 members. The constitution required elections to be by proportional representation, in part to satisfy Southern unionists, but it was also an electoral system supported in principle by Arthur Griffith and Sinn Féin. The

Oireachtas determined that there should be multimember districts. It was the electoral system proposed by the Irish Convention in 1918.

The Dáil was summoned by the Governor-General, and its maximum life was four years, "unless earlier dissolved" on the advice of the Executive Council.[65] The maximum term was extended to five years by the Electoral (Amendment) Act of 1927, which was itself authorized by the fourth amendment to the constitution earlier that year. The government argued that the change was necessary to give ministers more time to learn their jobs between general elections.[66] The dates of parliamentary sessions were set by the Dáil, with the assent of the Seanad in the case of its own adjournment.[67]

The upper house, the Senate, was also known in the English version by its Irish name, Seanad Éireann. In meetings with Southern unionists in November and December 1921 Arthur Griffith had agreed that the Seanad would provide a safeguard for unionists by checking hasty legislation, but when he met with the constitution drafting committee on 24 January 1922 he rejected the notion that there might be nominated unionist senators.[68] In May 1922, Lord Midleton, a Southern unionist leader, suggested that half the senators should be nominated from people prominent in the professions, commerce, and education, and the other half should be elected on a property franchise. Both principles of selection would have favored unionists, but they were rejected by the Provisional government, which prized popular sovereignty above all.[69]

The precise structure and powers of the Seanad were worked out in London on 14 June 1922 at a meeting of representatives of the Provisional government, the British government, and the Southern unionists.[70] They agreed on an elected Seanad of sixty members[71] serving twelve-year terms, one-quarter to be replaced every three years.[72] Elections were by proportional representation, with the Irish Free State as a single electorate. Sitting senators were permitted to nominate themselves for election; of the remaining candidates, two-thirds were nominated by the Dáil and one-third by the Seanad. Nominations were to be made "with special reference to the necessity for arranging for the representation of important interests and institutions in the country."[73]

The Southern unionists were not particularly happy with the settlement. They secured a sixty-seat Seanad, rather than the forty-seat body the Provisional government's draft constitution had proposed, but they had no reserved seats and the chamber had very limited powers. In particular, as we shall see, the Dáil was given the power to override a vote

of the Seanad. The unionists would have preferred that disputed measures be resolved, as in all the home rule bills, by a joint sitting of the
two chambers. Nor were the unionists pleased that the Seanad would
be popularly elected. They would have preferred the Southern Senate
of the 1920 Government of Ireland Act, which was a nominated house
representing a variety of interests.[74]

To placate the unionists in the short term, Article 82, one of the
"transitory provisions" of the constitution, provided that half of the
first Seanad would be elected by the Dáil and half would be nominated
by the President of the Executive Council, with "special regard to the
providing of representation for groups or parties not then adequately
represented in Dáil Éireann."[75] The nominated members would gradually be replaced by elected members, beginning in 1925.

When the Provisional government introduced the constitution to the
Dáil in September 1922, it insisted that the provisions on the Seanad
that had been agreed with the Southern unionists should be accepted
as matters of honor. The Dáil generally complied, making only the following minor changes. First, the proposal that there would be two senators from each of the Free State universities was abandoned when the
universities were assigned three seats each in the Dáil. Second, the Seanad was given twenty-one days, rather than fourteen, to consider a
money bill. Third, Article 57 was added to the constitution to permit a
minister to address the Seanad.[76]

As soon as the constitution was approved, the Dáil and President
Cosgrave moved quickly to select senators, and the house first sat on 11
December 1922.[77] Of the thirty senators nominated by the President,
sixteen were unionists in what Lyons called the "broad sense."[78] The
first Seanad also had twenty-four non-Catholics.[79]

One representational principle for the Seanad that the constitution
drafting committee had considered quite seriously before rejecting it,
was functional representation, which is to say, the explicit representation of significant functional or vocational groups in society. This principle had great support in the constitution committee because, as Darrell Figgis wrote, "We are more frequently, in the intake and output
of our lives, blacksmiths or architects, or whatever else, than we are
individuals or citizens."[80] An unsigned memorandum in Hugh Kennedy's papers, possibly from Figgis, argued that in Britain the executive
frequently made agreements with representatives of industry and labor
in which Parliament played no role. This could be avoided by bringing

such interests into the legislature. The memorandum suggested two models for Ireland, either a functional second chamber, a formula the Labour party supported,[81] or some extraparliamentary advisory bodies connected to the Oireachtas in some way, which the memorandum called the German model.[82] On 16 March 1922 Figgis called Collins's attention to Article 68 of the Polish constitution which provided for councils of agriculture, commerce, industry, skilled labor, salaried employees, and so on, "which shall form together the Supreme Economic Council of the Republic."[83]

Figgis himself abandoned the concept of a functional chamber when he came to recognize that only the professions of medicine and law were adequately organized for the purpose in Ireland. The principle was impractical, he wrote, "under the present organization of society."[84] But all three of the drafting committee's drafts contained provisions for *advisory* functional councils, and they identified agriculture, industry, labor, and other sectors of the economy as interests worthy of representation. Nonetheless, Article 45 of the constitution merely repeated the rather austere language of the Provisional government's draft: "The Oireachtas may provide for the establishment of Functional or Vocational Councils representing branches of the social and economic life of the Nation. A law establishing any such Council shall determine its powers, rights and duties, and its relation to the government of the Irish Free State (Saorstat Éireann)." Article 56 further provided that the legislation to create these councils might authorize them to nominate external ministers, but the advisory councils were not created by the Oireachtas and it was not until the constitution of 1937 was adopted that the principle of functional representation found its way into the constitution as the representational basis of the new Seanad Éireann.

Before closing the discussion of the legislature, I should note that Article 20 required each house to make its own rules and standing orders. These were modeled very closely on British practices, as was parliamentary etiquette.

## The Irish Free State's Powers

Article 12 of the constitution declared, "The sole and exclusive power of making laws for the peace, order and good government of the Irish Free State is vested in the Oireachtas." The words "sole and exclusive" were added for emphasis during the Dáil debate on the constitution.[85] The Governor-General had the powers of assent and reservation but no Free State bill was ever denied the royal assent or reserved on orders from the United Kingdom. The Judicial Committee of the Privy Council was expressly denied the right to hear appeals questioning the validity of Irish laws.[86] Article 65 provided that only the Irish High Court might question the constitutionality of a law.

Only the Oireachtas was empowered to make law for the Irish Free State, but there were some restrictions on its powers. First, Article 2 of the Constitution Act provided that the Anglo-Irish Treaty would become part of Irish constitutional law and this restricted the Free State in certain ways. It had to accept, for example, that it was a dominion in the Commonwealth, with a representative of the Crown and an oath of allegiance. It had to accept some liability for the United Kingdom public debt and war pensions, allow Britain to maintain military bases in Ireland, and restrict the Irish military to the same ratio of establishments to population as existed in Britain. The Free State also had to accept that it might not claim sovereignty over Northern Ireland without the assent of the Parliament of Northern Ireland. Finally, Article 8 of the constitution restated Article 16 of the Anglo-Irish Treaty, which guaranteed freedom of conscience and religion in the Free State and contained the prohibition against endowing or restricting religion that had been included in all the home rule bills and the 1920 Government of Ireland Act.

The Oireachtas was also obliged to respect certain rights of the citizen: to liberty in Article 6; to the inviolability of dwellings in Article 7; and to opinion, assembly, and association in Article 9. These rights reflected American and continental influences, and were unprecedented in British and dominion law. They were not protected by the Anglo-Irish Treaty and were therefore amendable, but absent a constitutional amendment they were protected by the courts.

The Irish Free State constitution was unique. Ostensibly it created an Irish constitutional monarchy, but by force of will the Provisional government ensured that key republican values were written into constitutional law for the first time, including popular sovereignty, parliamentary control of the war power, and entrenched civil rights. Under great pressure, the Provisional government and Dáil Éireann agreed to a significant role for the Crown in the constitution, but this made the document unacceptable to antitreaty republicans who were confirmed in the view that the Anglo-Irish Treaty was a binding agreement not to advance, rather than a stepping-stone to independence, as Collins alleged. But they were completely wrong. The constitution actually retained enough of the rejected Provisional government draft of May 1922 to undermine the Crown fatally in Ireland. As Kevin O'Higgins said in the Dáil, "Going through this constitution, you will find that whenever one side stood upon the law and said, 'The law in Canada is so-and-so,' we have in each case modified and corrected the acerbity of the law by setting out fully and clearly the usage and practice."[87] Nowhere was this more evident than in the sections dealing with responsible government, to which we turn next.

# CHAPTER 9

# The Irish Free State and Responsible Government

We have already seen that the core rules of responsible government were stated in the Dáil Éireann constitution of 1919. They were expanded in the constitution of 1922. J. S. Swift MacNeill, professor of law at University College, Dublin, paid tribute to that document in 1925 when he wrote: "[The Irish Free State constitution] might . . . be utilized as a valuable list of political maxims universally acknowledged and carried out in the practice of the British Constitution, but not found among the formal Acts of the British Legislature nor forming part of the law of Great Britain."[1] In 1932 Leo Kohn wrote in a similar vein, "[The constitution] mocked the time-honoured empiricism of the British Constitution by the enunciation of basic principles and the formulation of dogmatic definitions. . . . It reduced to precise terms the conventional rules of the British Constitution."[2] Both statements were basically true. The Free State constitution did write the conventions of British responsible government into law for the first time, but it also modified the British model in significant ways. In this chapter I will consider both of these elements of the 1922 constitution, using the eight characteristics of responsible government outlined in chapter 1 as a guide.

## The Constitution of 1922 and the Eight Characteristics of Responsible Government

### Fusion

Article 52 of the Irish Free State constitution provided for fusion between the executive and the legislature by requiring members of the Executive Council, the Cabinet, to sit in Dáil Éireann. The Provisional government's draft constitution of May 1922 specified that nonexecutive ministers, the so-called external ministers, would not have seats, but this was amended during the Dáil ratification debate to permit, but not require, them to sit in the Dáil, and all of them did. Amendment 15 to the constitution, passed in 1929, permitted one member of the Seanad to sit in the Executive Council, and one did, in 1932.

## Majority Government

Article 53 of the constitution recognized majority government by requiring the Governor-General to appoint the President of the Executive Council on the nomination of Dáil Éireann. In practice, the President was elected by the Dáil after each general election. He then nominated the other members of the Executive Council to the Governor-General, after securing the approval of the Dáil for his choices. The Dáil itself nominated the external ministers, on the recommendation of a Dáil committee.[3] In each of these appointments processes the majority in the Dáil prevailed. Article 53 also required the Executive Council to resign should the President "cease to retain the support of a majority in Dáil Éireann," but how this support would be measured was not specified. In 1930 President Cosgrave felt that he should resign after losing a vote on a relatively minor issue, but he was renominated by the Dáil without an intervening general election.[4] The Free State did not last long enough to build a body of precedent on the subject.

## The Primacy of the Lower House

Several provisions of the Free State constitution established the primacy of Dáil Éireann over the Seanad. We have already seen, for example, that the Dáil nominated the President of the Executive Council and could force his resignation by withdrawing its support. Article 51 made explicit what was implicit in these provisions, that the Executive Council was responsible only to the Dáil. Article 52 required all the members of the Executive Council to sit in the Dáil, and this number had to include the key officers, the President, Vice-President, and Minister for Finance.[5] Article 35 gave the Dáil exclusive control of money bills, defined to include taxation, charges on public monies, votes of supply, and public accounts. The Seanad was permitted twenty-one days to recommend changes to such bills, but amendments were not permitted. During its lifetime the Seanad recommended fifty-five changes, of which thirty-four were accepted,[6] but it only once sought to amend a money bill, when Senator Guiness successfully moved an amendment to a finance bill in committee on 14 June 1923. This was a constitutional error, which was not repeated.[7]

The Seanad was permitted to initiate, amend, or reject nonmoney bills, but the members of the constitution drafting committee agreed that the chamber should not have the power, by itself, to block a measure approved by the Dáil. They disagreed, however, on how a dispute between the two chambers might be resolved. Drafts A and B would have allowed the Dáil to override the Seanad's rejection of a bill after a 180-day period of delay, but Draft C preferred such a bill to become law only after a referendum. The Provisional government adopted a mixture of these two proposals. Article 38 provided that the Seanad might only delay a bill for 270 days, in normal circumstances,[8] but Article 47 permitted a majority of the Seanad, or two-fifths of the Dáil, to call for an additional 90-day delay during which time two-thirds of the Seanad or 5 percent of registered voters might call for a referendum on the measure. As Darrell Figgis described this provision, "The Senate and the people . . . are placed in a watchful alliance over the acts and proceedings of the Dáil."[9]

The Southern unionists had wanted conflicts between the two houses of the Oireachtas to be resolved by a vote of both houses in a joint sitting, a formula that had already appeared in colonial constitutions and all the home rule bills, but the Provisional government rejected this plan as an unacceptable limitation on the Dáil. Article 38 provided only that the two chambers might meet in joint session to debate a bill on which they disagreed, not to resolve it by a vote. This procedure was never used and was dropped from the constitution in 1928.[10] A standing order was adopted in both houses in 1924 that allowed a joint committee to be appointed to reconcile disagreements between the two houses, but it was only convened three times, in 1924, 1926, and 1929.[11]

Whether an upper house makes a useful contribution to legislation depends not only on its formal powers but on its composition. If it simply mirrors the lower house it is unlikely to have much effect. Every draft of the Free State constitution recognized that the Seanad should be very different from the Dáil and the constitution anticipated that it would be a chamber of distinction, capable of making a nonpartisan, if nonbinding, contribution to legislation. Article 30 stated, "Seanad Éireann shall be composed of citizens who have done honour to the Nation by reason of useful public service or who because of special qualities or attainment represent important aspects of the Nation's life." This proved to be a pious aspiration because of the selection process for senators that was adopted. Half of the first Seanad was nominated by the President of the Executive Council and half was elected by the Dáil but the constitution proposed that members of the first Seanad would be phased out in favor of popularly elected members, beginning in 1925.[12] These would be elected by the country at large from a panel of candidates prepared by the Oireachtas, two-thirds nominated by the Dáil and one-third by the sitting Seanad. This formula guaranteed the Dáil considerable influence in Seanad selection through the nominating process, but the sixth amendment to the constitution, passed in 1928, went much farther. It provided that the Dáil and the Seanad, voting together, would be the electorate for Seanad elections, rather than the country as a whole.[13] The party politics of the Dáil soon took charge of this electoral process, though its effects were delayed. Senators served long, fixed terms, twelve years at first and nine after the seventh amendment to the constitution was passed in 1928, with a proportion retiring every three years.[14] As a result, the character of the Seanad was slow to change, and when de Valera took office in 1932 he found himself faced with a Seanad still dominated by the opposition. Sinn Féin would have won control in time, of course, but de Valera decided to abolish the chamber in 1936.

The constitution very clearly assigned the Seanad a subordinate role in the Oireachtas, but Free State governments went out of their way to limit its role still further, in part, as O'Sullivan argues, because the country was in "an ultra-democratic phase which [forbade] the concession of any but minimum powers to any members of an upper house."[15] The Dáil was suspicious of the early Seanad because it contained no revolutionaries from the 1916 to 1921 years. There were, at best, some Redmondite nationalists, but the Protestants nominated by the President in 1922 tended to be wealthy and privileged, and there were eight peers in the house. Many senators were former unionists, including the Chairman, Lord Glenavy, a former Lord Chancellor of Ireland.[16]

Disdain for the Seanad was expressed in several ways. No senators were elected as external ministers by the Dáil, although the constitution permitted them to serve, or were appointed as Parliamentary Secretaries by the President, although the Ministers and Secretaries Act of 1924 permitted such junior minister appointments. The custom in other countries that the government party leader in the upper house sits in the Cabinet was never adopted in the Free State because the Executive Council wanted all ministers to face the risks of a general election after the dissolution of the Dáil.[17] In 1929, after the abolition of external ministers, the fifteenth amendment to the constitution permitted a member of the Seanad to sit in the Executive Council, but only one was appointed, in 1932, when President de Valera nominated a former minister, Senator Joseph Connelly.

Article 57, which was added during the Dáil ratification debate, permitted ministers with seats in the Dáil to attend the Seanad, and they often did, but in 1926 the Minister for Finance, Ernest Blythe, prevented the upper house from reviewing the Ultimate Financial Settlement with Britain by refusing to appear or to supply papers.[18] The custom of questioning ministers in Question Time was never extended to the Seanad, and it was not until 1930 that a Seanad standing order was adopted requiring a minister to open the debate on the second reading of a bill.[19]

The government, which controlled the flow of legislation, also had a habit of sending a large number of bills to the Seanad just before the Christmas and summer recesses, leaving the chamber with insufficient time to consider them in any detail. Only three government bills were ever introduced in the Seanad, all noncontroversial measures introduced in 1923, although this practice would have spread the burden of legislation more evenly through the session. In an attempt to prevent bills from being rushed through the house, the Seanad amended its standing orders in 1924 to prohibit more than one stage of a bill being dealt with in a single day, but the order could be set aside at the government's request.[20] Despite these handicaps, the Seanad offered many hundreds of amendments to government bills, most of which were accepted by the Dáil,[21] and President Cosgrave paid tribute to its valuable contributions.[22]

Government legislation dominated the Seanad's agenda but individual senators were permitted to introduce their own bills, although there was no Seanad draftsman to assist them. In fact, very few bills originated there, and of the fourteen sent from the Seanad to the Dáil, three were rejected, four were never considered, three were passed amended, and only four were passed unamended.[23]

## Party Government

Although there was a great deal of criticism of party government in the Dáil ratification debate, parties were very strong in the Irish Free State. Indeed, the troubled early period of the state was a particularly inauspicious time for experiments in nonpartisanship.

In January 1922 the Sinn Féin leadership divided over the legitimacy of the Anglo-Irish Treaty, and this division laid the foundation for a party system that still exists in Ireland. Fine Gael and Fianna Fáil, the two dominant parties in the Irish Republic, are the direct descendants of the protreaty and antitreaty factions of Sinn Féin that emerged in the vote on the treaty. From January 1919 to the general election of June 1922, Sinn Féin was the only party in the Dáil because unionists and members of the Irish Parliamentary party refused to sit, and the Irish Labour party chose not to contest elections for fear of splitting the nationalist vote. In May 1922, however, de Valera and Collins used the word "parties" in their preelection pact to describe the protreaty and antitreaty factions of Sinn Féin, and the latter referred to themselves as the Republican party. Sinn Féin itself was described as an "organization."[24] In January 1923 the protreaty faction began to organize a new party, Cumann na nGaedheal (League of Gaels), which was formally launched in April. In 1932 it joined with two smaller organizations, the National Guard, an association of ex-officers and men of the Free State Army better known as the "Blue Shirts," and the National Center party, a conservative party with particular interests in agriculture, to form Fine Gael.[25]

The antitreaty republicans left the Dáil after the general election of June 1922 and fought the 1923 general election as Sinn Féin on a platform of opposition to the treaty and abstention from the Dáil. The party splintered in March 1926, and in May Eamon de Valera organized a new party, Fianna Fáil. Forty-four of its members were elected in the general election of June 1927 and they took their seats in the Dáil in August.[26] Sinn Féin dwindled to a small minority in the south of Ireland and is best known now as the extreme Irish nationalist party in Northern Ireland.

The language used to describe the republican split in 1922, particularly the use of the terms "protreaty" and "antitreaty," suggests that the two sides parted company over the terms of the Anglo-Irish Treaty, but this is an oversimplification. No one on either side accepted the treaty as a just settlement. The issue that really divided them was whether to accept the treaty as the best that could be achieved at the time, or to reject it and continue the War of Independence. The majority view in the Cabinet, Dáil Éireann, and the electorate was that the Free State should make the best of a bad bargain and accept the treaty while continuing to work for change in peaceful ways.

As we shall see in chapter 11, the Cumann na nGaedheal government soon began to demonstrate that the Free State was truly independent of Britain, and one might have expected this to cause the antitreaty opposition to fade away, with other social or economic interests moving in to shape party politics, but this did not happen. As late as 1981, R. K. Carty found that Fianna Fáil and Fine Gael were "programmatically indistinguishable parties, each commanding heterogenous electoral support,"[27] and that their members were still differentiated, to a substantial degree, by their orientations to the treaty, whether as aged participants in the events of 1922 or as relatives of those who participated.[28] Both are "center-right" parties in the European context. Although Gallagher found that social class also had a measurable impact on partisanship in Ireland, he decided that it was much less evident than in other countries.[29]

There are a number of explanations for the persistent influence of the events of 1922 on Irish parties. Some argue, for example, that the split in Sinn Féin was built upon an existing cleavage in Irish society between the "center" and the "periphery"—between those who were established more or less securely in the modern economic system and were comfortable with the outside world, and those who lived in, or identified with, a traditional, Gaelic, precapitalist, isolated, and anti-British Ireland.[30] Thomas Garvin writes, "I would argue that the division between [Fine Gael and Fianna Fáil] actually reflects a profound distinction in Irish society, a distinction between those who, for class, cultural or other reasons, assume a natural affinity between Ireland and Britain and those who do not, or would rather such an affinity did not exist."[31]

Carty counters that it was Fianna Fáil's conduct, rather than a deep cleavage in Irish society, that best explains the continuing influence of the events of 1922.[32] He argues that de Valera used the symbols of the "center-periphery" cleavage to structure an artificial party competition in the Free State: "Fianna Fáil leaders re-created and maintained, at a *symbolic level*, the centre-periphery conflict that had structured Irish national competition for a century. Their political genius was in perpetuating the image of Fianna Fáil as the party of Ireland as a periphery within the British Isles, and so the logical government of the country."[33] De Valera was able to paint Cumann na nGaedheal, a party led by men with impeccable republican credentials, as the party of the British connection and his own Fianna Fáil as the party of the traditional Irish nation. The fact that many politicians of the revolutionary period were active into the 1950s helped to perpetuate the attitudes of the 1920s. The deaths of Michael Collins and Arthur Griffith in 1922 removed the two men who might have effectively challenged the distortions.[34]

Cumann na nGaedheal had no defense against Fianna Fáil's tactics. Its leaders had, after all, gone to war to defend the treaty. As Ronan Fanning reminds us,

All the bitterness and brutality of civil war reinforced the inhibitions of the Free State Ministers against tinkering with, let alone dismantling, the treaty for which they had fought and won. A treaty first perceived, even by its advocates, merely as a means to an end became an end in itself. The consequences for party politics in the new state proved lasting and profound.

Fanning concludes that "once Fianna Fáil entered the Dáil they could play the green card . . . with irresistible effect."[35] Fianna Fáil was able to declare that it would restore the Irish Republic that had been surrendered in 1921, something Cumann na nGaedheal, the "protreaty" party, could not do. Fianna Fáil also built an effective extraparliamentary organization on the basis of civil war units. Cumann na nGaedheal, which inherited the institutions of state without having to organize at the grass roots to seize power, neglected to do this in the early 1920s, and suffered for it thereafter.[36]

Whatever the explanation for the resilience of the treaty division, whether it was the result of a long-standing cleavage in Irish society or of the manipulation of the symbols of such a cleavage by Fianna Fáil, or some combination of the two, the practical effects were the same. The basic issue in Irish Free State politics after independence was what it had been before, Ireland's relationship with Britain. As a result, the treaty issue stifled political development in the Irish Free State in much the same way that home rule stifled political development in Ireland before 1922. Very much the same thing was happening in Northern Ireland too, where political parties were fixated on the British connection, both before and after partition.[37]

The belief of some of the Irish founding fathers that Dáil Éireann would demonstrate a new kind of nonpartisan parliamentary behavior was destroyed in this stormy environment, and the tendency to polarize the legislature into government and opposition, or winners and losers, which is inherent in responsible government, reinforced the party division, a process that accelerated after Fianna Fáil entered the Dáil in 1927.[38]

The Free State electoral system also helped to polarize the legislature. Article 26 of the constitution called for Dáil elections by proportional representation but allowed the Oireachtas to determine the number and character of constituencies, subject only to the rule that there should be not less than one deputy per thirty thousand electors, nor more than one per twenty thousand. The Oireachtas opted for multimember constituencies, but the degree to which election results would proportionally reflect the electorate would depend very largely on the number of Dáil seats per constituency. The larger the number, the more likely that minor parties and independents would win seats by proportional representation. The smaller the number, the more likely that the larger parties would dominate the result.

The Electoral Act of 1923 created a 153-member Dáil with some very large constituencies. One returned 9 members, three returned 8, and five returned 7. The remaining constituencies had 3, 4, or 5 members each. The 1935 Electoral Act eliminated the 8- and 9-member constituencies and two of the 7-member districts, and almost doubled the number of 3-seat constituencies, from 8 to 15. The changes worked to the advantage of the larger parties. Of the 45 seats available in the 3-member constituencies in the 1937 general election, for example, Fianna Fáil won 24, Fine Gael won 16, and Labour won 3.[39] Warner Moss identified ten parties that won seats in the Dáil between 1923 and 1932,[40] but Fianna Fáil and Fine Gael, or its predecessor, Cumann na nGaedheal, have actually dominated election results in independent Ireland, with Labour as a consistent third party.[41]

The effect of the emergence of a party system rooted in the conflict over the Anglo-Irish Treaty, coupled with the manipulation of the electoral system to the advantage of the larger parties, meant that proportional representation did not fragment the Dáil to the degree that it was impossible for a government to win the support of a majority, the fundamental condition for responsible government. As late as April 1926, in a memorandum prepared for the Amendments to the Constitution Committee, Ernest Blythe, the Minister for Finance, expressed the fear that proportional representation would produce indecisive government:

Good government and efficient administration require that there shall be a stable majority in parliament and that the Executive shall normally hold office for a reasonable term of years. It is only when these conditions exist that considered policies can be carried through. Where the Parliamentary majority is unstable and where measures are carried by transient combination of a number of groups there is little responsibility to the people and a consistent programme is impossible.[42]

Blythe's fears were unfounded.

Within the Oireachtas, party discipline was very strong, particularly after Fianna Fáil entered the Dáil in 1927. In part this was due to the relatively small membership of the chamber, but it was also due to the harsh, confrontational politics of the time, which provided an incentive for members to toe the line. Partisanship was even extended to the selection of the Chairman, or Speaker, of the Dáil. The second amendment to the constitution, passed in 1927, was designed to limit party politics in the matter of the Chair by permitting a sitting Chairman to be returned unopposed in his constituency at a general election.[43] In Britain, the practice was also to allow a Speaker to continue in office from Parliament to Parliament, but in 1932 the Cumann na nGaedheal Chairman, Michael Hayes, was defeated by the Fianna Fáil deputy, Frank Fahy, in an election for Chairman of the Dáil that followed the general election.[44] In their conduct of Dáil business both men were essentially nonpartisan, but the office itself was now regarded as a prize to be won, unlike the Speaker's chair in the British House of Commons.

## Cabinet Government

Article 12 of the constitution, copied from the constitutions of Britain's dominions, formally assigned to the Oireachtas the "sole and exclusive power of making laws for the peace, order and good government of the Irish Free State." But the rules of responsible government ensured that the Cabinet would actually dominate the proceedings.

The Irish Free State constitution provided explicitly for Cabinet government. Article 51 vested executive authority in the King but created an Irish Cabinet, the Executive Council, "to aid and advise" the Governor-General. It further stated that executive authority would be exercisable "in accordance with the law, practice and constitutional usage" of Canada. There was no doubt at all, in 1922, that the Canadian Cabinet controlled the executive through its advice to the Governor-General, and this is what Irish constitutional law, in an oblique way, provided.

Article 51 also defined the composition and collective responsibility of the Irish Cabinet: "The Executive Council shall be responsible to Dáil Éireann, and shall consist of not more than seven nor less than five Ministers appointed by the representative of the Crown on the nomination of the President of the Executive Council." Article 54 added: "The Executive Council shall be collectively responsible for all matters concerning the Departments of State administered by Members of the Executive Council. . . . [It] shall meet and act as a collective authority." External ministers were specifically exempted from collective responsibility by Article 54, and were not required to resign if the President lost the confidence of the Dáil.

What "collective authority" meant in practice was established by the Provisional government in August 1922 when it decided that dissents in the Cabinet would be recorded, but all decisions would be presented to the public as unanimous and Cabinet proceedings would be strictly confidential. G. Gavan Duffy, who had planned to make public his reasons for resigning from the government, agreed that he should not do so after this decision.[45] The Provisional government's policy was confirmed by the Free State Cabinet in 1924 when the Army Inquiry Committee asked for details of certain legal advice which the Cabinet had received, and Cosgrave refused, stating:

If such immunity from investigation and such mutual confidence are not maintained in respect of the deliberations of the Executive Council, no one could undertake the responsibility of Executive Government in the Saorstát. It would be against every canon of public policy to permit any breach of a protection so vital to the full and anxious exploration of the problems of Government by responsible ministers.[46]

In the same year the Executive Council refused to release department files on broadcasting to the Dáil.[47]

In the hostile party competition of the 1920s, collective responsibility was not difficult to maintain, although the Department of Finance complained that ministers of other departments were inclined to blame it in public for their inability to adopt popular programs. The primacy of Finance was accepted in the Free State, as in Britain, and the department had to approve the major expenditures of all government departments. It would have preferred every member of the government to defend its decisions, but accepted its role as scapegoat, Fanning says, with an "air of philosophic resignation."[48]

One aspect of collective responsibility was the requirement, expressed in Article 54, that the Executive Council would prepare estimates of the receipts and expenditures for the Free State and present them to the Dáil each year. Article 37 also required money bills to be "recommended by a message from the Representative of the Crown acting on the advice of the Executive Council." The Provisional government's draft of this article in May 1922 had made no reference to the Crown, but Britain wanted to retain at least some of the language of the dominion constitutions in which the Governor-General recommends money bills to Parliament. However, because the article also required the Governor-General to act on the advice of the Executive Council, the Irish constitution made the redundancy of the Crown explicit.[49] Similarly, Article 28 recognized the Governor-General's right to dissolve Dáil Éireann and call a general election, but only on the advice of an Executive Council.

The standing orders adopted by the Dáil added numerous other opportunities for the Cabinet to dominate the Oireachtas to those already identified in the constitution. Standing Order 18, for example, provided that the order of business each day would be set by the Chairman in consultation with the Committee on Procedure, a majority of whose members were nominated by the Executive Council. Standing Order 41 allowed disorderly members to be suspended on a motion by a member of the Executive Council, and Standing Order 46 permitted a minister to move closure, which is to say, end debate. When in session the Dáil sat from Tuesday to Friday, but Standing Order 74 confined the agenda to questions to ministers and ministerial business for most of each sitting. Private members' business came a distant third, being permitted only on Wednesday evenings after 7:00 P.M. and at the end of the day on Fridays. The standing orders permitted even this meager allocation of time to be preempted by ministerial business. Finally, Standing Order 90 provided that only a member of the Executive

Council might move an amendment to increase an amount of money identified in a money bill.[50]

The Dáil did the bulk of its committee work in committees of the whole house, which precluded the back-bench expertise and cross-bench collegiality that might have limited the Cabinet's control to a degree if specialist committees had been used more often.[51] The only standing committee in the Irish Free State was the Committee on Public Accounts, which reviewed government expenditures but did not enter into policy questions. A number of special and select committees were appointed to consider specific issues,[52] but the system of standing committees working in parallel with departments of government that existed in the first Dáil Éireann was not replicated in the Free State.

## A Strong Prime Minister

The Irish Free State constitution assigned a very powerful role to the Cabinet, the Executive Council, but it also identified the office of Prime Minister, the President of the Executive Council, for the first time in a British or dominion constitution, and clearly established his primacy in the Executive. The President was appointed by the Governor-General on the nomination of Dáil Éireann but he had sole responsibility for nominating his Vice-President and other members of the Executive Council to the Dáil.[53] He had no authority to dismiss a minister. The Amendments to the Constitution Committee, appointed by the Executive Council in 1925, recommended that he be given this power, but the recommendation was never implemented.[54] However, the Council was required to resign as a whole if the President lost the confidence of the Dáil or chose to resign, for any purpose.

There were several respects in which the Irish President was intended to be somewhat weaker than his counterparts in Britain and the dominions. The Provisional government's draft constitution would have allowed the President alone to select the members of the Executive Council, as was the general practice elsewhere, but this system was amended in the Dáil debate on the constitution to require the Dáil's assent to each nomination. As we have seen, there was also an ostentatious effort to stress the Council's collective responsibility for Departments of State, for preparing estimates, and for advising the Governor-General on money bills and dissolutions. Under the constitution of 1922, Farrell writes, "The President of the Executive Council was destined to be chairman of his cabinet, not its master."[55] In practice, however, the powers of the President depended on his character, as well as the constitution. De Valera dominated Irish politics for forty years from 1932, and served as head of the government for twenty-one years, sixteen of them continuously. His colleagues in Fianna Fáil called him "the chief" and he was very much more than a chairman.[56] Even William Cosgrave, the first President of the Executive Council, who became head of government only because of the deaths of his two more prominent colleagues, Griffith and Collins, was stronger than the constitution might suggest.[57]

## A Weak Head of State

The Provisional government's draft constitution of May 1922 gave the Representative of the Crown, styled the Commissioner of the British Commonwealth, no powers at all in Irish domestic affairs. Once it became clear that the Free State would have to accept the Crown, the Irish opted for the title Governor-General rather than Commissioner precisely because the powers of Governors-General were already understood to be largely obsolete in the dominions. Kevin O'Higgins told the Dáil, "When you call the man a Governor-General you stamp him and the limits of his powers of interference in a way that is readily understood in Canada and the other Dominions. . . . You call him a Commissioner, and the name conveys nothing in particular, and no one knows what are the limits of his powers."[58] The Irish were also very successful in limiting even the formal powers of the Governor-General. As Leo Kohn wrote, "The monarchical frame of Dominion status was taken over, but it was subjected—by the formal enunciation of its actual content—to so restrictive an interpretation as to nullify it both in form and content."[59] The Governor-General appointed, but had no responsibility for selecting, ministers, and there was not the slightest suggestion in law that they served at his pleasure. It is true that he had authority in Article 41 to refuse the royal assent, or reserve a bill for "signification of the King's pleasure," but even here he was required to act in accordance with the "law, practice, and constitutional usage" of Canada, where it was understood that the Governor-General accepted the advice of his ministers.

We must remember, however, that Britain had attempted to undermine this understanding when the first Governor-General, Timothy Healy, was obliged to promise that he would advise the Colonial Secretary regarding bills whose constitutionality he doubted so that they might be reserved to London.[60] In his first two years Healy twice balked at signing a bill on constitutional grounds. The first was the Public Safety (Emergency Powers) (No. 2) Act of 1923, which suspended habeas corpus in certain cases, a possible violation of Article 6 of the constitution. Kevin O'Higgins, the Minister for Justice, visited Healy to point out that the Executive Council had formally advised him to signify his assent and he had no choice but to do so. The second occasion was the Intoxicating Liquor Bill of 1924. Healy questioned whether he should sign a measure approved by a Dáil that had been dissolved before he had an opportunity to give his assent. The Attorney General advised, "In no portion of the Constitution is [the Governor-General] required to approve or authorized to disapprove of legislation."[1] His job, in other words, was to do what he was told, and this is what he subsequently did. So much for Healy's assurances to the Colonial Secretary. Fortunately, the Colonial Office agreed with the Irish government on these bills. It did not want to be seen to be deciding such issues for Ireland.[62]

In one other important respect the role of the Governor-General was unclear in the first year of the Free State. On 12 December 1922 Healy followed British and dominion precedent by formally opening the Oireachtas session with a speech outlining the government's legislative program. He did this again in October 1923, after the first Free State general election, but the major opposition party, the Labour party, boycotted both ceremonies and the government abandoned the practice. This diminished the Governor-General's ceremonial role in the state and ended the practice of proroguing the Oireachtas each summer, at the end of an annual session, pending a formal reopening the following autumn. The effect was to deny the legislature an annual debate on the Speech from the Throne, which is the opportunity for a major debate on government policy in Britain and the dominions at the beginning of each session. Since 1923 Irish parliamentary sessions have been continuous, for the life of a Parliament, though with periodic recesses.[63]

Healy's successor, James MacNeill, a former Indian civil servant, accepted the diminished role of the Governor-General and encountered no difficulties with the government until, as we shall see, de Valera became President of the Executive Council and launched a republican attack on the office of Governor-General itself.

## Concentration of Power

The seven characteristics identified above produced a system of government that concentrated Irish Free State authority in the hands of the Executive Council and its President. The constitution itself provided for fusion, majority government, Cabinet government, a prominent role for the President, and a minor role for the Governor-General. Party government and the centralization of power followed inevitably from these formal provisions. In 1932, Leo Kohn wrote:

The Irish Constitution and the Standing Orders adopted under its provisions did, indeed, eliminate certain archaic features of the British system, but that very simplification only reveals the essential acceptance of the British model. The characteristic feature of that system is the rigid concentration of the initiative and the control of parliamentary business in the hands of the Executive, which is practicable only when the latter is able to rely on a permanent and effective majority.[64]

In one very important respect, the Irish Free State constitution restricted the powers of government. Article 65 provided that the High Court might review the constitutionality of any law. This provision was very much less effective in the Free State than it was to be in the Irish Republic, in part because British-trained Irish judges were very conservative, and in part too because the constitution was amendable by ordinary law for the whole of its life, as we shall see in chapter 11. By 1937 forty-one of its original eighty-three articles had been amended.[65] In this environment, few constitutional cases reached the High Court, although there were important exceptions. In three cases heard in 1934 and 1935, for example, the Court was able to prevent the government from suppressing the Blue Shirts, a uniformed organization with neofascist characteristics. O'Sullivan describes the government's reverse in the third case, *The State (Eoin O'Duffy) v. Bennett and Others* (1935), as "a vitally important legal decision, which safeguarded the individual from the possible tyranny of the Executive."[66]

## *Modifications of Responsible Government in the Irish Free State Constitution*

It can be argued that those who drafted the Free State constitution did a brilliant job of rendering the conventions of British responsible government into legal form. One still finds constitution scholars in the British Commonwealth arguing that the conventions that regulate the Crown are too delicate, too subtle, or too nuanced to be written into constitutional law. What they are really saying is that Britain or Canada or Australia or New Zealand cannot possibly accomplish today what the Irish Free State managed to accomplish very well in 1922.[67] It should be added, however, that the Irish succeeded when they tried to codify existing British practice. But they failed when they tried to modify that practice.

A majority in the constitution drafting committee were anxious to use the Free State constitution to experiment with new constitutional forms or rules, and three of these are of particular interest to us: external ministers, the legislative initiative and referendum, and a qualified dissolution. By addressing these three issues, the Irish were trying to weaken collective responsibility, enhance the individual responsibility of ministers, restrict somewhat the powers of the President of the Executive Council, subdue party, and give substance to popular sovereignty. In effect, they were trying to reverse the concentrating tendencies of responsible government.

## The External Minister

The external minister concept involved a two-tier ministry with two quite different concepts of ministerial responsibility.[68] It was based on the belief that proportional representation would produce a Dáil with many parties, but dominated by none. Kevin O'Higgins, who managed the debate on the constitution for the government, told the Dáil, "Under Proportional Representation you will have not so many great solid parties like in England, which make the party system a fairly good working arrangement, but you will have rather a lot of groups in this Dáil not bound together particularly, but voting independently on the different issues that may arise."[69] O'Higgins believed that a Dáil with "a lot of groups" would not be controlled by one or two large parties, and this prospect made it possible for the Free State to experiment with two kinds of ministers, internal and external.

The concept of the external minister was introduced to the constitution drafting committee by James Douglas and was adopted in Drafts B and C.[70] Draft A called for an orthodox, single-tier ministry on the British model. Draft B was adopted by the Provisional government after a difficult debate in which Arthur Griffith supported Draft A.

Over his objections, the government proposed that the Executive Council would have two tiers: a small group of ministers selected from Dáil Éireann who would be collectively responsible to that chamber, and a second group of ministers selected from outside the Oireachtas who would not share in collective responsibility. The proposal was based on the assumption that there were two categories of government business. The first, the major issues of public policy, would be assigned to the first group of ministers, those collectively responsible to the Dáil, who could be voted out of office *en bloc* were they to lose the confidence of the Dáil. The second category of business was assumed to include noncontroversial or technical matters that did not need to be treated by the Dáil as issues of confidence. They would be entrusted to skilled administrators or technicians who would be individually responsible to the Dáil. This formula was approved by the British government in June 1922 but was challenged in the Dáil ratification debate in September and October. In fact, all the articles dealing with the executive were referred to a Dáil committee and its recommendations formed the basis of the constitution's amended provisions on a two-tier executive.

As finally adopted, Article 53 provided that only the first tier of the Free State government would be known as the Executive Council. It was composed of a President nominated by the Dáil, and between four and six other ministers nominated by the President and approved by the Dáil. In the language of Article 54, the Council was "collectively responsible for all matters concerning the Departments of State administered by Members of the Executive Council," and it was required to retire as a whole if the President lost the confidence of the Dáil. O'Higgins told the Dáil, "We never contemplated that one man of the group could be picked out and assailed and that the others would not go down with him. . . . That group must be a group representing the broad lines of policy, and it must stand together."[71] O'Higgins anticipated that Executive Council ministries would include at least Finance, Defence, Foreign Affairs, and Home Affairs.[72]

The second tier, identified in Article 55, was composed of ministers known popularly, but not in the constitution, as external or extern ministers. They did not sit in the Executive Council, and although they could be removed from office individually by a vote of the Dáil for malfeasance, incompetence, or failure to carry out the wishes of the Dáil, they were not required to resign after a vote of no-confidence in the

Executive Council. Their term of office was for the life of a Dáil, not the life of the Executive Council. The Dáil was free to reject items of an external minister's policies without forcing his resignation, or that of the ministry as a whole, and there was no presumption that an external minister would have to agree with every aspect of government policy. As O'Higgins said to the Dáil, "Why lose your best servant because he does not agree with you on matters outside the scope of his work?"[73]

External ministers were elected by Dáil Éireann, but the President determined how many there would be and which ministries they would lead.[74] O'Higgins anticipated that they might include Education, Industry, Trade, Commerce, Justice, the Postal Service, Local Government, Public Health, Agriculture, Labour, and Fine Arts.[75] No fixed number was set by the constitution but the total ministry, including the required five to seven members of the Executive Council, was not to exceed twelve.[76]

To insulate external ministers from party and electoral politics, the Provisional government's draft constitution proposed that they would not sit in the Oireachtas, but there was serious opposition to this proposal in the Dáil because it would have undermined the external minister's personal responsibility to the legislature. Deputies also foresaw that if an external minister were chosen from the Dáil, the by-election for the seat he would have to vacate to accept office might lead to a change in the balance of parties in the Dáil, given that general elections were by proportional representation in multimember constituencies and by-elections would necessarily be for single seats. The Dáil agreed to a compromise that permitted, but did not require, external ministers to sit in the Oireachtas,[77] and in fact, all of them did. In the first Irish Free State government of December 1922, the Dáil elected three external ministers, for Agriculture, the Postal Service, and Fisheries. After the general election of August 1923 President Cosgrave added Local Government to the list.[78]

Those who supported the two-tier executive believed that external ministers would escape from the stifling discipline imposed by what Deputy Thomas J. O'Connell described as "the pernicious doctrine of Collective Responsibility in the Ministry,"[79] which led almost every vote in the British Parliament to be treated not on its merits but as a way of testing the government's majority. Partisanship would be limited to only the most fundamental issues that define a government, those assigned to the Executive Council. Matters assigned to external ministers would be liberated from the shackles of party competition. O'Higgins knew that external ministers were strange to "minds which have been so much turned upon the British system of politics,"[80] but he insisted:

These proposals will make the Irish Parliament what the British Parliament is not. It will make it a deliberative Assembly that will weigh carefully on their merits the measures brought before it, and solely with an eye to the results of these measures in the country. . . . If we admit the evils of the British Party system of Government, if we can see them clearly, if we admit it is wrong to have a man, almost as a matter of routine, voting against his best judgement under the crack of a Party Whip, is it not worthwhile to try to get away from that, and try to forge here a system that will enable men to remain in politics and to remain honest?[81]

He also argued:

It is important that at the launching of a young state . . . a Minister should be able to bring forward proposals here and have them freely discussed by the Dáil without feeling that their rejection would endanger his whole Ministry and his whole administration, and endanger the President, and the policy that the President stood for.[82]

The Provisional government also recognized an incidental value of external ministers as it had proposed them in the draft constitution submitted to the British government in May. The draft proposed to exclude external ministers from the Oireachtas, and Collins believed that this would permit Eamon de Valera and his associates to serve as external ministers without swearing the oath of allegiance to the King required of all members of the Oireachtas by Section 4 of the Anglo-Irish Treaty. In September 1922 O'Higgins denied that this had been any part of the government's plan,[83] but in April, before the collapse of the Collins–de Valera pact, it had been a different story. Then, the committee members responsible for Draft B, Kennedy, Douglas, and France, had argued that de Valera would be able to serve as an external minister,[84] and Griffith made exactly this point when he met Churchill on 26 May. However, Griffith was forced to retreat in the face of British objections. The British insisted on the insertion of Article 55 of the constitution, which required that all members of the government must swear the oath of allegiance.[85]

Britain did not object to external ministers per se, and the proponents of the concept in the drafting committee clearly believed that it had merit in itself. It was modeled, very loosely, on a provision in the Swiss constitution, which was much admired by Professor O'Rahilly. Hugh Kennedy wrote, "The provisions [on the executive] in the Irish draft may be described as the Swiss system, altered and adapted to suit Irish conditions,"[86] but O'Rahilly quite correctly countered many years later that the Swiss contribution was swamped by the British in the finished constitution.[87] Some similarity survived, it is true, but not much. Article 96 of the Swiss constitution provided that all seven members of the Swiss Federal Council were elected by members of the two houses of Parliament, to which they were individually responsible, while Irish external ministers were elected by the Dáil, to which they were individually responsible. But there the similarity ends. External ministers were elected for the life of a Dáil, but the members of the Swiss Federal Council were elected to three-year terms. In practice, all the external ministers sat and voted in the Dáil, but the Swiss had no votes in Parliament. In Ireland, there was a two-tier ministry and the executive ministers were collectively responsible to the Dáil. In Switzerland, there was a single-tier ministry and every minister was individually responsible. Finally, the Swiss model was designed to meet the needs of a federation. One member of the Federal Council represented each canton. Ireland had no such restriction. The inspiration for external ministers may have been Swiss, therefore, but the final product was not.

## The Initiative and Referendum

The second feature of the 1922 constitution designed to inhibit the concentration of power was the legislative initiative, and its related provision, the referendum. Any attempt to give legislative power directly to the people impedes the concentration of power that is a characteristic of responsible government. This is precisely why the Free State constitution, influenced by Germany, Switzerland, and some the American states, included Article 48 which permitted the Oireachtas to create the legislative initiative and referendum. The procedure, if legislated, would have provided that fifty thousand registered voters might petition the Oireachtas to enact a measure, and if it failed to do so, the measure would be put to the people in a referendum.

The constitution envisaged that the referendum would be used in two other cases: to reverse an act of the Oireachtas and to approve constitutional amendments. Article 47, a very clumsy article, provided that a bill passed by the Oireachtas would be submitted to a referendum if it met two conditions. First, the bill would have to be suspended for 90 days at the request of two-fifths of the Dáil or a majority of the Seanad. Second, three-fifths of the Seanad or one-twentieth of all registered voters would have to request a referendum within that 90-day period. A majority of those voting in the referendum would decide the issue. Money bills, or "such Bills as shall be declared by both houses to be necessary for the immediate preservation of the public peace, health or safety," were excluded from such referenda. Note that this provision allowed two-fifths of the Seanad to delay legislation for 90 days beyond the 270 days provided in Article 38 of the constitution, even if no referendum were to materialize. This effectively extended the Seanad's period of delay to 360 days for contested bills. Article 50 required constitutional amendments to be approved by the Oireachtas and by either a majority of all registered voters or two-thirds of those actually voting in a referendum. We will see in chapter 11 that none of these three procedures calling for a referendum was ever used.

## The Qualified Dissolution

In an attempt to strengthen the Irish legislature against what was seen as the excessive power of the Cabinet in countries such as Britain, the customary dissolution procedure was qualified in the Free State constitution. Article 53 stated that "the Oireachtas shall not be dissolved on the advice of an Executive Council *which has ceased to retain the support of a majority in Dáil Éireann*" (emphasis added). In Britain and the dominions it was customary for the head of state to dissolve Parliament and call for a general election at any time on the advice of the Prime Minister, even if the government had lost the support of a majority in the lower house. Those who wrote the Irish constitution were suspicious of the power this procedure gave to the Prime Minister. They reasoned that a Prime Minister who had actually lost the confidence of the House of Commons might be able to win a formal vote of confidence by threatening to dissolve Parliament, were he to lose. Faced with the possibility of losing their seats in the general election that would follow, some M.P.'s, perhaps enough to tip the scales, might be bullied into supporting the government. As J. G. Swift MacNeill put it, "The power of Ministers, when defeated in the House of Commons, to appeal to the country . . . immensely increases the power of a Ministry over the House of Commons which has appointed that Ministry and whose servant it is."[88]

Article 53 of the Free State constitution eliminated this possibility by denying a President the right to call an election if he had already lost the confidence of the Dáil. In effect, it was left to the Dáil, not the defeated President, to decide whether to call a general election after the fall of a government. Only an Executive Council possessing the confidence of the majority was entitled to advise the Governor-General to dissolve the Dáil. This meant that the Dáil could nominate a new President either to form a new ministry for the long term, or to recommend a dissolution immediately.

Responsible government was very much a part of the Irish Free State constitution, as it had been of the Dáil Éireann constitution which it succeeded, but as I have shown, those who drafted the 1922 constitution made significant efforts to modify the model in ways that would limit the powers of party and Cabinet government. These modifications did not survive for very long, or very long in their original forms, because by 1925 the Cumann na nGaedheal government had already begun the process of eliminating what it regarded as unnecessary impediments to Cabinet government imposed by the constitution. External ministers were effectively excluded from the government in 1927, the legislative initiative and referendum was abandoned in 1928, and the qualified dissolution provision was modified when de Valera introduced a new constitution in 1937. In each case, the effect of the change was to strengthen the government by bringing the Irish model into greater conformity with responsible government as it was practiced in Britain and the dominions.

# CHAPTER 10

# Amending the Irish Free State Constitution, 1922–1936

The Irish Free State was born in very troubled times. The civil war lasted until April 1923 and was followed by a long period of unrest. There was no peaceful transition to independence, but there were a number of forces working in favor of the new state. The government had considerable legitimacy after its general election victory in June 1922, and it was supported by an experienced civil service and judiciary. By the time of partition, in 1921, both had been substantially penetrated by Irish nationalists and it proved to be much easier to recruit officials and judges for the south than for the north. "The vast majority of Irish civil servants," McBride writes, "wanted no connection with the Northern government."[1] The Free State also benefited from the first major reorganization of the Irish civil service which Sir Warren Fisher, the permanent head of the British Treasury, had completed in 1920. As a result, O'Halpin writes, "[The] Irish state which came into being in 1922 inherited not an outmoded, ramshackle, demoralized administrative machine but one which had just been thoroughly overhauled along the most modern lines."[2]

The Irish Free State also began its life with a very serviceable constitution, and the Dáil debate on ratification shows that many deputies had a sophisticated understanding of constitutional matters. The constitution was adopted in haste, however, and it contained a number of experimental features. Not surprisingly, there were changes in the fifteen years before it was replaced by the constitution of 1937. These changes addressed two major subjects, the constitutional relationship between the United Kingdom and Ireland, and the institutions of responsible government.

In this chapter I will consider constitutional change between 1922 and 1936. Before I begin, I must point out that the subject involves more than the Irish Free State constitution alone. Because the Irish Free State was a dominion under the Crown, its constitutional law was affected by developments in the Commonwealth. Broadly speaking, therefore, constitutional change could be accomplished in two ways, either externally, by altering the relationship between the United Kingdom and the dominions, or internally, by amending the constitution. We will find that during the period when William Cosgrave led the Executive Council, from 1922 to 1932, changes in the Free State's constitutional relationship with the United Kingdom were accomplished externally and changes in responsible government were accomplished internally. During the period of de Valera's government, from 1932 to 1937, both kinds of change were achieved internally by amending the constitution.

The constitution could be amended quite easily. Article 50 provided that amendment would be by ordinary law for a transition period of eight years. Thereafter it would require both an act of the Oireachtas and the assent of two-thirds of the voters in a referendum. In 1929 the sixteenth amendment to the constitution, itself passed by ordinary legislation under Article 50, doubled the transition period to sixteen years. This meant that for its entire history the 1922 constitution was amendable by the Oireachtas alone.

## The Cosgrave Ministry, 1922–1932

### The Constitutional Relationship with the United Kingdom

The Irish Free State was created as a dominion but we have already seen that the precise constitutional meaning of dominion status was unclear in 1922. The British insisted that imperial policy would be made jointly, in meetings of Commonwealth ministers, but this procedure was always unrealistic. The Imperial War Cabinet, a true policymaking body during World War I, was not reconvened as a peacetime institution and the Imperial Conferences that were convened in the postwar period were primarily concerned with intra-Commonwealth matters, not with Commonwealth foreign and defense policies. Indeed, the conferences were primarily used by the dominions to assert their independence from Britain, with the Irish Free State playing a leading role.

David Harkness describes the Commonwealth policy of the Cosgrave government as follows: "Their objective was full and unrestricted sovereignty: their method became the peaceful transformation of the British Empire so that the definition of Dominion status might be synonymous with fullest freedom."[3] The Irish government had no particular desire to leave the Commonwealth. Indeed, Mansergh argues that the "strategic aim" of Terence O'Higgins, the Vice-President of the Executive Council, was a genuinely dual monarchy, in which all sense of Irish subordination to the United Kingdom would be absent.[4] But the government did want to assert Ireland's independence. In 1928, for example, Ernest Blythe, Vice-President and Minister for Finance, said in the Dáil, "Are we seeking a Republic? We are not. We believe that this country as a member of the British Commonwealth of Nations can enjoy greater freedom and greater security than she could outside the British Commonwealth of Nations, and our policy within it is really to remove anomalies that exist in the relationship between the members of it."[5]

Britain's own indifference to shared Commonwealth policies encouraged the dominions in their quest for unrestricted sovereignty. Britain signed the Treaty of Lausanne in 1923. In 1924 it recognized the U.S.S.R. and negotiated with Germany concerning reparations. It did not seek the prior agreement of the dominions for these policies, and when it signed the Locarno Treaty in 1925 it specifically exempted the dominions from any treaty obligations.[6]

The Irish Free State never accepted what J. P. Walshe, the Secretary of the Department of External Affairs, described as Britain's "pet principle of the oneness of the sovereignty of the Commonwealth."[7] It joined the League of Nations as a fully sovereign state in September 1923,[8] and in July 1924, over strong British objections, registered the Anglo-Irish Treaty with the Treaty Registration Bureau of the League of Nations as an agreement between two states.[9] In October 1924 T. A. Smiddy was appointed "Minister Plenipotentiary" to the United States, the first dominion diplomat accredited to a foreign country, and an American Minister was received in Dublin in 1927.[10] The Free State issued its own passports from April 1924, again over British objections, rather than accept British nationality for this purpose.[11] In 1928 the Paris Treaty for the Renunciation of War, the Kellogg-Briand Pact, was the first treaty signed by the King on the advice of Irish ministers.[12] In 1929, the Free State signed the optional clause of the Permanent Court of International Justice, which obliged it to commit even an intra-Commonwealth dispute to the jurisdiction of the Court, something Britain and the other dominions were not prepared to do.[13] And in 1931 the Free State was the first dominion to use its own seal on a treaty, the Treaty of Commerce and Navigation with Portugal. The Irish Foreign Minister, Patrick McGilligan, rather than a British minister, went to Buckingham Palace to secure the King's signature.[14]

With acts such as these the Irish Free State and other dominions laid the foundation for an assault on the role of the Crown in dominion constitutions. The Canadian Prime Minister, McKenzie King, was particularly anxious for reform after he was denied a dissolution by the Governor-General, Lord Byng, in June 1926, despite having the support of a majority in the House of Commons. Byng granted a dissolution to the man he appointed as King's successor, Arthur Meighan, who did not have the confidence of the house, but King was reelected in the subsequent general election.[15] These events could not have happened in Ireland, where the Governor-General was obliged to appoint a President nominated by Dáil Éireann, but it was worrying that a Governor-General had resurrected powers thought to be obsolete in Canada, the dominion used as a model for the Irish Free State in the constitution.

The issue of reform was taken up at the Imperial Conference of 1926 where, Harkness argues, "Ireland alone had a consistent and practical program."[16] Britain agreed that henceforward the Governors-General would act only on the advice of the dominion governments and would be agents of the Crown, not of the British government. High Commissioners were appointed to represent Commonwealth governments in their relations with each other. In 1930 the Imperial Conference accepted the principle that the Governor-General should be appointed on the advice of the dominion government, a rule practiced by the Irish Free State since 1922.[17] In 1929 the Imperial Conference on the Operation of Dominion Legislation and Merchant Shipping Legislation found that the powers of reservation and disallowance were obsolete in the dominions.[18] Their only remaining purpose was to ensure that the law of the Crown would be uniform throughout the Commonwealth, and in their place the conference suggested that "any alteration in the law touching the Succession to the Throne or the Royal Style and Titles shall hereafter require the assent as well of the Parliaments of all the dominions as of the Parliament of the United Kingdom."[19] These recommendations were approved by the Imperial Conference of 1930[20] and implemented in the comprehensive Statute of Westminster, which the United Kingdom Parliament approved in 1931. The statute stated that the Colonial Laws Validity Act of 1865, which established the primacy of British over dominion law in cases of conflict, would no longer apply and that no new British law would extend to a dominion unless at its own request. Any continuing constitutional dependence on Britain by a dominion would therefore be by its own decision.[21]

By 1931, then, the Imperial Conferences and the Statute of Westminster had established that the dominions were completely independent of Britain, if they chose to be so, but Fianna Fáil professed not to be impressed with what Cosgrave and his dominion colleagues had achieved. "What one British Parliament has enacted another British Parliament can repeal . . . without the consent of the Parliament of this State or of that Dominion," de Valera's deputy, Seán Lemass, argued. He also asked the question that was to divide Fianna Fáil from Fine Gael for the next few years. Was the Free State now free to eliminate the Crown and the Anglo-Irish Treaty from the constitution?[22] Cosgrave thought not, because the treaty was a binding agreement between states, but Fianna Fáil answered affirmatively when it came to power in 1932.

## Amendments to Responsible Government

There were sixteen amendments to the constitution between 1926 and 1931, and eleven of these were recommended, in whole or part, by the Amendments to the Constitution Committee, which the Executive Council created in 1925. The committee reported in 1926 and its most important recommendations had a substantial impact on responsible government in the Free State, and specifically on (1) the external minister, (2) the Seanad, and (3) the legislative initiative and referendum.[23] These reforms illustrated the tension that existed in the Irish Free State between those who favored strong, Cabinet government on the British model, and those who favored a more balanced constitution, with power shared by the Cabinet, Parliament, and the people.

EXTERNAL MINISTERS. The first major change recommended by the committee became the fifth amendment, passed in 1927, which in effect eliminated external ministers from the government. The external minister provision had been opposed by the three members of the constitution drafting committee in 1922 responsible for Draft A, including Darrell Figgis, as well as by Arthur Griffith in the Provisional government. When he first saw the proposal Griffith penciled against it the words, "impossible" and "against all precedent."[24] Griffith died in August but Figgis and other deputies continued the attack in the Dáil when it debated the constitution in September and October 1922. They argued that the concept of external ministers, particularly of ministers selected from outside the Oireachtas, as the Provisional government draft constitution at first provided, challenged the executive's responsibility to the legislature.[25] When the Dáil decided that external ministers might sit in the Oireachtas, opponents replied that it would be strange if a government were not to use its majority in the Dáil to select external ministers from its own supporters there, which would negate the purpose of the provision.[26] "I see no indication in this Dáil or outside of it that there is going to be any cessation of party organization in the near future,"[27] said Deputy Seán Milroy; Deputy J. Burke added, "We all know very well that the Dáil is controlled by a majority, and that majority is controlled by the Ministry."[28]

During their short lifespan, three lines of criticism were opened against external ministers: the difficulty of identifying which ministries were suitable for external ministers, the partisan character of Dáil elections for external ministers, and the lack of coherence in the executive caused by external ministers. Each criticism attacked the assumption that two kinds of ministries could be identified, those which, because of their importance, were particularly appropriate for Executive Council ministers, and those which were best led by external ministers.

Early experience showed that there was no simple rule for identifying which departments should be included in the Executive Council and which should not. For example, when Cosgrave decided that education should have an executive minister, he was charged by Deputy T. J. O'Connell with politicizing education, a department O'Connell insisted should be "kept as far as possible from politics or political concerns." O'Connell argued:

[The Minister of Education] cannot do that if he is a member of the Executive Council, because it would mean if the proposal that he brings forward happens to be defeated, and happens not to meet with the wishes of the Dáil, it is immediately a question of policy, and as the Minister is a member of the Executive Council, the Council stands or falls, the Government stands or falls, on this educational proposal.[29]

But Cosgrave did not accept the idea that education should be nonpolitical. It was so vital to the reconstruction of the nation and the "Gaelicisation . . . of our whole culture," he insisted, that the Executive Council should be collectively responsible for education policy.[30]

Agriculture was another controversial ministry. Cosgrave included the Minister for Industry and Commerce in the Executive Council but consigned Agriculture to an external minister, much to the annoyance of Deputy Wilson, of the Farmers' party, who pointed out that five-sixths of the working population were engaged in agriculture or related industries. Agriculture should therefore be in and Industry and Commerce should be out.[31]

In his reply to these criticisms Cosgrave unwittingly betrayed the inherent impracticality of the two-tier Cabinet. There could be no automatic agreement on which departments should or should not be represented in the Executive Council, Cosgrave argued, because the decision might hinge on the status of the minister, not the work of the department. "With the exception possibly of two or three Ministries," he said, "the selection of the Executive Council is not a matter of particular Ministries, but the inclusion of certain persons."[32] Whichever department these "certain persons" were best suited to administer would be included in the Executive Council. This destroyed the basis of the external minister concept, that certain ministries should be external, and not covered by collective responsibility, because their functions were essentially nonpolitical.

The selection process revealed the second problem for external ministers. The Dáil was supposed to select the best qualified candidates, whether from inside or outside the Dáil, and quite independent of party considerations. Cumann na nGaedheal never gave the experiment a chance. With 63 seats and a divided opposition, the party had a large majority in the 153-seat Dáil after the 1923 general election because the antitreaty republicans refused to take the 44 seats they had won.[33] With this advantage, it would not have harmed Cosgrave's government to comply with the spirit of the constitution by appointing specialist, nonpartisan, external ministers. Instead, the government manipulated the selection process to ensure that party loyalists would be selected from the Dáil.

When the Dáil nominating committee reported its nominees for external ministers in October 1923, after the August general election, opposition members of the committee disclaimed any responsibility for the choices because the government majority had preselected its candidates at party meetings. Thomas Johnson, the Labour leader complained, "The decisions were made at Party meetings beforehand and the names were tabled. . . . A decision had been made and the committee was a farce."[34] Another member of the committee, Deputy William Redmond, the son of John Redmond, elected as an Independent, added, "Of course, the Government, having a majority in this House, naturally had a majority upon the Committee, and, therefore, I want it to be realized that these gentlemen, strictly speaking, are Government nominees."[35] President Cosgrave denied the charge, alleging that the opposition had failed to propose alternative candidates to the committee,[36] but the truth is that Cumann na nGaedheal had prepared a slate of candidates and had made no attempt to search, in a collegial way, for talented, nonpartisan external ministers. Should we be surprised? Deputy O'Mahony thought not: "Surely all this is a pretence of piety. I wonder what would the Labour members do if they were a majority? I wonder what would the Farmers do if they were in a majority? I wonder what would the Independents do if they were in a majority? They would do exactly what they accuse the Government members of having done last week."[37]

The third problem with external ministers was the perceived incoherence of government. For example, all the ministries spent public money but only the members of the Executive Council were collectively responsible for finance, and it was sometimes difficult to make the external ministers respect the Executive Council's decisions. In its submission to the Amendments to the Constitution Committee, the Department of Finance said, "It is thought that proper financial control of all matters, including control of staff, cannot be maintained under a system of extern Ministers individually responsible to Dáil Éireann."[38] In a 1923 debate President Cosgrave expressed his displeasure at the performance on financial matters of the external Minister of Fisheries, Finian Lynch, and in 1927 the external Minister for Posts and Telegraphs, J. J. Walsh, who was also Chairman of Cumann na nGaedheal, publicly disagreed with the government on trade policy, accusing it of allowing "free trade civil servants" to sabotage policy.[39]

The government accepted the recommendation of the Amendments to the Constitution Committee that the external minister provision of the constitution should be amended. In November 1926 Kevin O'Higgins, now Minister for Justice, presented a bill that became the fifth amendment to the constitution to the Dáil. It permitted all twelve ministers to be members of the Executive Council, and in effect left the decision on whether to have any external ministers to the President. If he chose to nominate twelve ministers to the Executive Council there would be no room for external ministers.[40]

O'Higgins made four points when he presented the amendment to the Dáil.[41] First, with a maximum membership of only seven, the Executive Council was too small to accommodate all who should be members. Second, while external ministers were required to participate in decisions of importance to the whole government, particularly financial decisions, they did not share in the collective responsibility of the Executive Council. Third, lacking collective responsibility, they had no incentive to cooperate with the Executive Council. Fourth, the two-tier ministry denied the President the flexibility he needed in the assignment of portfolios. The government's amending bill was approved by the Oireachtas with very little opposition in April 1927. Thereafter, while the possibility of external ministers existed in law until the new constitution of 1937, no new ones were appointed. The Executive Council was expanded to twelve members in 1927.

The external minister concept was an imaginative attempt to curb the excesses of party government, but it was misguided because it denied the imperatives inherent in responsible government. Simply stated, responsible government is party government and it was naive of those who drafted the constitution to suppose that the majority party would not use its power to control the selection of external ministers. Leo Kohn was quite correct when he wrote, in 1932, that the failure of the external minister experiment illustrated "the inevitability of the structural design of the British system of parliamentary government when once its fundamental framework has been accepted."[42]

THE SEANAD.    A second major reform of responsible government in the Cosgrave years concerned the Seanad. Cumann na nGaedheal allowed the upper house to perform only the minimum functions required by law. When senators sought a constitutional amendment in 1926 to allow them to sit in the Executive Council, a change recommended by the Amendments to the Constitution Committee,[43] Kevin O'Higgins replied that any senator with ministerial aspirations should run for election to the Dáil.[44] It was not until the fifteenth amendment to the constitution was passed in 1929 that a member of the Seanad was permitted to sit in the Executive Council, and only one was appointed, in 1932.

Fianna Fáil would have abolished the Seanad, and at the very least wanted it to be cowed.[45] In 1928 Seán Lemass said, "We are in favor . . . of the abolition of the Senate, but if there is to be a Second House, let it be a House under our thumb. Let it be a group of individuals who dare not let a squeak out of them except when we lift our fingers to give them breath to do it."[46] He described the Seanad as a body created not to improve the machinery of government "but to give political power to a certain class that could not get that power if they had to go before the people at a free election."[47]

The constitution provided that the first Seanad would be a transitional body. Half of its members were nominated by the President and half were elected by the Dáil, but these members were to be phased out at three-year intervals. The first Seanad triennial election was held in 1925, and proved a great disappointment. The Irish Free State as a whole was the constituency and the electorate was faced with a ballot containing seventy-six candidates for nineteen seats. Thirty-eight were Dáil nominees, nineteen were Seanad nominees, and nineteen were retiring senators who had nominated themselves. Only 25.5 percent of registered voters participated in the vote and it is clear that they were very confused. They found it impossible to rank seventy-six names in order of preference, and few people indicated more than a few. It took sixty-seven counts over a fourteen-day period to decide the winners.[48]

Rather than break the country into manageable constituencies for future Seanad elections, the Amendments to the Constitution Committee recommended that popular elections for the second chamber be abandoned altogether. It argued that because two elected chambers can each claim popular legitimacy, serious difficulties might result for a government responsible to only one. It therefore recommended, in what became the sixth amendment in 1928, that senators should be elected by the Dáil and the Seanad voting together, rather than by the electorate as a whole. The legislators would use proportional representation and select from a joint list of candidates produced by the two houses.[49]

The new nomination and election systems meant that the parties in the Oireachtas were able to control the Seanad selection process very directly and the chamber lost whatever legitimacy it might have gained from popular elections. Furthermore, given the party composition of the two chambers, candidates were able to calculate their chances of success with some accuracy, and this meant that few people were willing to have their names placed in nomination for an election they knew they would lose. For example, only twenty-eight candidates were nominated for twenty-three vacancies in 1931.[50]

LEGISLATIVE INITIATIVE AND REFERENDUM. A third constitutional amendment of importance to responsible government was the elimination of the legislative initiative and referendum provisions in Articles 47 and 48 of the constitution. Article 47 provided that a bill approved by the Oireachtas that was neither a money bill nor a bill declared by both houses "to be necessary for the immediate preservation of the public health and safety," would be "submitted by Referendum to the decision of the people" at the request of three-fifths of the Seanad or not less than 5 percent of registered voters. Article 48 allowed the Oireachtas to provide a procedure for the initiation of a bill by the people in a petition signed by not less than fifty thousand registered voters.

The arguments used to support these provisions in 1922 were philosophical. It was argued, for example, that they would enhance popular sovereignty. By 1926, however, before they had ever been used, they were being attacked on very practical grounds.[51] The Amendments to the Constitution Committee concluded, for example, "It has been found by experience that if a substantial number of voters require any matter brought before the Dáil, this can always be done. The right of petition given in [Article 48] is consequently unnecessary."[52] The committee also argued that legislative referenda would be excessively expensive to run and that it would be difficult to frame legislation in the simple "yes/no" terms required by a ballot.[53] The Cosgrave government had already been advised to remove these provisions by 1926, therefore, and had itself decided in 1927 that this should be done before the issue was forced the following year.[54]

Article 48 only permitted the Oireachtas to legislate to create the legislative initiative; it did not require it. By 1927 the Oireachtas had still not acted. The article also provided that a petition of seventy-five thousand registered voters could force it to act. Late in 1927 it became clear that Fianna Fáil had the necessary support for such a petition. At the Fianna Fáil party conference of November 1927 de Valera announced his intention to use the initiative to remove the oath of allegiance from the constitution, in violation of the Anglo-Irish Treaty and Article 2 of the Constitution Act. On 23 May 1928 Fianna Fáil presented a petition with ninety-six thousand signatures supporting the removal of the oath. The government responded on 7 June by introducing the tenth amendment, to abolish Articles 47 and 48. By 12 July, after a fierce debate, the bill had passed through both houses, with the rider that it was necessary for the preservation of public peace. This meant that the petition and referendum in Article 47, which in normal circumstances would have permitted 5 percent of the electorate to challenge a bill approved by the Oireachtas, could not be used to prevent the Oireachtas from abolishing Article 47 itself.[55]

Cumann na nGaedheal used its party advantage very crudely on this occasion to defeat Fianna Fáil, but it had actually decided that the initiative and referendum provisions should be abolished before Fianna Fáil presented its petition in 1928. The fact of the matter is that the government was uncomfortable with the prospect of loss of control represented by the initiative and referendum, and when it moved to delete them from the constitution it ignored the recommendation of the Amendments to the Constitution Committee that safeguards should be placed in the constitution to replace the Seanad's right, in Article 47, to call for a referendum on an act passed over its opposition. The government would only agree to the thirteenth amendment, which created a new Article 38A. This extended the Seanad's power to delay a non-money bill from nine months to twenty.[56] If, after eighteen months, the Seanad failed to pass a bill sent to it by the Dáil, the Dáil could again send it to the Seanad, and it would become law without the Seanad's approval after a further sixty days.

By 1932, when it lost office, the Cosgrave government had substantially revised the Free State constitution by eliminating most of the devices introduced in 1922 to curb party government: external ministers, a Seanad of men above party, and the initiative and referendum. One commentator, Andrew Malone, writing in 1929, argued that these changes would play into de Valera's hands were he to be elected to office. He wrote, "Many parliamentary precedents have been created by Mr. Cosgrave in the heat of party battle which will serve Mr. de Valera well in any future revolutionary adventure which he may decide to undertake." He concluded that this would not have happened "had the spirit and the letter of the constitution been adhered to rigidly."[57] But Malone missed an important point. The amendments introduced by

Cosgrave were not designed to frustrate Fianna Fáil "in the heat of party battle." They were all meant to bring the Irish constitution into compliance with what Cosgrave now believed, from his experience in government, responsible government should be. In other words, they were designed to make it easier for the Executive Council to govern.

## The De Valera Ministry, 1932–1937

### The Constitutional Relationship with Britain

De Valera and his colleagues abstained from participating in Dáil Éireann until August 1927 because of their objections to the oath of allegiance, but they contested elections as plebiscites on the legitimacy of the state. In 1927 the Oireachtas passed the Election Amendment Act, in the aftermath of the assassination of Kevin O'Higgins, which required all candidates for the Dáil to declare that if elected they would swear the oath. Fianna Fáil was therefore faced with a choice. It could either enter the Dáil or play no further part in elections. De Valera made the decision to enter the Dáil. Fortunately, the oath was inscribed in a book and deputies had simply to sign their names, a less traumatic experience for de Valera than raising his hand and repeating the oath in public. The lack of ceremony also helped him to disparage the process. On 10 August 1927 he said, "The Fianna Fáil deputies would certainly not wish to have the feeling that they are allowing themselves to be debarred by nothing more than an empty formula from exercising their functions as public representatives."[58] What had been an issue worth fighting a war for in 1922 was now, it appeared, "nothing more than an empty formula."

De Valera entered the Dáil but still did not accept the constitution as wholly legitimate. He said, "In so far as there is any part of it which can be regarded as having been freely accepted by the Irish people or their representatives, we accept it. But that part of the Constitution which has been imposed upon this country has always been opposed by us."[59] Once in the Dáil he refused to serve as Chairman of the Public Accounts Committee, a post traditionally occupied by a leading member of the major opposition party in the British Parliament, because he wanted no part in operating the parliamentary system.[60] Thomas Johnson, until 1927 the leader of the Labour party, accepted the chairmanship, and Denis Gwynn writes that he "regarded the position of

Leader of the Opposition as involving responsibilities scarcely less than those of the Prime Minister."[61]

Cosgrave's position as President of the Executive Council was always tenuous after Fianna Fáil entered the Dáil in 1927. In the general election of August 1927 Fianna Fáil, with fifty-seven seats, only trailed Cumann na nGaedheal by five seats and the government survived a vote of confidence only with the casting vote of the Chairman.[62] But it was defeated in the general election of 16 February 1932 and Eamon de Valera became President of the Executive Council with the support of the Labour party. Cosgrave respected the rules of the constitution and handed power over to a man who had led a civil war against the state in 1922.[63] Another general election followed, in January 1933. This time Fianna Fáil won an overall majority of one, but with one of its members in the Chair it maintained a majority only with the support of the Labour party.

The Free State's relationship with Britain descended into an economic war in the summer of 1932. De Valera's government decided not to send Britain the "land annuities," revenues collected in Ireland from farmers as payments for loans made under the terms of Irish Land Acts enacted before independence. The payments had been agreed to by the Cosgrave government in the Ultimate Financial Settlement of 1926 but de Valera would not accept that obligation, which had not been submitted to Dáil Éireann. Britain's response was to raise customs duties on Irish goods, and the economic war was on. It lasted until 1938.[64]

During this period de Valera was ready to play the constitutional game for what he might gain. If it failed him, he appeared ready to act unconstitutionally. Fortunately, Cosgrave had already made a major breakthrough in the Free State's constitutional relationship with Britain, and de Valera was able to concede that "there have been advances made that I did not believe would be made at the time."[65] He was prepared, therefore, to continue to advance incrementally and constitutionally toward an Irish republic. In April 1933 he stated his new position:

Let it be made clear that we yield no willing assent to any symbol that is out of keeping with Ireland's right as a sovereign nation. Let us remove these forms one by one, so that this State that we control may be a Republic in fact; and that, when the time comes, the proclaiming of the Republic may involve no more than a ceremony, the formal confirmation of a status already attained.[66]

He began by attacking the oath of allegiance and the role of the Anglo-Irish Treaty in the constitution.

THE OATH OF ALLEGIANCE AND THE ANGLO-IRISH TREATY.    The oath was central to the split in Sinn Féin in 1921, and in 1932 the Free State High Commissioner in London described it as "an intolerable burden, a relic of medievalism, a test imposed from the outside under the threat of war."[67] De Valera himself called it "an intolerable burden to the people of this State."[68] Cosgrave fully understood the incendiary potential of the oath and unsuccessfully tried to negotiate new wording with the British.[69] Their intransigence played into Fianna Fáil's hands, and after his election de Valera moved quickly, with Labour's support, to eliminate both the oath and the Anglo-Irish Treaty from the constitution.

De Valera introduced the Constitution (Removal of Oath) Bill, effectively the eighteenth amendment, on 20 April 1932. Section 1 of the bill deleted the oath of allegiance from Article 17 of the constitution. Section 2 deleted Section 2 of the Constitution Act, which gave the Anglo-Irish Treaty the force of law in the Free State and prohibited constitutional amendments that were repugnant to the treaty. Section 3 deleted the first part of Article 50 of the constitution which permitted constitutional amendments only if they were "within the terms of" the treaty.[70] In defense of the amendments, de Valera argued that the Statute of Westminster in 1931 had confirmed Ireland's right to amend any part of its constitution.[71] Britain disputed this view. It insisted that Article 50 was entrenched and unaffected by the statute. Cosgrave also challenged de Valera's interpretation. He believed that the treaty was an international obligation. It followed that the Statute of Westminster, which permitted a dominion to override existing British law in its territory, was irrelevant because a treaty was at issue, not a British law. Professor A. B. Keith, the leading Commonwealth lawyer of his time and an adviser to British governments, supported this view.[72]

The amendment bill passed the Dáil but was amended by the Seanad which was determined to preserve the treaty in the constitution until such time as Britain should consent to its deletion.[73] The Dáil refused to accept the amendments and sent the bill back in March 1933. This time the Seanad refused to consider the bill "until it has been made the subject of negotiation between the Executive Council and the British Government with a view to an amicable settlement."[74] The Dáil over-rode these objections and the bill received the royal assent on 3 May 1933. The Free State then adopted a new oath, the one de Valera had offered in 1922, which required members of the Oireachtas to pledge their allegiance to the Irish Free State, to the British Commonwealth, and to the Crown as a symbol of the Commonwealth so long as the Free State should remain a member.[75] The issue was settled as far as Britain was concerned by the Judicial Committee of the Privy Council's finding in 1935 "that the Statute of Westminster gave to the Irish Free State a power under which they could abrogate the Treaty."[76]

THE GOVERNOR-GENERAL.    Having begun by deleting the oath and the Anglo-Irish Treaty from the constitution, de Valera next moved against the Governor-General. Fianna Fáil was not inclined to permit the Governor-General so much as the modest role in public affairs he had assumed in the Cosgrave years, and the British government even worried that de Valera would appoint "some rebel or murderer" to the office. The British Attorney General, Sir Thomas Inskip, indicated that while only the Irish Free State might advise the King on the appoint-ment, he was not obliged to accept it.[77]

The Governor-General when de Valera came to power was James MacNeill. As a member of the 1922 constitution committee he had written the first memorandum on the powers of a Governor-General, and he was the Free State's first High Commissioner to London.[78] He was nominated by Cosgrave in 1928 to succeed Timothy Healy, but de Valera treated him derisively. MacNeill was instructed not to invite ministers to his functions, and three of them snubbed him by leaving a ball at the French legation when MacNeill arrived. De Valera admitted that the incident was "unfortunate and regrettable" and recommended that further embarrassment could be avoided if MacNeill would advise the government of his engagements in advance. MacNeill was also in-structed not to host a reception at the Vice-Regal Lodge for the Cardinal Legate and other participants at the Eucharistic Congress, which was held in Ireland in July 1932. MacNeill complained to de Valera in writing, demanding an apology for what he termed "ill-con-ditioned bad manners," but received no satisfaction. He then ignored instructions from de Valera not to publicize the dispute and handed the correspondence to the press.[79]

MacNeill clearly had to go, but he refused to resign. In September, therefore, de Valera asked the King to recall him. The King agreed but no replacement was announced until 26 November.[80] In the interim de Valera invited Hugh Kennedy to serve as both Chief Justice and Governor-General, but Kennedy declined to serve out the remainder of Mac-Neill's five-year term because he wanted to maintain the separation of powers between the executive and the judiciary. However, he advised a course that had been suggested to him, he said, by an Englishman he did not name "who formerly held position of great importance and influence." His proposal was to treat the governor-generalship as a purely formal office, with no social or ceremonial responsibilities. It could be carried on by an ordinary Irishman living somewhere in the city.[81] De Valera accepted the advice, but only after the British government rejected his proposal to combine the presidency and the governor-generalship for a temporary period. Britain argued that this would violate Articles 2 and 3 of the Anglo-Irish Treaty, which required the Governor-General to be appointed as in Canada.[82]

De Valera recommended the appointment of a relative nonentity to the office, a Maynooth grocer named Domhnall ó Buachalla (Donal Buckley), who had been a member of the first Dáil. He assumed office on 25 November 1932 and lived in the anonymity of a Dublin suburban house, traveling into the city to sign papers. He enjoyed some perquisites of office, including a handsome salary, a chauffeur, private secretary, cook, maid, gardener, and bodyguard. He did everything required of him by the constitution, strictly on the advice of the Executive Council, and had no official social or ceremonial life.[83]

The Crown remained in the constitution, however, and de Valera conceded that it was not yet possible to abolish the office of Governor-General. In the Dáil on 14 July 1933 he stated, "If the office of Governor-General is retained today, it is because there is a fear in certain people's minds that, if it were abolished, you would have a renewal of some war."[84] In the Dáil the following year he added, "We would get rid of [the Governor-General] tomorrow if there were not certain obligations involved in the Treaty, in the first instance, and in the Constitution, in the second instance. It is our hope to end them."[85] It was odd to hear de Valera concede that the Free State had obligations under the treaty. However, in December 1936 the office of Governor-General disappeared, it appears inadvertently, when the Crown was removed from the constitution.

THE CROWN. By 1936 de Valera had eliminated most of the powers of the Crown from the constitution. In November 1933 the twentieth amendment to the constitution transferred to the Executive Council the Governor-General's formal responsibility for recommending financial measures to the Oireachtas under Article 37, and the twenty-first amendment eliminated the Governor-General's power to withhold his assent to Irish bills or reserve them to London for the royal assent under Article 41.[86] His sole remaining legislative responsibility was to sign bills presented to him by the Executive Council.

In December 1936 the Irish government used the confusion caused by the abdication of King Edward VIII to eliminate all remaining references to the Crown.[87] The British government advised that a new succession act was necessary in each dominion to accommodate the unprecedented circumstances of George VI's accession to the throne. The Statute of Westminster now required each dominion to pass such a law, and de Valera used the opportunity to rush two bills through the Dáil. Although they had nothing specifically to do with the succession, they had the effect of defining the responsibilities of the new King.

King Edward VIII abdicated on 10 December 1936. That day, deputies, who were in recess, received telegrams summoning them to a session of the Dáil at 3:00 P.M. the following day. Those who were at home to receive the morning's post on 11 December received copies of the bills that the government proposed to introduce that afternoon, but those who left home early did not see the bills until they arrived for the debate. By the following day, 12 December, the bills had been rammed through the Dáil by use of a guillotine procedure that limited debate to just a few hours. They became law immediately because, as we shall see below, the Seanad had been abolished earlier in the year.[88]

The first of the two bills, the Constitution (Amendment No. 27) Act, deleted all references to the King and the Governor-General from the constitution. Bills now became law on the signature of the Chairman of the Dáil, who was also called upon to summon and dissolve the Oireachtas on the advice of the Executive Council. One of the deleted references was Article 60, which required the Governor-General to be appointed "in like manner as the Governor-General of Canada." On 22 December 1936 Michael McDunphy, the Assistant Secretary in the Department of the President, wrote a memorandum regarding the circumstances surrounding the twenty-seventh amendment in which he said:

It was believed at the time of its introduction that its effect, as far as the Governor-General was concerned, would be to remove him from the specific functions mentioned. After its passage into law, however, the President was advised by the Department of External Affairs that the amendment to that Act, by deleting Article 60 of the Constitution, had abolished the Governor-General.[89]

The Governor-General had been abolished by accident! The Executive Power (Consequential Provisions) Act of May 1937 tidied up the loose ends of the twenty-seventh amendment by assigning what remained of the Governor-General's powers to the Executive Council.[90]

The second of the two bills passed on 12 December 1936 was the Executive Authority (External Relations) Act. One of the provisions of the twenty-seventh amendment was an extraordinarily clumsy amendment to Article 51 of the constitution that permitted the Free State to use "any organ used as a constitutional organ for the like purpose" by the other dominions "for the purposes of the appointment of diplomatic and consular agents and the conclusion of international agreements." The External Relations Act made this provision effective. It stated that so long as the Free State was associated with the Commonwealth, the King, who was the "organ used as a constitutional organ for the like purpose" by the other dominions, would appoint diplomatic and consular agents and sign international agreements on behalf of the Free State, on the advice of the Executive Council.[91]

When proposing to delete the Crown from the constitution in 1936, de Valera argued, "It is very much better that our people should see clearly, with no fog and no mist of constitutional theory about it, what the situation is."[92] But the amendment to Article 51 and the External Relations Act actually created an extraordinary situation. They permitted the Sovereign, King George VI, who was no longer mentioned in the constitution, to act for the Irish Free State in foreign affairs. As John Costello, the Cumann na nGaedheal Attorney General from 1926 to 1932, pointed out in the Dáil, "[For] one purpose we have no head of this State and for another purpose we have a foreign King as the head of our State."[93]

The two acts appeared to have been prepared very quickly by the government in response to the abdication, but this was not really the case. The terms of the External Relations Act had already been suggested by John J. Hearne, the legal adviser to the Department of External Affairs, in September 1936, during the drafting of the 1937 constitution. In hopes of improving the prospects of drawing Northern Ireland into a united Ireland, de Valera wanted to delete the Crown from the new constitution without severing the connection to the British Commonwealth. Hearne proposed that a Foreign Relations Bill might be passed that would allow the King to act for the Free State in foreign relations, and this was the substance of the External Relations Act passed some months later.[94] The abdication crisis allowed the government to accomplish in 1936 what it had already decided to do in a new constitution. When the 1937 constitution was adopted, it restated, in Article 29.4.2°, the permissive authority to use the King as an agent that had been added to Article 51 of the 1922 constitution in December 1936, and the External Relations Act continued in effect as before. (The degree sign ° indicates a subparagraph.) It remained so until its repeal in 1948.

Precisely what the External Relations Act meant for the Irish Free State's position in the Commonwealth was unclear. On the day the bill was introduced, William Cosgrave asked de Valera if it was his intention to sever the connection with the Crown, and if the Free State government had consulted other members of the Commonwealth about the change. De Valera admitted that he had not consulted Britain or the other dominions, and he denied that the country was leaving the Commonwealth. After all, Article 1, which stated that the Irish Free State was a member of the Commonwealth, remained in the constitution.[95] The question of whether Ireland had become a republic in 1936 was not resolved because de Valera thought it inappropriate to raise the issue specifically at a time when he still hoped for reconciliation with Northern Ireland. In 1948 Irish ministers said that the Free State had left the Commonwealth in 1936, but that is not what the constitution said.[96]

LEGAL APPEALS TO THE PRIVY COUNCIL. None of de Valera's amendments to the constitution concerning the oath, the Governor-General, and the Crown discussed above changed the reality of Irish government in any way. They simply recognized in Irish Free State constitutional law certain conventions of the constitution concerning the executive that had long been practiced in Britain and the dominions, and certain changes in the status of the dominions that had been agreed to by Britain by 1931. The one change that did not fit this pattern was the abolition of legal appeals to the Privy Council in 1933. This involved a substantial change in constitutional practice.

The right of legal appeal from the Irish Free State to the Judicial Committee of the Privy Council was not required by the Anglo-Irish Treaty and was not included in the first draft constitution presented by the Provisional government in May 1922. However, the British government cited two reasons for insisting that this provision be included in the constitution. First, as a monarchy, the Free State had to accept the Common Law principle that justice is a prerogative of the King. Second, the Privy Council was an appropriate forum for the adjudication of intra-Commonwealth disputes.

One can understand why the Irish were sensitive about this issue. Not only was the Privy Council a manifestation of the Crown but in 1922 three of its members were known opponents of Irish nationalism. Lords Sumner, Carson, and Cave had each spoken against the Anglo-Irish Treaty in the House of Lords. Carson had also led the Ulster rebels in 1912, and Cave had presided at the trial of Sir Roger Casement in 1916.[97] Nonetheless, the Provisional government capitulated and the right of appeal to the Privy Council was included as Article 66 of the Free State constitution. Kevin O'Higgins told the Dáil that, "inasmuch as we have accepted the King, then we have to accept the special prerogative of that King, and grant, in very special cases, the right of appeal." He also said that the Provisional government had been assured that appeals would only be allowed "in very special cases, raising matters other than purely Irish interests, raising international issues of first importance."[98] This interpretation was confirmed by Lord Haldane, a member of the Judicial Committee of the Privy Council, in a discussion with Hugh Kennedy, the legal adviser to the Free State government, in July 1923. Haldane explained that the Judicial Committee was not an English court but a council to the King that could sit anywhere and might include dominion judges. He pointed out that the constitutional evolution of the dominions had led to a very substantial decline in cases heard by the Judicial Committee. He anticipated that the Sovereign, meaning the Judicial Committee through its advice to the Sovereign, would apply a "general principle of restriction" on Irish appeals, and that "we shall look somewhat strictly at all Applications for Leaves to Appeal" from Ireland. So satisfied was Kennedy with this assurance that he wrote to President Cosgrave, "The result of the proceedings at the Privy Council is to establish our position in this matter rigidly, and I need hardly say that this is a matter where, if they had been so dishonestly minded, the British side could have eaten into our rights very substantially."[99] The Free State government was also reassured by the fact that the first three Applications for Leaves to Appeal from Ireland were dismissed by the Crown.[100]

In 1925, however, the Free State government was astonished when the Privy Council allowed an appeal in an Irish civil case that had no international implications, as it did again in 1930.[101] In 1926 and 1930 the Free State failed to win the agreement of Imperial Conferences for the proposition that each dominion should decide for itself the extent of the Privy Council's jurisdiction in its domestic affairs.[102] The Cosgrave government therefore decided to act unilaterally, using the freedom it believed it had acquired from the Statute of Westminster in 1931. It could delete this provision from the constitution, it believed, because legal appeals to the Privy Council were not mentioned in, and therefore not protected by, the Anglo-Irish Treaty. The Cosgrave government was in the process of preparing a constitutional amendment bill when it fell in 1932, and it was de Valera who completed the task with the twenty-second amendment to the constitution. This abolished the right of appeal to the Privy Council in 1933. The amendment was tested in 1935 when the Privy Council accepted yet another case on appeal from Ireland, this one concerning fishing rights on the River Ernle in County Donegal.[103] In deciding the case, the Judicial Committee ruled, "The simplest way of stating the situation is to say that the Statute of Westminster gave to the Irish Free State a power under which they could abrogate the Treaty, and that, as a matter of law, they have availed themselves of that power."[104]

THE BRITISH REACTION.    Even before the adoption of the new Irish constitution in 1937, the Free State had managed to eliminate the British connection from the constitutional law of the Irish Free State. All that remained was a link with the King in his capacity as head of the Commonwealth. Britain was thoroughly dismayed by this development. It had thought the Irish problem solved by the Anglo-Irish Treaty, which Lionel Curtis, the Second Secretary to the British delegation, described as "one of the greatest achievements in the history of the Empire."[105] So alarmed was the British Cabinet by what was happening in 1932 that it established an Irish Situation Committee, chaired by the Prime Minister, which met, albeit infrequently, from March 1932 until 1938.[106] In 1933 the Dominions Secretary, J. H. Thomas, argued that it was not possible for the Free State to be a member of the Commonwealth for some purposes, but not for others, and he condemned the amendments to the Irish constitution that eliminated provisions of the Anglo-Irish Treaty.[107] However, his case was destroyed in 1935 by the Judicial Committee of the Privy Council's finding that the Statute of Westminster permitted the Free State to eliminate the treaty from the constitution.

Lloyd George had promised the House of Commons in December 1921 that if the Free State were to break the treaty, Britain would act,[108] but how could it do so, and when? In the 1930s the British government could not quite decide what the constitutional implications of the Free State's actions were, and hence could think of little to do. The Attorney General, Sir Thomas Inskip, believed that the abolition of the oath of allegiance in 1933 violated the treaty, but he did not think it was, in itself, either a repudiation of allegiance or an act of secession.[109] This appeared to mean that the Irish could gradually whittle away the link with the Crown because no one knew where the breaking point lay. By not withdrawing from the Commonwealth or declaring the Free State a republic, de Valera refused to settle the issue finally himself.

The Irish Free State was actually demonstrating the structural weaknesses of the post–World War I Commonwealth, and by 1936, Deirdre McMahon concludes, "the chickens of 1921 were coming home to roost with a vengeance."[110] The British could only dither, in part, of course, because from 1931 to 1940 the National governments of Ramsey MacDonald, Stanley Baldwin, and Neville Chamberlain received most of their support in the House of Commons from Conservatives who would not accept de Valera's sensible compromise of external association because it did not provide a traditional role for the Crown in Ireland. Conservatives such as Winston Churchill also feared the effects that constitutional concessions to Ireland would have elsewhere in the empire, in India particularly.[111] But the Dominions Secretary from 1935 to 1938, Malcolm MacDonald, reminded his colleagues that the constitutional arrangements of the British Empire were constantly evolving.[112] The Cabinet decided to accept his advice that the Irish Free State should not be treated as having withdrawn from the Commonwealth, and its precise status should be left unclear.[113] This, quite simply, was appeasement.

## Reform of Responsible Government

The elimination of the Crown from the constitution in 1936 affected the definition of the executive in Ireland, but not the operation of responsible government. Because it was already clear in the constitution that the Governor-General could act only on the advice of the Executive Council, it mattered little that his office disappeared. However, one Fianna Fáil reform, the abolition of the Seanad, did affect responsible government in a fundamental way.

The Free State began its life with the very strong sense that the Executive Council was responsible to the Dáil and the Dáil was responsible to the people. In this formulation there was never a comfortable role for the Seanad. Cosgrave respected its work but never encouraged it to do more than the minimum required by the constitution, and in 1928 he moved to bring the chamber more directly under the control of the Dáil by having it elected by the Dáil and Seanad voting together. The Seanad became progressively more partisan as Independents were eliminated. Table 10.1 details the shrinkage of Independents from 1928 to 1934. In time, Fianna Fáil would have controlled the Seanad, and its supporters used this fact to argue that their objection to the chamber was theoretical, not partisan. When supporting the bill for its abolition in 1934, Seán Lemass argued that the issue was popular sovereignty, not Fianna Fáil's desire for power. "It is about time," he said, "that the Irish people became masters in this country. This is a Bill to make them masters."[114]

In its lifetime the Seanad did a great deal of useful work, notwithstanding the poor attendance records of many senators.[115] Its Clerk,

TABLE 10.1
State of the Parties after Seanad Elections

|  | 1928 | 1931 | 1934 |
|---|---|---|---|
| Cumann na nGaedheal/Fine Gael | 19 | 21 | 22 |
| Fianna Fáil | 7 | 13 | 19 |
| Independent Group of Ex-Unionists | 12 | 10 | 7 |
| Independents | 15 | 9 | 4 |
| Labour | 6 | 6 | 7 |
| Chairman | 1 | 1 | 1 |
| Totals | 60 | 60 | 60 |

Donal O'Sullivan, records that in its thirteen and a half years, it received 489 nonmoney bills from the Dáil and amended 182. In all it produced 1,831 amendments, the vast majority of which were accepted by the Dáil. Those that the Dáil refused to accept were generally withdrawn by the Seanad, so it could not be charged with obstruction. Even in the triennial period from 6 December 1931 to 5 December 1934, essentially the first three years of de Valera's administration, the Dáil accepted all but 47 of the more than 500 amendments offered by the Seanad.[116] In most matters, including legislation to implement the economic war, which a majority of the Seanad opposed, the government was allowed to have the measures it wanted,[117] and in its lifetime the Seanad only forced the government to the full suspensory period eleven times.[118]

Unfortunately, by blocking even a very small proportion of Fianna Fáil bills, the Seanad led de Valera to demand its abolition. In 1932 it voted against the amendment to remove the oath and the treaty from the constitution. In 1933 it challenged two bills that changed the local government franchise to the advantage of Fianna Fáil. And in 1933 it challenged the Constitution (Amendment No. 19) Bill, which proposed to reduce the Seanad's suspensory period from twenty to five months.[119]

Fianna Fáil senators had never done anything to make the Seanad an effective chamber. They took almost no part in revising legislation, other than to introduce government-sponsored amendments,[120] and one of their number admitted, "When I came in here, I came in on the definite understanding that when the time arose I was here to do my bit to wreck this House."[121] His opportunity came on 21 March 1934 when the Seanad rejected the Wearing of Uniform (Restriction) Bill, a measure, targeted at the conservative Blue Shirts movement, which de Valera insisted was necessary for law and order. On 22 March he introduced the Constitution (Amendment No. 24) Bill, to abolish the Seanad.[122] "The Second Chamber," he said, "as at present constituted, appears to me to be an absolute menace to this country."[123]

In the debate de Valera said he could find no sound argument in history for second chambers, other than in federal states. Elsewhere they were remnants of ascendancy classes, designed to protect vested interests and privilege. The Irish Free State Seanad, he argued, was a partisan chamber that favored Fianna Fáil's opponents and thwarted the wishes of the popularly elected chamber.[124] Indeed, de Valera could see no clear role at all for a second chamber in responsible government. If it had the same party composition as the Dáil, it was redundant, but if it had a different composition it was mischievous.[125]

Much of what de Valera said was true. The Seanad was controlled by his opponents, and in responsible government it is difficult to construct a second chamber which has some power but not so much as to be able to thwart a government responsible to the first chamber. Furthermore, it is difficult to select a second chamber that is representative in some sense without thereby allowing it the legitimacy to challenge the authority of the first chamber. But what most offended de Valera's opponents was that he offered no guarantees for democratic or minority rights in a political system with only one legislative chamber, a system dominated, furthermore, by one party and one man whose attachment to democratic values was suspect.

De Valera rejected the argument that he was opening the door to his own dictatorship: "We hear talk of a dictatorship—one-man rule and so on—as if everybody in this Assembly of 153 individuals had not a voice and as if everybody here was inanimate and took no part, and played no part, in upholding the views he believed in, and the views of the people he represented."[126] But de Valera was being disingenuous. He was too skilled a political operator not to understand the reality of party government and the power it gave to a Cabinet. Furthermore, his promise to use the time before the abolition measure finally passed through the Oireachtas to introduce measures to protect democratic rights in the constitution was never fulfilled.[127] The only change he accepted, under pressure from the opposition, was that the Comptroller and Auditor-General and members of the judiciary would be removable from office only by a four-sevenths majority of the Dáil.[128] In the 1922 constitution they were removable by simple majorities of the Dáil and the Seanad.

The Seanad abolition bill was approved in the Dáil by fifty-four votes to thirty-six but was defeated in the Seanad by thirty-three votes to fifteen. It was presented to the Seanad again in December 1935, defeated again, and became law over the Seanad's opposition.[129] The chamber went out of existence on 29 May 1936.[130] Ironically, the Wearing of Uniform Bill, which had provoked the abolition, was not pressed by the government after its rejection by the Seanad.[131]

One thing more should be said about the Seanad. A second chamber was an important part of the agreement that Arthur Griffith reached with southern unionists in June 1922. So too was university representation in the Oireachtas, because Dublin University was expected to elect Protestants. The three Dublin University members of the Seanad, while nominally independent, consistently opposed Fianna Fáil, and this was also true of at least one of the National University members.[132] In 1934 the government introduced the Constitution (Amendment No. 23) Bill to eliminate the university seats, and it became law in 1936 over the objections of the Seanad. With the university seats and the Seanad gone from the constitution, all that remained of the agreement with the southern unionists was the principle of elections by proportional representation.[133]

By early 1937, then, the Irish Free State already had a republican constitution in all but name. The links to Britain and the Commonwealth had dwindled to almost nothing as de Valera and Fianna Fáil passed constitutional amendments that translated the sovereignty of the dominions into Irish constitutional law. Cosgrave and de Valera had also reworked the 1922 constitution so that responsible government was reduced to its most basic elements, fusion of the executive and the legislature in a single parliamentary chamber. The primacy of the first house had been established beyond question by the simple expedient of abolishing the second. The dominance of Cabinet government was clearly established by the elimination of external ministers and the provisions for legislative initiatives and referenda. The primacy of the President of the Executive Council was exemplified by a man whose colleagues called him "chief," and any challenge from the head of state had been met by first amending the Governor-General's powers in the constitution, and then by eliminating the Crown altogether. De Valera, as the head of a well-disciplined party that controlled a unicameral parliament, was by 1937 in possession of virtually dictatorial powers. However, he had already determined that there should be a new constitution that would step back from the rather alarming model of responsible government, with enormous concentration of power, that he and Cosgrave had created.

# CHAPTER 11

# The 1937 Constitution

The committee that drafted the 1922 constitution was broadly based and was given a relatively loose rein by the Provisional government. This was not the case with the 1937 constitution, which was written by civil servants working under Eamon de Valera's close supervision. The constitution is known justifiably as de Valera's constitution, so tightly did he control the process, and his opponents were extremely skeptical of his motives. They did not consider de Valera a democrat and regarded his stubborn dedication to principle since 1922 as destructive egoism. They were wrong to be suspicious because the new constitution he shaped confirmed his strong commitment to democracy as expressed through his interpretation of the rules of responsible government. When he purged the Free State constitution of the Governor-General and the Seanad it was not to establish himself as an Irish führer, but to assert a strong preference for the Cabinet, rather than Parliament, as the most important organ of governance. In this interpretation, Dáil Éireann is elected by the people not to govern but to elect a government which, once in power, must be allowed to govern. De Valera did not oppose a head of state, per se, or a Senate, but he believed that neither must be permitted to impede the work of the Cabinet. He carried this belief into the 1937 constitution.

The process of drafting a new constitution began in 1934 when a committee of civil servants was appointed to advise the Executive Council on those articles of the Free State constitution that were of fundamental importance. The committee included John Hearne, legal adviser to the Department of External Affairs.[1] De Valera was the minister of that department as well as President of the Executive Council. In late April 1935 he asked Hearne to prepare a new constitution. De Valera himself took little part in the technical work of preparation but gave instructions to Hearne and responded to the numerous drafts that Hearne and his civil service associates presented. The first draft was submitted to de Valera on 18 May 1935,[2] and only when his papers on the constitution were opened in 1987 did the names of the civil servants who actually drafted the document become generally known.[3]

The constitution was introduced into the Dáil on 10 May 1937 and received final approval on 14 June. An act was also passed that provided for a plebiscite on the document at the following general election, which was held on 1 July 1937. The constitution was approved by a vote of 685,105 to 526,945, and came into operation on 29 December 1937.[4]

## The Constitution of 1937

The constitution of 1937 has only fifty articles but they are more elaborately subdivided than were the eighty-three articles of the Free State constitution, which was actually about 40 percent shorter. The new constitution was innovative in many respects because de Valera was determined that it should be the constitution he would have proposed himself in 1922, had he been in power. Articles 1 through 8 and 41 through 44 therefore identify Ireland as a sovereign, independent, democratic, Gaelic, and Catholic country, and assert a claim to Northern Ireland. Article 8 indicates that Irish is the first official language, with English as the second, and in this spirit several provisions require that Irish terms shall be used for political institutions even in the English version. "Oireachtas" is used for "Parliament," "Dáil Éireann" for "House of Representatives," and "Seanad Éireann" for "Senate," as they were in the 1922 constitution, but de Valera added "Taoiseach" for "Prime Minister" and "Tánaiste" for "Deputy Prime Minister." The Irish for "President," "Uachtarán," is not used in the English text, de Valera told the Dáil, "[b]ecause it is difficult to get the word after the article in Irish without a change in form."[5]

All that was missing from de Valera's 1937 definition of Ireland was the word "republic," a deliberate omission to encourage Northern Ireland to accept a united Ireland. "If the Northern problem were not there," he said, "in all probability there would be a flat, downright proclamation of a republic."[6] The state was renamed Éire (Ireland) in Article 4 because the name Saorstát Éireann (the Irish Free State) was unacceptable to Fianna Fáil, and "Éire" was commonly used in English conversation until the name of the country was changed to "Republic of Ireland" by law in 1949.[7] The word "republic" has never been written into the constitution, although this was recommended by the Committee on the Constitution in 1967,[8] but the document is thoroughly republican in content.

De Valera clearly intended the constitution to make a statement about his vision of Ireland. John Kelly, a distinguished constitutional lawyer, disapprovingly described some articles as "a manifesto rather than . . . bare law."[9] In its treatment of responsible government, however, de Valera's constitution was resolutely oldfashioned. Indeed, by strengthening the role of the Prime Minister it brought the Irish constitution into greater conformity with responsible government as practiced in Britain and the Commonwealth.

Since its adoption, the 1937 constitution has been amended only nine times and none of the amendments has had any significance for responsible government.[10] Amendment is not the easy process it was in the Free State. Article 51 provided that amendment would be by ordinary legislation for a period of only three years, and since 1941 it has required the approval of the Oireachtas and a referendum.

A committee sat in 1940 to review the early working of the constitution, and minor amendments were enacted, but there has since been only one comprehensive review.[11] In 1966 Taoiseach Seán Lemass established an informal, all-party Committee on the Constitution chaired by George Colley, Minister for Industry and Commerce. Lemass himself joined the committee after his resignation as Taoiseach. The committee reported in 1967, but most of the issues it raised were sufficiently controversial that the arguments it adduced for and against reform canceled each other out. Reference will be made to this report under various headings below, in chapter 13.

## The Executive of Éire and the Republic of Ireland

Article 28 of the 1937 constitution vests executive authority not in the head of state, who is the President, but in a Cabinet known formally as "the Government," a body of not less than seven and not more than fifteen members of the Oireachtas. In practice, fifteen are always appointed, plus an Attorney General who sits with the government but is not formally a member.[12] He is not required to sit in the Oireachtas. By ordinary law, up to fifteen Ministers of State, or junior ministers, are also appointed. They were known until 1977 as Parliamentary Secretaries.[13] The number of government departments is also set by law, and is currently seventeen, including the Department of the Taoiseach, which means that some ministers are responsible for more than one department.[14]

Article 13.1 of the constitution provides that the head of the government, the Taoiseach, is appointed by the President on the nomination of Dáil Éireann, as was the case in the Free State. Other members of the government are appointed by the President on the nomination of the Taoiseach, with the previous approval of Dáil Éireann. The Taoiseach nominates one of the ministers to be his deputy, the Tánaiste. Members of the government must be members of either the Dáil or the Seanad, but no more than two may sit in the Seanad. The Taoiseach, Tánaiste, and Minister of Finance must always sit in the Dáil.

The President is not formally described as head of state, but Article 12.1 provides that he "shall take precedence over all other persons in the State." In 1967 the Committee on the Constitution recommended that there should be amendments to recognize that the President exercises executive powers on the advice of the government. This has not been done, and while it would bring Ireland into line with Britain and the dominions, it would add nothing of significance to the constitution. It would also detract from the unique character of the Irish constitution, in that, unlike its British and dominion counterparts, it locates the formal executive at the site of the real executive, the government.[15]

Article 12 states that the President is elected by direct vote of the people for a seven-year term. De Valera had intended that there would be no restriction on the President's right to run for reelection, but Fine Gael argued that such a person would perform his functions with an eye to reelection. De Valera compromised by agreeing to a two-term limit.[16] The President can only be removed from office by impeachment "for stated misbehaviour," a procedure never invoked. It requires at least two-thirds of the members of one house of the Oireachtas to charge the President with an offense, and two-thirds of the members of the other house to convict. The Supreme Court is given responsibility for determining if a President is permanently incapacitated from carrying out the office. Article 14 provides that if the President fails to carry out his responsibilities, whether because of death, removal from office, or any other reason, his functions will be carried out by a commission composed of the Chief Justice, and the Chairmen of Dáil Éireann and the Seanad. The President's powers are discussed below in chapter 13, but we should note here that most of them may be exercised only on the advice of the government or Dáil Éireann.

## The Legislature in Éire and the Republic of Ireland

The Parliament is referred to in both the English and Irish versions of Article 15 of the 1937 constitution by its Irish name, the Oireachtas, which is defined as the President, Dáil Éireann, and Seanad Éireann. The definition follows the tripartite British model, with the head of state and two chambers, which was also used by the Free State.

The composition of the Dáil is determined by Article 16 of the constitution, which uses the Free State model. The number of Dáil constituencies is set by ordinary law but the constitution specifies their character and mode of elections. The number of deputies must be not less than one per thirty thousand of the population and not more than one per twenty thousand. Constituencies must be revised periodically by the Oireachtas to accommodate population changes. Members must be elected by proportional representation using the single transferable vote, and each constituency must have at least 3 seats. There were 138 seats in 1937, a number set by the Electoral Act of 1935, and there are 166 seats today. The number of constituencies has varied from thirty-four in 1937 to forty-two in 1969 and 1974. Currently there are forty-one.[17] The constitution sets the maximum term of a Dáil at seven years, or a shorter period set by law. The maximum term set by law, in the 1963 Electoral Act, is five years, but there is no minimum term and the President may dissolve the Dáil at any time on the advice of the Taoiseach.

The composition of the Dáil posed no problems for de Valera. He simply accepted the Free State model. He also recognized that Irish public opinion favored a second house, even a bad one,[18] but its composition was much more problematical, for two reasons. First, de Valera refused to replicate the Free State Seanad he had abolished because he thought it unrepresentative and obstructive. Second, and more fundamentally, he recognized the theoretical difficulty inherent in forming a responsible government second chamber. As he said in 1934, "[It] is either of the same political complexion as the Lower House, in which case it is not an effective check, or . . . it is opposed to the majority in the Lower House, in which case it acts from political motives . . . and is mischievous. Our experience here proves that."[19] In 1936, when moving to abolish the Free State Seanad, he said he hoped to be able to present a new constitution to the Dáil, but added, "Whether that Constitution is to be based on the principle of a Single Chamber or two will depend upon whether it is possible to devise a Second Chamber which can be of value and not a danger."[20]

Hearne's first draft constitution, dated 17 May 1935, contained no Seanad,[21] but other drafts prepared in 1936 provided that one might be created by law after the enactment of the constitution.[22] This proposal was probably made in anticipation of the report of the Commission on the Second House, chaired by Chief Justice Hugh Kennedy, which de Valera had appointed. Fine Gael refused to cooperate with the commission, but it had more than twenty members, including Conor Maguire, the Attorney General, John Hearne, Justice G. Gavan Duffy, Professor Alfred O'Rahilly, of the 1922 constitution drafting committee, and Thomas Johnson, a veteran of the Labour party. It reported in time to influence the drafting of the constitution.

The commission's task was very difficult. The Seanad had to have some legitimacy, but not so much as to challenge the authority of the responsible chamber, the Dáil. It also had to have some powers, but not too many. The members of the commission agreed that it should have the power to delay nonmoney bills that was possessed by the 1922 Seanad, but with a much shorter period of delay, only ninety days rather than the twenty months the Free State Seanad had when it was abolished.[23] The commission disagreed, however, on the composition and selection of the Seanad. Preferred sizes ranged from forty to one hundred. Preferred selection systems ranged from election by the Dáil and the sitting Seanad to a plan, offered by Deputy Frank MacDermott for sixty senators to be drawn by lot from candidates nominated by vocational, professional, and other groups, including the Turf Club and the Royal Dublin Society. The most popular arrangement appeared to be a mix of senators, some elected and some nominated by the President, a proposal first made by the Amendments to the Constitution Committee in 1927.[24]

On 30 September 1936 Justice Kennedy sent de Valera a majority report, a minority report, a solo report prepared by himself, and a minor dissent by Thomas Johnson.[25] The reports agreed that representation of vocational groups in the Seanad was desirable in principle, but they disagreed over whether this could be accomplished in statutory form. Kennedy, for example, echoed the majority view of the 1922 constitution committee when he argued, "Economic life in the Saorstát is not organized on what is called a 'functional' basis. . . . There is no prospect of a functional basis for our National economic life arising in the near future at all."[26] The commission's majority report preferred that it should be left to a Dáil nominating committee and the President to ensure vocational representation by selecting senators "on account of their ability, character, experience and knowledge of public affairs."[27] However, the minority report proposed that vocational representation should be clearly identified in the constitution itself. It proposed a fifty-member chamber serving for the life of the Dáil with ten senators nominated by the President and forty elected by Dáil Éireann to five-year terms from panels prepared by groups representing different vocational interests in the community.[28]

De Valera accepted this vocational framework, although he enlarged the chamber to sixty. As early as June 1933 he had expressed some support for vocational representation: "[It] would be very much more valuable . . . if we could have a chamber with differentiated functions. . . . I can imagine a Seanad, for instance, in which the members would represent vocational groups."[29] By 1937 he was ready to accept such a chamber, although he told the Fianna Fáil´Ard Fhéis, the annual convention, in November 1936 that he was not convinced that Ireland was yet sufficiently organized for functional representation. Nonetheless, he thought the Seanad might develop into an acceptable functional chamber.[30]

As it finally emerged, Article 18 of the constitution called for a Seanad with sixty members, with eleven nominated by the President and three each elected by graduates of the National University of Ireland and the University of Dublin, a process that excludes the two new (1989) universities, Dublin City University and Limerick University. The balance of forty-three members is elected from five panels by procedures determined by law. The panels are expected to produce "persons having knowledge and practical experiences" in five broad areas: (1) national language and culture, literature, art, education; (2) agriculture and allied industries, and fisheries; (3) labor, "whether organized or unorganized"; (4) industry and commerce; and (5) public administration and social services, including voluntary services. Article 19 provides that some members of the Seanad might be directly elected by functional or vocational organizations in the future, a provision also recommended by the minority report of the commission. "If there was a voluntary development in that direction," de Valera said, "I think most people would welcome it."[31] Lee argues that by leaving this issue to be decided in the future, de Valera was handling "the vocationalist threat with consummate skill,"[32] but de Valera's expressions of support over the years suggest that he believed the idea had some promise, if it were not forced. In fact, functional organizations have not yet been established.

The choice of a Seanad selected largely from vocational panels was influenced to a modest degree by European corporatist and Catholic thought, particularly the 1931 encyclical of Pope Pius XI, *Quadragesimo Anno*.[33] Many in Fine Gael supported corporatism in the 1930s, particularly party members who had been in the Blueshirt movement, but vocational representation had actually been considered, and rejected, by the constitution drafting committee of 1922. It is also the case that Irish vocationalism was very different from continental corporatism. The Italians saw "corporations" as associations combining employers and trades unions from the same trade or profession. The Irish assigned employers and labor to separate Seanad panels. Furthermore, interest representation per se, a feature of corporatism, was specifically rejected in Ireland. Speaking for the whole Commission on the Second House, the majority report noted:

[The] selection of members of the Second House on a basis of vocations or occupations was not contemplated for the purpose of making the Second House a body to represent such vocations or occupations . . . but rather that it might be possible by selecting for a Panel persons who had attained positions of responsibility and distinction in their own particular vocations or occupations to afford a wide choice of persons certainly qualified . . . for membership of the House, and that the selection of members might not be made on a political party basis.[34]

In this sense, the Seanad had more in common with the second chamber recommended by the Irish Convention in 1918 than with corporatism.[35] It was not meant to represent interests but to provide a way of selecting a group of senators whose prominence in various walks of life would enable them to contribute to the well-being of the whole society. De Valera confirmed this interpretation in the Dáil in 1945.[36]

De Valera at first adopted the electoral system for the Seanad suggested by the majority report, which was an electoral college composed of all the candidates at the preceding Dáil election. This scheme was abandoned during the Dáil debate and the completed constitution left the form of Seanad elections to be determined by law. After some changes, the law now provides for elections by members of the Oireachtas and county and county borough councils, a group of about 960. They select from two subpanels in each vocational group, one nominated by members of the Oireachtas and one nominated by recognized vocational bodies on the Register of Nominating Bodies. The registration process is governed by electoral acts. The Seanad election must be held not later than ninety days after the Dáil general election.[37] There are substantial discrepancies in the ratios of councillors to populations in Irish local councils, but all local councillors vote in Seanad elections. This therefore has the effect of biasing election results. As John Colgan describes it:

The least favoured half of the electorate—those in Dublin and in Counties Cork, Kerry, Kildare, Donegal and Wexford—have only 31 percent of the councillor voting strength in the Seanad elections. The other half have 69 per cent of the votes. The effect is the election of a rurally-based Seanad with unrepresentative, predominantly rural values and interests.[38]

## The Powers of the State in Éire and the Republic of Ireland

Article 6.1 of the 1937 constitution states, "All powers of government, legislative, executive and judicial, derive, under God, from the people." Article 6.2 adds, "These powers of government are exercisable only by or on the authority of the organs of State established by this constitution." These two articles essentially restate Article 2 of the Free State constitution, with the addition of the obeisance to God. The provisions establish unequivocally that Ireland is sovereign and they are not compromised by the recognition of royal prerogatives that caused such irritation in 1922.

The state's powers are not unlimited, however, because certain rights of citizens are entrenched in the constitution. Article 40, for example, contains a "bill of rights" that is very similar to Articles 6, 7, and 8 of the Free State constitution. It guarantees equality before the law; due process of law; the right of habeas corpus; the inviolability of dwellings; and freedom of expression, assembly, and association. The constitutionality of acts of the Oireachtas can be tested against these and other provisions of the constitution, either by an appeal in a particular case to the High Court[39] or by a reference from the President to the Supreme Court before he signs a bill.[40] In addition, Ireland is now bound by the laws of the European Community and the Single European Act, obligations that were approved by referenda in 1972 and 1987.

## The Constitutional Relationship with Britain

Article 1 of the Irish Free State constitution, which defined the state as a "co-equal member of the Community of Nations forming the British Commonwealth," was not restated in the 1937 constitution. Nonetheless, the new document contained residual signs of the relationship with Britain that had so long dominated Irish constitutional thought. The word "republic" was not mentioned in the constitution because de Valera was anxious not to alienate Northern Ireland. He also wanted the constitution to be capable of meeting two sets of circumstances, one in which the country was associated with the British Commonwealth, and the other in which it was not.[41] These exclusions and ambiguities made it difficult for him to define the head of state. He asked Hearne to draft articles that would provide a President to perform purely internal functions while retaining the King as a constitutional officer in international relations.[42] As we have seen, this paved the way for the decision, during the abdication crisis of 1936, to remove all references to the Crown from the 1922 constitution and to amend Article 51 to permit the Free State to adopt any "organ, instrument, or method of procedure" used for purposes of international relations by any group with which it might be associated. The group identified in the External Relations Act of December 1936 was the Commonwealth, and the "organ, instrument, or method" was King George VI, who was authorized to appoint diplomatic and consular agents and sign international agreements on behalf of the Free State.[43] As a result, the President is mentioned in the constitution, but not the King, although de Valera fully intended that the King would continue to act for Éire in international relations. Article 29.4.2° of the 1937 constitution restated the amendment to Article 51 of the 1922 constitution which enabled the External Relations Act to remain in effect under a new authority.

The External Relations Act enabled, but did not require, Éire to maintain an association with Britain and the Commonwealth. At any time, the act could have been repealed and the association severed without a constitutional amendment, but for the moment de Valera was anxious not to completely sever the relationship. He was even prepared to consider a permanent military relationship with Britain if it would agree to cede Northern Ireland to Éire.

How did the British government respond to this calculated constitutional ambiguity? First, it informed the Irish government that the new constitution departed from the Anglo-Irish Treaty and should have been the subject of prior consultation,[44] but faced with the gathering storm in Europe, and anxious not to alienate Ireland, it subsequently settled again on appeasement. Paul Canning writes, "Issues once thought so important had . . . become 'constitutional niceties.' All that now mattered was whether or not Ireland wished to remain a member of the Commonwealth, and this was recognized as being up to her to decide."[45] On 30 December 1937 the British government stated that while it recognized no change in the status of Northern Ireland as a part of the United Kingdom, it was prepared to regard the new constitution as not affecting a fundamental alteration in the position of Éire as a member of the British Commonwealth.[46]

Simultaneously, however, Britain undermined one pillar of de Valera's policy, his assumption that Britain might trade Northern Ireland to Éire in return for a permanent military relationship.[47] As Germany occupied Austria in March 1938, Britain agreed not only to end the economic war but also to withdraw from the treaty ports, naval facilities retained in Ireland by Britain after 1921, which it had decided were too expensive to maintain and had unnecessarily alienated the Irish people.[48] On 25 April, therefore, the two governments signed, in effect, a new Anglo-Irish Treaty.[49] In so doing, Éire lost any leverage the treaty ports might have given it in dealing with Britain on Northern Ireland. Winston Churchill, always a staunch defender of the original 1921 Anglo-Irish Treaty, objected in Parliament to the new agreement,[50] but by 1938 no British government would have gone to war to defend military bases its own military planners no longer regarded as essential. Furthermore, there had been a change of heart. Most members of the British government had finally come to recognize what Irish nationalists since the time of Grattan had been arguing: that Ireland treated as a disaffected colony was a greater threat than an independent Ireland tied to Britain by good will and common interests. Unfortunately, partition still clouded the relationship, and this led to Éire's decision to remain neutral after the outbreak of the European war in September 1939.

The British government's response to Éire's neutrality demonstrated that it had not understood the recent constitutional developments in Ireland. In the Cabinet, Winston Churchill, now First Lord of the Admiralty, insisted that the neutrality policy was illegal because the King was still the head of the Irish state and Germany was the King's enemy.[51] In fact, of course, the King was not the head of state in Éire. He was simply "an organ, instrument, or method" in the terms of the constitution. Anthony Eden, the Dominions Secretary, was as confused as Churchill. He wrote, "We do not want formally to recognize Éire as a neutral while Éire remains a member of the British Commonwealth. To do this would be to surrender the hitherto accepted constitutional theory of the indivisibility of the Crown."[52] De Valera still considered Éire to be associated with the Commonwealth but had categorically rejected the concept of the indivisibility of the Crown in 1936.

Whatever Eden wanted to believe, the reality, of course, is that Éire was neutral and Britain had to respond to this reality in some way. By agreement with the dominions, it had already decided in 1937 that Éire should not be cast out of the Commonwealth, in part because this would have changed the legal status of Irishmen living in the United Kingdom, making them neutral aliens in time of war, for example.[53] Britain decided to maintain this policy.[54] It chose not to challenge Éire's neutrality in any formal way and the External Relations Act continued in effect throughout the war, although this meant that Éire could not replace its recently withdrawn ambassador to Germany because it could not ask the King to sign letters of credence.[55]

Éire's neutrality was relatively benevolent, and British and Irish military authorities planned joint responses to potential German attacks on Ireland,[56] but when Churchill became Prime Minister in May 1940 the War Cabinet applied economic pressure on Éire in an attempt to force a change of policy.[57] They also raised the possibility of a united Ireland. This initiative, which was attempted several times, failed, in large part because de Valera was asked to abandon Éire's neutrality without first being given an absolute guarantee that a united Ireland would follow. Furthermore, Britain had not seriously attempted to pressure Northern Ireland to support the deal. The Northern Irish had made it clear that they would not voluntarily discuss concessions unless de Valera were first to abandon Éire's neutrality, something he would never do.[58]

Éire's wartime neutrality set a precedent for its postwar foreign policy, even when de Valera's government was replaced in 1947. Indeed, it was the Fine Gael–led coalition of John Costello that refused to sign the North Atlantic Treaty in 1949,[59] and that finally completed Éire's separation from Britain and the Commonwealth. As Mansergh describes the decision:

De Valera delayed his decision, seemingly continuing to hope that, if formal secession could be deferred, republicanism and unity might ultimately be reconciled, while his more conservative, traditionally pro-Commonwealth critics, with long years in the political wilderness behind them, insisted on an end to all prevarication and procrastination on the issue.[60]

In November 1948 the Republic of Ireland Bill was introduced, which Costello said would "end forever, in a simple, clear and unequivocal way this country's long and tragic association with the institution of the British Crown."[61] The association was severed by the Republic of Ireland Act, and by the repeal of the External Relations Act. Éire became the Republic of Ireland on Easter Sunday, 1949.[62] De Valera took no part in the celebration because it was not yet the republic which Pearse had declared in 1916.[63]

Britain's initial reaction to this definitive act of separation was that it should treat the Republic of Ireland henceforward as a foreign state in every respect. However, in response to an appeal from Dr. H. V. Evatt, the Foreign Minister of Australia, and other Commonwealth ministers, Britain agreed, in the Ireland Act of 1949, to allow Irish citizens to retain the benefits of Commonwealth citizenship, including the right to vote in the United Kingdom.[64] It was only in 1984 that the Irish constitution was amended to allow British citizens to vote in Ireland.[65] The Ireland Act was also used to reassure the people of Northern Ireland that they would never be abandoned. It stated: "It is hereby declared that Northern Ireland remains part of His Majesty's dominions and of the United Kingdom and it is hereby affirmed that in no event will Northern Ireland or any part thereof cease to be part of His Majesty's dominions and of the United Kingdom without the consent of the Parliament of Northern Ireland."[66] The effect, therefore, of abandoning the strange constitutional formula that had kept Éire in an association with the Commonwealth from December 1936 was to strengthen Britain's commitment to the status quo in Northern Ireland.

## A Catholic Constitution

The 1922 constitution departed from British precedents by protecting fundamental civil rights in Ireland and providing for the judicial review of legislation, but the 1937 constitution departed yet again by endorsing specifically Catholic religious values concerning marriage and the family. Indeed, the family is described in Article 41 as "a moral institution possessing inalienable and imprescriptible rights antecedent and superior to all positive law." Implicit in this language is the Thomistic view that natural law takes precedence over positive law. Article 41.3 requires the state to "guard with special care the institution of Marriage," and prohibits a civil divorce. Article 42 acknowledges that the "primary and natural educator of the child is the Family" and recognizes the parents' right to select a school, a provision that supports the system of Catholic education in Ireland. Article 43, reminiscent of papal encyclicals, acknowledges that man has a natural right, again antecedent to positive law, to the private ownership of property. Article 40 was added to the constitution after a referendum in 1983 and acknowledges the right to life of the unborn, "with due regard to the equal right to life of the mother." The 1937 constitution also recognized, in the original Article 44.1.2°, "the special position of the Holy Catholic and Roman Church as the guardian of the Faith professed by the great majority of the citizens," but this section was deleted, with the support of the Catholic church, after a referendum in 1972. It was thought unnecessarily offensive to non-Catholics although it actually created no rights or obligations and was followed by Article 44.1.3°, which recognized "the Church of Ireland, the Presbyterian Church in Ireland, the Methodist Church in Ireland, the Religious Society of Friends in Ireland, as well as the other religious dominations existing in Ireland." By recognizing Irish churches other than the Catholic church, this clause had offended the Vatican in 1937. It too was deleted in 1972 by the referendum. Article 44.2.1°, which guaranteed "freedom of conscience and the free profession and practise of religion," remains in the constitution.

The Catholic content of the constitution, and de Valera's motives for including it, have been treated adequately in other places.[67] For my purposes it will suffice to say that it added a novel dimension to the Irish constitutional tradition, one that has attracted more public and scholarly attention than any other part of the constitution. However, it affected responsible government, the central concern of this book, in only two respects. First, as we saw above,[68] continental corporatist and Catholic thought influenced the vocationalist basis of the Seanad to a degree, but this should not be exaggerated. We will see in the following chapter that vocationalism was to be a particularly ineffective element of the constitution. Second, the inclusion in the constitution of specific policies regarding marriage and the family has limited the freedom of the Oireachtas to legislate in those areas without constitutional amendments and referenda. The government has discovered several times in recent years how intense the battles over such constitutional amendments can be. The referendum on the eighth amendment to the constitution in 1983, which introduced the prohibition on abortion, was the first such battle, and it was followed by the refusal of the electorate to remove the prohibition on divorce from the constitution in the 1986 referendum. Both were hotly contested.[69]

At the General Election of 25 November 1992 three more controversial referenda were put to the people. They all arose out of a case, *The Attorney General versus X and Others*, in which the Attorney General, by arguing that abortion is illegal in Ireland, secured an interim injunction in the High Court to prevent a young girl who had become pregnant by rape from traveling to England for an abortion. On appeal, the Supreme Court found that the girl could have an abortion because a psychologist had testified that she was in danger of taking her own life. Article 40.3.3° requires the right to life of the mother to be considered as well as the rights of the unborn.[70] The injunction was lifted and the girl was permitted to travel to England.

The first of the three referenda that followed from this decision proposed that Article 40.3.3° should not limit a woman's freedom to travel to another state. The second proposed that the article should not limit the freedom to obtain or make available "information relating to services lawfully available in another state." Abortion services were implied. The third referendum proposed that Article 40.3.3° should be amended so that a pregnancy might only be terminated if the threat to the life of the mother arose from "an illness or disorder . . . not being a risk of self-destruction."[71] On 25 November, the first proposal was accepted by 62.3 percent of the voters, thereby permitting Irish women

to travel abroad for abortions. The second proposal was accepted by
59.9 percent of the voters, thereby permitting the Irish to obtain abortion information in Ireland. But the third proposal received only 34.6
percent of the vote, which means that the Supreme Court's interpretation of Article 40.3.3° in the "X" case stands. Conservatives had opposed the proposal because it would have permitted abortion, albeit in
more limited circumstances than those permitted by the Supreme
Court, but Liberals opposed it because it was far too restrictive. The
Catholic bishops, fearing the Supreme Court's interpretation as much
as the proposed amendment, agreed that Catholics might in conscience
vote either way.[72] In the confusion, the preferred status of abortion in
Ireland went unresolved, and it will fall to another government to devise a wording that can win the support of a majority. The government
knows that any proposal will divide the electorate into angry camps yet
again.

In 1928 the Cumann na nGaedheal government removed the popular initiative and referendum from the constitution because it could not
control the outcome of a referendum campaign on a contentious issue,
the oath of allegiance, which was bound to arouse great passions in the
electorate. Today such passions are directed at referenda on portions
of the 1937 constitution that fix the moral values of the majority in
constitutional law.

# CHAPTER 12

# The 1937 Constitution and Responsible Government

The 1937 constitution made no fundamental changes in the basic model of responsible government that had been practiced by the first Dáil Éireann and the Irish Free State since 1919, although there were some changes in the institutions of government, most notably the introduction of the office of President of Ireland. The constitution restated the Irish Free State article that "the sole and exclusive power of making laws for the State is hereby vested in the Oireachtas"[1] but it simultaneously affirmed the essential rules of responsible government that have the effect of concentrating power in the Cabinet, not the Oireachtas. This chapter will consider the first seven characteristics of responsible government as they are represented in Ireland today under the 1937 constitution. The eighth characteristic, the concentration of power which follows from the first seven, will be the subject of the final chapter.

## Fusion

Article 28 of the 1937 constitution provides for fusion of the executive and the legislature. The executive, known formally as the government, is responsible to Dáil Éireann, and the Taoiseach, Tánaiste, and Minister for Finance must be members of the Dáil. All other members of the government must be members of the Oireachtas, although no more than two may sit in the Seanad. These provisions essentially reproduce the provisions of the Free State constitution after external ministers were removed from the Executive Council by constitutional amendment in 1927 and senators were admitted to the Council in 1929.

## Majority Government

Majority government is identified in two articles reproduced from the 1922 constitution. First, Article 13.1.1° requires the President to appoint the Taoiseach on the nomination of Dáil Éireann. Other members of the government are appointed by the President on the new Taoiseach's nomination, subject to the approval of the Dáil. Second, Article 28.10 requires the Taoiseach to resign on ceasing to retain the support of a majority in Dáil Éireann. It is therefore illegal in the Republic of Ireland for the government to govern, other than in an interim capacity, without the support of a majority in the legislature. The 1937 constitution fails, as did its predecessor, to specify exactly how to measure the government's majority, a problem to which I will return in the discussion of the President.[2]

Majority government does not mean that a party or coalition must always have an overall majority of seats in the Dáil in order to form a government. Rather, it means the government must win the support of a majority on critical votes, particularly votes of confidence, even if this means relying on independents or small parties, described by Chubb as "camp followers,"[3] with whom it has no formal relationship. Ireland often has minority governments that secure the majorities they require in this way. Of course, responsible government works most easily with only two parties in the legislature because the majority is always clear, absent a tie, but government formation has never been this simple in Ireland.

Both the 1922 and 1937 constitutions required elections to be by proportional representation and such elections have permitted considerable fragmentation in the Dáil, with a substantial number of parties and independents being represented. Twenty-five governments have been installed in Dublin after general elections since 1922. Only nine of these were single-party governments with overall majorities in the Dáil,[4] and only de Valera's Fianna Fáil administration in 1938 won both a majority of seats and a majority of the popular vote. Of the nine, three can be considered single-party majority governments only with qualifications. The 1922 protreaty government and the 1923 Cumann na nGaedheal government had majorities only because the antitreaty deputies refused to take their seats. The 1965 Fianna Fáil government of Seán Lemass, with exactly half the seats in the Dáil, had a majority only when a Labour deputy, Patrick Hogan, was elected Chairman.

Of the remaining sixteen governments formed since 1922, six were coalitions in which the coalition partners had an overall majority of seats in the Dáil. All were formed since 1948, four by Fine Gael and two, in 1989 and 1993, by Fianna Fáil. This leaves ten governments that lacked overall majorities and depended on the votes of other parties or independents for their majorities on major votes. All but one of these, the 1981 Fine Gael-Labour coalition, were single-party governments and they include the Fianna Fáil government of 1937 that won half the seats in the Dáil but lost its overall majority when one of its members sat as Chairman. Table 12.1 offers a detailed picture of majority and minority Irish governments since 1922.

The large number of coalition and minority governments in Ireland

TABLE 12.1.
Majority and Minority Governments since 1922

| Election | Government | Maj/Min | Govt/Dáil |
|----------|------------|---------|-----------|
| 1922 | Protreaty Repubs. | Majority | 58/128 |
| 1923 | Cumann na nGaedheal | Majority | 63/153 |
| 1927 (June) | "      "      " | Minority | 47/153 |
| 1932 (Sept.) | "      "      " | Minority | 62/153 |
| 1932 | Fianna Fáil | Minority | 72/153 |
| 1933 | "    " | Majority | 77/153 |
| 1937 | "    " | Minority | 69/138 |
| 1938 | "    " | Majority | 77/138 |
| 1943 | "    " | Minority | 67/138 |
| 1944 | "    " | Majority | 76/138 |
| 1948 | Coalition | Majority | 79/147 |
| 1951 | Fianna Fáil | Minority | 69/147 |
| 1954 | Coalition | Majority | 74/147 |
| 1957 | Fianna Fáil | Majority | 78/147 |
| 1961 | "    " | Minority | 70/144 |
| 1965 | "    " | Majority | 72/144 |
| 1969 | "    " | Majority | 75/144 |
| 1973 | Coalition | Majority | 73/144 |
| 1977 | Fianna Fáil | Majority | 84/148 |
| 1981 | Coalition | Minority | 80/166 |
| 1982 (Feb.) | Fianna Fáil | Minority | 81/166 |
| 1982 (Nov.) | Coalition | Majority | 86/166 |
| 1987 | Fianna Fáil | Minority | 81/166 |
| 1989 | Coalition | Majority | 83/166 |
| 1993 | Coalition | Majority | 101/166 |

under proportional representation can be compared with governments in the United Kingdom, which has elections in single-member constituencies with plurality voting. The twenty-five United Kingdom general elections between 1900 and 1992 produced eighteen single-party majority governments, five single-party minority governments, and only two coalitions. Margaret Thatcher was able to form three Conservative governments with substantial overall majorities in the House of Commons despite winning only 43.9 percent of the popular vote in 1979, 42.4 percent in 1983, and 42.3 percent in 1987.[5] In 1992 John Major formed a Conservative government with a twenty-one-seat majority based on only 41.9 percent of the popular vote.[6] By contrast, Charles Haughey, who formed two Fianna Fáil minority governments and one Fianna Fáil–Progressive Democrat majority coalition, never won a majority of seats in Dáil Éireann although his party received 47.3 percent of the popular vote in February 1982, 44.1 percent in 1987, and 44.4 percent in 1989.[7] Table 12.2 offers a comparison of United Kingdom and Irish governments.

In addition to the large number of coalition and minority governments in Ireland, there have been frequent alternations in power, particularly in recent years, suggesting considerable electoral volatility. The sitting government has lost office in thirteen of the twenty-five general elections since independence, including all eight since 1973.

The difficulty experienced in forming single-party, majority governments in Ireland led the Informal Committee on the Constitution in 1966 to hear arguments for and against proportional representation, but it could not agree on a recommendation for reform. Opponents argued that proportional representation fragments the vote and fosters instability; that the postelection coalitions that often result from proportional representation are unrepresentative because electors do not

TABLE 12.2.
Governments Formed after Elections

|  | Independent Ireland | United Kingdom |
|---|---|---|
| No. of elections | 25 (1922–92) | 25 (1900–1992) |
| Single-party majority govts. | 9 | 18 |
| Majority coalitions | 6 | 2 |
| Minority governments | 10 | 5 |

knowingly vote for them at a general elections; and that deputies are too distant from the people for effective representation in large multimember districts. Supporters of proportional representation argued that parties have not multiplied unmanageably in Ireland and there has been no serious government instability.[8] It is true that single-party governments generally survive longer than coalitions, but all Irish governments have been able to govern effectively for reasonable lengths of time and have rarely been defeated in the Dáil.

Fianna Fáil, the largest party in the state, is most likely to form a single-party majority government, and is the only party to have done so since 1933, but it has been frustrated so many times by the electoral system in its quest for a Dáil majority that in 1959 and 1968 it sponsored constitutional amendments to abandon proportional representation and adopt single-member districts and plurality voting on the British model. A skeptical electorate voted "no" on both occasions. It was clear that Fianna Fáil stood to gain substantially from the adoption of the British system because, as the largest party, it would have won a disproportionate number of elections in single-member constituencies contested by three or more parties.[9] Michael Gallagher has argued that the Irish electoral system produces one of the fairest results in the world, measured by the degree to which popular support for parties is reflected in their representation in the legislature,[10] but the extreme difficulty experienced in forming governments after the elections of 1989 and 1992 is likely to revive the debate over proportional representation.

Article 16.2.5° calls for constituencies to be revised at least once every twelve years in response to population shifts, which gives the government of the day an opportunity to seek marginal advantages by changing constituency sizes in the Irish equivalent of the American gerrymander. In the 1960s, for example, the Fianna Fáil Minister for Local Government, Kevin Boland, the minister responsible for redistricting, increased the number of four-seat constituencies in the Dublin area, where his party stood to win about half the seats with about two-fifths of the vote. He concentrated three-seat constituencies in the west where Fianna Fáil stood to win two-thirds of the seats with less than half of the vote. The Fine Gael–Labour coalition Minister, James Tully, redrew the constituencies in his "Tullymander" of 1974, ostensibly to Fine Gael's advantage, but that exercise unexpectedly rebounded to the party's disadvantage in the 1977 general election. The practice of gerrymandering was subsequently abandoned by the Fianna Fáil Taoiseach, Jack Lynch, and there followed the first redistricting by an independent commission with neutral terms of reference in 1979.[11] In 1988 the minority Fianna Fáil government of Charles Haughey sought to return to the old practice by instructing the commission to reduce the number of five-seat constituencies, to the disadvantage of small parties and independents. The commission recommended reducing the number of such constituencies by only two, but its report was shelved by the government in the face of Dáil opposition.[12]

Proportional representation remains in the constitution and Ireland therefore seems destined to continue to experience difficulties in government formation. Indeed, the problem has worsened in recent years. Until 1989, it was always possible for the Dáil to elect a Taoiseach at its first meeting, two to three weeks after a general election, but that year and again in 1992 several adjournments of the new Dáil were required before the parties could agree on a Taoiseach. Because of these unprecedented delays in forming the government, a procedure was devised within the constitution that allows the state to continue to function in the period between the first sitting of a new Dáil and the delayed election of a new Taoiseach. The Dáil is summoned, members are seated, and a Chairman is elected who conducts the election for Taoiseach. Article 28.10 requires the Taoiseach to resign "upon his ceasing to retain the support of a majority in Dáil Éireann unless on his advice the President dissolves Dáil Éireann," but Article 28.11.1° requires the government to remain in office until its successor has been appointed. With the Dáil formally seated, a Chairman elected, and an interim government in place, the Dáil is in a position during this interim period to process necessary business, with the cooperation of the major parties, and deputies can claim their salaries. Meanwhile, negotiations can take place on the formation of a new government.

In the election of 15 June 1989 Fianna Fáil won only seventy-seven seats, a net loss of four seats which was seven short of an overall majority. Table 12.3 details the composition of the 1989 Dáil Éireann. When the ballot for Taoiseach was held on Thursday, 29 June, none of the party leaders could win a majority and Haughey secured an adjournment. He secured adjournments again, on 3 July and 6 July, while interparty negotiations on a new government took place. Haughey's failure to win reelection had made it immediately obvious on 29 June that he did not have the support of a majority in the Dáil. It was also obvious that he could not go to the President to request a dissolution because coalition possibilities had not yet been thoroughly explored. Haughey resisted resigning immediately after the vote, arguing that "time is not of the essence" in the matter, but under pressure from opposition leaders he did resign that evening.[13] He remained in office as caretaker Taoiseach.

Fianna Fáil's standing policy was to refuse to participate in coalitions, and Haughey rejected a Fine Gael proposal for a Fianna Fáil–Fine Gael government that would have shared ministerial portfolios equally between the two parties and alternated the office of Taoiseach annually between the party leaders. But to remain in office, Haughey was forced to abandon the no-coalition policy and on 12 July he announced a coalition with the Progressive Democratic party, which had lost eight of its fourteen seats in the election. The price he paid was high. Three of the six Progressive Democrats in the Dáil received posts in the government, Desmond O'Malley and Bobby Molloy as full ministers and Mary Harney as Minister of State. Only then was Haughey reelected Taoiseach, by a vote of eighty-four to seventy-nine, with two abstentions. The crisis was over. A majority had been found.[14]

The general election of 25 November 1992 produced an even less decisive outcome. At a time of national economic distress and substantial dissatisfaction with the two major parties, Fianna Fáil polled its lowest vote since 1927 and won only sixty-eight seats, a net loss of

TABLE 12.3.
Seats in the 26th Dáil Éireann, June
1989

| | |
|---|---|
| Fianna Fáil | 77 |
| Fine Gael | 55 |
| Labour | 15 |
| Workers | 7* |
| Progressive Democrats | 6 |
| Independents | 2 |
| Independent Fianna Fáil | 1 |
| Green | 1 |
| Democratic Socialist | 1 |
| Ceann Comhairle (Chairman) | 1 |
| Total | 166 |

* Six members of the Workers' party formed a new
political party during the 26th Dáil, the Democratic
Left.

nine. Fine Gael polled its lowest vote since 1948 and won only forty-five seats, a net loss of ten. The major beneficiary was the Labour party which polled its highest vote ever and won thirty-three seats, a net gain of eighteen. The Progressive Democrats, with ten seats, gained four, and the Democratic Left, with four seats, lost two.[15] Table 12.4 details the party composition of the 1992 Dáil Eireann. Taoiseach Albert Reynolds, who had succeeded Haughey in January, failed to secure a majority at the first meeting of the new Dáil on 14 December and resigned immediately, remaining in office on an interim basis. The new Dáil was able to approve Supplementary Estimates and Appropriations bills, and it also approved measures required by the Single European Act,[16] but the task of finding a new government was complicated by many factors, including the mutual antipathies of the party leaders.

Accepting that his government had lost the election, Reynolds allowed the other major parties the first shot at forming a coalition, but many Fianna Fáil deputies believed the party should go into opposition, where it could regroup while others grappled with the enormous economic problems facing Ireland.[17] It was only after the leaders of Fine Gael, Labour, and the Progressive Democrats made no progress in their negotiations that Fianna Fáil took the initiative to form a government.

Fine Gael had made it clear during the election campaign that it was prepared to enter a coalition with Labour and the Progressive Democrats, but Labour would have none of this and refused to be taken for granted. It had bad memories of the very harsh budgets offered by John Bruton, the Fine Gael leader, when he was the coalition's Finance Minister in the 1980s and it did not welcome having to work with the eco-

TABLE 12.4.
Seats in the 27th Dáil Éireann,
November 1992

| | |
|---|---|
| Fianna Fáil | 68 |
| Fine Gael | 45 |
| Labour | 33 |
| Progressive Democrats | 10 |
| Democratic Left | 4 |
| Independent | 4 |
| Green | 1 |
| Ceann Comhairle (Speaker) | 1 |
| Total | 166 |

nomically conservative Progressive Democrats in a coalition. Labour also knew that its newfound electoral strength might weaken were the party to enter a coalition in a clearly subordinate position, as happened during the coalition years in the 1980s. It therefore outlined radical economic and social policies, and demanded that the office of Taoiseach be rotated between the Labour and Fine Gael parties, terms that were unacceptable to Fine Gael.[18] One possible outcome of Labour's tough bargaining strategy, a historic Fianna Fáil–Fine Gael "Grand Coalition," would not have worried Labour at all because it would have left Labour as the major opposition party in the Dáil. Such a coalition would have ended the long era of Anglo-Irish Treaty and civil war politics, a benefit in itself, but it would also have blurred the distinction between the two center-right parties, which Labour anticipated would lead to Fine Gael's replacement by Labour as the second party in the state.[19]

In his column in the *Irish Times* on 12 December, former Fine Gael Taoiseach Garret FitzGerald spoke for many in his party when he strongly opposed a "Grand Coalition." He agreed that there were no fundamental differences on economic and social policies between the two parties but insisted that Fianna Fáil still adhered to "a deeply traditional single-ethos nationalism" that was unacceptable to the "instinctive pluralism" of the other parties. In other words, Fianna Fáil was still playing the "green card," what FitzGerald described as "historical Catholic, Gaelic nationalism." But one might equally argue that a coalition agreement between Fianna Fáil and Fine Gael would necessarily have required Fianna Fáil to eschew the politics of republican nationalism. Perhaps it was FitzGerald himself, therefore, who was keeping the "green card" in play, to save Fine Gael.

Fine Gael refused to commit suicide by joining a coalition with Fianna Fáil, but Dick Spring, supported by polls showing him to be the most popular party leader in the country,[20] refused to be drawn into a coalition. In the circumstances there really was only one way out of the crisis, short of another general election: a Fianna Fáil–Labour coalition. This was the outcome Spring probably anticipated all along because it made sense. By 1992 Labour was closer to Fianna Fáil on economic policy, its first priority, than to Fine Gael and the Progressive Democrats. Furthermore, on nationalist issues, which had previously divided Fianna Fáil from the other parties in the Dáil, Taoiseach Reynolds had already shown some moderation. As I demonstrated in chapter 6, Fianna Fáil agreed in the summer of 1992 that Articles 2 and 3, with their claim to Northern Ireland, might be removed from the constitution as part of a comprehensive agreement with Britain on Northern Ireland. A Fianna Fáil–Labour coalition was approved by the Dáil on 12 January 1993. Labour secured six of the fifteen full ministerial positions, including Tanaiste and Minister for Foreign Affairs for Spring himself, and the new post of Minister for Employment and Enterprise for Ruari Quinn.

Coalition government contains pitfalls, particularly for smaller parties, which suffer if the electorate fails to differentiate between the weaker and stronger members of the partnership, as happened to Labour during its coalitions with Fine Gael. This is precisely why many members of the Labour party are hostile to coalitions. In 1957 the annual conference voted not to participate in coalitions, and this remained the party's policy until 1973, when it signed a preelection pact with Fine Gael. The two parties subsequently formed a government and campaigned together, though unsuccessfully, for reelection in 1977. Labour did not sign a preelection pact in 1981 and the Fine Gael–Labour coalition of that year was the result of postelection negotiations. The coalition lost the February 1982 election. The next general election was in November 1982 and by then the annual conference of the Labour party had decided that a special delegate conference, rather than party leaders, would decide whether to enter a coalition. This prompted the resignation of the party leader, Michael O'Leary, but after the election the party did enter another coalition with Fine Gael which survived until the election defeat of 1987, the year Labour won only 6.4 percent of first-preference votes. Since then the party has avoided preelection pacts, and in 1992 it polled 19.3 percent. It will be interesting to see if the party will retain its popularity as a coalition member.

Fine Gael has been more sympathetic to coalitions, other than coalitions with Fianna Fáil, because it anticipates being the dominant party in such arrangements and sees little possibility of taking power on its own. For a preelection pact in 1989 it turned to the Progressive Democratic party, which had temporarily displaced Labour as the third largest party in the state, but that agreement held only through the first ballot for Taoiseach in the Dáil. Thereafter, the Progressive Democrats joined in government with Fianna Fáil.

Coalition government is rarely easy. It is difficult for opponents in bitterly contested election campaigns to put aside their enmities to work together, and there is always a period of hard bargaining on the elements of a joint program for government before the coalition is cemented. Once a government is formed, it may be difficult for its members to pull together. It was, for example, Labour's opposition to cost cutting by the Fine Gael majority in 1987 that led to the collapse of the Fine Gael–Labour coalition in 1987.[21] The 1989–92 Fianna Fáil–Progressive Democrat coalition proved difficult for both parties. In October 1990 the Progressive Democrats threatened to leave the government if Taoiseach Haughey did not dismiss the Tánaiste, Brian Lenihan, who appeared to have lied about his involvement in events surrounding the dissolution of the Dáil in 1982. Haughey reluctantly complied.[22] Then, in January 1992, he found himself embroiled in a controversy with the Fianna Fáil Chairman of the Seanad, Seán Doherty, over Doherty's allegation that the Taoiseach was aware of illegal wiretaps of journalists and members of the Oireachtas some years before. Once again, the Progressive Democrats placed the coalition on the line, and this time Haughey himself had to resign. His successor, Albert Reynolds, was elected by the Dáil on 11 February 1992,[23] but Reynolds's government was destroyed by the resignation of the Progressive Democrats on 4 November 1992. They voted against Reynolds during a vote of confidence the following day.[24]

It seems likely that the Irish electorate will continue to oppose the abolition of proportional representation and that party fragmentation in the Dáil will also continue. Irish political parties will therefore have no choice but to continue to engage in interparty maneuvering as they strive for Dáil majorities or try to negotiate the unpleasant compromises involved in coalition formation. In this process, the character of the parties themselves will play a critical role. Ireland remains unusual in Europe in that class-based ideologies play a relatively minor role in its political parties. Marsh and Sinnott note that a number of opinion polls put questions about issues to Irish voters during the 1989 election campaign that allowed them to differentiate themselves on the customary left-right, class-based, party continuum—questions about cuts in government spending, for example. The responses showed no clear, class basis in party support. Marsh and Sinnott conclude, "The most striking thing about the results is not any left-right divide but the substantial degree of consensus which exists."[25] The agendas of voters on the left differed somewhat from those of others, but "these differences were of degree rather than of kind, with all political groups in substantial agreement about the relative importance of the major issues."[26] They also observed that all social classes are represented in all parties. Fianna Fáil, for example, is "an almost completely cross-class party," and while Fine Gael has a bias toward professional and middle-class voters, the pattern is not overwhelming.[27]

Such a level of cross-class support for parties and cross-party consensus by voters on major issues suggests that a variety of postelection coalition combinations is possible in Ireland, and that Fianna Fáil, having surrendered its long-standing anticoalition policy in 1989, is well positioned as the largest party to continue to be the dominant force in government formation. Nonetheless, the atavistic mutual antipathy of Fine Gael and Fianna Fáil; Fine Gael's move to the right on economic issues, which makes it harder than before for the party to work with Labour; the newfound strength of Labour itself; and the persistence of the Progressive Democrats and the Democratic Left, with fourteen seats between them in the twenty-seventh Dáil, suggest that negotiations may be difficult. Furthermore, because it was accepted for the first time in 1989 that a new government need not be identified before the first meeting of a new Dáil, negotiations might well be very lengthy. The major weakness in the procedure for interim government used in 1989 and 1992 is that the constitution sets no limit to such government. It could well take a very long time to elect a Taoiseach in the future, and although the state would continue to function in the interim, it would lack direction or mandate. The four-week delay in 1989 before a new Taoiseach was selected was considered a minor crisis at the time, but after the election of 25 November 1992 it took seven weeks to resolve the Dáil's postelection stalemate. There is no guarantee that even longer delays will not be experienced in the future.

## The Primacy of the Lower House

The 1937 constitution continues the primacy of the Dáil established in 1922. It specifies that the government is responsible only to Dáil Éireann,[28] which selects the Taoiseach and approves his nominees for ministers.[29] The Taoiseach, Tánaiste, and Minister for Finance must sit in the Dáil and no more than two senators may sit in the government, although ministers may speak in either house.[30] Only two senators have sat in the government since 1937 and the Irish Free State convention persists that ministers should sit in the responsible chamber.

The primacy of the Dáil is also reflected in the limited legislative powers of the Seanad, which are very much those of the Free State Seanad. It has coordinate powers with the Dáil in only very limited cases, namely, to remove judges[31] and declare an emergency "in time of war or armed rebellion,"[32] but it may not initiate or amend a money bill, and has only twenty-one days in which to recommend changes to the Dáil.[33] It may amend a nonmoney bill, but has only ninety days to consider the matter, a much shorter period than in the Free State Seanad. Its amendments can be overridden by resolutions of the Dáil[34] and the ninety-day period of delay can be abridged by the President, at the request of the Taoiseach, "for the preservation of the public peace and security or by reason of the existence of a public emergency, whether domestic or international."[35] Bills passed by this abbreviated procedure lapse after ninety days unless both houses agree to their extension. Because de Valera believed the Dáil should always prevail, there is no procedure for resolving disputes between the two houses in the constitution, not even the mild consultation provided in Article 38 of the Free State constitution. However, often representatives of the two houses do meet informally to iron out conflicts without reference to the constitution.[36]

As we can see, the 1937 constitution thoroughly establishes the formal primacy of the Dáil in the Oireachtas, but the austere language of the law does not reflect the degree to which the Seanad is subordinated in practice. The Free State Senate was abolished because it challenged de Valera, but the new Seanad has never even tried to challenge the government. There appear to be four reasons for its passivity. First, by design the electoral cycles for the two chambers are roughly the same. Irish Free State senators served long fixed terms, with a proportion retiring every three years, and when de Valera came to office in 1932 he found that the chamber was controlled by the opposition. He decided in 1937 that the whole Seanad would be replaced at each election precisely to diminish its chances of becoming an opposition chamber. Elections for all the elected seats in the Dáil must therefore be held within ninety days of Dáil elections[37] and both chambers therefore tend to reflect the mood of the moment. Second, Article 18 requires the Taoiseach to nominate eleven senators. De Valera admitted that this article was included to ensure that the government can control the chamber, even though it might not win a majority of the elected seats.[38] Third, the Seanad nomination and election processes are dominated by partisan politics directed by the party leaders in the Dáil, and party discipline operates in both chambers. The elections for the vocational seats in 1989, for example, produced a party-dominated chamber. Fianna Fáil won twenty-four, Fine Gael won fifteen, and Labour won four. The Taoiseach's nominees were all party politicians, eight from Fianna Fáil and three from the Progressive Democrats, so that only the six university members refused to accept a party whip.[39] Fourth, senators accept socialization into a subordinate role and are loathe to obstruct the government, even when they might do so. The Taoiseach has often nominated two or three independents, including some from Northern Ireland, knowing that even were the government to have a minority in the Seanad, its policies would not be obstructed.[40] In 1991 the leader of the opposition Fine Gael in the Seanad, Maurice Manning, said, "Certainly it is not our job to frustrate the other House," as the 1934 Seanad had done. He added, "Looking back on that, I think that Mr. de Valera was absolutely right."[41]

The Seanad is a useful debating chamber but the government has lost only three divisions there, in 1958, 1964, and 1990, and the Seanad has never used the power in Article 27 by which two-thirds of the Seanad and one-third of the Dáil can request the President to call a referendum on an item of legislation.[42] Nor has the Seanad been active as a revising chamber. David Gwynn Morgan records that of the approximately 300 bills passed by the Seanad in the years 1971 to 1980, only 33 were amended, for a total of 184 amendments. Most of the amendments were initiated by the government to improve bills already approved by the Dáil. The Seanad is limited to "recommending" changes for money bills, and between 1938 and 1982 it did so only seven times in 400 bills, six of which were accepted by the government.[43] Despite the pressure of business in the Dáil, very few bills originate in the Seanad, although the pattern was broken for a short while by the Fine Gael–Labour coalition in the 1980s. Of 39 bills passed by the Oireachtas in 1986, for example, 12 originated in the Seanad, and in 1987 the proportion was 14 to 34.[44] The Seanad's schedule has always been very variable. It sat for only twenty-eight days in 1980, for example, and for twenty-two days in 1982, but in 1986 it sat for seventy-eight days, and in 1990 for sixty. It has always sat less frequently than the Dáil, how-

ever, which averaged eighty-four days of sittings in the period 1980–
90, and has increased sitting days substantially since then.[45]

The secondary role the Seanad plays is reflected in its composition.
Many eminent people have served there, but not many party politicians
who were, during their Seanad careers, of the very first rank. Chubb
describes many senators as "rising, falling, or resting" politicians, and
only two have sat in the government since 1937: Seán Moylan, Fianna
Fáil Minister for Agriculture who had recently lost his Dáil seat, in
1957, and James Dooge, Fine Gael Minister for Foreign Affairs, who
was a particularly close associate of the Taoiseach, Garret FitzGerald,
in 1981.[46]

The constitutional provisions on the Seanad have not been altered
since 1937 although the ambivalence that surrounded the chamber
when the constitution was debated has surfaced several times. In 1943,
for example, the Commission on Vocational Organization proposed
that popularly elected vocational councils should elect the Seanad and
recommend economic and social policy to the Oireachtas, but the proposal was ignored by the government.[47] In 1944 de Valera himself expressed dissatisfaction with the chamber but recognized that only a federal state could support a truly effective second chamber.[48] In 1958 he
appointed the Seanad Electoral Law Commission which recommended, in 1961, that twenty-three of the forty-three vocational seats
should be elected, and not simply nominated, by a vocational process.
By then, however, de Valera had resigned and Garret FitzGerald, a
member of the commission, tells us that the new Taoiseach, Seán Lemass, was not interested in the issue.[49]

In 1967 a majority of members of the Informal Committee on the
Constitution criticized the Seanad but recognized that it had public
support. They could suggest no reformulation of its powers that would
be compatible with responsible government. For example, they specifically rejected direct elections for senators: "We feel . . . that, whatever Constitutional provisions may be enacted to the contrary, there is
always the possibility of conflict arising when each of the two different
houses of the legislature is elected directly by the people, and thus in a
position to claim an equal mandate."[50] They rejected a system of rotation, with half the Seanad elected at each election, because the chamber
might not adequately reflect changes in popular opinion, and this
"could, possibly, give rise to a situation in which the two houses of the
legislature find themselves frequently at loggerheads."[51] They rejected

any strengthening of vocationalism in the Senate: "We think it is necessary always to guard against any suggestion that the members of the
Seanad should not be in the fullest sense politicians rather than delegates of particular interests in the national life."[52] And finally, when
considering Article 19 of the constitution, which provided that vocational groups might be given the power to elect members of the Seanad,
the committee concluded, "We are unanimous in the view that all suggestions of this kind should be rejected, mainly on the ground that if
such an arrangement were introduced the political parties would find
it necessary to take a much greater interest in the internal affairs of the
Nominating Bodies."[53]

The Seanad Electoral Law Commission had come to quite the opposite conclusion in 1961, as did Fine Gael in its reform proposals of
1990.[54] Indeed, Fine Gael proposed to make Seanad reform a major
priority when it returns to government, arguing that "Fianna Fáil has
consistently failed to recognize the potential of the Seanad and through
failure of leadership has prevented the Seanad from developing the distinctive role which is one of the main reasons for the existence of Upper
Houses."[55] The Progressive Democrats, on the other hand, have proposed that the Seanad be abolished.[56]

## Party Government

Parties are necessary in responsible government. In the Republic of
Ireland, for example, they offer candidates for election to the Oireachtas and structure the electorate so that a vote for a Dáil candidate ex-
presses a preference for a government. In the Dáil party discipline is
essential if governments are to be formed and are to survive. The need
for discipline in the government party or parties conditions the behavior of the major opposition parties too. With few exceptions, as during
the period 1987 to 1989, when Fine Gael adopted the "Tallaght Strategy," which required it to support the government during a period of
severe national economic difficulty, the major opposition parties oppose the government in a vigorous way on the presumption that a government that cannot supply its own majority should make way for one
that can.

Adversarial politics in the Dáil actually conceals a degree of cooperation behind the scenes that indicates acceptance of certain rules of parliamentary behavior. Because opposition leaders are the government-

in-waiting, there is a degree of self-interested reciprocity in their relationship with the sitting government. In particular, they accept the idea that a government that has the support of a majority must be permitted to govern, after an appropriate period of opposition harassment, and they expect the same courtesy when they enter government themselves. Government and opposition leaders therefore collaborate in scheduling Dáil business so that the government can complete its agenda while allowing the opposition recognized opportunities to attack. Furthermore, in recognition of their role in the governing process, allowances are provided to all the major parties to pay for administration and research. In 1992 Fianna Fáil received Ir£ 125,130, Fine Gael received Ir£ 248,205, and Labour received Ir£ 123,313.[57] The governing party, Fianna Fáil, received proportionately less because the civil service provides ministers with administrative and policy support. Minor parties with fewer than seven seats and independents receive no special support, although they may hold the balance in the Dáil.

Each party requires its candidates for the Dáil to sign a pledge to support the party, and both Fianna Fáil and Labour deputies agree to resign their seats if so instructed by the National Executive.[58] Members are not precisely instructed on how to vote in the Dáil, but they understand that membership in the parliamentary party can be withdrawn if they deviate from the party line, and this will cost them the party's endorsement at the following general election. Late in 1986, as his government was threatened by the defection of a number of deputies, Taoiseach FitzGerald announced that any Fine Gael deputy who did not obey the party whip would not be ratified as a party candidate at the next general election.[59] Expulsions by a party are rare, but not unknown. Indeed, Desmond O'Malley formed the Progressive Democratic party after being expelled from Fianna Fáil in 1984.[60] Fine Gael and Labour have both recognized that a member may vote his conscience, rather than the party line, on certain issues, the 1974 bill permitting the importation and sale of contraceptives, for example, but Fianna Fáil, with occasional exceptions, has resisted this concession.[61]

A party's firm hold on deputies is illustrated by the behavior of ministers forced out of government. In 1970 two Fianna Fáil Cabinet ministers, Charles Haughey and Neil Blaney, were dismissed by the Taoiseach, Jack Lynch, for their alleged roles in importing arms for use in Northern Ireland. Three other ministers resigned. When the opposition moved a vote of no confidence in the Taoiseach for his handling of the arms affair, he won only because the former ministers voted for him.[62] As the *Irish Times* of 11 May 1970 reported, "The name of the game was survival." More recently, in October 1990, Taoiseach Charles Haughey won a confidence vote by three votes on the issue of his dismissal of the Tánaiste, Brian Lenihan, and both Lenihan and his sister, Deputy Mary O'Rourke, voted with the government.[63]

In Ireland the government is only responsible to Dáil Éireann but the atmosphere of party competition extends to every level of electoral politics, including the Seanad. It begins, of course, with the President's eleven appointees, whose primary purpose is to ensure that the government can control the upper house, but it extends to the forty-three elected vocational senators too. They may be nominated by any four members of the Oireachtas or by registered vocational nominating bodies, of which there were seventy-two in 1982.[64] The Oireachtas part of this nominating process is highly partisan, of course, but partisanship has also infiltrated the nominating bodies. Furthermore, the electorate for these seats comprises members of the Oireachtas and local governments, who are themselves highly partisan. J. J. Lee concludes, "'Vocationalism' was left to the tender mercies of party politicians. The designated electorate took to its task with a will. Genuine vocational representatives were swamped beneath the avalanche of party loyalists."[65] The Commission on Vocational Organization found as early as 1943 that those involved in the Seanad nominating process "tend to nominate not those who are most eminent in their professions or calling, but those who are most likely to be acceptable to the political parties."[66] In October 1944 Dr. T. F. O'Higgins, the Fine Gael leader, described the system as "a mere sham and humbug" because the Seanad electors "are the most politically minded electorate that it would be possible to get in this country."[67] And James Dillon of Fine Gael insisted that "the present Seanad has been used for the purpose of shameless jobbery."[68]

The constitution made the election of the President a party political matter too. A candidate for the presidency, other than an incumbent who nominates himself, as Patrick Hillery did in 1983, has to be nominated by twenty or more members of the Oireachtas or four or more county or county borough councils. The process is likely to be dominated by party considerations.[69] Fianna Fáil downplayed partisanship when it nominated the founder of the Gaelic League, Douglas Hyde, who was unopposed for the presidency,[70] but between 1945 and 1990 every President was a former Fianna Fáil party politician. The fact that Presidents O'Kelly in 1952, Ó Dálaigh in 1974, and Hillery, in 1976 and 1983, were unopposed indicates that Fine Gael knew it could not win. The four contested elections held before 1990 were won by Fianna Fáil candidates: Seán T. O'Kelly in 1945, Eamon de Valera in 1959 and 1966, and Erskine Childers in 1973.[71] Only in the 1990 election was Fianna Fáil's hold on the presidency broken, by the Labour-supported candidate, Mary Robinson. She lost to Fianna Fáil's Brian Lenihan on the first count and won on the second count with the redistributed votes of the third candidate, Fine Gael's Austin Currie (see Table 12.5 for a detailed picture of the election results). Her victory also owed a great deal to a scandal, discussed below, that engulfed the Fianna Fáil candidate in the last month of the campaign.

The 1990 election campaign provided ammunition for those who believe that the popular election of the President politicizes an office that should be nonpartisan.[72] The election became a plebiscite on the government, and by embroiling the presidency in matters that it cannot affect it did the office a great disservice. Robinson spoke harshly, for example, of the "grinding and humiliating poverty" in Ireland, and of the need to protect the environment, neither of which she can affect in any appreciable way as President.[73] But unless the system of presidential selection is changed, the temptation will always exist to include the President in partisan politics.

## Cabinet Government

The 1937 constitution assigns greater responsibilities to the head of government than did the 1922 Irish constitution but it also speaks more often of the government, the Cabinet, as a collective body than did its predecessor, and to a very considerable degree collective government is

TABLE 12.5.
Presidential Election Results, 1990

| First Count | | Second Count | |
| --- | --- | --- | --- |
| Lenihan | 44.1% | Robinson | 52.6% |
| Robinson | 38.9% | Lenihan | 47.2% |
| Currie | 17.0% | | |

Source: Irish Times, 10 November 1990.

practiced.[74] The Irish government has never used committees to the degree that they are used in Britain, where they make most decisions on behalf of the full Cabinet, although Garret FitzGerald records that he sat on three committees during the 1973–77 coalition, the Economic, Social, and Education Committees, and he attended the Security Committee whenever an external issue was being discussed.[75] Nonetheless, most matters are decided by the full government, which makes for overloaded agendas at the two meetings it holds each week.[76]

A number of the constitution's provisions on the government's collective powers were drawn from the 1922 constitution, including Article 28.4.2°: "The Government shall meet and act as a collective authority, and shall be collectively responsible for the Departments of State administered by the members of the Government." As in 1922, appropriations may only be recommended to Dáil Éireann by the government, although it no longer has to use the Governor-General as a conduit,[77] and the government must submit estimates of department receipts and expenditures each financial year to Dáil Éireann.[78] Judges are appointed on the advice of the government.[79]

Government powers that are mentioned for the first time in 1937 generally fill constitutional gaps left by the elimination of the Crown in 1936 and the introduction of the President in 1937. Articles 13.9 and 13.11, for example, require the President to act on the advice of the government in all matters other than those specifically identified as being at his or her discretion. It is the government that permits the President to leave the state[80] and address a message to the nation,[81] and the government that recommends that the period for the Senate's consideration of a bill should be abridged by the President because of some public emergency.[82] The executive power of the state in external relations is vested in the government,[83] rather than the Crown, and while only Dáil Éireann may declare war, the government is empowered to act if an invasion of Ireland occurs before such a declaration.[84]

The constitution recognizes the collective responsibility of ministers to the Dáil, but the Ministers and Secretaries Act of 1924 recognizes each minister as an individual "corporation sole," which David Gwynn Morgan describes as "an artificial legal entity distinct from the holder of the office."[85] The minister is not only the head of the department, but as a corporation sole personifies the department in law. T. J. Barrington writes that "the legal personality is the Minister and the department is no more than the legal extension of that personality."[86] It is also the practice in Ireland, as in Britain, for the minister to represent his or her department in the Dáil, at Question Time, for example, and in debates. The 1937 constitution contains no equivalent of Article 56 of the Free State constitution, that each minister is individually as well as collectively responsible to the Dáil, and it remains an open question, because untested, whether the Dáil can force an individual minister to resign by a personal vote of no confidence. But as Chubb realistically points out, "The truth is that a Minister can be forced to resign by the Dáil only if the government or the Taoiseach with government support decides to abandon him."[87]

In practice the combination of collective responsibility, ministerial responsibility, and corporation sole has the effect of erecting a formidable barrier between the legislature and the government. Both the Oireachtas and the public are denied access to government deliberations on the ground that knowledge of internal divisions would undermine collective responsibility. It was established in 1922 that collective responsibility requires all government decisions to be presented publicly as if taken unanimously, and in 1924 that the details of government discussions would not be released to the Dáil.[88] Since then many ministers have resigned because of differences with the government they could not express while in office. In 1983 government secrecy was formalized in the fourth edition of *Government Procedure Instructions*. After each meeting of the government a designated minister briefs the government Press Secretary on what can be released to the press.[89]

The government is determined to defend its secrecy. When a former minister, Raymond Burke, was questioned about government discussions during a judicial inquiry into the beef processing industry in July 1992, the chairman of the tribunal, Mr. Justice Hamilton, ruled that Burke should answer, but the government challenged the ruling in the Supreme Court and won. The Court, in a three-to-two ruling which seriously hampered the work of the tribunal, stated: "The members of Government must meet and act as a collective authority. This involves an obligation to accept collective responsibility for decisions, and the non-disclosure of dissenting or different views of members of Government prior to the making of decisions."[90]

On at least one occasion, a government appears to have waived confidentiality. The *Irish Times* of 27 August 1992 reported that the Fianna Fáil–Progressive Democrat government of Charles Haughey chose not to block the publication of Gemma Hussey's diaries, *At the*

*Cutting Edge: Cabinet Diaries, 1982–87* (Dublin: Gill and Macmillan, 1990), although Hussey was a minister in FitzGerald's Fine Gael–Labour coalition and her diaries describe Cabinet proceedings. Ireland has now entered the age of political memoirs, which may put some strain upon the principle of Cabinet confidentiality.

Ministerial responsibility and corporation sole are also used to shield the civil service from public scrutiny, something the civil service values highly. Government departments speak and act in the name of the minister, and civil servants are free only to represent official department policy at committee hearings. Ireland therefore shares with other parliamentary systems a powerful tradition of civil service secrecy, reinforced in 1963 by the adoption of the Official Secrets Act, which prohibits civil servants from unofficially communicating official information.[91]. The corollary to shielding the civil service is that ministers have a virtual monopoly on information and support from the departments they head, a powerful weapon in their dealings with the legislature and the public.

The power of the government is particularly evident in its control of the Dáil agenda. Standing Order 25 permits the Taoiseach to determine the order in which government business shall be taken each day, and Standing Order 86 allows a minister to move, without notice, that a private member's time be preempted by government business.[92] Such business therefore dominates the agenda. Government bills may originate in a party's electoral program or with a minister, but many originate in the civil service, which plays a vital role in identifying problems and options. It consults with outside experts and interest groups, and drafts the bills.[93] The initiating department will have to clear each bill with the Department of Finance and other affected departments. By the time a bill arrives in the Dáil for the first time, therefore, most of its features will have been decided within the executive, and while the time table for its consideration is usually set by agreement with the opposition, the government can use its majority to vote to "guillotine," which sets a time limit for debate, or vote closure, which immediately ends debate on a measure.[94] It is clear, therefore, that the Dáil—which encounters legislation very late in the legislative process, operates under tight party discipline, and is restricted by standing orders—can never do more than influence legislation on the margins.

Department estimates of receipts and expenditures for each financial year are similarly dominated by the government and the civil service.

Article 17.1.2° of the constitution, copied from Article 36 of the Free State constitution, requires the Oireachtas to approve department estimates within the year of the expenditure, and the Central Fund (Temporary Provisions) Act of 1965 allows a minister to spend up to 80 percent of the previous year's appropriation before the vote. The financial year is always well under way, therefore, before estimates are brought in for votes, between March and June, and only after the estimates are approved does the Oireachtas pass an appropriations bill.[95] Most estimates receive no parliamentary discussion at all, and as Collins and McCann have noted, "Once the cabinet and civil servants, working in confidence, have arrived at a pattern of expenditure and taxation involving intense bargaining and compromise, it is difficult to find room for significant adjustments."[96]

Article 17.2, reinforced by Standing Orders 122 to 125, provides that money bills may only be presented to the Dáil by the government. Other kinds of legislation may be introduced by the government or nongovernment deputies, but the latter are rarely successful. Private members' bills occupy only a few hours of debate a week, and this time can be preempted by government business on the motion of a minister.[97] Dáil standing orders require that a private member's bill must have seven sponsors, which gives control of the very limited time to the front benches of the major opposition parties, much to the annoyance of independents and small parties. Proinsias de Rossa of the Workers party, now leader of the Democratic Left, complained in 1983: "Private members' time is regarded as the preserve of the major party in Opposition. In the last Dáil it was the preserve of Fine Gael and Labour. Neither Independents nor Workers' party Deputies were allowed [to] initiate motions for Private Members' Time."[98]

Each party may move only one private member's bill at a time, and debate on the second stage is limited to six hours, after which the government will, except in the rarest of cases, defeat the measure. Fine Gael's proposal in 1989, the Judicial Separation and Family Law Reform Act, which provided for judicial separation in a marriage that has broken down irretrievably, was an exception. Between 1937 and 1991 only eight private members' bills became law.[99]

Perhaps the best-known parliamentary instrument available to the ordinary deputy in the Dáil is Question Time, but although a minister's reputation can be helped or harmed by this ritual, it does little to make the government accountable to the Dáil and is not available in the

Seanad. An hour and a quarter each sitting day is reserved for questions to ministers, with questions to the Taoiseach having priority on Tuesday and Wednesday. Other ministers are questioned in rotation, generally one per day, so that they each appear approximately every five weeks. "Priority questions" may be asked by a deputy representing a "group," in practice a front-bench opposition leader. Dáil standing orders require that a question must be "to elicit information upon or to elucidate matters of fact or policy," and must relate to the business of a minister's department. It cannot deal with, among other matters, the advice given to a minister by civil servants, interdepartment communications, or matters affecting the conduct of state-sponsored bodies. There is nothing in standing orders to compel ministers to reply, but they do, orally, or in writing if there is insufficient time. Unless recognized as urgent by the Chairman, questions are asked with three working days notice for priority questions, and four for nonpriority questions, so that when called by the Chairman to reply, the minister has been well prepared to read, usually monotonously, a reply prepared by civil servants. Supplementary questions may be asked at the discretion of the Chairman, but they can be answered evasively by all but the most inept minister.[100]

It also has to be said that deputies do not make the best use of Question Time. Opposition deputies often use questions to club ministers verbally while government backbenchers lob friendly questions designed to present the government in a favorable light. Furthermore, a great many questions deal with detailed constituency problems that could be dealt with quite effectively by phone calls or letters to a department. They serve primarily to show constituents that their deputies are on the job in Dublin.[101] By far the largest number of questions is directed to the Minister for Local Government and the Environment.[102]

Question Time aside, there are a few other opportunities for deputies to challenge the government. There are, for example, brief opportunities prior to the adjournment each day during which members can raise issues, and ministers can reply, but no votes are taken. There is a provision for special hour-and-a-half adjournment debates on matters of urgency, but the Chairman interprets "urgent" very narrowly and few such debates are permitted.[103] Richard Humphreys has recently written of a number of procedural ways deputies can obstruct business in the Dáil—challenges to the order of business, adjournment motions, quorum calls, and so on—but the government invariably prevails in the end, and obstruction is rarely constructive.[104]

Government dominance is clearly established by the constitution and reinforced by standing orders, but it is also powerfully affected by the composition of the government benches in the Dáil. Fifteen ministers, all but 2 of whom must sit in the Dáil, and 15 Parliamentary Secretaries supply the solid core of the government's votes in a chamber of only 166 members. Furthermore, backbenchers are fully aware that their promotion into government depends on their compliant behavior in the Dáil. Although party meetings are held every one to two weeks during the session, to which deputies, senators, and members of the European Parliament are invited, the Taoiseach's patronage power and the need for party discipline gives the government an enormous advantage.[105]

Two other characteristics of Irish politics might be cited as contributing to the dominance of the government: the facilities available to members of the Dáil and "clientalism." First, deputies do not have the resources with which to compete with the government in the power stakes. Until 1975 deputies had no secretaries. That year they were assigned one per seven deputies, and in 1981 one each, but this secretary is the sum of a deputy's personal staff. Furthermore, until 1983 there were very few committees in the Oireachtas in which members could become experts in a particular subject field or contribute to framing legislation. The committee system will be discussed at length in the final chapter; it is enough to say at this point that despite the establishment of many new committees in recent years, they have not substantially changed the distribution of power between the government and the legislature.

Second, Irish politicians have what has been called a "clientalist" or "brokerage" view of their roles. Deputies spend enormous amounts of time acting as brokers by interceding with the civil service, or in Chubb's pejorative phrase, "persecuting civil servants,"[106] on behalf of constituents in order to win votes. Lee Komito concludes that election rhetoric revolves around special influence and past favors, as politicians compete to encourage voters to believe that a politician's assistance is the best guarantee of receiving state benefits.[107] He found that 60 percent of a sample of voters from Dublin saw brokerage as more important than policymaking by deputies, although only 17 percent had actually contacted a politician for assistance. Significantly, he found "the greater the need for state services, the greater the dependence on politicians as brokers."[108] The bulk of deputies' attention is focused on the Department of Social Welfare, which accounts for more than 25 percent of current government spending. It receives about forty thousand representations from deputies each year, and answers about four thousand parliamentary questions.[109]

Deputy Michael Keating confessed in 1983, "The majority of the letters that all of us write amount to no more than our participating in a massive deceit on the public—that we are engaged in some type of procurement of an advantage for them which otherwise would not come their way."[110] But in a study of Galway, Valerie Kelly confirms Komito's finding that those most in need of help from the state turn to local deputies when state agencies fail them, and the deputy's intervention produces substantial results.[111] There is a substantial opportunity cost, however. Deputies do not have much time for other things. Basil Chubb concludes:

The poor performance of the Oireachtas arises partly because it is badly equipped and poorly informed. But more fundamentally, poor performance results from, firstly, a general acceptance by members of the dominant role of the government as policy maker, and, second, the preoccupation of many members with their own local positions.[112]

Governments are not equally powerful, of course, and coalitions put considerable strain on government unity. In the multiparty governments of 1948 to 1951 and of 1954 to 1957, for example, open votes, without party discipline, were sometimes allowed in the Dáil to keep the government intact.[113] The Fine Gael–Labour coalitions of more recent years were more cohesive, although Garret FitzGerald points out that meetings of his governments were often long and tedious because of the need to bring both coalition parties into agreement.[114] During Cosgrave's coalition government in 1974, a free vote had to be called on the Control, Importation, Sale and Manufacture of Contraceptives Bill, which was introduced by the Minister of Justice, Patrick Cooney, as a private member's bill, but the disagreements were not interparty. The Taoiseach, Liam Cosgrave, joined six Fine Gael colleagues in voting against the measure, with no warning to his colleagues. Garret FitzGerald writes that this "caused a sensation and damaged the Government." He adds, "Our insistence that it was not a Government Bill binding all Government Ministers in collective responsibility was regarded as sophistry, and we were accused of having thrown this crucial constitutional doctrine overboard."[115] A more reasonable interpretation of what happened is that a new constitutional convention emerged: the rule in Article 28.4.2°, "The Government shall meet and act as a collective authority," does not apply in a free vote on a private member's bill.

It is clear that the 1989–92 Fianna Fáil–Progressive Democrat coalition was a particularly stormy one. The partners differed on several items of policy. The Progressive Democrats, for example, favored eliminating Articles 2 and 3 and the prohibition of divorce from the constitution, policies that Taoiseach Haughey would not concede.[116] As a measure to control AIDS, the Progressive Democrats favored making condoms available to men as young as sixteen, but Fianna Fáil took a more conservative approach to sexual hygiene.[117] At the Progressive Democrat's annual conference in April 1991, Desmond O'Malley criticized his own government's policy on taxes and spending, and in the summer of 1992 he took the witness stand at a judicial inquiry into the beef processing industry to criticize the Taoiseach, Albert Reynolds, for failing to fulfill his statutory duties as Minister for Industry and Commerce in 1987 and 1988.[118] Finally, having forced Tánaiste Lenihan out of office in 1990 and Taoiseach Haughey out in February 1992, the Progressive Democrat ministers brought the government down by resigning in November 1992. In the Dáil confidence debate O'Malley argued that he and his colleagues had been forced to resign by Fianna Fáil's refusal to consult them and by public criticism of O'Malley by the Taoiseach. For his part, the Taoiseach appeared relieved that the coalition was over and pointedly argued that coalitions do not work if the junior partner holds the senior to ransom.

These examples make it obvious that coalition government puts great strain on Article 28.4.2°, which requires the government to "meet and act as a collective authority," but while the result is a government weaker than might otherwise be, no other institution, the Dáil for example, is empowered as a result.

## A Strong Prime Minister

It was clear to the opposition parties in 1937 that de Valera was proposing to create a Prime Minister with substantially more authority than the President of the Executive Council had exercised under the 1922 constitution, and this aroused their suspicions. They would have been even more alarmed had they seen an early draft of the Taoiseach's powers, which de Valera rejected: "The [Prime Minister] shall exercise a general authority over all Departments of State and the Minister in charge of any Department of State shall report to the Prime Minister as and whenever desired by him so to do on any matter relating to the administration of such Department."[119] This, at least, was abandoned in favor of collective supervision, but the role of the Prime Minister was strengthened in 1937 and this was reflected in the attention de Valera paid to finding a new Irish name for the office.

Under the 1922 constitution, the Prime Minister, the President of the Executive Council, was known in Irish as Uachtarán,[120] but this title was transferred to the President of Ireland in the 1937 constitution. For Prime Minister de Valera could have taken Príomh-Aire from the 1919 Dáil, or Árd-Aire, which was used in early drafts of the new constitution. *Aire*, meaning nobleman, denotes minister, and *Príomh* and *Árd* are prefixes denoting high or first. But de Valera wanted to be more than "first" or "high" minister. He settled on *Taoiseach*, which is Irish for chieftain or captain, and both the Irish and English versions of the constitution require that the Príomh-Aire, translated as Prime Minister, shall be called Taoiseach.[121]

De Valera was not seeking glory for himself in the title. It actually reflects the primacy de facto of the Prime Minister in 1937, but there were some in the press who hoped that Taoiseach Costello would cease to use the title when he took office in 1948 because it was reminiscent of such discredited foreign titles as "Duce," "Führer," and "Caudillo." "Quidnunc," writing in the *Irish Times* on 30 March 1948, noted that when the Lord Mayor of Dublin addressed Costello as "Prime Minister" at the opening of a new cinema, "A woman in the audience . . . remarked, 'Sure they couldn't call him Taoiseach or everybody would think it was Dev they meant.' "[122] But the Irish title was not abandoned and it is used exclusively in Ireland today, by speakers in Irish and in English.

Several provisions relating to the Prime Minister were carried over from Article 53 of the 1922 constitution. The Taoiseach is appointed on the nomination of Dáil Éireann and the survival of the government is personalized because the Taoiseach must resign upon ceasing to retain the support of a majority of Dáil Éireann. Once he resigns, the other members of the government are deemed to have resigned too.[123] The Taoiseach nominates fellow members of the government, with the approval of the Dáil,[124] and in practice he also identifies the ministers' portfolios when seeking this approval. The creation of departments is formally decided by the Oireachtas, in ordinary law,[125] but the Taoiseach makes ministerial assignments. He usually operates with some restraints, of course. In a coalition, some ministers will be chosen by agreement with the leader of the coalition partners, and even when a single-party government is formed there are party leaders who cannot be ignored by the Taoiseach and geographical areas he will often try to represent. In the end, however, the nominations are his to make, and they give him extraordinary influence.

The 1937 constitution departs from its predecessor in three very important respects concerning the Prime Minister, two of which were recommended by the Amendments to the Constitution Committee in 1927, but not acted upon.[126] First, the Taoiseach may request a minister to resign "at any time, for reasons which to him seem sufficient," or have him dismissed by the President if he fails to comply.[127] Fine Gael and the Labour party both attacked this provision in 1937 because it violated the spirit of collective responsibility. John Costello of Fine Gael complained of "the very humiliating position" of the government under the constitution,[128] and William Norton, the leader of the Labour party, described the provision as "calculated to make yes-men out of the . . . Government"[129] because every minister would serve at the Taoiseach's pleasure. They preferred the 1922 constitution which did not allow the President of the Executive Council to dismiss ministers, and therefore permitted them to oppose him in the Council without fear of reprisal.

De Valera's own experience taught him otherwise. He insisted that the responsibility of a head of government is to assemble ministers who can work as a team, and to do that he must be able to dismiss those who do not fit. In the Dáil he denied that a Taoiseach would act capriciously: "He is not dealing with children. . . . Do you think it would be possible for a Taoiseach, in a purely arbitrary way, to compel the resignation of a member unless there was concurrence on the part of the other members of the Government? Of course it would be impossible."[130]

Since 1937 no Taoiseach has used his powers to dismiss a minister in an indefensible way, although dismissals are often controversial. For example, Charles Haughey and Neil Blaney were dismissed by Taoiseach Jack Lynch in 1970 because of suspicions that they were involved in a scheme to supply arms to nationalists in Northern Ireland. Brian Lenihan, the Tánaiste, was dismissed by Haughey in 1990 at the insistence of Fianna Fáil's coalition partners, the Progressive Democrats, because of an incident during the 1990 presidential election (discussed below).[131] Albert Reynolds and Pádraig Flynn were dismissed by Haughey for opposing his leadership in a vote of Fianna Fáil deputies.

The second new power recommended by the Amendments to the Constitution Committee in 1927 and adopted in 1937 is the Taoiseach's power to advise the President to dissolve the Dáil, even if he has lost the support of the majority. The convention in Britain and elsewhere is that the Prime Minister may secure a dissolution at any time, but as we saw earlier, the Provisional government believed such a power was open to abuse.[132] Article 53 of the 1922 constitution specifically denied the right to a dissolution to the President of an Executive Council who had ceased to retain the support of a majority in Dáil Éireann. It was left to the Dáil to elect a new President without an intervening election. In 1927 the Amendments to the Constitution Committee saw the weakness in this arrangement: the Dáil might be unable to agree on a new President following a vote of no confidence. The committee recommended that a defeated President should have a qualified right to a dissolution. He should be permitted to ask for a dissolution but it could be denied by the Governor-General at the request of both houses of the Oireachtas.[133] That is to say, the Oireachtas might insist that an alternative government was available. This proposal was not accepted, but Article 13.2.2° of the 1937 constitution uses the President of Ireland to accomplish a similar end. It allows a Taoiseach who has lost his majority to advise a dissolution but allows the President to refuse, "in his absolute discretion." In other words, if the President concludes that an alternative government can, and should, be formed without a general election, he can deny the dissolution and call upon the Dáil to elect a new Taoiseach.

This article was thought to have given the President a significant power, but, as we shall see in the discussion of the President, this has not been the case. No Taoiseach, having lost a vote in the Dáil, has ever been denied a dissolution by a President. Indeed, it is believed by some that a dissolution should only be denied in some dire emergency.[134]

The third new provision on the Taoiseach adopted in 1937, one not recommended by the Amendments to the Constitution Committee, is the personal right of a Taoiseach who retains the support of a majority in the Dáil to advise the President to dissolve the Dáil. In the Free State constitution this power was vested in the Executive Council collectively.

In addition to the Taoiseach's powers in the constitution, which are formidable, he derives power from the fact that he controls the agenda of government meetings and his department provides the government secretariat, preparing agendas, serving committees, and overseeing the implementation of policy. A number of agencies also report to the Department of the Taoiseach, including the National Museum, the National Library, Government Information Services, and the National Economic and Social Council. The Fianna Fáil Taoiseach has had two Ministers of State to assist him, one of whom serves as government Chief Whip with responsibility for managing government business in the Dáil.

A number of circumstances have combined to strengthen the hand of the Taoiseach within the government since the 1970s. These include the strong personalities of Charles Haughey and Garret FitzGerald; the economic crisis that overcame the country in the 1980s, which required the Taoiseach's close supervision; the new prominence of the Taoiseach as a European Community head of government; and his special role in British–Irish negotiations and Northern Ireland policy.[135]

Finally, we must recognize that the Taoiseach is a party leader, the President of a national party organization with its attendant powers and visibility. In a television age, elections are personalized as trials of strength between party leaders, and although the annual conference of the party, the Ard Fhéis, is formally the party's supreme policymaking body, in practice it is the occasion for demonstrations of loyalty to the party leader.[136]

The party leader is elected by members of the Dáil, in the case of Fianna Fáil and Labour, and by members of the Dáil and the Seanad in the case of Fine Gael, but procedures for deposing leaders are less clear. Since 1971 Fine Gael has selected, or reselected, a leader within two months of a general election, unless the party has entered government. Fianna Fáil and Labour have no rules for reselection, but three attempts were made by Fianna Fáil deputies to vote Haughey out of office in 1982 and 1983, and another in 1991, all unsuccessful.[137]

## A Weak Head of State

De Valera described the new office of President of Éire as heir to the "rightful chiefs" of Ireland,[138] but he gave the title Taoiseach, or Chief, to the Prime Minister. The Irish President's powers are very limited, though they are substantially more in practice than those of the British Sovereign or her/his Governors-General.

The Taoiseach is required to inform the President on matters of domestic and international policy,[139] but what this means in practice is unclear. Taoiseach Haughey told the Dáil, "It would not be appropriate—nor would it be in keeping with the dignity of the office—to give precise details."[140] Joe Carroll of the *Irish Times* reports that the Taoiseach met President de Valera monthly during de Valera's two terms as President, but Taoiseach Liam Cosgrave saw President Ó Dálaigh only four times in two years.[141] Taoiseach Reynolds reportedly briefs President Robinson every five weeks or so.[142] The President has no legal recourse should the Taoiseach decide to communicate little or nothing, and the President has no right to see confidential government papers.

The President has three classes of powers. In the first class, identified in Article 13, the President is specifically directed to act in certain matters on the advice of the Taoiseach, the Government, the Dáil, or as specified by law. The most important is that the President must appoint the Taoiseach on the nomination of Dáil Éireann, and appoint ministers on the Taoiseach's nomination. The President also summons and dissolves Dáil Éireann on the advice of the Taoiseach and may communicate with the Oireachtas or the nation, "on a matter of national or public importance," only with the approval of the government, a provision which de Valera believed would enable the government to present an important message to the people in a nonpartisan fashion.[143] The constitution does not address the limits, if any, on the President's freedom to address audiences other than the Oireachtas or the nation, but in practice all the President's major speeches are cleared by the government. The President appoints the Attorney General on the advice of the Taoiseach,[144] and the Comptroller and Auditor-General on the advice of Dáil Éireann.[145] The President is also Supreme Commander of the Defence Forces, as regulated by law, now the Defence Act of 1954.[146]

In the second class of presidential powers, most of which are also stated in Article 13, there is no specific requirement that the President must act on advice but the powers are all governed by two general rules, stated in Articles 13.9 and 13.11. Article 13.9 provides that, with the exception of certain discretionary powers, the President's constitutional powers "shall be exercisable and performable by him only on the advice of the Government." For example, the President signs and promulgates laws, pardons criminals, commutes or remits sentences for criminal offenses, and appoints judges.[147] Article 13.11 was added during the Dáil debate on the constitution when it was noticed that new presidential powers might be created under Article 13.10 that would not be regulated by Article 13.9, which only speaks of powers conferred by the constitution. Members of the opposition, suspicious of de Valera, argued that new, and even dictatorial, powers might be conferred on the President by law that would not be subject to the advice of the Dáil or the government.[148] It would be, said Deputy Costello, of Fine Gael, "a very serious menace in the future."[149] De Valera thought this absurd. He foresaw only very limited uses for Article 13.10, to empower the President to appoint visitors to new universities, for example,[150] but he had already taken steps to draft what became Article 13.11 to quell the fears.[151] The article reads, "No power or function conferred on the President by law shall be exercisable or performable by him save only on the advice of the Government."

The third class of presidential powers lies within the discretion of the President. There are seven of these; as de Valera explained to the Dáil, they require the President to be "an umpire, so to speak, to see that the Lower House acts in accordance with the spirit of the constitution."[152] They are designed, he said, "to guard the people's rights and . . . the constitution."[153] Five of these powers are exercisable only after consultation with the Council of State, but the President is not bound by its advice. The Council was established by Article 31 "to aid and counsel" the President. It has a number of statutory members: Taoiseach, Tánaiste, Chief Justice, President of the High Court, Chairmen of Dáil Éireann and Seanad Éireann, Attorney General, and "every person able and willing to act" who has held office as Taoiseach or Chief Justice. The President may also appoint up to seven members at his or her absolute discretion, and may convene the Council "at such times and places" as he or she shall determine.

The five powers that require prior consultation with the Council of State are as follows. First, the President may, at any time, convene a meeting of either or both of the Houses of the Oireachtas.[154] Second, at the request of the Taoiseach and the Dáil, the President may, in the interests of public peace and security, abridge the maximum period provided in the constitution for the Seanad to consider a bill.[155] Third, there is a procedure by which one-third of the Seanad may challenge the certification of a money bill by the Chairman of the Dáil and it is the President's responsibility to decide if a Committee of Privileges should be appointed to rule on the challenge.[156] Fourth, if a bill becomes law over the objections of the Senate, the President may call for a referendum on the measure at the request of a majority of the Senate and not less than one-third of the Dáil.[157] Fifth, the President may test the constitutionality of a bill by referring it to the Supreme Court before adding his or her signature. This provision does not apply to money bills, bills to amend the constitution, or bills sent to the Seanad under the abridged procedure for reasons of public peace and security.[158]

The President has only two powers that are exercisable at his or her "absolute discretion," that is to say, without advice and without consulting the Council of State. The first, of course, is to appoint up to seven members of the Council of State.[159] The second is to dissolve, or refuse to dissolve, the Dáil on the advice of a President who has lost the support of a majority in Dáil Éireann.[160]

It is to the third class of powers, the seven discretionary powers, that we must look for evidence of the President's independent authority. Three have never been invoked, because the President has to respond to requests from others that have never been made. These are to abridge the Seanad's time to consider a bill, to appoint a Committee of Privileges to consider a challenge to the certification of a money bill, and to call a referendum on a bill passed by the Oireachtas.

The President has exercised four discretionary powers. First, the President has, of course, routinely appointed members to the Council of State. Second, the power to call the houses of the Oireachtas into session has been used once, to convene a purely ceremonial joint session on the occasion of the fiftieth anniversary of the first Dáil, in January 1969. It is difficult to imagine a contingency in which the President would summon either house without advice, or what might be accomplished in such a session. The third and fourth powers are much more significant. The third is the President's power to refer Oireachtas bills to the Supreme Court for constitutional rulings under Article 26.1.1°, and the fourth is his or her discretion to grant a dissolution at the request of a Taoiseach who has lost his majority, under Article 13.2.2°.

The President had referred eight bills to the Supreme Court by 1992, beginning with President Hyde in 1940, and on three occasions the Court found a bill to be unconstitutional.[161] One of these referrals provoked the only moment of real tension between a government and a President and led to the resignation of President Cearbhall Ó Dálaigh in 1976.

At a time of many I.R.A. attacks in the Republic of Ireland in 1976, which included the murder of the British Ambassador, Christopher Ewart-Biggs, the Fine Gael–Labour coalition of Liam Cosgrave secured passage of the Emergency Powers Bill, which President Ó Dálaigh referred to the Supreme Court for an opinion.[162] The President was an experienced lawyer, having served as Fianna Fáil Attorney General, Chief Justice of the Irish Supreme Court, and member of the European Court of Justice, but speaking in Mullingar on 18 October 1976, Patrick Donegan, the Minister for Defence, described Ó Dálaigh as "a thundering disgrace" for his action. Ó Dálaigh treated the insult as an attack on the office of President by a member of the government. Donegan quickly offered his resignation to the Taoiseach, Liam Cosgrave, who refused it and advised Donegan to apologize to the President instead. This Donegan did, abjectly, but Ó Dálaigh would accept nothing but a resignation. On 21 October Fianna Fáil moved a motion in the Dáil calling for Donegan's resignation. It was defeated by a vote of sixty-three to fifty-eight, which the President took to mean that the Dáil had taken sides against him. He decided to resign, and by the time Cosgrave accepted Donegan's resignation, on 22 October, Ó Dálaigh had submitted his own resignation.[163]

The crisis had been unnecessary. The Supreme Court found the bill to be constitutional. Donegan had spoken rashly and was right to offer his resignation. Cosgrave should have accepted the resignation and the Dáil should never have been placed in a position in which a partisan vote of confidence in a minister could be interpreted as a vote of no confidence in the President. In the aftermath, the coalition government accepted Fianna Fáil's nominee for President, Patrick Hillery, a former Fianna Fáil Foreign Minister and Ireland's European Commissioner. The crisis certainly strengthened the presidency because it is unlikely that a minister will insult the President again, and inconceivable that a

Taoiseach will not resolve the problem very quickly by accepting the minister's resignation.

The fourth discretionary power that has been used is the President's absolute discretion to grant or refuse a dissolution to a Taoiseach who has lost the support of the majority in the Dáil. No President has ever refused a Taoiseach a dissolution but the opportunity has arisen several times. One problem the President faces in applying this provision is the lack of clarity in Article 13.2.2°, which states, "The President may in his absolute discretion refuse to dissolve Dáil Éireann on the advice of a Taoiseach who has ceased to retain the support of a majority in Dáil Éireann." What exactly does "ceased to retain the support of a majority" mean? A government defeat on a motion of confidence is a clear-cut case, as when Haughey lost a vote of confidence in the autumn of 1982 and Reynolds in November 1992. But would a defeat on another kind of motion be presumptive evidence that the government had lost the confidence of the Dáil?

In 1938 de Valera was defeated by a single vote on a minor matter, and President Hyde agreed to a dissolution, as he did again, in similar circumstances, in 1944. Hyde's Secretary, Michael Dunphy, discussed the latter case in two memoranda he prepared in 1944 and 1945. Following the 1944 defeat de Valera asked for a dissolution and made it clear that he regarded the President as having discretion in the matter. Hyde agreed to dissolve the Dáil because he believed there was no reasonable prospect of forming an alternative to de Valera's minority Fianna Fáil government in the existing Dáil. With 65 seats, Fianna Fáil was by far the largest party in the 138-seat chamber and the opposition was badly fragmented. In his 1945 memorandum, however, Dunphy explained that he was no longer satisfied that the President had acted correctly in 1944. He reasoned that had de Valera returned to the Dáil he would probably have won a vote of confidence, and could have continued to govern. "Such a possibility," Dunphy argues, "raises a very serious doubt as to the value of a single defeat as evidence of loss of confidence."[164]

The most controversial dissolution came in 1982, although it did not become a matter of dispute until 1990. On 27 January 1982 Taoiseach FitzGerald's minority Fine Gael–Labour coalition government, which had clung to power since 1981 with the support of independents, was defeated by eighty-two to eighty-one on a vote on a portion of the budget. FitzGerald believed he had no choice but to resign, and he advised the President to dissolve the Dáil. He told journalist Raymond Smith, "Under our Constitution, it has always been accepted that if you lose a Dáil division on a Budget measure, you have no option but to seek a dissolution. To try to remain on would leave a Government in an impossible position."[165]

Within two hours of his decision, FitzGerald arrived at the President's house to request the dissolution, but Charles Haughey, the Fianna Fáil leader, was willing to try to form a government without an intervening election and had already issued a very circumspect statement, which included the following: "It is a matter for the President to consider the situation which has arisen now that the Taoiseach has ceased to retain the support of a majority in Dáil Éireann. I am available for consultation with the President should he so wish."[166] Less circumspect was a series of telephone calls that Haughey and other party leaders, including, it appears, the Tánaiste, Brian Lenihan, made to the President's house to try to communicate with President Hillery, who was, FitzGerald records, "disturbed and indeed quite angry" at what he took to be pressure.[167] Hillery decided to grant the dissolution.

The telephone calls to the President, which Raymond Smith described at length in a biography of FitzGerald published in 1985,[168] became a hot political issue in October 1990, during the presidential election campaign, when Fine Gael launched a concerted attack on the Fianna Fáil candidate, Lenihan. Austin Currie, the Fine Gael candidate, was reported as saying that Lenihan "sought to interfere with the constitutional independence of the President by pressuring him into not granting a dissolution of the Dáil."[169] FitzGerald was reported as describing the President as "unmoved by these improper attempts to intimidate him into a decision."[170] In the Dáil Alan Dukes, the Fine Gael leader, accused Lenihan of trying "to interfere with the President's absolute discretion in deciding whether to grant a dissolution of the Dáil."[171] A week later he said it was Fianna Fáil's harassment of the President, not its offer to form a government, that was at issue.[172]

Fianna Fáil could have defused the issue by conceding that calls had been made to inform the President of Haughey's availability, while denying that harassment had taken place. Instead, a Fianna Fáil spokesman said there was "not a scintilla of truth" in FitzGerald's story[173] and Lenihan said, "Nothing like that ever happened."[174] Unfortunately, Jim Duffy, a graduate student in politics at University College, Dublin, possessed a tape recording of an interview in which Lenihan confirmed that he and others had made the telephone calls and that he himself had talked to the President, "who was clearly annoyed at the whole bloody lot of us."[175] When the contents of the tape were published, Lenihan denied that he had spoken to the President and insisted that the interview had been recorded when he was under the influence of antirejection drugs, taken to protect a liver transplant.[176]

The Haughey government now came under pressure from its coalition partners, the Progressive Democrats, to dismiss Lenihan. When he refused to resign, he was dismissed by the President on the advice of the Taoiseach. The government then won a vote of confidence in the Dáil by eighty-three votes to eighty.[177] Lenihan went on to lose the presidential election to Mary Robinson.

Whatever the truth about the alleged harassment, it is clear that in 1982 Haughey and Lenihan believed President Hillery should use his power under Article 13.2.2° to deny FitzGerald's request for a dissolution and invite Fianna Fáil to form the government. They certainly did not claim at the time that there was a political crisis of some sort to justify such a decision. During the presidential campaign of 1990, however, Lenihan argued the reverse case. He insisted now that a President might only deny a dissolution "in a case of a very serious state of anarchy." It would be, he said, "an intolerable situation under our circumstances at the present time and in the foreseeable circumstances for a President to refuse the application of a Taoiseach requesting dissolution of the Dáil."[178] Furthermore, in the Duffy tape he concedes that it had been a mistake to press Hillery to deny a dissolution in 1982, "because Paddy Hillery would be very (what's the word) strict or conventional in that way."[179]

Although it was he who advised Hillery to dissolve the Dáil in 1982, Garret FitzGerald does not take Lenihan's restrictive view of the President's power. In 1990 he argued that a President may refuse a dissolution if "there is an alternative Government available in the House, not anarchy,"[180] and Dick Spring, the Labour leader, agreed.[181] The Dáil record certainly supports FitzGerald, not Lenihan. In 1937 de Valera clearly stated that the President might refuse a dissolution to a Taoiseach who lacked a majority, and he made no mention of the need for "a serious state of anarchy."[182] Furthermore, having lost his own majority, de Valera twice asked the President for a dissolution himself, in 1938 and 1944, in circumstances falling far short of anarchy, and he accepted the principle that the President had the authority to refuse.

The constitution would have been more helpful, of course, had it clearly identified what would constitute loss of support in the Dáil, a vote of confidence, for example, but in the absence of such clarity there is no reason to accept the restrictive Fianna Fáil view of the President's power of dissolution. For example, had Taoiseach Haughey requested a dissolution in July 1989, after the Dáil refused to renominate him as Taoiseach, as he threatened to do at one point during his negotiations on the coalition with Progressive Democrats,[183] President Hillery would have been perfectly justified in denying the request. It would have come soon after the June general election when all the possibilities of forming an alternative government had not yet been explored, whether a Fianna Fáil–Fine Gael coalition or a government led by someone other than Haughey. Or the Dáil might have been able to emulate the Dáil of 1948 when six parties and a number of independents formed a coalition under John Costello in order to deny Eamon de Valera office, even though Fianna Fáil was only six votes short of forming a government.[184] In 1989, however, Haughey finally cobbled together a coalition with the Progressive Democrats and the crisis was averted.

Some have suggested that the President should have the power to nominate a Taoiseach if the parties in the legislature are unable to agree on a choice within a reasonable time following a general election, as was nearly the case in 1989 and 1992–93. Indeed, this possibility was discussed by the Informal Committee on the Constitution in 1967, which adduced arguments both for and against such a change before deciding not to recommend a constitutional amendment. In favor of the new presidential power, the committee argued:

It is not difficult to imagine a situation arising in which the three main political parties are so represented in the House that each of their candidates for the office of Taoiseach can be defeated by the combined strength of the other two. If candidates are put forward in circumstances of this kind under the existing Constitution provisions, an acrimonious debate might well take place which might reduce considerably the possibility of any agreement being subsequently arrived at by the parties. Such a debate might not arise in the event of the President being given the power to appoint the person most likely to secure the confidence of the house.

Opposing a change, the committee argued that new powers would risk the President's involvement in party politics. It expressed confidence that "the good will of the parties could be relied on to secure agreement beforehand on a candidate who would succeed in procuring nomination by a majority at the time of voting in the Dáil . . . without the intervention of the President." [185]

The President has only once, so far as I know, come close to involving himself directly in the election of the Taoiseach. In 1987 the outgoing Taoiseach, Garret FitzGerald, who had not won a majority of seats at the general election, thought that there might be no agreement on a successor when the new Dáil assembled, and he discussed with President Hillery how he should proceed. The President advised FitzGerald not to announce his resignation or to seek another dissolution. Instead, he was advised to announce that he was going to visit the President to discuss the situation. Then, as FitzGerald describes the plan,

After visiting him, I was to go back to the Dáil and attempt, by knocking heads together, to get a resolution of the deadlock. If I failed in this attempt I was to return to the President once again, at which point he would publicly instruct me to make a further effort, acting on his authority. We both hoped that the mounting pressure thus created would resolve the problem should it arise. [186]

In the event, because of the decision of the independent, Tony Gregory, to abstain, Haughey was elected on the first ballot, with a minority government and the President did not have to use his influence. In 1989 and 1992–93 the Dáil was able to sort out the problem for itself when the crisis envisaged by the Committee on the Constitution actually occurred, but only after weeks of indecision and without the "agreement beforehand" the committee had anticipated.

Many of those who debated the constitution in 1937 would be surprised that Presidents have been so docile, either in exercising their discretionary powers or accumulating new ones. Professor Alfred O'Rahilly, for example, wrote, "Whatever we may prescribe on paper, we cannot prevent the growth of constitutional usage and convention. And there is very little doubt that a president, claiming a direct popular authority, can and will develop his power and prestige." [187] This was a widespread opinion in 1937, and it explains why the provisions on the President were controversial during the Dáil debate on the new constitution. But by 1967 some members of the Committee on the Constitution wanted to abolish the office because it was so weak. It survived primarily because of its ceremonial functions and its role as guardian of the constitution. [188] However, if the crises of government formation experienced in 1989 and 1992–93 become the rule in Ireland, we can anticipate that forceful Presidents will be tempted to intervene, as even President Hillery, a man with a very conservative view of the office, was tempted to do in 1987.

The issue of reform of the presidency was revived during the 1990 presidential election when the President's lack of power and prestige was a central issue in the campaign. Indeed, because President Hillery's presidential entertainment allowance had remained unchanged at Ir£ 15,000 during his fourteen years in office, even his level of activity was questioned.[189] But the recommendations for change voiced in the campaign clashed with the rules of responsible government, as we will see in the final chapter.

## Concentration of Power

We are left, then, with one final characteristic of responsible government in the 1937 constitution to discuss, the concentration of power in modern Ireland. This is the dominant characteristic of contemporary Irish politics because the provisions of the constitution have allowed the government to accumulate policymaking and administrative powers that are matched in few other democracies. This important development deserves extended consideration, and it is an appropriate theme for the final chapter of this book in which I address how responsible government has influenced the distribution of political power in contemporary Ireland.

# CHAPTER 13

# Conclusion: The Concentration of Power in Modern Ireland

Ironically, the concentration of political power characteristic of responsible government ultimately destroys the literal meaning of the term "responsible government." Power is concentrated in the hands of the government and its partner, the civil service, and leads to the consequent diminution of the power of the legislature. Parliament becomes the instrument of the government rather than its master. This is very different from the original meaning of responsible government. The term was used in the mid-nineteenth century to identify a model in which the executive was both selected by and responsible to the legislature. In his book *The English Constitution*, published in 1867, Walter Bagehot described the Cabinet as "a board of control chosen by the legislature," and as a "committee of the legislative assembly."[1] "The House of Commons," he wrote, "lives in a state of perpetual potential choice; at any moment it can choose a ruler and dismiss a ruler."[2] To illustrate that Bagehot was describing the real world, we should note that between 1832 and 1867 seven Cabinets lost the confidence of the House of Commons and were replaced without an intervening general election.[3]

The power of the House of Commons was never absolute, of course. Bagehot argued that the Prime Minister's power to advise Queen Victoria to dissolve Parliament, and thereby put parliamentary seats at risk, enabled him to put substantial pressure on members of Parliament. He wrote that members "are *collected* by a deferential attachment to particular men, or by a belief in the principles those men represent, and they are *maintained* by fear of those men—by the fear that if you vote against them, you may yourself soon not have a vote at all."[4] Nonetheless, Bagehot saw the House of Commons, in a very real sense, as an "electoral chamber."[5]

Bagehot's perceptive book suffered by being published at the very end of the era he was describing, just as mass-based political parties were about to usurp the electoral function of the House of Commons. Bagehot conceded the need for a degree of party discipline in the legislature. "Efficiency in an assembly," he wrote, "requires a solid mass of steady voters."[6] But he abhorred the prospect that constituency-based political parties might dictate what members of Parliament should do. He wrote, "Constituency government is the precise opposite of Parliamentary government. It is . . . the judgement of persons judging in the last resort and without a penalty, in lieu of persons judging in fear of a dissolution, and ever conscious that they are subject to an appeal."[7] The threat was greater than Bagehot imagined. Quite soon after he wrote, constituency parties were merged into national parties, led by famous parliamentary leaders such as Disraeli and Gladstone. These parties were mobilized in national campaigns to win the majorities in the House of Commons that were necessary to support Cabinets. Ministers came to be men with multiple sources of power. They were, simultaneously, (1) government ministers controlling the executive, the civil service, and key constitutional levers; (2) leaders of disciplined parliamentary parties; and (3) leaders of mass-based national parties. As a result, the character of the House of Commons, the "club" Bagehot so admired, changed drastically. It remained a reservoir and training ground for ministers and governments, a debating chamber, and an arena for the struggle between government and opposition, but the independence of members virtually disappeared in the face of powerful Cabinets and disciplined parliamentary parties. The House also lost its electoral role. Henceforward, the government would be determined by general elections.

Responsible government had evolved to this point long before the Irish Free State was born in 1922, and its characteristics were understood by most of those who wrote the 1922 constitution, but they did not approve of everything they saw. Many of the founders of the Irish Free State had a populist streak and were determined to limit the excesses of what they called British "party government." They therefore denied a government that had lost its majority the right to dissolve the Dáil. They sought to enhance the independent role of the legislature by creating external ministers answerable to the Dáil, not to the Cabinet.

They also tried to empower citizens by giving them a direct role in legislation through the processes of legislative initiative and referendum. But the imperatives of responsible government, and the highly charged partisanship of the early years of the state, soon combined to defeat these reforms, which were eventually repealed or modified.

The constitution of 1937 does not return to all of the principles of 1922. It draws its inspiration from the Free State constitution as it had been amended by 1936 and it therefore provides the framework for an extremely concentrated form of government. Power is concentrated in the hands of the Taoiseach and the government, who dominate the Oireachtas agenda, the budget process, and legislation. By appealing to collective responsibility, the government is able to shield itself from outside inspection, and while the civil service has taken on an ever-increasing role in devising and administering public policies in the age of the welfare state, it is largely screened from parliamentary and public view by ministerial responsibility and the doctrine of corporation sole. Brian Farrell writes, "It is this tradition of executive secrecy, buttressed by the doctrine of collective responsibility, which has done much to reduce the role of parliament from the parliamentary body envisaged in the Constitution."[8] An emasculated Dáil is no match for the government in such a system, and neither the Seanad nor the President have sufficient powers in law to enable them to provide some balance.

## Other Centralizing Forces

Responsible government is primarily responsible for this concentration of power, but there are three other aspects of the Irish political system that magnify the process: local government, state-sponsored bodies, and the social partnership.

### Local Government

The Republic of Ireland has a layered system of government rising from thirty town commissions, six boroughs, forty-nine urban district councils, five county boroughs, and twenty-seven councils to a number of regional boards, including eight regional health boards, and more than one hundred state-sponsored bodies.[9] What characterizes the system as a whole is the large degree of central government control or influence at each level. T. J. Barrington argues, "Centralized government in a small state is very widely believed to be more efficient than decentralized government."[10] He adds, "[Ireland] has a very inadequate acceptance of the democratic value of the directly elected local representative, and of the significance for a developed democracy of increased local discretion."[11] This has been true ever since the founding of independent Ireland in 1922.

The number and type of local authorities and their powers is determined by the Oireachtas and can be changed at any time. In 1969, for example, the Dublin City Council was suspended for nonperformance of its duties,[12] and in 1990 the five-year local authority elections were postponed until 1991 because the government was considering a new, three-tier, system of local administration. At the time of writing (1993) the new system had not been adopted by the Oireachtas. Certain matters that are locally controlled in many countries, the police, for example, are controlled by central government in the Republic of Ireland, and even in the areas of local responsibility, such as public housing, roads, water, and sanitation, the central government, particularly the Department of the Environment, exercises a great deal of influence. Most importantly, the government controls much of the funding available to local authorities. Rates, or property taxes, on agricultural land and domestic dwellings were abolished in 1978 and this seriously undermined the financial independence of local councils.[13] In addition, the Republic of Ireland has a city and county manager form of local government that was adopted from the United States in the 1920s, with professional managers exercising executive functions that in England are the preserve of executive committees of elected councillors. Managers are nominated by a central state body, the Local Appointments Commission. Finally, most Dáil deputies serve on local councils and see them as sources of services and benefits for their Dáil constituents. In October 1990 deputies held 114 seats on county or city councils, and senators held 39. Deputies held 23 seats on regional health boards and senators held 9.[14] Local authorities are therefore integrated into the clientalist system of politics, serving deputies' careers in the Oireachtas. It was only in 1991 that ministers were precluded by law from serving on local authorities.[15]

Layered above city and county councils are regional boards, for example, eight regional health boards that were established in 1970 to administer services on a multicouncil basis. These boards include elected representatives of local authorities and nominees of professional organizations, but each also has three ministerial nominees and the bodies operate under the supervision of the central government.

## State-Sponsored Bodies

State-sponsored bodies are permanent, autonomous, public authorities operating under the direction of boards appointed by ministers.[16] There has never been an authoritative definition of the term, and in 1976 the Minister for the Public Service confessed that he could think of none.[17] Dooney and O'Toole list six methods of establishing such bodies but identify no criteria by which one method is preferred to another.[18] The bodies are engaged in a variety of activities. Many are commercial, including Aer Lingus and the Electricity Supply Board. Some provide marketing, promotional, development, or research services, such as Bord Fáilte Éireann (the Irish Tourist Board) and the Industrial Development Authority. Others are engaged in the regulation of professions or economic activities, such as the Dublin Dental Board and the Local Government Staff Negotiations Board. Still others provide or administer health or environmental services, the National Social Service Council, for example. Many would be termed "nationalized industries" in Britain, and others would be covered there by the acronym QUANGO, meaning QUasi-Autonomous NonGovernmental Organization. Problems of definition mean that there is no agreement on how many state-sponsored bodies exist. John Bruton, in a 1980 Fine Gael report, identified 30 commercial bodies and 57 noncommercial bodies,[19] but Dooney and O'Toole list a total of 133, based on information supplied in ministers' answers to parliamentary questions in 1991.[20] In 1992, Basil Chubb, who counted only 96 bodies, reported that they employed seventy-nine thousand people and were responsible for 30 percent of total public-sector employment.[21] In 1991 David Kennedy estimated that the commercial bodies alone employed approximately seventy-three thousand people and produced approximately 10 percent of Irish GDP.[22]

State-sponsored bodies are not expressions of Irish socialism. A major role for the state in the economy is widely accepted on pragmatic grounds in Ireland and is supported by Article 45 of the constitution, the "Directive Principles of Social Policy." Although Article 45 is not enforceable by any court, its endorsement of state activity is clear. The state, it says, "shall strive to promote the welfare of the whole people . . . [and] shall favour and, where necessary, supplement private initiative in industry and commerce."

From their inception in 1927, with the Electricity Supply Board and the Agricultural Credit Corporation, state-sponsored bodies have posed a significant problem for parliamentary government. Their boards are appointed by ministers, to whom they report, and it is the responsibility of ministers to ensure that government policies, particularly policies on spending, are adhered to. However, the Oireachtas has never been able to review their activities adequately, in part because they were established as autonomous bodies precisely to free them from day-to-day state control. For this reason, ministers do not answer parliamentary questions on the routine operations of state-sponsored bodies, and although relevant annual reports and accounts are presented to the Oireachtas, their activities are very rarely debated in the Dáil. Because they are so important in Irish life, however, populists have targeted them for some kind of parliamentary control. In 1978 the Fine Gael–Labour coalition government established what is now known as the Joint Oireachtas Committee on Commercial State-Sponsored Bodies to review the accounts and activities of twenty-six trading and commercial bodies, but the noncommercial bodies were, and are still, excluded.

David Kennedy, a former Chief Executive of Aer Lingus, a commercial state body, has argued that state interference in the management of such enterprises makes it extremely difficult for them to operate in a totally commercial manner. Major financial questions, for example, must be made by the Department of Finance, and because of its concern for the size of state debt the department is loathe to endorse large equity investments. Given their lack of public accountability and their inability to function as purely commercial operations, the commercial state-sponsored bodies might be more comfortably accommodated in the private sector, but to date the resistance of trades unions and the unwillingness of governments to depart from long-established tradition has limited privatization to two companies, Irish Sugar and the Irish Life Assurance Company.[23]

The growth of state-sponsored bodies in Ireland is an example of the paradox Ira Sharkansky discusses in his book *Wither the State?* (1979). Sharkansky argues, "Modern states are both growing and withering. They grow in response to incessant demands for more services; they wither as officials assign important activities to bodies that enjoy formal grants of authority from the state."[24] It is difficult for governments, let alone members of the Oireachtas, to comprehend the full extent of "the state" in this context, and the democratic principle of accountability is eroded by the incoherence of the process.

## The Social Partnership

Professor J. J. Lee has pointed to the practice that developed in Ireland in the 1960s by which the government and its "social partners," representatives of employers and trades unions, began to determine national wage agreements and other national policies without reference to the Oireachtas. Lee called this the "new corporatism" and concluded that it "diminished even further the authority of the Dáil."[25] This practice has now taken on enormous significance. Since 1987 the government and the social partners, meeting in the National Economic and Social Council, have prepared reports on the Irish economy without reference to the Oireachtas or political parties. The *Irish Times* labeled the Council "The Alternative Parliament."[26] In 1991 the Council not only agreed to a three-year plan of pay increases and tax cuts, but to a comprehensive strategic program for the 1990s. The program, which was debated in the Oireachtas only after its publication, dealt with macroeconomic and tax policies, social reform and welfare, health, education, housing, transport, construction, commercial state bodies, the environment, arts and culture, agriculture, forestry, and other matters.[27] Fine Gael and the Labour party both attacked the government for excluding them from the process, and the Fine Gael leader in the Senate, Maurice Manning, argued, "There must always be dialogue within any Government or any political party and the major social interest groups in society but it is a very bad development that this dialogue becomes institutionalized and virtually takes the place of the policy-making process which should rightfully be decided finally in the Houses of Parliament."[28] The government replied that there could have been no agreement on a plan if all the political parties had been involved.[29] Perhaps so, but one has to worry about the implications for democracy of such thinking. Who needs the Oireachtas?

## Countervailing Forces

### Judicial Review

All this is not to say that there are no countervailing forces to those of the government in contemporary Ireland, and no significant attempts to reform the system. Both exist. Acts of the legislature can be reviewed by the courts, for example. As the Attorney General, Peter Sutherland, wrote in 1988, "The Irish Constitution makes clear that there are limits to what the elected representatives of the people may do, and that these limits are to be enforced by the courts."[30] Article 15.4.1° provides that the Oireachtas shall not enact any law that is repugnant to the constitution, and under Article 34.3.2° acts of the Oireachtas may be challenged on constitutional grounds in the High Court or the Supreme Court. The President may also refer a bill to the Supreme Court for an opinion before signing it into law under Article 26.1.1°.

De Valera could not have anticipated the great effect judicial review would have on the evolution of Irish law. The personal rights enumerated in Articles 40 to 43 of the constitution correspond closely to Catholic thinking in the 1930s, as it was expressed in a number of papal encyclicals, which means that they reflect the Thomistic view that natural law takes precedence over positive law.[31] As Anthony Coughlin argues, "People have rights as persons as well as citizens."[32] This theory opens the way for "judicial law-making," which is to say, for judges to recognize specific new rights by appealing to general principles of natural law.[33] Attorney General Sutherland has pointed to the difficulties that unenumerated general rights raise for governments that are forced to respond to court decisions with new legislation.[34] The Health (Family Planning) Act of 1979, which legalized the sale of contraceptives, was made necessary by a Supreme Court decision, for example.[35] Other new rights have been recognized as a result of the application of European Community law and the European Convention on Human Rights. European law, for example, calls for equal pay for equal work.

What was required for new rights to emerge from the constitution and European law was judges prepared to decide cases creatively, and litigants prepared to bring the right kinds of cases to trial. Both began to appear in the 1960s. Judges were appointed who were no longer tied to their training in the conservative British legal system, and Irish society began to change in response to economic forces, European law, and the Irish feminist movement. Today's courts do not assume a static constitution or a static society because, as Justice Brian Walsh has said, "The courts see the Constitution as a contemporary fundamental law that speaks in the present tense. As a document it speaks from 1937, but as law it speaks from today."[36] As a result of these circumstances, a right of privacy was recognized that led to the notion of marital privacy and the right to import contraceptives. The mothers of illegitimate children and their offspring now have recognized rights. The right to travel outside the country and possess a passport has been established. Sex discrimination in employment has been found to be illegal, as has discrimination against women in the tax code, and so on.[37] Mary Robinson, now the President of Ireland, was a counsel in several important cases. Yvonne Scannell argues that, with the exception of the Succession Act of 1965, "it is difficult to identify any major piece of legislation relevant to the rights of women that was not forced on our representatives by the courts, the women's movement or the EC."[38]

## The Ombudsman

A second countervailing force is the office of the Ombudsman. As civil servants assumed ever greater powers in modern welfare states, without a corresponding increase in parliamentary scrutiny, an "Ombudsman" movement developed in many countries, beginning in Scandinavia, the source of the title. The Ombudsman is a person to whom the public may turn if entitlements are neglected or denied by the civil service. In Ireland such an office was suggested by the Public Services Organization Review Group, the "Devlin Committee," in 1969.[39] The issue was raised again in a private member's motion offered by Deputy Fergus O'Brien in May 1975, and an informal, all-party committee established by the Fine Gael–Labour coalition recommended an Irish ombudsman.[40] The coalition fell in 1977, before the passage of its bill, but Fianna Fáil introduced the necessary legislation in 1980.[41] The first Irish Ombudsman, Michael Mills, political correspondent of the *Irish Press*, was appointed by a Fine Gael–Labour government after consultation with the leader of the opposition, Charles Haughey, in October 1983 and he began work on 1 January 1984.[42] A measure of his independence from the government is his six-year term. The act provides that in Ireland a citizen or deputy may initiate an inquiry. In Britain only a member of Parliament may do so. The Ombudsman has no power to redress a grievance, only to suggest a course of action to a responsible minister.[43]

The Irish Ombudsman has been starved of funds during the period of financial hardship in Ireland suffered by all government departments, although some took this to be a Fianna Fáil attack on the principle of the Ombudsman. Many back-bench deputies also see the Ombudsman as a threat to clientalist politics because he offers citizens a new means of securing redress.[44] But this suspicion is almost certainly misplaced. The Ombudsman is likely to focus on significant failures in the bureaucracy, not on the myriad cases that deputies succeed in "fixing" for unskilled constituents which informed citizens might resolve for themselves.

## Efforts at Reform

### The Oireachtas

Some countervailing power does exist in Ireland, therefore, but it does not change the reality that responsible government has concentrated enormous power in the hands of the government. In recognition of this fact there has been a fairly continuous drumbeat for reform in Ireland for many years, as elsewhere where responsible government is practiced. Early examples in Ireland were the Public Services Organization Review Group in 1969 and the Informal Committee on Dáil Procedure in 1972. The problem for reformers is to identify reforms that will empower members of the Oireachtas and the public without undermining the ultimate control of the legislature that every Cabinet feels it must have in responsible government. Britain and Canada have gone much further in this direction than has Ireland. In both countries, for example, opposition parties are permitted to control debating time in the House of Commons for about 30 days in a legislative year of about 160 days. "Opposition days" are not recognized in Ireland where party leaders have to use private members' time for opposition motions. In addition, quite complex parliamentary committee systems have been created in Britain and Canada to allow structured opportunities for ordinary members to participate in framing legislation and reviewing the work of government departments.

Members of the Dáil have called for a committee system since 1919, when Deputy James J. Walsh first raised the issue.[45] The argument is made, often with envious glances at the United States, that deputies should be assigned to parliamentary committees that will be able to consider legislation and monitor the activities of the government in particular subject areas. The competence and influence of ordinary deputies will be enhanced by committees, it is argued, and the state will be enriched by using to the full the talents of deputies who would otherwise languish on the back benches.

Unfortunately, proponents of committee systems have underestimated the difficulties of combining committees with responsible government. Committees flourish in the United States because Congress is independent of the executive. It uses committees and an army of support staff to compete with the executive branch in a system of separation of powers. Parliamentary committees have been resisted in countries practicing responsible government, however, because they have the effect of creating sources of information, expertise, power, collegiality, and prestige in the legislature that can be used to challenge the government's control of that body. As J. L. McCracken wrote in 1958, "The practice of retaining practically all bills in committees of the whole house strengthens the [Irish] government by enabling it to use its majority more effectively than it might be able to do in a standing committee."[46]

The Oireachtas has always had two types of committees, standing and select, although it would be an exaggeration to speak of a committee system. Standing committees are used for the third, or committee, stage of certain noncontroversial bills, the line-by-line scrutiny that follows the second-stage debate on principles, but between 1937 and 1983 only twenty of twelve hundred government bills received this treatment.[47] Most bills are considered in committees of the whole house.

Select committees are established annually with specialized functions, and until 1983 their use was rather limited. The older ones include those that are routinely reestablished each year, including the Dáil and Senate Procedure and Privileges Committees, the Joint Services Committee, and the Dáil Public Accounts Committee, the only committee charged with scrutinizing the government.[48] Chaired, as in Britain, by a leading member of the opposition, the limited charge of the committee is to monitor that the government spends funds in ways authorized by law. It does this by considering reports on government spending prepared by the Comptroller and Auditor-General, an official appointed by the President on the recommendation of the Dáil. It has no authority to consider government policies, per se. In 1968, with the support of deputies from all sides, the Public Accounts Committee successfully asserted its right to call for government witnesses and review government papers and records, but the government would not agree to recognize this right in law.[49] Occasionally the government appoints a select committee to investigate a specific issue of public policy; such committees disband on completing their work.

The Fine Gael–Labour coalition of 1973 to 1977 began to use committees more often. Both parties had long opposed the extreme concentration of power favored by Fianna Fáil. When he entered the Seanad in 1965, for example, Garrett FitzGerald noted a marked difference between the inclinations of Fine Gael and Fianna Fáil:

Fianna Fáil, possibly because it had been in office for twenty-seven of the previous thirty-three years, tended to favour an approach that gave maximum power to the executive, a position that most civil servants also tended to favour. Fine Gael, by contrast, had, and has retained, an instinct for a more open and democratic approach, and for conceding a greater role to bodies independent of Government.[50]

Labour's position was stated in a 1975 article by Deputy Barry Desmond: "Inside our parliamentary system, the role of the Dáil as the supreme law-making body should be critical, responsive, and constructive." The reality, he noted, was very different:

Dáil Éireann is . . . to many observers a sleepily middle class, quasi-professional, male dominated, conservatively deliberative, poorly attended debating assembly. Deputies play less and less a role in the formulation and enactment of legislation and more and more occupy their time in the pretence of political favour peddlers, consumer representatives, and clerical messenger boys on behalf of constituents.[51]

Desmond favored establishing a new set of standing committees to consider legislation and budget estimates.

The coalition began to grope toward a more substantial role for the Oireachtas in 1976. That year deputies were given clerical assistants for the first time at a rate of one per seven deputies. The sums made available to the leaders of parliamentary parties for administration and research were also substantially increased. The opposition Fianna Fáil party received Ir£ 55,000 in 1976, as compared with the Ir£ 10,000 shared by Fine Gael and Labour in opposition in 1972.[52] The government also created two new committees. The first was the Joint Committee on State-Sponsored Bodies, a committee of the Dáil and Seanad charged with examining the accounts and reports of twenty-six state-sponsored bodies engaged in trading or commercial activities.[53] It was renamed the Joint Committee on Commercial State-Sponsored Bodies in 1981. The second new committee was the Joint Committee on the Secondary Legislation of the European Community, charged with reviewing rules issued by the Irish government to implement the legislation of the European Community, as required by Section 4 of the European Communities Act of 1972.[54] There was as yet no comprehensive committee system, however, and the government encountered considerable resistance to the use of standing committees from Fianna Fáil in the Dáil. John Kelly, who was government Whip at the time, recalled how difficult it was for the coalition to send bills to standing committees because the coalition had a very small majority and Fianna Fáil was determined to break the government in the Dáil by refusing to facilitate government business in the customary way:

If a Bill was not contentious, and if there was no publicity mileage in it and one could persuade a few simple-minded Deputies to participate, that was fine. It would go into committee, be discussed in one of the back rooms, and would go through in jigging time. But with a serious Bill where there was mileage to be got out of it by way of attracting the interest of the press or breaking the necks of the Government front bench, there was no question of sending it to committee, and it did not matter what the consequences were for Dáil business.[55]

Further reforms of the Oireachtas were introduced by Garrett Fitz-Gerald's first, short-lived, Fine Gael–Labour coalition of June 1981 to February 1982 and his longer lived coalition of 1983 to 1987. The reforms were based on a report drafted by John Bruton and adopted by the Fine Gael parliamentary party late in 1979. Bruton summarized the problem faced by the Oireachtas as he saw it:

Under the Constitution the Oireachtas has the "sole and exclusive power of making laws for the state." Nonetheless in practice it plays practically no effective part in either the making of laws or even the expert criticism of them. One of the most disciplined party systems in Europe has ensured that it is the Government, not the Oireachtas, that exercises the power. Members of the Government do have to account for themselves subsequently in the Dáil but this is only after decisions have already been made. Even this negative accountability is being diminished by the fact that nowadays the Government does not act alone. Most of its decisions are taken as a result of confidential bargaining with representatives of the major interest groups in the Community—Trade Unions, Employers, Farmers Organizations etc. Thus, in contrast to the democratic theory that decisions be taken in the open in a popularly elected parliament, they nowadays are being taken in private in consultation with groups whose mandate is limited and not governed by law. . . . The result of this process has been worse not better Government. . . . A radical reform of the Oireachtas would shift back to an open public forum many of the decisions now taken in private.[56]

The report made a number of recommendations for reforms of the committee system and the budget process. These included a large increase in committees to consider legislation, review the activities of noncommercial state-sponsored bodies, and approve departmental estimates. The report argued that committees would enable estimates to be approved by December preceding the year of the expenditures, rather than in May or June of the expenditure year. It also proposed that the government submit capital spending and borrowing plans to the Dáil for the first time.

Fine Gael also recommended a number of reforms addressed to the powers of deputies. It proposed, for example, that the rules on private members' bills should be changed, on the British model, so that three members of the Dáil would be selected by lot each year to introduce their own private members' bills. It also proposed that any seven members, not simply any party with seven or more members, as in the existing rule, should be able to introduce a private members' bill. Deputies should be allowed to put written questions to ministers during the recess, and Question Time should be extended by an hour and a half a week, with state-sponsored bodies receiving full state funding to be the subjects of questions for the first time. To open up the Oireachtas to public scrutiny, Fine Gael also proposed that its proceedings should be televised. To accommodate many of these changes, it proposed that the parliamentary session should be extended by two weeks by cutting short the summer recess.

During FitzGerald's first government each deputy was assigned a full-time clerical assistant, who may work in Dublin or in the constituency,[57] and four new Oireachtas committees were proposed: women's rights, youth affairs, development cooperation, and marriage breakdown. The Fianna Fáil leader, Haughey, approved only the Committee on Development Cooperation before the government fell in February 1982, and no new committees were actually established.[58]

When Fine Gael returned to power with Labour in December 1982, Bruton, now Minister for Industry and Energy, was appointed Leader of the House by Taoiseach FitzGerald, a new position with responsibility for parliamentary reform. On 22 January 1983 he moved a general resolution that the procedures of Dáil Éireann "should be reformed to improve efficiency and its control over public finances."[59] A second motion, which Bruton introduced in June, focused on the creation of committees. Both motions were approved without a division[60] but in the debates a sharp line was drawn between Fine Gael and Labour on one side, both of which supported measures to empower deputies, and Fianna Fáil, which wanted to tone down the expectations of the reformers.

Fianna Fáil raised two very significant obstacles to a committee system, one practical and one theoretical. The practical obstacle was that the system would impose unacceptably heavy burdens on deputies. Fianna Fáil Deputy Ahern, for example, argued:

Deputies are almost totally engaged in working for their constituents and while the problem has been eased slightly by the provision of one secretary for each non-office holder, Deputies do not have research facilities and any work they carry out must be done in their own time. . . . I agree with many of [Bruton's] ideas but they will be workable only if people have time to devote to the matter.[61]

The leader of Fianna Fáil, Charles Haughey, expressed "qualified, cautious approval" for committees, but identified three existing committees and ten proposed new committees that would have to be filled by only 130 or so nongovernment deputies. "I know," he said, "that the problem is to get Deputies to man these committees once they are established."[62]

The theoretical obstacle to committees was addressed most directly by Haughey and Brian Lenihan, both of whom argued that responsible government is primarily a system of government by the executive, not by Parliament. In February 1983 Lenihan described very precisely the model of government that Fianna Fáil had supported since de Valera came to power in 1932:

Whatever we do here as parliamentarians must be regarded essentially as a kind of subsidiary or advisory function. . . . Fundamentally, what we are all concerned about in a representative democracy is electing people who will come here and elect a Government. . . . I would not agree with any committee system that would in any way intrude on or obstruct the basic decision-making process of politicians elected to Government. . . . I am in favour of setting up a committee who know their terms of reference but not a committee set up as an alternative Government.[63]

In the June debate on committees Lenihan argued, "It is the people's right at election time to elect a Government through the House and to be drawn from this House. From there on policy making, the raising of finances and expenditure relating to policy making . . . resides firmly within the compass of the Government."[64] Charles Haughey endorsed this view:

Basically, decisions have to be taken by the Government. Those of us who have been in Government know that is the reality. We can get things examined by interdepartmental committees, or committees of this House or committees of any other sort, but the running of the country, particularly the running of the economy, is a matter for clear hard decisions by the Government. I do not want us to indulge in some sort of self-deception that by setting up these committees we are going to avoid the hard crunch difficult decisions because they have been discussed in some committee perhaps on a non-party basis. I want to make the point that it is the business of the Government to govern and it is the business of the Government to take the executive decisions that have to be taken, and that we should not think for one moment that we are going to obviate that hard central need by establishing these committees.[65]

Despite these reservations by the leaders of the opposition, the coalition established nine new select committees in 1983, two in the Dáil and seven joint committees, with the three major parties sharing committee and subcommittee chairmanships.[66] It was anticipated that some of the new committees would be renewed each year and become permanent fixtures, the Joint Committee on Legislation, for example, and the Dáil Committee on Public Expenditure. Others were meant to dissolve after reporting on a particular topic, for example, the Joint Committee on Marriage Breakdown.[67] Committees were not authorized to monitor the work of government departments, a common task of committees elsewhere, because the Irish felt that they would become advocacy groups seeking funds from departments. Each committee was assigned a clerk and such full-time or part-time consultants as it could justify to the Minister for the Public Service, an unsubtle check on committee activities. The Dáil Committee on Public Expenditure also had access to a large advisory panel of academics and business leaders.[68]

How did the new committees work? In a 1988 study Joseph Zimmerman identified some things that worked well.[69] There was an absence of hostile partisanship in committees, for example, perhaps because many of the topics selected for investigation were highly technical. Committees also appeared to contribute to a division of labor in the Oireachtas and to the education of members on issues such as crime, development aid to the third world, and the status of women. On the debit side, however, committee reports did not lead to legislation and were not debated in the Dáil under either Fine Fáil–Labour or Fianna Fáil governments. Only the Seanad scheduled time to debate joint committee reports.[70] The disinclination to schedule debates predated the creation of the new committees in the 1980s because the Dáil has not debated the reports of the Joint Committee on Commercial State-Sponsored Bodies, which was established in 1978. Furthermore, the extraordinary number of reports published by the new committees, most of them prepared by consultants, essentially precludes debate. Only the legislation creating the Committee on Public Expenditure required the government to schedule debates on its reports, but that requirement was rescinded by the coalition in November 1986.

Zimmerman noted that some departments had refused to allow officials to appear before committees, and for those who did testify the principle of "corporation sole" was strictly applied. The Department of the Public Service reminded civil servants in 1984 that they could only present their departments' views, not their own personal views, at hearings. Civil servants were also warned not to provide information that the rules of the Dáil would allow a minister to refuse to provide in answer to a parliamentary question. This is a formidable list that includes advice given by civil servants to their ministers and interdepartment communications.

Audrey M. Arkins's study of committees in the Twenty-fourth Oireachtas, from 1983 to 1987, confirms Zimmerman's analysis.[71] On the positive side she finds that committees directed attention to important issues, provoked questions to ministers, and helped in the formulation of private members' bills. They also influenced some department policies. On the debit side, however, she finds that "[w]hat should have begun as a modest experiment blossomed into an uncoordinated mishmash of committees. The potential effectiveness of the new committees was immediately undermined by their superabundance."[72] They strained the accommodation and staff of Leinster House; at one point seventeen committees or subcommittees were meeting simultaneously.[73] Their reports descended in such an avalanche—113 in all during the Twenty-fourth Oireachtas, from 1983 to 1987—that it was impossible for the Dáil or the Senate to debate them.

Fianna Fáil abandoned important elements of the new committee system when it returned to power in 1987. From the beginning it had argued that the Committee on Public Expenditure was unacceptably intrusive on government, and it was not reappointed in 1987. Even Fine Gael felt that the committee tended to overlap the activities of the Public Accounts Committee and had suggested merging the two in a new Committee of Public Management. Fianna Fáil also abandoned the Joint Committee on Legislation and a majority of the topical select committees. Only the Joint Committees on Women's Rights, the Irish Language, and Commercial State-Sponsored Bodies were reconstituted.[74]

In summary, therefore, reform of the committee system has done very little to challenge the government's control of the legislative process. The burden of committee work descends on members who have one clerical assistant each but no research assistants and no access to a comprehensive legislative research service. Members also have a tradition of intensive constituency service that takes up most of their time. The coalition created too many committees in 1983. They were understaffed, there were too few members to serve on them, and too few rooms to house them.[75] While committees provided a substantial measure of government oversight that had been lacking before, they did not empower the Oireachtas in any significant way.

Fine Gael remains dissatisfied with the pace of Oireachtas reform. It was unable to implement a large number of its 1980 recommendations between 1983 and 1987, including a Committee on Non-Commercial State-Sponsored Bodies, an extended Question Time, a lottery system for private members' bills, and an extension of the Dáil year. Furthermore, some of the coalition's new committees were abandoned by Fianna Fáil in 1987. In May 1988, therefore, the party initiated yet another review. A report was published in the summer of 1990, based on a paper by Senator Maurice Manning, a political scientist, which restated many of the criticisms and recommendations of Fine Gael's 1979 report and raised again the disadvantages of a political system excessively dominated by the government.[76] Once again it proposed that several members should be chosen by lottery to introduce private members' bills each year, that Question Time be extended by one-and-a-quarter hours a week, and that members be allowed to put written questions to ministers during recess.

The most comprehensive of Fine Gael's 1990 new proposals was that three new Dáil Standing Committees, or Business Committees, should be established, for Economic Affairs, Social Affairs, and General Affairs. They would have three tasks. First, every bill introduced into the Dáil would be assigned to an appropriate committee for its committee stage, with provision being made for interests groups and non-committee deputies to testify. Several bills could be processed simultaneously in this way, and it would be easier for ministers to accept amendments in committee than in the confrontational setting of the Dáil as a whole. Second, each department's estimates would be referred to one of these committees for a detailed review. Third, each committee would exercise general oversight of the policies of departments assigned to it.

Fine Gael also proposed the creation of two new committees outside the Business Committee framework. One would be a Dáil Foreign Affairs Committee, which would take over the responsibilities of two existing sessional committees, the Overseas Development Committee and the Committee on Secondary Legislation of the European Community. The second new committee would be a Joint Committee on the Environment. In February 1992 the Fianna Fáil government agreed to create a Dáil Foreign Affairs Committee, a dramatic reversal of policy from a year earlier, when the Minister of State at the Department of Foreign Affairs, Seán Calleary, had argued that such a committee would be "a major handicap to any Government" because "the flow of information to the Department of Foreign Affairs and our missions abroad would soon dry up if it found its way into the public domain."[77] The committee was finally established in the summer of 1993, with Brian Lenihan as chairman.

The 1990 Fine Gael report also proposed that there should be a relationship between the Oireachtas and the European Community. An enormous amount of new law is coming from Europe but the Oireachtas is left out of this process except in so far as the Joint Committee on the Secondary Legislation of the European Community reviews rules made in Ireland to implement European Community decisions. Fine Gael proposed that the constitution be amended to permit Irish members of the European Parliament to sit in the Seanad ex officio, that they be permitted to address the proposed Dáil Foreign Affairs Committee, and that members of national parliaments be permitted to participate in the proceedings of committees of the European Parliament. Finally, it recommended an annual two-hour Dáil debate on European affairs, a token gesture.

Fine Gael also reiterated its long-standing position that the nominating process for the Seanad should be changed to strengthen the vocational aspect of representation, and proposed that there be Question Time in the Seanad. In a 1991 debate, Senator Manning, the Fine Gael leader in the house, made it clear that his party does not advocate additional formal powers for the Seanad. Rather it wants the house to scrutinize legislation more effectively than in the past, by using committees and being given more time by the government to consider each measure. Fine Gael would also like to see more time provided in the Seanad for private members' bills beyond the one and a half hours or so each week at present.[78] Senator John Murphy argued in 1991, "All Governments have treated this House with contempt when they want business done,"[79] but this state of affairs has improved recently. In 1992 the Fianna Fáil leader in the Senate, G. V. Wright, was working closely with his Fine Gael counterpart in scheduling business, for example.

Because Fine Gael's proposals would place new burdens on the Oireachtas, it again proposed that the Dáil week be extended from the customary three or four days to five, with committee hearings being held on Mondays and part of each Friday being used for private members' bills. It proposed to increase the staff of the Oireachtas, particularly the Parliamentary Draftsman's Office, and make larger grants to the opposition parties. It also proposed that voting in the Dáil should be by roll call rather than division, in order to save time. Finally, it called for a longer legislative year, with the Dáil reassembling in September rather than October after its summer recess. In 1983 Senator Manning, the prime author of the 1990 report, explained that the inordinate length of summer recess was due to the fact "that Governments of all parties do not like the inconvenience of the Dáil sitting too frequently."[80]

Fianna Fáil did not endorse Fine Gael's proposals, but in October 1991 its coalition partners the Progressive Democrats made reform of the Dáil a condition of renewing the coalition, and the government agreed to a series of reforms. These included a shorter summer recess, greater use of Fridays for debate, greater use of committees for the third stage of bills, and additional time for members to raise topical matters for discussion in the Dáil. The effect will be to raise the number of sitting days by thirty or more a year. The government also agreed to consider the introduction of electronic voting.[81]

## The Presidency

Reform of the Oireachtas is one way reformers hope to attack the government's dominance of the political process in Ireland. Another is to strengthen the role of the President, the central issue in the presidential election campaign in 1990 when Labour and Fine Gael each put forward a candidate who promised to change the role of the President.

The Labour-supported candidate, Mary Robinson, won the election. She is a brilliant barrister who understands the value of a political pulpit. As a senator for Dublin University for many years she used the Seanad as a platform to champion liberalization of laws relating to divorce, contraception, mixed marriage adoptions, and homosexuality. Few doubt that she was influential in changing public attitudes on these matters, and she appeared to view the presidency as an office from which to continue her activism.[82] She promised to "restore" an active presidency, although an active presidency has never existed. Indeed, Garrett FitzGerald records that Erskine Childers, President for eighteen months in 1973 and 1974, was distressed when the government refused to allow him to establish a "think-tank" on the long-term needs of the country, as he had promised in his election campaign.[83] Robinson also proposed to appoint an ad hoc emigrant's council to advise on the welfare of Ireland's emigrants,[84] and to address issues such as the "grinding and humiliating poverty" in Ireland, the environment, culture, and artistic excellence.[85] In a lecture at Queen's University, Belfast, she promised to extend the hand of friendship to Northern Ireland.[86] She proposed to make the Council of State a broad advisory council with representatives of women, farmers, the young, and other groups.[87] She was also reported as saying, "As President, directly elected by the people of Ireland, I will have the most democratic job in the country. I'll be able to look [Taoiseach] Charlie Haughey in the eye and tell him to back off if necessary because I have been directly elected by the people as a whole and he hasn't."[88] De Valera would have been astounded at this interpretation of the 1937 constitution, and it is inconceivable that President Robinson could have looked "Charlie Haughey in the eye" and escaped unscathed. However, during the campaign she also agreed that the President has no executive role and must defend the constitution, not lobby for constitutional change.[89] In October 1990 she said, "I have been making it clear for the past five months that I will restore

the Presidency to an active 'value for money' role within the Constitution. At no stage during that time have I suggested an executive role for
the President."[90]

By the end of the presidential election campaign the kind of presidency Mary Robinson envisaged was not entirely clear. In the *Irish
Times* David Gwynn Morgan suggested that she might play "the Prince
Charles role,"[91] that is, the head of state as gadfly, goading the government on public issues, but no Irish government has ever tolerated such
interference in public affairs from a head of state. Article 7 of the Irish
Constitution requires that the President's messages "to the Nation"
must be approved by the government, and while this has never meant
that every utterance must be cleared in advance, no government would
permit the President to criticize its record in public or suggest new public policies.

Austin Currie, the Fine Gael candidate for President, a former Social
and Democratic Labour party politician from Northern Ireland, also
campaigned for an expanded presidency. He too promised to appoint
a presidential commission on immigration,[92] and he too wanted the
presidency to be the focal point of the nation, the center of excellence
in commerce, sports, communications, and other areas of life.[93]

Robinson and Currie left Brian Lenihan, the Fianna Fáil candidate,
with little choice but to promise that he too would be an active President. The presidency would be the focus, he said, "for all that is good
in Irish life," but only within the framework of the constitution.[94] He
agreed with Taoiseach Haughey, who said on 7 October 1992, "To
suggest, as some are now doing, that the President should take on some
new kind of executive role and exercise additional powers is dangerous
nonsense. It would completely disrupt the constitutional balance and
cause legal chaos."[95]

A few weeks later, on 24 October, Alan Dukes, the Fine Gael leader,
attempted to boost Currie's flagging presidential campaign by introducing a private member's motion in the Dáil to expand the powers of
the President. "My party believe that while the President symbolizes
the nation, the office of President should not itself be regarded as purely
symbolic,"[96] Dukes said. He proposed that the President should chair
the Overseas Development Aid Commission "in a manner which is
above party politics," and should initiate the process of consultations
through which the Bar Council and the Incorporated Law Society rec-

ommend candidates for the judiciary to the government. The President should also chair a Judicial Commission, an Environmental Council, and a National Sports and Recreation Council, and should preside over a system of national awards to recognize excellence in all areas of Irish life. Finally, the President should address both houses of the Oireachtas annually. In a display of pure hyperbole, Dukes forecast that this address would mark the dawn of a new presidency! He recognized, of course, that Article 13.11 would require all of these new powers to be exercised on the advice of the government, but assured the Dáil, "The fact that in the exercise of such powers the President is subject to the Constitution does not prevent meaningful executive work from being entrusted to him by law."[97]

There are some minor precedents for creating new responsibilities for the President, to appoint members of the Council of the Institute for Advanced Studies and the Governor of the Central Bank, for example, but Dukes was proposing a much more profound change in the presidency and Fianna Fáil found it very easy to attack on constitutional grounds. The Minister for the Environment, Mr. Flynn, led the charge, pointing out that the proposed new functions would be redundant because they could only be performed on the advice of the government. The chairmanship of the Overseas Development Aid Commission, for example, "would place the President in a position of allocating money which the Government has provided in the way in which the Government advised."[98] With respect to judicial appointments, "the Government would have to advise the President as to whom he should advise the Government to advise him to appoint."[99] Not only would it be redundant for the President to chair assorted commissions, Flynn argued, it would be politically dangerous:

The President chairing these commissions could, constitutionally, act only on the advice of the Government: it is not hard to see, however, the seeds of conflict in a proposal to have him chair . . . high profile councils or commissions, when he himself, as the holder of high constitutional office, cannot determine the resources he can commit or how they are to be allocated. It is clear, in particular, that an environmental council chaired by the President could not be apolitical and it would inevitably become involved in controversy.[100]

Flynn quoted with approval from Professor Ronan Fanning's column in the Sunday Independent:

The notion of a populist President, of a new-style President inspired by a sense of purpose separate from the purpose of the elected government, is nonsense. And, in so far as it flies in the face of the letter and of the spirit of the Constitution, it is a potentially dangerous nonsense. . . . The Presidency should serve as the source of stability, not as a force for change. To suggest otherwise is utterly to misrepresent the nature of the office.[101]

Dukes's motion was defeated by Fianna Fáil in a party line vote.[102]

Since taking office President Robinson has begun to transform the presidency, as she promised she would do in her campaign. Unlike her predecessor, she is an active head of state, traveling widely in Ireland and abroad; her entertainment expenses were raised from Ir£ 15,000, the sum alloted in 1973, to Ir£ 100,000 in 1992 to accommodate a more active office.[103] On 8 July she addressed a joint session of the Oireachtas, only the second time this has happened and the first such speech in the Dáil chamber itself.[104] She spoke on "The Irish Identity in Europe," but because she was making a formal address to the nation the speech had to be approved by the government. She appointed four women and three men to the Council of State who represent a diversity of interests. They include feminists, one of whom is a farmer, a disabled journalist, a representative from Northern Ireland, and T. K. Whitaker, author of the famed Whitaker Report which recast Irish economic planning in the 1950s.[105] President Robinson's speeches and press interviews raise important issues, about AIDS, women's rights, poverty, the crisis in Somalia (where she visited in October 1992), and Ireland's place in the world, for example. In September 1992 she paid an official visit to Northern Ireland. But her activities are necessarily nonpartisan and circumspect, and her activism is more muted than the presidential campaign suggested. Were she to challenge the government directly on a matter of policy, the Taoiseach would be bound to assert the government's authority, and both sides would suffer in a confrontation. Taoiseach Haughey refused to allow her to deliver the BBC's annual Dimbleby Lecture in England,[106] but his successor, Albert Reynolds, appears to accept the idea that the new-style presidency is an asset for Ireland. Indeed, a British journalist, comparing President Robinson with the present unhappy condition of the British monarchy, writes, "She represents an image of Ireland that the Irish find deeply flattering to themselves—intelligent, cultured, modern, liberal."[107]

## Conclusion

There have been substantial changes in Irish life in recent years—in the courts, the Oireachtas, and the presidency—that have changed the tone of Irish politics and opened up the political process a little, but they have not eroded the power of the Taoiseach and the government appreciably. The system remains one of the most highly centralized in the democratic world.

Does this book exaggerate the government's power? Perhaps, to a degree. There are always informal constraints inside a political system that it is difficult for an observer to capture, and this book has covered too much ground to capture every nuance. Certainly those who govern are rarely as impressed by their alleged omniscience as are those they govern, and few members of the Oireachtas will concede that they are as superfluous to policymaking as this account suggests. They will point to the fact that there are always discussions between a government and its supporters, whether informally or in regular Oireachtas party meetings, and that the government often yields to persuasion. But there is a very uneven balance in the relationship. Members of the Oireachtas lack the information and civil service support available to the government, and those with political ambitions on the government back benches are sensitive to who controls patronage and the instruments of party discipline. It remains unarguably the case, therefore, that responsible government has concentrated political power in the government in Ireland, and particularly in the Taoiseach. Brian Farrell writes, "It is the Taoiseach who exercises ultimate authority. It is a function not merely of the office but of the multiplicity of roles thrust upon him—simultaneously chief executive, government chairman, party leader, national spokesman, principal legislator, electoral champion and media focus."[108]

There have been reforms in recent years designed to break down the government's domination to a degree, most of them introduced by Fine Gael–Labour coalitions since 1973, but a skeptic might say that reform is to be expected from parties that are more often in opposition than in power themselves. When Fine Gael's predecessor, Cumann na nGaedheal, was in office for ten years, from 1922 to 1932, it behaved much as Fianna Fáil has since 1932 to enhance the power of the government. Furthermore, the coalition's reforms were not as far-reaching as Fine Gael and Labour had proposed when in opposition.

Fianna Fáil, the dominant party in Ireland since 1932, has always resisted reform because it believes responsible government should be Cabinet government, not parliamentary government. Any empowerment of deputies, the Oireachtas, or the President challenges that belief. However, Fianna Fáil's precarious electoral position in recent years, and its need to join in coalitions with the more reformist Progressive Democrat and Labour parties, has made the party more malleable. It accepted some of the Fine Gael–Labour coalition's reforms on returning to office in 1987, including clerical assistants for deputies, and some committees, and under pressure from its coalition partners, the Progressive Democrats, it implemented some opposition initiatives in the period 1989–92, televising Oireachtas proceedings begun in 1991, for example, and lengthening the Dáil year.

There is room for further change, of course. The process by which the Oireachtas approves department estimates each year should be overhauled. Members of the Oireachtas could be allowed more committees, as in Britain and Canada, particularly if they were assigned more personal staff, as in Canada and Australia, to help them with their workloads. They could be given access to an Oireachtas legislative research staff. The opposition could be assigned Opposition Days, as in Britain and Canada, and the Dáil could consider more private members' bills. In Britain, using a lottery system, approximately twenty private members' bills are introduced each year, with up to sixteen Friday afternoons being set aside for debates. Many of these bills have been enacted, with the acquiescence of the government, often on sensitive moral and legal issues such as divorce, abortion, obscenity, homosexuality, and the death penalty.[109] British back-bench politicians are frustrated at having so little private members' time, but in the Parliament of a large industrial state they still have far more than their counterparts in Ireland, where private members' time is monopolized by the leaders of the largest opposition parties.

In the end, however, the Irish model of government will ensure that reform will always be on the margins. No government will allow the Dáil to usurp the legislative and executive powers that have been concentrated in the Cabinet in every country that practices responsible government, and party discipline will always be invoked to ensure that the government prevails. It was thoroughly disingenuous of John Bruton to say, in 1983, that "[t]he central objective of the reform of the Dáil is to enable this House to take the leadership in public affairs [which] it should be capable of doing as the elected assembly of the people."[110] Governments provide leadership in responsible government, not the Dáil, as Bruton well knows.

The Seanad is also unlikely to see major reforms, although the continuing novelty of vocational representation will protect the house from the fate of the New Zealand upper house, the Legislative Council, which was abolished as redundant in 1950. Vocationalism has not worked successfully as a principle of representation, but strengthening it, as Fine Gael proposes to do in some unspecified way, will not enhance the Seanad's legislative role in any substantial way. Some procedural changes, more committees, for example, and improvements in the flow of business from the Dáil, would permit the Seanad to review legislation and debate issues more effectively than it does now, but given the essential priority of the lower house in responsible government, and the model's antipathy to second chambers, it is inconceivable that a government would agree to strengthen the Seanad's powers in ways that might allow it to obstruct government programs. It is also inconceivable that the government will approve any reforms to enhance the formal powers of the President, no matter how successful Mary Robinson is in enhancing the symbolic character of the office. Such reforms too would interfere with the government's control of the political system.

Those who want more power to be given to the people, or to the Oireachtas, or to the President in order to counter the powers of the government, have a very difficult task ahead in Ireland because they are swimming against the current of responsible government as well as the conservative traditions laid down by Cumann na nGaedheal and Fianna Fáil governments since 1922. To achieve even modest reforms they will have to swim with the current, channeling rather than fighting the flow. This means finding ways to help the government do its job better rather than trying to substitute for the government. For its part, the government will have to recognize that it has an interest in this kind of reform. A less confrontational style of politics in the Dáil would be a good start which need not lead to any substantial weakening in the government's ability to govern. But we should not expect too much. In 1980 Professor Basil Chubb wrote:

The three factors that most inhibit the development of the potential of the Oireachtas are . . . the view of all political leaders when in government that they must have a monopoly of initiative, the practice of strictly competitive politics in dealing with parliamentary business, and the acceptance by most members of the present meager role of the Oireachtas in the political system.[111]

The Fine Gael–Labour coalition's initiatives will have changed this description a little since 1980, but lurking behind Chubb's argument is the logic of responsible government, a powerful model that conditions and channels political behavior in certain ways. It cannot be willed away.

*Appendices*

# The Irish Free State Constitution, 1922, and Responsible Government

The Irish Free State Constitution was the First Schedule to the Constitution of the Irish Free State (Saorstát Éireann) Act of 1922. It had eighty-three articles. The Second Schedule is a restatement of the Anglo-Irish Treaty of 6 December 1921. The following articles dealing with responsible government and the British connection are drawn from the unamended constitution of 1922.

## Constitution of the Irish Free State

ARTICLE 1

The Irish Free State (otherwise hereinafter called or sometimes called Saorstát Éireann) is a coequal member of the Community of Nations forming the British Commonwealth of Nations.

ARTICLE 2

All powers of government and all authority legislative, executive, and judicial in Ireland, are derived from the people of Ireland and the same shall be exercised in the Irish Free State (Saorstát Éireann) through the organizations established by or under, and in accord with, this Constitution.

. . .

ARTICLE 12

A Legislature is hereby created to be known as the Oireachtas. It shall consist of the King and two Houses, the Chamber of Deputies (otherwise called and herein generally referred to as "Dáil Éireann") and the Senate (otherwise known and herein generally referred to as "Seanad Éireann"). The sole and exclusive power of making laws for the peace, order and good government of the Irish Free State (Saorstát Éireann) is vested in the Oireachtas.

. . .

ARTICLE 26

Dáil Éireann shall be composed of members who represent constituencies determined by law. The number of members shall be fixed from time to time by the Oireachtas but the total number of members of Dáil Éireann (exclusive of members for the Universities) shall not be fixed at less than one member for each thirty thousand of the population, or at more than one member for each twenty thousand of the population. . . . The members shall be elected upon principles of Proportional Representation.

. . .

ARTICLE 28

. . . Dáil Éireann may not at any time be dissolved except on the advice of the Executive Council.

. . .

ARTICLE 30

Seanad Éireann shall be composed of citizens who shall be proposed on the grounds that they have done honour to the Nation by reason of useful public service or that, because of special qualifications or attainments, they represent important aspects of the Nation's life.

ARTICLE 31

The number of members of Seanad Éireann shall be sixty. . . . Subject to any provisions for the constitution of the first Seanad Éireann the term of office of a member of Seanad Éireann shall be twelve years.

ARTICLE 32

One-fourth of the members of Seanad Éireann shall be elected every three years from a panel constituted as hereinafter mentioned at an election at which the area of the jurisdiction of the Irish Free State (Saorstát Éireann) shall form one electoral area, and the elections shall be held on the principles of Proportional Representation.

. . .

ARTICLE 35

Dáil Éireann shall in relation to the subject matter of Money Bills as hereinafter defined have legislative authority exclusive of Seanad Éireann. . . .

. . .

ARTICLE 37

Money shall not be appropriated by vote, resolution or law, unless the purpose of the appropriation has in the same session been recommended by a message from the Representative of the Crown acting on the advice of the Executive Council.

ARTICLE 38

Every bill initiated in and passed by Dáil Éireann shall be sent to Seanad Éireann and may, unless it be a Money Bill, be amended in Seanad Éireann and Dáil Éireann shall consider any such amendment; but a Bill passed by Dáil Éireann and considered by Seanad Éireann shall, not later than two hundred and seventy days after it shall have been first sent to Seanad Éireann, or such longer period may be agreed upon by the two Houses, be deemed to be passed by both Houses in the form in which it was last passed by Dáil Éireann: Provided that every Money Bill shall be sent to Seanad Éireann for its recommendations and at a period not longer than twenty-one days after it shall have been sent to Seanad Éireann, it shall be returned to Dáil Éireann which may pass it, accepting or rejecting all or any of the recommendations of Seanad Éireann, and as so passed or if not returned within such period of twenty-one days shall be deemed to have been passed by both Houses. When a Bill other than a Money Bill has been sent to Seanad Éireann a Joint Sitting of the Members of both Houses may on a resolution passed by Seanad Éireann be convened for the purpose of debating, but not of voting upon, the proposals of the Bill or any amendment of the same.

. . .

## ARTICLE 40

A Bill passed by either House and accepted by the other House shall be deemed to be passed by both Houses.

## ARTICLE 41

So soon as any Bill shall have been passed or deemed to have been passed by both Houses, the Executive Council shall present the same to the Representative of the Crown for the signification by him, in the King's name, of the King's assent, and such Representative may withhold the King's assent or reserve the Bill for the signification of the King's pleasure: Provided that the Representative of the Crown shall in the withholding of such assent to or the reservation of any Bill, act in accordance with the law, practice, and constitutional usage governing the like withholding of assent or reservation in the Dominion of Canada.

A Bill reserved for the signification of the King's Pleasure shall not have any force unless and until within one year from the day on which it was presented to the Representative of the Crown for the King's assent, the Representative of the Crown signifies by speech or message to each of the Houses of the Oireachtas, or by proclamation, that it has received the Assent of the King in Council.

. . .

## ARTICLE 45

The Oireachtas may provide for the establishment of Functional or Vocational Councils representing branches of the social and economic life of the Nation. . . .

. . .

## ARTICLE 47

Any Bill passed or deemed to have been passed by both Houses may be suspended for a period of ninety days on the written demand of two-fifths of the members of Dáil Éireann or of a majority of the members of Seanad Éireann presented to the President of the Executive Council not later than seven days from the day on which such Bill shall have been so passed or deemed to have been so passed. Such a Bill shall in accordance with regulations to be made by the Oireachtas be submitted by Referendum to the decision of the people if demanded before the expiration of the ninety days either by a resolution of Seanad Éireann assented to by three-fifths of the members of Seanad Éireann, or by a petition signed by not less than one-twentieth of the voters then on the register of voters, and the decision of the people by a majority of the votes recorded on such Referendum shall be conclusive. These provisions shall not apply to Money Bills or to such Bills as shall be declared by both houses to be necessary for the immediate preservation of the public peace, health or safety.

## ARTICLE 48

The Oireachtas may provide for the Initiation by the people of proposals for laws or constitutional amendments. Should the Oireachtas fail to make such provisions within two years, it shall on the petition of not less than seventy-five thousand voters on the register, of whom not more than fifteen thousand shall be voters in any one constituency, either make such provisions or submit the question to the people for decision in accordance with the ordinary regulations governing the Referendum.

Any legislation passed by the Oireachtas providing for such Initiation by the people shall provide (1) that such proposals may be initiated on a petition of fifty thousand voters on the register, (2) that if the Oireachtas rejects a proposal so initiated it shall be submitted to the people for decision in accordance with the ordinary regulations governing the Referendum; and (3) that if the Oireachtas enacts a proposal so initiated, such enactment shall be subject to the provisions respecting ordinary legislation or amendments of the Constitution as the case may be.

ARTICLE 49

Save in the case of actual invasion, the Irish Free State (Saorstát Éireann) shall not be committed to active participation in any war without the assent of the Oireachtas.

. . .

ARTICLE 51

The Executive Authority of the Irish Free State (Saorstát Éireann) is hereby declared to be vested in the King, and shall be exercisable, in accordance with the law, practice and constitutional usage governing the exercise of the Executive Authority in the case of the Dominion of Canada, by the Representative of the Crown. There shall be a Council to aid and advise in the government of the Irish Free State (Saorstát Éireann) to be styled the Executive Council. The Executive Council shall be responsible to Dáil Éireann, and shall consist of not more than seven nor less than five Ministers appointed by the Representative of the Crown on the nomination of the President of the Executive Council.

ARTICLE 52

Those Ministers who form the Executive Council shall all be members of Dáil Éireann and shall include the President of the Council, the Vice-President of the Council and the Minister in charge of the Department of Finance.

ARTICLE 53

The President of the Council shall be appointed on the nomination of Dáil Éireann. He shall nominate a Vice-President of the Council, who shall act for all purposes in the place of the President, if the President shall die, resign, or be permanently incapacitated, until a new President of the Council shall have been elected. The Vice-President shall also act in the place of the President during his temporary absence. The other Ministers who are to hold office as members of the Executive Council shall be appointed on the nomination of the President, with the assent of Dáil Éireann, and he and the Ministers nominated by him shall retire from office should he cease to retain the support of a majority in Dáil Éireann, but the President and such Ministers shall continue to carry on their duties until their successors shall have been appointed: Provided, however, that the Oireachtas shall not be dissolved on the advice of an Executive Council which has ceased to retain the support of a majority in Dáil Éireann.

ARTICLE 54

The Executive Council shall be collectively responsible for all matters concerning the Departments of State administered by Members of Executive Council. . . .

ARTICLE 55

Ministers who shall not be members of the Executive Council may be appointed by the Representative of the Crown and shall comply with the provisions of Article 17 of this Constitution. Every such Minister shall be nominated by Dáil Éireann on the recommendation of a Committee of Dáil Éireann chosen by a method to be determined by Dáil Éireann, so as to be impartially representative of Dáil Éireann. . . .

## ARTICLE 56

Every Minister who is not a member of the Executive Council shall be the responsible head of the Department or Departments under his charge, and shall be individually responsible to Dáil Éireann alone for the administration of the Department or Departments of which he is the head: Provided that should arrangements for Functional or Vocational Councils be made by the Oireachtas these Ministers or any of them may, should the Oireachtas so decide, be members of, and be recommended to Dáil Éireann by, such Councils. The term of office of any Minister, not a member of the Executive Council, shall be the term of Dáil Éireann existing at any time of his appointment. . . .

## ARTICLE 57

Every Minister shall have the right to attend and be heard in Seanad Éireann.

. . .

## ARTICLE 60

The Representative of the Crown, who shall be styled the Governor-General of the Irish Free State (Saorstát Éireann) shall be appointed in like manners as the Governor-General of Canada and in accordance with the practice observed in the making of such appointments. . . .

. . .

## ARTICLE 65

The judicial power of the High Court shall extend to the question of the validity of any law having regard to the provisions of the Constitution. . . .

## ARTICLE 66

The Supreme Court of the Irish Free State (Saorstát Éireann) shall, with such exceptions (not including cases which involve questions as to the validity of any law) and subject to such regulations as may be prescribed by law, have appellate jurisdiction from all decisions of the High Court. . . . Provided that nothing in this Constitution shall impair the right of any person to petition His Majesty for special leave to appeal from the Supreme Court to His Majesty in Council or the right of His Majesty to grant such leave.

. . .

# The Constitution of Ireland, 1937, and Responsible Government

The following articles from the 1937 constitution deal with responsible government in the Republic of Ireland.

## The Constitution of Ireland

### The State

ARTICLE 6

1. All powers of government, legislative, executive and judicial, derive, under God, from the people, whose right it is to designate the rulers of the State and, in final appeal, to decide all questions of national policy, according to the requirements of the common good.

### The President

ARTICLE 12

1. There shall be a President of Ireland (Uachtarán na hÉireann), hereinafter called the President, who shall take precedence over all other persons in the State and who shall exercise and perform the powers and functions conferred on the President by this Constitution and by law.

2.1° The President shall be elected by direct vote of the people.

3.1° The President shall hold office for seven years from the date upon which he enters upon his office. . . .

2° A person who holds, or who has held, office of President, shall be eligible for re-election to that office once, but only once.

. . .

4.2° Every candidate for election, not a former or retiring President, must be nominated either by:

i. not less than twenty persons, each of whom is at the time a member of one of the Houses of the Oireachtas, or

ii. by the Councils of not less than four administrative Counties (including County Boroughs) as defined by law.

. . .

4° Former or retiring Presidents may become candidates on their own nomination.

5° Where only one candidate is nominated for the office of President it shall not be necessary to proceed to a ballot for his election.

. . .

9. The President shall not leave the State during his term of office save with the consent of the Government.

10.1° The President may be impeached for stated misbehaviour.

. . .

ARTICLE 13

1.1° The President shall, on the nomination of Dáil Éireann, appoint the Taoiseach, that is, the head of the Government or Prime Minister.

2° The President shall, on the nomination of the Taoiseach with the previous approval of Dáil Éireann, appoint the other members of the Government.

3° The President shall, on the advice of the Taoiseach, accept the resignation or terminate the appointment of any member of the Government.

2.1° Dáil Éireann shall be summoned and dissolved by the President on the advice of the Taoiseach.

2° The President may in his absolute discretion refuse to dissolve Dáil Éireann on the advice of a Taoiseach who has ceased to retain the support of a majority in Dáil Éireann.

3° The President may at any time, after consultation with the Council of State, convene a meeting of either or both of the Houses of the Oireachtas.

. . .

4. The supreme command of the Defence Forces is hereby vested in the President.

5.1° The exercise of the Supreme command of the Defence Forces shall be regulated by law.

6. The right of pardon and the power to commute or remit punishment imposed by any court exercising criminal jurisdiction are hereby vested in the President, but such power of commutation or remission may, except in capital cases, also be conferred by law on other authorities.

7.1° The President may, after consultation with the Council of State, communicate with the Houses of the Oireachtas by message or address on any matter of national or public importance.

2° The President may, after consultation with the Council of State, address a message to the Nation at any time on any such matter.

3° Every such message or address must, however, have received the approval of the Government.

. . .

9. The powers and functions conferred on the President by this Constitution shall be exercisable and performable by him only on the advice of the Government, save where it is provided by this Constitution that he shall act in his absolute discretion or after consultation with or in relation to the Council of State, or on the advice or nomination of, or on receipt of any other communication from, any other person or body.

10. Subject to this Constitution, additional powers and functions may be conferred on the President by law.

11. No power or function conferred on the President by law shall be exercisable or performable by him save only on the advice of the Government.

. . .

## The National Parliament

### Constitution and Powers

ARTICLE 15

1.1° The National Parliament shall be called and known, and is in this Constitution generally referred to, as the Oireachtas.

2° The Oireachtas shall consist of the President and two Houses, viz.: a House of Representatives to be called Dáil Éireann and a Senate to be called Seanad Éireann.

. . .

2.1° The sole and exclusive power of making laws for the State is hereby vested in the Oireachtas: no other legislative authority has power to make laws for the State.

. . .

3.1° The Oireachtas may provide for the establishment or recognition of functional or vocational councils representing branches of the social and economic life of the people.

. . .

4.1° The Oireachtas shall not enact any law which is in any respect repugnant to this Constitution or any provision thereof.

. . .

6.1° The right to raise and maintain military or armed forces is vested exclusively in the Oireachtas.

. . .

7. The Oireachtas shall hold at least one session every year.

. . .

### Dáil Éireann

ARTICLE 16

2.1° Dáil Éireann shall be composed of members who represent constituencies determined by law.

2° The number of members shall from time to time be fixed by law, but the total number of members of Dáil Éireann shall not be fixed at less than one member for each thirty thousand of the population, or at more than one member for each twenty thousand of the population.

. . .

5° The members shall be elected on the system of proportional representation by means of the single transferable vote.

6° No law shall be enacted whereby the number of members to be returned, for any constituency shall be less than three.

. . .

3.2° A general election for members of Dáil Éireann shall take place not later than thirty days after the dissolution of the Dáil.

. . .

5. The same Dáil Éireann shall not continue for a longer period than seven years from the date of its first meeting; a shorter period may be fixed by law.

6. Provision shall be made by law to enable the member of Dáil Éireann who is the Chairman immediately before a dissolution of Dáil Éireann to be deemed without any actual election to be elected a member of Dáil Éireann at the ensuing general election.

. . .

ARTICLE 17

2. Dáil Éireann shall not pass any vote or resolution, and no law shall be enacted, for the appropriation of revenue or other public moneys unless the purpose of the

appropriation shall have been recommended to Dáil Éireann by a message from the Government signed by the Taoiseach.

## Seanad Éireann

### ARTICLE 18

1. Seanad Éireann shall be composed of sixty members, of whom eleven shall be nominated members and forty-nine shall be elected members.

. . .

3. The nominated members of Seanad Éireann shall be nominated, with their prior consent, by the Taoiseach who is appointed next after the re-assembly of Dáil Éireann following the dissolution thereof which occasions the nomination of the said members;

4.1° The elected members of Seanad Éireann shall be elected as follows:—

i. Three shall be elected by the National University of Ireland.

ii. Three shall be elected by the University of Dublin.

iii. Forty-three shall be elected from panels of candidates constituted as hereinafter provided.

. . .

5. Every election of the elected members of Seanad Éireann shall be held on the system of proportional representation by means of the single transferable vote, and by secret postal ballot.

6. The members of Seanad Éireann to be elected by the Universities shall be elected on a franchise and in the manner to be provided by law.

7.1° Before each general election of the members of Seanad Éireann to be elected from panels of candidates, five panels of candidates shall be formed in the manner provided by law containing respectively the names of persons having knowledge and practical experience of the following interests and services, namely:—

i. National Language and Culture, Literature, Art, Education and such professional interests as may be defined by law for the purpose of this panel;

ii. Agriculture and allied interests, and Fisheries;

iii. Labour, whether organized or unorganized;

iv. Industry and Commerce, including banking, finance, accountancy, engineering and architecture;

v. Public Administration and social services, including voluntary social activities.

7.2° Not more than eleven and, subject to the provisions of Article 1 hereof, not less than five members of Seanad Éireann shall be elected from any one panel.

8. A general election for Seanad Éireann shall take place not later than ninety days after a dissolution of Dáil Éireann, and the first meeting of Seanad Éireann after the general election shall take place on a day to be fixed by the President on the advice of the Taoiseach.

. . .

### ARTICLE 19

Provision may be made by law for the direct election by any functional or vocational group or association or council of so many members of Seanad Éireann as may be fixed by such law in substitution for an equal number of the members to be elected from the corresponding panels of candidates constituted under Article 18 of this Constitution.

## Legislation

ARTICLE 20

1. Every Bill initiated in and passed by Dáil Éireann shall be sent to Seanad Éireann and may, unless it be a Money Bill, be amended in Seanad Éireann and Dáil Éireann shall consider any such amendment.

2. 1° A Bill other than a Money Bill may be initiated in Seanad Éireann, and if passed by Seanad Éireann, shall be introduced in Dáil Éireann.

2° A Bill initiated in Seanad Éireann if amended in Dáil Éireann shall be considered as a Bill initiated in Dáil Éireann.

3. A Bill passed by either House and accepted by the other House shall be deemed to have been passed by both Houses.

## Money Bills

ARTICLE 21

1. 1° Money Bills shall be initiated in Dáil Éireann only.

2° Every Money Bill passed by Dáil Éireann shall be sent to Seanad Éireann for its recommendations.

2. 1° Every Money Bill sent to Seanad Éireann for its recommendations shall, at the expiration of a period not longer than twenty-one days after it shall have been sent to Seanad Éireann, be returned to Dáil Éireann, which may accept or reject all or any of the recommendations of Seanad Éireann.

. . .

ARTICLE 22

2. 1° The Chairman of Dáil Éireann shall certify any Bill which, in his opinion, is a Money Bill to be a Money Bill, and his certificate shall, subject to the subsequent provisions of this section, be final and conclusive.

2° Seanad Éireann, by a resolution, passed at a sitting at which not less than thirty members are present, may request the President to refer the question whether the Bill is or is not a Money Bill to a Committee of Privileges.

3° If the President after consultation with the Council of State decides to accede to the request he shall appoint a Committee of Privileges consisting of an equal number of members of Dáil Éireann and of Seanad Éireann and a Chairman who shall be a Judge of the Supreme Court: these appointments shall be made after consultation with the Council of State. In the case of an equality of votes but not otherwise the Chairman shall be entitled to vote.

. . .

## Time for Consideration of Bills

ARTICLE 23

1. This Article applies to every Bill passed by Dáil Éireann and sent to Seanad Éireann other than a Money Bill or a Bill the time for the consideration of which by Seanad Éireann shall have been abridged under Article 24 of this Constitution.

1° Whenever a Bill to which this Article applies is within the stated period defined in the next following sub-section either rejected by Seanad Éireann or passed by Seanad Éireann with amendments to which Dáil Éireann does not agree or is neither passed (with or without amendment) nor rejected by Seanad Éireann within the stated period, the Bill shall, if Dáil Éireann so resolves within one hundred and eighty days after the expiration of the stated period be deemed to have been passed by both houses of the Oireachtas on the day on which the resolution is passed.

2° The stated period is the period of ninety days commencing on the day on which the Bill is first sent by Dáil Éireann to Seanad Éireann or any longer period agreed upon in respect of the bill by both Houses of the Oireachtas.

. . .

## ARTICLE 24

1. If and whenever on the passage by Dáil Éireann of any Bill, other than a Bill expressed to be a Bill containing a proposal to amend the Constitution, the Taoiseach certifies by messages in writing addressed to the President and to the Chairman of each House of the Oireachtas that, in the opinion of the Government, the Bill is urgent and immediately necessary for the preservation of the public peace and security, or by reason of the existence of a public emergency, whether domestic or international, the time for the consideration of such Bill by Seanad Éireann shall, if Dáil Éireann so resolves and if the President, after consultation with the Council of State, concurs, be abridged to such period as shall be specified in the resolution.

. . .

## ARTICLE 26

This Article applies to any Bill passed or deemed to have been passed by both Houses of the Oireachtas other than a Money Bill or a Bill expressed to be a Bill containing a proposal to amend the Constitution, or a Bill the time for the consideration of which by Seanad Éireann shall have been abridged under Article 24 of this Constitution.

1.1° The President may, after consultation with the Council of State, refer any Bill to which this Article applies to the Supreme Court for a decision on the question as to whether such Bill or any specified provision or provisions of such Bill is or are repugnant to this Constitution or to any provision thereof.

. . .

## Reference of Bills to the People

### ARTICLE 27

This Article applies to any Bill, other than a Bill expressed to be a Bill containing a proposal for the amendment of this Constitution, which shall have been deemed, by virtue of Article hereof, to have been passed by both Houses of the Oireachtas.

1. A majority of the members of Seanad Éireann and not less than one-third of the members of Dáil Éireann may by a joint petition addressed to the President by them under this Article request the President to decline to sign and promulgate as a law any Bill to which this Article applies on the ground that the Bill contains a proposal of such national importance that the will of the people thereon ought to be ascertained.

. . .

3. Every such petition shall contain a statement of the particular ground or grounds on which the request is based, and shall be presented to the President not later than four days after the date on which the Bill shall have been deemed to have been passed by both Houses of the Oireachtas.

4.1° Upon receipt of a petition addressed to him under this Article, the President shall forthwith consider such petition and shall, after consultation with the Council of State, pronounce his decision thereon not later than ten days after the date on which the Bill to which such petition relates shall have been deemed to have been passed by both Houses of the Oireachtas.

. . .

5.1° In every case in which the President decides that a Bill the subject of a petition under this Article contains a proposal of such national importance that the will of the people thereon ought to be ascertained, he shall inform the Taoiseach and the Chairman of each House of the Oireachtas accordingly in writing under his hand and Seal and shall decline to sign and promulgate such Bill as a law unless and until the proposal shall have been approved either

i. by the people at a Referendum in accordance with the provisions of section 2 of Article 47 of this Constitution within a period of eighteen months from the date of the President's decision, or

ii. by a resolution of Dáil Éireann passed within the said period after a dissolution and re-assembly of Dáil Éireann.

. . .

## The Government

ARTICLE 28

1. The Government shall consist of not less than seven and not more than fifteen members who shall be appointed by the President in accordance with the provisions of this Constitution.

2. The executive power of the State shall subject to the provisions of this Constitution be exercised by or on the authority of the Government.

3.1° War shall not be declared and the State shall not participate in any war save with the assent of Dáil Éireann.

2° In the case of actual invasion, however, the Government may take whatever steps they may consider necessary for the protection of the State, and Dáil Éireann if not sitting shall be summoned to meet at the earliest practicable date.

. . .

4.1° The Government shall be responsible to Dáil Éireann.

2° The Government shall meet and act as a collective authority, and shall be collectively responsible for the Departments of State administered by the members of the Government.

3° The Government shall prepare Estimates of the Receipts and Estimates of the Expenditure of the State for each financial year, and shall present them to Dáil Éireann for consideration.

5.1° The head of the Government, or Prime Minister, shall be called, and is in this Constitution referred to as, the Taoiseach.

2° The Taoiseach shall keep the President generally informed on matters of domestic and international policy.

6.1° The Taoiseach shall nominate a member of the Government to be the Tánaiste.

. . .

7.1° The Taoiseach, the Tánaiste and the member of the Government who is in charge of the Department of Finance must be members of Dáil Éireann.

2° The other members of the Government must be members of Dáil Éireann or Seanad Éireann, but not more than two may be member of Seanad Éireann.

8. Every member of the Government shall have the right to attend and be heard in each House of the Oireachtas.

9.1° The Taoiseach may resign from office at any time by placing his resignation in the hands the President.

2° Any other member of the Government may resign from office by placing his resignation in the hands of the Taoiseach for submission to the President.

3° The President shall accept the resignation of a member of the Government, other than the Taoiseach, if so advised by the Taoiseach.

4° The Taoiseach may at any time, for reason which to him seem sufficient, request a member of the Government to resign; should the member concerned fail to comply with the request, his appointment shall be terminated by the President if the Taoiseach so advises.

10. The Taoiseach shall resign from office upon his ceasing to retain the support of a majority in Dáil Éireann unless on his advice the President dissolves Dáil Éireann and on the reassembly of Dáil Éireann after the dissolution the Taoiseach secures the support of a majority in Dáil Éireann.

11.1° If the Taoiseach at any time resigns from office the other members of the Government shall be deemed also to have resigned from office, but the Taoiseach and the other members of the Government shall continue to carry on their duties until their successors shall have been appointed.

2° The members of the Government in office at the date of a dissolution of Dáil Éireann shall continue to hold office until their successors shall have been appointed.

12. The following matters shall be regulated in accordance with law, namely, the organization of and distribution of business amongst Departments of State, the designation of members of the Government to be the Ministers in charge of the said Departments, the discharge of the functions of the office of a member of the Government during his temporary absence or incapacity, and the remuneration of the members of the Government.

## International Relations

ARTICLE 29

4.1° The executive power of the State in or in connection with its external relations shall in accordance with Article 28 of this Constitution be exercised by or on the authority of the Government.

2° For the purpose of the exercise of any executive function of the State in or in connection with its external relations, the Government may to such extent and subject to such conditions, if any, as may be determined by law, avail of or adopt any organ, instrument, or method of procedure used or adopted for the like purpose by the members of any group or league of nations with which the State is or becomes associated for the purpose of international co-operation in matters of common concern.

. . .

5.1° Every international agreement to which the State becomes a party shall be laid before Dáil Éireann.

. . .

## The Attorney General

ARTICLE 30

2. The Attorney General shall be appointed by the President on the nomination of the Taoiseach.

. . .

4. The Attorney General shall not be a member of the Government.

. . .

5.4° The Attorney General shall retire from office upon the resignation of the Taoiseach, but may continue to carry on his duties until the successor to the Taoiseach shall have been appointed.

. . .

## The Council of State

ARTICLE 31

1. There shall be a Council of State to aid and counsel the President on all matters on which the President may consult the said Council in relation to the exercise and performance by him of such of his powers and functions as are by this Constitution expressed to be exercisable and performable after consultation with the Council of State, and to exercise such other functions as are conferred on the said Council by this Constitution.

2. The Council of State shall consist of the following members:

i. As *ex-officio* members: the Taoiseach, the Tánaiste, the Chief Justice, the President of the High Court, the Chairman of Dáil Éireann, the Chairman of Seanad Éireann, and the Attorney General.

ii. Every person able and willing to act as a member of the Council of State who shall have held the office of President or the office of Taoiseach, or the office of Chief Justice, or the office of President of the Executive Council of Saorstát Éireann.

iii. Such other persons, if any, as may be appointed by the President under this Article to be members of the Council of State.

3. The President may at any time and from time to time by warrant under his hand and Seal appoint such other persons as, in his absolute discretion, he may think fit, to be members of the Council of State, but not more than seven persons so appointed shall be members of the Council of State at the same time.

. . .

8. Meetings of the Council of State may be convened by the President at such times and places as he shall determine.

. . .

## The Courts

ARTICLE 34

3.2° Save as otherwise provided by this Article, the jurisdiction of the High Court shall extend to the question of the validity of any law having regard to the provisions of this Constitution. . . .

3° No Court whatever shall have jurisdiction to question the validity of a law, or any provision of a law, the Bill for which shall have been referred to the Supreme Court by the President under Article 26 of this Constitution, or to question the validity of a provision of a law where the corresponding provision in the Bill for such law shall have been referred to the Supreme Court by the President under the said Article 26.

. . .

4.1° The Court of Final Appeal shall be called the Supreme Court.

. . .

4° No law shall be enacted excepting from the appellate jurisdiction of the Supreme Court cases which involve questions as to the validity of any law having regard to the provisions of this Constitution.

5° The decision of the Supreme Court on a question as to the validity of a law having regard to the provisions of this Constitution shall be pronounced by such one of the judges of that Court as that Court shall direct, and no other opinion on such question, whether assenting or dissenting, shall be pronounced, nor shall the existence of any such other opinion be disclosed.

# Notes

## Preface

1. Emmet Larkin, "The Irish Political Tradition," in Thomas E. Hachey and Lawrence J. McCaffrey, eds., *Perspectives on Irish Nationalism* (Lexington: University of Kentucky Press, 1989), 99–120.

## Introduction. Responsible Government

1. A. V. Dicey, *Lectures Introductory to the Study of the Law of the Constitution* (London: Macmillan, 1885), 24–25.

2. See Alan J. Ward, "Exporting the British Constitution: Responsible Government in New Zealand, Canada, Australia and Ireland," *Journal of Commonwealth and Comparative Politics* 25, no. 1 (1987): 3–11.

3. New Zealand Statutes, no. 114 of 1986.

4. Leo Kohn, *The Constitution of the Irish Free State* (London: Allen and Unwin, 1932), 80.

5. Walter Bagehot, *The English Constitution*, ed. R. H. Crossman (Ithaca, N.Y.: Cornell University Press, 1963), 65.

6. Alan J. Ward, "Challenging the British Constitution: The Irish Free State Constitution and the External Minister," *Parliamentary History* 9, pt. 1 (1990): 116–28.

7. An exception is Section 22D of the New South Wales Constitution which requires that a casual vacancy in the Legislative Council, caused by the removal, resignation, or death of a member, shall be filled by someone from the same group or party.

8. Bagehot, *English Constitution*, 51.

9. Dicey, *Law of the Constitution*, 351.

10. John Manning Ward, *Colonial Self-Government: The British Experience, 1759–1856* (London: Macmillan, 1976), 172–208.

11. John Mackintosh writes that George I did not meet with his Cabinet because "he was both ignorant of English affairs and stupid." George III was subject to periodic fits of insanity. See John P. Mackintosh, *The British Cabinet*, 2d ed. (London: Methuen, 1968), 51, 69.

12. Mackintosh, *British Cabinet*, 56.

13. E. C. S. Wade and G. Godfrey Phillips, *Constitutional and Administrative Law*, 9th ed. (London: Longman, 1977), 17.

14. Ibid., 195–96.

15. Robert McKenzie, *British Political Parties* (London: Mercury Books, 1964), 2.

16. J. M. Ward, *Colonial Self-Government*, 177.
17. Bagehot, *English Constitution*, 111.
18. Ibid., 98.
19. McKenzie, *British Political Parties*, 6.
20. J. M. Ward, *Colonial Self-Government*, 278.

## Chapter 1. "Independent Parliament"

1. F. X. Martin, "The Coming of Parliament," in Brian Farrell, ed., *The Irish Parliamentary Tradition* (Dublin: Gill and Macmillan, 1973), 40.
2. W. E. H. Lecky, *A History of Ireland in the Eighteenth Century*, abridged by L. P. Curtis, Jr. (Chicago: University of Chicago Press, 1972), 201.
3. R. B. McDowell, *Ireland in the Age of Imperialism and Revolution, 1760–1801* (Oxford: Clarendon Press, 1979), 107–20.
4. Edith Johnston, *Great Britain and Ireland, 1760–1800* (London: Oliver and Boyd, 1963), 268; McDowell, *Ireland in the Age of Imperialism*, 121–25.
5. Johnston, *Great Britain and Ireland*, 118.
6. A. P. W. Malcomson, *John Foster: The Politics of the Anglo-Irish Ascendancy* (Oxford: Oxford University Press, 1978), 235–36.
7. Edith Johnston, *Ireland in the Eighteenth Century* (Dublin: Gill and Macmillan, 1974), 133.
8. Johnston, *Great Britain and Ireland*, 3.
9. Ibid., 273.
10. Edmund Curtis and R. B. McDowell, *Irish Historical Documents, 1172–1922* (London: Methuen, 1968), 83.
11. Brendan Bradshaw, "The Beginnings of Modern Ireland," in Farrell, ed., *Irish Parliamentary Tradition*, 70.
12. Curtis and McDowell, *Irish Historical Documents*, 187.
13. Thomas Bartlett, review of Gerard O'Brien, *Anglo-Irish Politics in the Age of Grattan and Pitt* (Dublin: Irish Academic Press, 1987), *Irish Literary Supplement* 7, no. 2 (Fall 1988): 45.
14. Maurice R. O'Connell, *Irish Politics and Social Conflict in the Age of the American Revolution* (Philadelphia: University of Pennsylvania, 1965), 18; McDowell, *Ireland in the Age of Imperialism*, 131.
15. Gerard O'Brien, *Anglo-Irish Politics in the Age of Grattan and Pitt* (Dublin: Irish Academic Press, 1987), 32.
16. Vincent T. Harlow, *The Founding of the Second British Empire, 1763–1793*, 2 vols. (London: Longmans, 1952), 1:493–501.
17. Leonard W. Larabee, *Royal Government in America: A Study of the British Colonial System before 1783* (New Haven, Conn.: Yale University Press, 1930), 220–22.
18. Ibid., 35.
19. O'Connell discusses the influence of the American Revolution on the Patriots; see particularly "Irish Opinion on the American Revolution," in his *Irish Politics and Social Conflict in the Age of the American Revolution*, 25–36. Also see McDowell, "The American War and the Volunteers," in *Ireland in the Age of Imperialism*, 239–74.
20. McDowell, *Ireland in the Age of Imperialism*, 254–62; Johnston, *Ireland in the Eighteenth Century*, 150–51.
21. Curtis and McDowell, *Irish Historical Documents*, 233–34. Catholic relief was only endorsed by the Volunteers in Ulster; see Marianne Elliott, *Wolfe Tone: Prophet of Independence* (New Haven, Conn.: Yale University Press, 1989), 113.

22. O'Brien, *Anglo-Irish Politics*, 35; McDowell, *Ireland in the Age of Imperialism*, 283–84.

23. Curtis and McDowell, *Irish Historical Documents*, 203, 222–24.

24. See McDowell, *Ireland in the Age of Imperialism*, 284, and his *Irish Public Opinion, 1750–1800* (London: Faber and Faber, 1964), 74.

25. O'Brien, *Anglo-Irish Politics*, 42; McDowell, *Ireland in the Age of Imperialism*, 287–88.

26. Lecky, *History of Ireland*, 197; O'Connell, *Irish Politics and Social Conflict*, 333–42; Curtis and McDowell, *Irish Historical Documents*, 187–88.

27. The American precedent is discussed in Harlow, "The Irish Revolution as an Imperial Problem," in *Founding of the British Empire*, 1:493–557.

28. McDowell, *Ireland in the Age of Imperialism*, 132–33.

29. Harlow, *Founding of the British Empire*, 1:532–33.

30. Ibid., 1:501.

31. Ibid., 1:493.

32. Ibid., 1:495–500.

33. O'Connell, *Irish Politics and Social Conflict*, 343.

34. O'Brien, *Anglo-Irish Politics*, 60; McDowell, *Ireland in the Age of Imperialism*, 289.

35. Malcomson, *John Foster*, 49–58; McDowell, *Ireland in the Age of Imperialism*, 330–37.

36. Pitt to Orde, October 1784, quoted in O'Brien, *Anglo-Irish Politics*, 66.

37. Foster to Grattan, 20 January 1785, quoted in Malcomson, *John Foster*, 50.

38. Ibid., 52.

39. O'Brien, *Anglo-Irish Politics*, 81.

40. Memorandum, February 1886, Gladstone Papers, Add. 44632, F103–4, British Library.

41. McDowell, *Irish Public Opinion*, 77.

42. Ibid., 78; O'Brien, *Anglo-Irish Politics*, 89.

43. Johnston, *Great Britain and Ireland*, 34–35.

44. G. C. Bolton, *The Passing of the Act of Union* (Oxford: Oxford University Press, 1966), 6.

45. Lecky, *History of Ireland*, 198.

46. Harlow, *Founding of the British Empire*, 631–38; Malcomson, *John Foster*, 65–68; McDowell, "The Catholic Agitation," in *Ireland in the Age of Imperialism*, 390–421.

47. Malcomson, *John Foster*, 47–48; Bolton, *Passing of the Act of Union*, 6–9; R. F. Foster, *Modern Ireland, 1600–1972* (London: Allen Lane/Penguin Press, 1988), 233; Johnston, *Great Britain and Ireland*, 89–96.

48. Malcomson, *John Foster*, 48.

49. Charles Sheridan to Richard Brinsley Sheridan, 10 March 1784, quoted in O'Brien, *Anglo-Irish Politics*, 95.

50. Harlow, *Founding of the British Empire*, 1:551–57.

51. Ibid., 1:644–45.

52. Ibid., 1:616–22; McDowell, *Ireland in the Age of Imperialism*, 339–42; Denis Kennedy, "The Irish Whigs and the Regency Crisis in Ireland, 1788–1789," *Eire-Ireland* 18, no. 3 (Fall 1983): 54–70.

53. Harlow, *Founding of the British Empire*, 1:619.

54. Ibid., 1:621.

55. Ibid., 1:619–20.

56. Ibid., 1:628–29; Johnston, *Ireland in the Eighteenth Century*, 159–62.
57. Johnston, *Great Britain and Ireland*, 221.
58. Malcomson, *John Foster*, 351.
59. Ibid., 61–62.
60. Ibid., 93, 98.
61. Ibid., 76.
62. McDowell, *Ireland in the Age of Imperialism*, 342–44.
63. Kennedy, "Irish Whigs," 55.
64. O'Brien, *Anglo-Irish Politics*, 101–7.
65. Ibid., 130.
66. McDowell, *Ireland in the Age of Imperialism*, 290–91.
67. Malcomson, *John Foster*, 90–91.
68. Bolton, *Passing of the Act of Union*, 5; O'Brien, *Anglo-Irish Politics*, 85.
69. Ibid., 86.
70. Foster, *Modern Ireland*, 171n.
71. Ibid., 246; McDowell, *Ireland in the Age of Imperialism*, 285.
72. Johnston, *Great Britain and Ireland*, 270.
73. Bolton, *Passing of the Act of Union*, 16.
74. Ibid., 23–24.
75. Foster, *Modern Ireland*, 244.
76. McDowell, "The Union," in *Ireland in the Age of Imperialism*, 678–704.
77. Curtis and McDowell, *Irish Historical Documents*, 227–33.
78. Bolton, *Passing of the Act of Union*, 114.
79. Ibid., 18; McDowell, *Ireland in the Age of Imperialism*, 445–61; Johnston, *Great Britain and Ireland*, 104–16.
80. McDowell, *Ireland in the Age of Imperialism*, 686.
81. Bolton, *Passing of the Act of Union*, 218.
82. Cited in McDowell, *Ireland in the Age of Imperialism*, 680.

## Chapter 2. Incomplete Union

1. B. McDowell, *The Irish Administration, 1801–1914* (London: Routledge and Kegan Paul, 1964), 19.
2. Ibid., 3.
3. Edward Brynn, *Crown and Castle: British Rule in Ireland, 1800–1830* (Dublin: Obrien Press, 1978), 45.
4. Ibid., 25, 44.
5. McDowell, *Irish Administration*, 65.
6. Brynn, *Crown and Castle*, 44.
7. McDowell, *Irish Administration*, 56–57.
8. Brian Jenkins, *Era of Emancipation: British Government of Ireland, 1812–1830* (Montreal: McGill-Queen's University Press, 1988), 57.
9. Brynn, *Crown and Castle*, 49.
10. McDowell, *Irish Administration*, 57–58.
11. Brynn, *Crown and Castle*, 48–52.
12. Robert Carl Shipkey, *Robert Peel's Irish Policy, 1812–1846* (New York: Garland, 1987), 3–4.
13. Brynn, *Crown and Castle*, 42.
14. McDowell, *Irish Administration*, 63; Brynn, *Crown and Castle*, 45–46.
15. Eunan O'Halpin, *The Decline of the Union: British Government in Ireland,*

*1892–1920* (Syracuse, N.Y.: Syracuse University Press, 1987), 5–6; Lawrence W. McBride, *The Greening of Dublin Castle* (Washington, D.C.: The Catholic University of America Press, 1991), 118–19.

16. McDowell, *Irish Administration*, 58–62.

17. For example, Lord Carnarvon in 1885; see Alan O'Day, *Parnell and the First Home Rule Episode* (Dublin: Gill and Macmillan, 1986), 61.

18. McDowell, *Irish Administration*, 56.

19. Ibid., 72.

20. McDowell, *Ireland in the Age of Imperialism*, 682–83; Jenkins, *Era of Emancipation*, 54.

21. Ibid., 125.

22. Brynn, *Crown and Castle*, 24.

23. Jenkins, *Era of Emancipation*, 38.

24. Ibid., 101–2.

25. Brynn, *Crown and Castle*, 103.

26. McDowell, *Irish Administration*, 52.

27. Great Britain, *Parliamentary Debates*, 2d series, vol. 9, 25 June 1823, col. 1213.

28. Ibid., col. 1227.

29. Kevin Nowlan, *The Politics of Repeal: A Study in the Relations between Great Britain and Ireland, 1841–1850* (London: Routledge and Kegan Paul, 1965), 59.

30. Great Britain, *Parliamentary Debates*, 3d series, vol. 111, 17 May 1850, col. 209.

31. Great Britain, *Parliamentary Debates*, 3d series, vol. 146, 7 July 1857, col. 1105.

32. McDowell, *Irish Administration*, 68.

33. Ibid., 65–71.

34. Ibid., 67.

35. Great Britain, *Parliamentary Debates*, 3d series, vol. 111, 17 May 1850, col. 173.

36. McDowell, *Irish Administration*, 67; Great Britain, *Parliamentary Debates*, 3d series, vol. 111, 17 May 1850, col. 181.

37. Ibid., col. 172.

38. Ibid., col. 175.

39. Ibid., cols. 232–34.

40. McDowell, *Irish Administration*, 68.

41. Great Britain, *Parliamentary Debates*, 3d series, vol. 112, 27 June 1850, cols. 468–69.

42. Ibid., col. 471.

43. Great Britain, *Parliamentary Debates*, 2d series, vol. 24, 11 May 1830, col. 574. Also see Oliver MacDonagh, *The Emancipist: Daniel O'Connell, 1830–1847* (London: Weidenfeld and Nicolson, 1989), 63.

44. Great Britain, *Parliamentary Debates*, 3d series, vol. 111, 17 May 1850, col. 180.

45. Lord Kimberly memorandum, 28 June 1871, Add. MSS. 44224, British Library.

46. Memo from Dublin Castle, 16 October 1871, Add. MSS. 44617, British Museum. McDowell, *Irish Administration*, 70, attributes the memorandum to H. Y. Thompson. See also Lord Bessborough to Gladstone, 26 May 1871, cited in *Irish Administration*, 69.

47. Memorandum by Gladstone on his discussion with the Queen, 25 June 1871, Add. 44760, F40, British Library.

48. Jenkins, *Era of Emancipation*, 5.

49. Ibid., 27.

50. McDowell, *Ireland in the Age of Imperialism*, 684.

51. Fergus O'Ferrall, *Catholic Emancipation: Daniel O'Connell and the Birth of Irish Democracy, 1820–30* (Dublin: Gill and Macmillan, 1985), 318–23.

52. K. Theodore Hoppen, *Elections, Politics, and Society in Ireland, 1832–1885* (Oxford: Clarendon Press, 1984), 1.

53. Jenkins, *Era of Emancipation*, 177.

54. Ibid., 8.

55. Ibid., 303.

56. Ibid., 39–42, 192–93.

57. John Coakley, "Constituency Boundary Revision and Seat Re-Distribution in the Irish Parliamentary Tradition," *Administration* 28, no. 3 (1980): 293–94.

58. Hoppen, *Elections, Politics, and Society*, 31–32, 87–88.

59. Jenkins, "The Catholic Association," in *Era of Emancipation*, 216–44.

60. MacDonagh, *The Emancipist*, 33.

61. Foster, *Modern Ireland*, 290.

62. Nowlan, *Politics of Repeal*, 8.

63. Ibid.

64. Angus Macintyre, *The Liberator: Daniel O'Connell and the Irish Party, 1830–1847* (London: Hamish Hamilton, 1965), 15.

65. Ibid., 73–76.

66. Ibid., 43.

67. Ibid., 301–2.

68. Ibid., 58.

69. Ibid., 69.

70. Richard Dunlop, "Daniel O'Connell," in *Dictionary of National Biography* (1895), 383.

71. MacDonagh, *The Emancipist*, 84.

72. Nowlan, *Politics of Repeal*, 7.

73. Precursor Association, *Five Reports of the Committee of the Precursor Association* (Dublin: Richard Grace, 1839), iii.

74. MacDonagh, *The Emancipist*, 63, 101–5, 124.

75. O'Connell to P. V. FitzPatrick, 22 April 1835, quoted in Maurice O'Connell, ed., *The Correspondence of Daniel O'Connell*, 8 vols. (Dublin: Blackwater, 1972–74), 5:296.

76. MacDonagh, *The Emancipist*, 68.

77. Lawrence McCaffrey, *Daniel O'Connell and the Repeal Year* (Lexington: University of Kentucky Press, 1966), *passim*; MacDonagh, "The Big Bang," in *The Emancipist*, 219ff.

78. McCaffrey, *Daniel O'Connell*, 211; MacDonagh, *The Emancipist*, 244–51; Macintyre, *The Liberator*, 278–79, 288.

79. Great Britain, *Parliamentary Debates*, 3d series, vol. 9, 4 July 1831, col. 652.

80. W. J. Fitpatrick, ed., *Correspondence of Daniel O'Connell*, 2 vols. (London: John Murray, 1888), 1:305.

81. Precursor Association, *Five Reports*, v.

82. For example, see "First Letter to the People of Ireland," 4 April 1833, in M. F.

Cusack, ed., *The Speeches and Public Letters of the Liberator*, 2 vols. (Dublin: McGlashan and Gill, 1875), 2:371–72.

83. Charles Chevenix Trench, *The Great Dan: A Biography of Daniel O'Connell* (London: Jonathan Cape, 1984), 193.

84. MacDonagh, *The Emancipist*, 85.

85. Ibid., 186–87.

86. A. D. Macintyre, "O'Connell and British Politics," in Kevin B. Nowlan and Maurice R. O'Connell, eds., *Daniel O'Connell: Portrait of a Radical* (Dublin: Appletree Press, 1984), 11.

87. Richard Davis, *The Young Ireland Movement* (Dublin: Gill and Macmillan, 1987), 212.

88. *Nation*, 10 June 1843.

89. Daniel O'Connell to the Secretary of the Loyal National Repeal Association, 12 October 1844, in Fitzpatrick, ed., *Correspondence*, 2:433–47.

90. J. G. V. Porter, *Ireland* (London: Ridgeway, 1844), *passim*.

91. Fitzpatrick, ed., *Correspondence*, 2:445.

92. Foster, *Modern Ireland*, 308–9.

93. See John Kendle, *Ireland and the Federal Solution: The Debates over the United Kingdom Constitution, 1870–1921* (Montreal: McGill-Queen's University Press, 1989), 9–10. As Kendle points out, Crawford's scheme was actually an example of devolution rather than federation and foreshadowed home rule.

94. MacDonagh, *The Emancipist*, 257; Macintyre, *The Liberator*, 280; Trench, *The Great Dan*, 293–94.

95. Davis, *Young Ireland Movement*, 63–65.

96. Nowlan, *Politics of Repeal*, 74.

97. Trench, *The Great Dan*, 267.

98. Ibid., 206.

99. Ibid.

100. Nowlan, *Politics of Repeal*, 13.

101. Ibid., 13.

102. Ibid.

103. Great Britain, *Parliamentary Debates*, 3d series, vol. 23, 25 April 1834, col. 89.

104. Great Britain, *Parliamentary Debates*, 3d series, vol. 69, 9 May 1843, col. 24.

105. Macintyre, *The Liberator*, 14.

106. MacDonagh, *The Emancipist*, 81–82.

107. Ibid., 82.

108. Foster, *Modern Ireland*, 316.

109. Macintyre, *The Liberator*, 288–89.

110. Ibid., 278.

111. Ibid., 294.

112. Nowlan, *Politics of Repeal*, 171–72.

113. Foster, *Modern Ireland*, 312.

114. Trench, *The Great Dan*, 193.

## Chapter 3. The Legislation

1. John Whyte, *The Independent Irish Party* (London: Oxford University Press, 1958), *passim*.

2. Kendle, *Ireland and the Federal Solution*, 4.

3. Ibid., 32.

4. John Vincent, *Gladstone and Ireland* (London: British Academy/Oxford University Press, 1977), 219; Kendle *Ireland and the Federal Solution*, 33.

5. The 52 percent of Scottish voters who supported the devolution proposal fell well short of the referendum requirement that 40 percent of the electorate must vote yes. In Wales only 20 percent of those who voted supported the proposal.

6. Vincent, *Gladstone and Ireland*, 228; see also 220.

7. Arthur Balfour, *Nationality and Home Rule* (London: Longmans Green, 1914), 19.

8. Patricia Jalland, *The Liberals and Ireland: The Ulster Question in British Politics to 1914* (New York: St. Martin's Press, 1980), 23–24.

9. David Butler and Anne Sloman, *British Political Facts, 1900–1979* (London: St. Martin's Press, 1980), 206.

10. Lawrence J. McCaffrey, *Irish Federation in the 1870s: A Study in Conservative Nationalism* (Philadelphia: American Philosophical Society, 1962), 8.

11. David Thornley, *Isaac Butt and Home Rule* (London: Macgibbon and Kee, 1964), 97.

12. McCaffrey, *Irish Federation in the 1870s*, 7–8.

13. Ibid., 15–19; Curtis and McDowell, *Irish Historical Documents*, 276–78.

14. McCaffrey, *Irish Federation in the 1870s*, 21.

15. Ibid., 24–25.

16. Thornley, *Isaac Butt*, 97.

17. Kendle, *Ireland and the Federal Solution*, 12–15.

18. Thornley, *Isaac Butt*, 100–101.

19. Ibid., 98–99.

20. Ibid., 101.

21. Ibid., 100.

22. Great Britain, *Parliamentary Debates*, 3d series, vol. 218, 20 March 1984, cols. 110ff.

23. Great Britain, *Parliamentary Debates*, 3d series, vol. 220, 30 June 1874, cols. 700–716.

24. Ibid., col. 701.

25. Ibid., cols. 717–29.

26. Ibid., col. 717.

27. Quoted in Kendle, *Ireland and the Federal Solution*, 15. See also Thornley, *Isaac Butt*, 102–3.

28. Great Britain, *Parliamentary Debates*, 3d series, vol. 230, 30 June 1876, cols. 738–64.

29. McCaffrey, *Irish Federation in the 1870s*, 39–41.

30. Ibid., 48; Alan J. Ward, *The Easter Rising: Revolution and Irish Nationalism* (Arlington Heights, Ill.: Harlan Davidson, 1980), 40–41.

31. McCaffrey, *Irish Federation in the 1870s*, 48; Foster, *Modern Ireland*, 418–19.

32. Ibid., 415–18.

33. O'Day, *Parnell*, 27.

34. Foster, *Modern Ireland*, 416.

35. O'Day, *Parnell*, 92.

36. Gladstone to Mrs. O'Shea, 22 December and 24 December 1885, Add. MSS. 44269, F258–9 and F266, British Library.

37. Gladstone to Parnell, 30 August 1889, Add. MSS. 44507, F203.

38. O'Day, *Parnell*, 141.

39. Ibid.

40. Great Britain, *Parliamentary Debates*, 3d series, vol. 304, 8 April 1886, cols. 1042, 1045, 1081–82; Curtis and McDowell, *Irish Historical Documents*, 287–92.

41. Catherine Shannon, *Arthur J. Balfour and Ireland, 1874–1922* (Washington, D.C: The Catholic University of America Press, 1988), 125.

42. The formation of the Gaelic Athletic Association in 1884 and the Gaelic League in 1893 were symptoms of the growth of Irish nativism.

43. For a good, brief discussion of the Ulster Unionist mind, see Patrick Buckland, *Irish Unionism 2: Ulster Unionism and the Origins of Northern Ireland, 1886–1922* (Dublin: Gill and Macmillan, 1973), xxx–xxxvi.

44. See O'Halpin, *Decline of the Union, passim,* and McBride, *Greening of Dublin Castle, passim.*

45. O'Halpin, *Decline of the Union,* 215.

46. Ibid., 207–9.

47. Ibid., 215.

48. O'Day, *Parnell,* 142–77.

49. Ibid., 179.

50. Ibid.

51. G. Gavan Duffy, "A Fair Constitution for Ireland," *Contemporary Review* 52 (September 1887): 303.

52. G. Gavan Duffy, "The Road to Australian Federation," *Contemporary Review* 57 (February 1890): 153–69.

53. G. Gavan Duffy, "The Humble Remonstrance of an Irish Nationalist," *Contemporary Review* 59 (May 1891): 656.

54. For examples see correspondence in Add. MSS. 44262 and 44269, British Library. Also see James Loughlin, *Gladstone, Home Rule, and the Ulster Question, 1882–93* (Atlantic Highlands, N.J.: Humanities Press International, 1987), 53–57.

55. Unsigned memo, Add. MSS. 44771, British Library. The proposal was unsigned, but Kendle attributes it to Parnell; see Kendle, *Ireland and the Federal Solution,* 41.

56. Gladstone to O'Shea, 16 December 1885, Add. MSS. 44269, F249, British Library.

57. Curtis and McDowell, *Irish Historical Documents,* 282–84.

58. Copy of Parnell to Capt. O'Shea, 14 December 1885, Add. MSS. 44262, British Library.

59. Parnell to J. J. O'Neill Daunt, 15 July 1885, Parnell MSS, National Library, Dublin.

60. O'Day, *Parnell,* 189.

61. Ibid., 170–71.

62. Kendle, *Ireland and the Federal Solution,* 41, 43.

63. Philip Magnus, *Gladstone* (London: John Murray, 1954), 77.

64. Draft by Gladstone, 7 May 1846, Add. MSS. 44735, F195, British Library.

65. Gladstone memorandum, n.d., Add. MSS. 44738, F234–63, British Library.

66. Vincent, *Gladstone and Ireland,* 196.

67. See, for example, Add. MSS. 44632, F107–30, Add. MSS. 44772, F4ff., British Library.

68. Great Britain, *Parliamentary Debates*, 3d series, vol. 304, 8 April 1886, col. 1080.

69. Vernon Bogdanor, *Devolution* (Oxford: Oxford University Press, 1979), 14.

70. Notes by Gladstone, 18 March 1886, Add. 44772, F64, British Library.

71. Bogdanor, *Devolution*, 10–41. The bills are printed in Great Britain, House of Commons, *Sessional Papers*, 1886 (181-Sess.I) vol. 2, 461ff.; 1893–1894 (201), vol. 3, 251ff.; 1912–1913 (136), vol. 2, 505ff.; 1914 (326), vol. 3, 1ff.

72. 1886 bill, Section 7.2.

73. Parnell to J. J. O'Neill Daunt, 15 July 1885, Parnell MSS. 5934, National Library, Dublin.

74. Great Britain, *Parliamentary Debates*, 3d series, vol. 304, 8 April 1886, col. 1059.

75. Great Britain, *Parliamentary Debates*, 3d series, vol. 306, 7 June 1886, col. 1172.

76. Ward, "Exporting the British Constitution," 7.

77. For example, a draft bill, February or March 1886, Add. 44771, British Library.

78. See discussion in chapter 8.

79. Minutes of a secret meeting of Irish party leaders in Dublin, 18 November 1892, Add. MSS. 44774, F152, British Library.

80. Minutes of a secret meeting of Irish party leaders in Dublin, 1 December 1892, Add. MSS. 44774, F169–71, British Library.

81. Clause 23.2.

82. Gladstone comments on the minutes of a secret meeting of Irish party leaders in Dublin, 5 December 1892, Add. MSS. 44774, F175–76, British Library.

83. Clause 4.4b.

84. Clause 7.1.

85. Clause 7.2.

86. G. Gavan Duffy, "Mr. Gladstone's Irish Constitution," *Contemporary Review* 49 (1886): 618.

87. Gladstone note, n.d., 1886, Add. MSS. 44771, British Library.

88. Great Britain, *Parliamentary Debates*, 3d series, vol. 306, 7 June 1886, col. 1172.

89. Minute of a secret meeting of Irish party leaders in Dublin, 16–18 November 1892, Add. MSS. 44774, F147–48, British Library.

90. Clause 23.

91. Clause 9.

92. Clause 11.

93. Clause 10.

94. The Preamble and Clause 1.2 in 1893; Clause 2 in 1914.

## Chapter 4. The Debates

1. Kendle, *Ireland and the Federal Solution*, 21.

2. Bogdanor, *Devolution*, 19–35, discusses these flaws in similar terms.

3. Kendle, *Ireland and the Federal Solution*, 17–18.

4. Notes for Gladstone's speech introducing home rule on 8 April 1888, Add. MSS. 44672, British Library.

5. Gladstone draft, February or March 1886, Add. MSS. 44771, F186–87, British Library.

6. Loughlin, *Gladstone, Home Rule, and the Ulster Question*, 76–80.

7. Ibid.

8. Great Britain, *Parliamentary Debates*, 3d series, vol. 304, 8 April 1886, col. 1055.

9. Ibid., col. 1059.

10. See speech by Lord Randolph Churchill, in Great Britain, *Parliamentary Debates*, 3d series, vol. 304, 12 April 1886, col. 1321.

11. Great Britain, *Parliamentary Debates*, 4th series, vol. 8, 13 February 1893, col. 1266.

12. Clause 10.

13. A. V. Dicey, *A Leap in the Dark* (London: John Murray, 1893), 49.

14. Great Britain, *Parliamentary Debates*, 4th series, vol. 8, 14 February 1893, cols. 1414–15.

15. A. V. Dicey, "Home Rule from an English Point of View," *Contemporary Review* 52 (1882): 85.

16. Great Britain, *Parliamentary Debates*, 3d series, vol. 304, 8 April 1886, col. 1209.

17. Great Britain, *Parliamentary Debates*, 3d series, vol. 304, 9 April 1886, col. 1272.

18. Clause 13.

19. Clause 26.3.

20. F. S. L. Lyons, *Charles Stewart Parnell* (London: Collins, 1977), 346.

21. Great Britain, *Parliamentary Debates*, 3d series, vol. 304, 8 April 1886, col. 1059.

22. Great Britain, *Parliamentary Debates*, 3d series, vol. 304, 9 April 1886, cols. 1207ff.

23. Great Britain, *Parliamentary Debates*, 4th series, vol. 8, 14 February 1893, cols. 1469–76. He was representing the views of a secret meeting of Irish party leaders held in Dublin in November 1892.

24. Patricia Jalland, "Irish Home Rule Finance: A Neglected Dimension of the Irish Question," *Irish Historical Studies* 23, no. 91 (1983): 235–36; O'Day, *Parnell*, 101–2; Kendle, *Ireland and the Federal Solution*, 45.

25. Gladstone draft, 18 March 1886, Add. 44772, F49, British Library.

26. Clauses 12 to 17.

27. Great Britain, *Parliamentary Debates*, 3d series, vol. 304, 8 April 1886, cols. 1124ff.; Jalland, "Irish Home Rule Finance," 235–36; Curtis and McDowell, *Irish Historical Documents*, 284–87.

28. Cited by Lawrence, in *Government of Northern Ireland*, 188.

29. Bogdanor, *Devolution*, 28.

30. Clauses 11 to 20.

31. Jalland, "Irish Home Rule Finance," 237; Bogdanor, *Devolution*, 31.

32. Great Britain, *Parliamentary Debates*, 3d series, vol. 8, 14 February 1893, cols. 1463ff.; Lawrence, *Government of Northern Ireland*, 188.

33. Gladstone to Sir William Harcourt, 16 January 1893, Add. 44203, British Library.

34. Jalland, "Irish Home Rule Finance," 238.

35. Ibid., 238–39.

36. Ibid., 242.

37. Ibid., 238.

38. Lawrence, *Government of Northern Ireland*, 189.

39. Ibid., 9.

40. Dicey, "Home Rule from an English Point of View," 82.

41. Great Britain, *Parliamentary Debates*, 3d series, vol. 305, 10 May 1886, col. 582.

42. Gladstone memorandum, March 1986, Add. MSS. 44772, British Library.

43. Brigid Hadfield, *The Constitution of Northern Ireland* (Belfast: SLS Legal Publications, 1989), 10–13.

44. Minutes of a secret meeting of Irish party leaders in Dublin, 16–18 November 1892, Add. MSS. 44774, F147–48, British Library.

45. Minutes of a secret meeting of Irish party leaders in Dublin, 1 December 1892, Add. MSS. 44774, F168.

46. Hadfield, *Constitution of Northern Ireland*, 19, 24–25.

47. Great Britain, *Parliamentary Debates*, 4th series, vol. 8, 14 February 1893, col. 1427.

48. J. E. Redmond, "Notes on the Home Rule Bill: Part 2, The Mutual Safeguards," *Contemporary Review* 63 (1893): 313–14.

49. Bogdanor, *Devolution*, 34.

50. Great Britain, *Parliamentary Debates*, 3d series, vol. 304, 8 April 1886, cols. 1120–21.

51. Great Britain, *Parliamentary Debates*, 4th series, vol. 8, 17 February 1893, col. 1722.

52. Kendle, *Ireland and the Federal Solution*, 122.

53. Shannon, *Balfour and Ireland*, 76.

54. London *Times*, 16 April 1912.

55. Notes by Gladstone, n.d., 1893, Add. MSS. 44677, British Library.

56. Lord Thring, "Home Rule and Imperial Unity," *Contemporary Review* 51 (1887): 304.

57. G. Gavan Duffy, "A Fair Constitution for Ireland," *Contemporary Review* 52 (1887): 301–32. Also see his "Mr. Gladstone's Irish Constitution," *Contemporary Review* 49 (1886): 609–20, and "An Australian Example," *Contemporary Review* 53 (1888): 1–31.

58. Great Britain, *Parliamentary Debates*, 3d series, vol. 304, 8 April 1886, col. 1119.

59. Goldwin Smith, "The Canadian Constitution," *Contemporary Review* 52 (1887): 2–3.

60. Ibid., 3.

61. Ibid.

62. A. V. Dicey, "Ireland and Victoria," *Contemporary Review* 49 (1886): 171–72.

63. Note by Gladstone, "The Colonies No Parallel," n.d., 1893, Add. MSS. 44677, British Library.

64. Dicey, *A Leap in the Dark*, 74.

65. Great Britain, *Parliamentary Debates*, 3d series, vol. 302, 9 April 1886, col. 1263.

66. See Gladstone Papers, Add. MSS. 44772, British Library.

67. Lawrence McCaffrey, *Ireland: From Colony to Nation State* (Englewood Cliffs, N.J.: Prentice-Hall, 1979), 108.

68. Oliver MacDonagh, *Ireland* (Englewood Cliffs, N.J.: Prentice-Hall, 1968), 57.

69. J. E. Redmond, "Notes on the Home Rule Bill, Part 2," 313.

70. Paul Bew, *C. S. Parnell* (Dublin: Gill and Macmillan, 1980), 70.

71. See Ian Malcolm, M.P., "Home Rule All Round," *Nineteenth Century* 68 (1910): 791–99.

72. Cited by Ian Malcolm, M.P., in Great Britain, *Parliamentary Debates*, 5th series, vol. 21, 15 February 1911, col. 1076.

73. Cited by Ian Malcolm, in "Home Rule All Round," 791–99.

74. Montreal *Daily Star*, 21 November 1901.

75. Great Britain, *Parliamentary Debates*, 5th series, vol. 21, 7 February 1911, col. 207.

76. Great Britain, *Parliamentary Debates*, 5th series, vol. 21, 15 February 1911, cols. 1102 and 1105.

77. John A. Murphy, "One Hundred Years of 'Ulster Says No,' " *Irish Times*, 9 June 1986.

78. Chamberlain speech in Birmingham, 4 June 1885, Add. MSS. 44770, British Library.

79. Chamberlain speech to a Cobden Club dinner, 13 June 1885, Add. MSS. 44770, British Library.

80. Chamberlain to W. H. Duignan, 17 December 1884, in C. H. D. Howard, ed., "Documents Relating to the Irish 'Central Board' Scheme, 1884–1885," *Irish Historical Studies* 8 (1952–53): 241.

81. Kendle, *Ireland and the Federal Solution*, 58.

82. Chamberlain to W. H. Duignan, 17 December 1884, in Howard, ed., "Documents," 240–41.

83. Chamberlain speech in Birmingham, 4 June 1885, Add. 44770, British Library.

84. C. H. D. Howard, "Joseph Chamberlain, Parnell and the Irish 'Central Board' Scheme, 1884–1885," *Irish Historical Studies* 8 (1952–53): 360n.

85. Chamberlain memorandum, 25 April 1885, in Howard, ed., "Documents," 256–57.

86. Chamberlain to John Morley, 21 January 1885, in Howard, ed., "Documents," 249.

87. Parnell to Capt. O'Shea, 5 January 1885, in Howard, ed., "Documents," 242.

88. Parnell to Capt. O'Shea, 13 January 1885, in Howard, ed., "Documents," 245–46.

89. Memorandum by Chamberlain, 25 April 1885, in Howard, ed., "Documents," 257; J. L. Garvin, *The Life of Joseph Chamberlain* (London: Macmillan, 1932), 600.

90. Chamberlain speech in Birmingham, 29 January 1887, Add. 44770, British Library.

91. Howard, ed., "Documents," 256.

92. Garvin, *Life of Joseph Chamberlain*, 604.

93. Howard, ed., "Documents," 258.

94. Great Britain, Parliament, House of Commons, *Sessional Papers*, 1907 (182), vol. 2, 481.

95. In 1904–5 MacDonnell had been associated with Lord Dunraven in a devolution plan that had led to uproar in the Conservative party, the resignation of the Chief Secretary, George Wyndham, and the revival of militant Ulster unionism; see O'Halpin, *Decline of the Union*, 41–51.

96. Great Britain, House of Commons, *Sessional Papers*, 1907 (182), vol. 2, 481.

97. Kendle, *Ireland and the Federal Solution*, 101; McBride, *Greening of Dublin Castle*, 131–40.

98. Great Britain, *Parliamentary Debates*, 3d series, vol. 304, 9 April 1886, col. 1200.

99. Ibid., cols. 1734–35.

100. Kendle, *Ireland and the Federal Solution*, 29.

101. Great Britain, *Parliamentary Debates*, 3d series, vol. 304, 9 April 1886, col. 1200.

102. Kendle, *Ireland and the Federal Solution*, 61.

103. Ibid., 80–81.

104. Ibid., 65.

105. Ibid., 72, 81.

106. Alvin Jackson, *The Ulster Party: Irish Unionism in the House of Commons, 1884–1911* (Oxford: Clarendon Press, 1989), 284–326.

107. Jalland, *The Liberals and Ireland*, 55.

108. Curtis and McDowell, *Irish Historical Documents*, 304.

109. Buckland, *Irish Unionism* 2, 61.

110. Memorandum by the Army Council, 4 July 1914, CAB 37/120 (81), Public Records Office, London.

111. Buckland, *Irish Unionism* 2, 9.

112. Robert Blake, *Unrepentant Tory* (New York: St. Martin's Press, 1956), 130.

113. Buckland, *Irish Unionism* 2, 13.

114. Harold Nicolson, *King George V: His Life and Reign* (New York: Doubleday, 1953), 222–29.

115. Jalland, *The Liberals and Ireland*, 83.

116. Shannon, *Balfour and Ireland*, 148–58.

117. Bogdanor, *Devolution*, 36.

118. Kendle, *Ireland and the Federal Solution*, 106–7.

119. See Balfour, *Nationality and Home Rule, passim*; Shannon, *Balfour and Ireland*, 67–68, 150.

120. Kendle, *Ireland and the Federal Solution*, 137.

121. Winston Churchill memorandum, "Devolution," 1 March 1911, CAB 37/1045, no. 16, Public Records Office, London; Kendle, *Ireland and the Federal Solution*, 138.

122. Ibid., 137.

123. Ibid., 138. Parnell had proposed to Gladstone in 1882 that the committee stage for Irish bills be taken by an Irish Grand Committee composed of the Chief Secretary, the Lord Lieutenant, Law Officers of the Crown in Ireland, and Irish M.P.'s. See Mrs. O'Shea to Gladstone, 6 October 1882, Add. MSS. 44269, British Library.

124. Kendle, *Ireland and the Federal Solution*, 140.

125. Jalland, *The Liberals and Ireland*, 39.

126. Great Britain, *Parliamentary Debates*, 5th series, vol. 36, 11 April 1912, col. 1403.

127. Kendle, *Ireland and the Federal Solution*, 33.

128. See Alan J. Ward, "Frewen's Anglo-American Campaign for Federalism," *Irish Historical Studies* 15, no. 59 (1967): 256–75.

129. Kendle, *Ireland and the Federal Solution*, 81–82.

130. Nicholas Mansergh, *The Unresolved Question: The Anglo-Irish Settlement and Its Undoing, 1912–1972* (New Haven, Conn.: Yale University Press, 1991), 44.

131. Jalland, *The Liberals and Ireland*, 107.

132. Ibid., 92–93.

133. Ibid., 108–9.

134. Ibid., 120, 129.

135. Ibid., 28, 67–71.

136. Ibid., 142–260; Mansergh, *Unresolved Question*, 61–75; John D. Fair, *British Interparty Conferences* (Oxford: Clarendon Press, 1980), 105–19.

137. Ibid., 114–19.

138. George Dangerfield, *The Damnable Question: A Study of Anglo-Irish Relations* (Boston: Little, Brown, 1976), 119–20.

139. Mansergh, *Unresolved Question*, 85.

140. Jalland, *The Liberals and Ireland*, 98.

141. Denis R. Gwynn, *The Life of John Redmond* (London: G. Harrap, 1932), 232.

142. Kendle, *Ireland and the Federal Solution*, 162–63.

143. Dangerfield, *Damnable Question*, 118.

144. McBride, *Greening of Dublin Castle*, passim.

145. Ibid., 187–88, 200–201; O'Halpin, *Decline of the Union*, 97–98.

146. McDowell, *Irish Convention*, 2–3.

147. Nicholas Mansergh, *The Commonwealth Experience*, 2 vols., 2d ed. (London: Macmillan, 1932), 1:225.

148. Nicholas Mansergh, *The Irish Question, 1841–1921*, 3d ed. (London: George Allen and Unwin, 1975), 137.

149. Great Britain, *Parliamentary Debates*, 4th series, vol. 8, 14 February 1893, col. 1437.

150. London *Times*, 16 January 1913.

151. O'Day, *Parnell*, 207.

152. Ibid., 199.

153. Alan J. Ward, "Models of Government and Anglo-Irish Relations," *Albion* 20, no. 1 (Spring 1988): 34.

## Chapter 5. Government of Ireland Act

1. F. S. L. Lyons, "The Meaning of Independence," in Farrell, ed., *Irish Parliamentary Tradition*, 227.

2. F. S. L. Lyons, "Dillon, Redmond, and the Irish Home Rulers," in F. X. Martin, ed., *Leaders and Men of the Easter Rising: Dublin 1916* (Ithaca, N.Y.: Cornell University Press, 1967), 35.

3. Curtis and McDowell, *Irish Historical Documents*, 314–17.

4. For a discussion of wartime opinion in the United States, see Alan J. Ward, *Ireland and Anglo-American Relations* (London: London School of Economics/Weidenfeld and Nicolson, 1969), 126–65.

5. McBride, *Greening of Dublin Castle*, 212–14.

6. The proposals were presented to Parliament as *Headings of a Settlement as the Government of Ireland*, Cmd. 8310, 1916. See Sir Arthur Quekett, *The Constitution of Northern Ireland*, 3 vols. (Belfast: His Majesty's Stationery Office, 1928), 1:12–13. See also Mansergh, *Unresolved Question*, 92–100.

7. R. B. McDowell, *The Irish Convention, 1917–1918* (London: Routledge and Kegan Paul, 1970), passim; Fair, *British Interparty Conferences*, 198–223; Mansergh, *Unresolved Question*, 103–7.

8. Ireland, *Report of the Proceedings of the Irish Convention*, 3.

9. See Alan J. Ward, "Lloyd George and the 1918 Irish Conscription Crisis," *Historical Journal* 17, pt. 1 (1974): 113.

10. Ibid., 107–29.

11. Mansergh, *Unresolved Question*, 120.

12. Kendle, *Ireland and the Federal Solution*, 196–209.

13. First Report of the Cabinet Committee on the Irish Question, 4 November 1919, C.P. Paper 56, CAB 24/92, Public Records Office, London; Kendle, *Ireland and the Federal Solution*, 226.

14. Ibid., 227–29.

15. Buckland, *Irish Unionism* 2, 95.

16. Ibid., 115–17.

17. Ibid., 117–19; Hadfield, *Constitution of Northern Ireland*, 31; Kendle, *Ireland and the Federal Solution*, 230.

18. Mansergh, *Unresolved Question*, 125.

19. Section 14.3.

20. Section 13 and Third Schedule.

21. Section 13 and Second Schedule; Buckland, *Irish Unionism* 2, 124–25.

22. Memorandum by Sir F. Greer considered by the Cabinet Committee on Ireland, 2 November 1920, CAB 27/68, Public Records Office, London.

23. Section 2.

24. Section 7.1.

25. Section 10.1.

26. Section 10.2.

27. Section 3.

28. Section 36; Harry Calvert, *Constitutional Law in Northern Ireland: A Study in Regional Government* (London: Stevens/Northern Ireland Legal Quarterly, 1968), 41.

29. Section 72; Calvert, *Constitutional Law*, 42.

30. Joseph Curran, *The Birth of the Irish Free State, 1921–1923* (University: University of Alabama Press, 1980), 52.

31. Quekett, *Constitution of Northern Ireland*, 1:18; Calvert, *Constitutional Law*, 48–49.

32. Hadfield, *Constitution of Northern Ireland*, 34–35.

33. Calvert, *Constitutional Law*, 118.

34. Ibid., 44–46, 113; Hadfield, *Constitution of Northern Ireland*, 39–41.

35. J. J. Lee, *Ireland: 1912–1985* (Cambridge: Cambridge University Press, 1989), 77.

36. Quekett, *Constitution of Northern Ireland*, *passim*; Curtis and McDowell, *Irish Historical Documents*, 297–303.

37. Calvert, *Constitutional Law*, 348–53.

38. Section 18.1 and 2.

39. Calvert, *Constitutional Law*, 324–30.

40. Section 8.5.

41. Section 8.4b.

42. Minute, Cabinet Committee on Ireland, 2 November 1920, CAB 27/68, Public Records Office, London.

43. Section 1.1.

44. Section 13.1.

45. Section 14.3.

46. Martin Wallace, *Northern Ireland: Fifty Years of Self-Government* (New York: Barnes and Noble, 1971), 29.

47. Section 14.4.

48. Section 17.
49. Quekett, *Constitutional Law*, 1:27; Calvert, *Constitutional Law*, 156–58.
50. Section 4.
51. Section 21.
52. Calvert, *Constitutional Law*, 221–50.
53. Section 9.2 and 3.
54. Section 5.1; Calvert, *Constitutional Law*, 251–72; Hadfield, *Constitution of Northern Ireland*, 79, 91–92n. Section 5 also prohibited the taking of property without compensation, a provision not limited to religious property, which was dropped in 1962. Sections 64, 65.2, and 68 further prohibited laws affecting certain provisions relating to Queen's University, Belfast, the Grand Lodge of Ancient Free and Accepted Freemasons of Ireland, and certain pensioned officers of local authorities and Queen's University; see Calvert, *Constitutional Law*, 285–86, and Hadfield, *Constitution of Northern Ireland*, 80.
55. Section 51; Calvert, *Constitutional Law*, 288–301.
56. Derek Birrell and Alan Murie, *Policy and Government in Northern Ireland: Lessons of Devolution* (Dublin: Gill and Macmillan, 1980), 33.
57. Section 13.3 and Fourth Schedule.
58. Section 14.4.
59. Section 16; Calvert, *Constitutional Law*, 155–56.
60. Section 17.
61. Third Schedule, Part II.
62. Section 18.4.
63. Birrell and Murie, *Policy and Government*, 30, 33; Butler and Sloman, *British Political Facts*, 390.
64. Calvert, *Constitutional Law*, 141.
65. Birrell and Murie, *Policy and Government*, 64–65.
66. Butler and Sloman, *British Political Facts*, 391; Patrick Buckland, *The Factory of Grievances: Devolved Government in Northern Ireland, 1921–1939* (Dublin: Gill and Macmillan, 1972), 26–29.
67. Mansergh, *Unresolved Question*, 253–56.
68. Ibid., 28, 230–36.
69. Birrell and Murie, *Policy and Government*, 94–95.
70. Buckland, *Factory of Grievances*, 28.
71. Birrell and Murie, *Policy and Government*, 33.
72. Section 8.3. Departments were renamed Ministries in 1946. Hadfield, *Constitution of Northern Ireland*, 61.
73. McBride, *Greening of Dublin Castle*, 295.
74. Buckland, *Factory of Grievances*, 9–10. For a full list of all ministers, 1921 to 1972, see Butler and Sloman, *British Political Facts*, 389–90.
75. Birrell and Murie, *Policy and Government*, 32.
76. Section 16.2.
77. Birrell and Murie, *Policy and Government*, 53–55; Buckland, *Factory of Grievances*, 26–27.
78. Birrell and Murie, *Policy and Government*, 52.
79. See Birrell and Murie, *Policy and Government*, 50–64, and Calvert, *Constitutional Law*, 150–61, for discussions of the operations of the Northern Ireland Parliament.
80. Michael J. Cunningham, *British Government Policy in Northern Ireland, 1969–1989* (Manchester, England: Manchester University Press, 1991), 44.

81. Birrell and Murie, *Policy and Government*, 65–66.

82. Buckland, *Factory of Grievances*, 10.

83. Birrell and Murie, *Policy and Government*, 48–49.

84. Calvert, *Constitutional Law*, 355–56.

85. Section 63.

86. Buckland, *Factory of Grievances*, 45.

87. Calvert, *Constitutional Law*, 352.

88. Section 8.3.

89. Birrell and Murie, *Policy and Government*, 41; Buckland, *Irish Unionism 2*, 128–29.

90. Birrell and Murie, *Policy and Government*, 41–42.

91. Ibid., 44, 47.

92. Ibid., 42. See also Brian Barton, *Brookeborough: The Making of a Prime Minister* (Belfast: Queen's University, 1988), 152–54, 195–229.

93. Butler and Sloman, *British Political Facts*, 389.

94. Gladstone draft, February or March 1886, Add. 44771, British Library.

95. Section 19a.

96. Hadfield, *Constitution of Northern Ireland*, 59.

97. Ibid., 88n.

98. Butler and Sloman, *British Political Facts*, 207–9.

99. Calvert, *Constitutional Law*, 81–84.

100. Lawrence, *Government of Northern Ireland*, 11.

101. The financial provisions were Sections 20 to 36. For discussions of Northern Ireland and finance, see Buckland, *Factory of Grievances*, 81–104; Birrell and Murie, *Policy and Government*, 15–23; and Lawrence, *Government of Northern Ireland, passim*.

102. Mansergh, *Unresolved Question*, 246.

103. Buckland, *Factory of Grievances*, 150–51; Birrell and Murie, *Policy and Government*, 16–18; Lawrence, *Government of Northern Ireland*, 163.

104. Wallace, *Northern Ireland*, 166.

105. Mansergh, *Unresolved Question*, 246.

106. Birrell and Murie, *Policy and Government*, 280–81.

107. Ibid., 225, 294.

108. Terence O'Neill, *Ulster at the Crossroads* (London: Faber and Faber, 1969), 32.

109. Birrell and Murie, *Policy and Government*, 273, 282.

110. O'Neill, *Ulster at the Crossroads*, 112–46, 155–76.

111. Hadfield, *Constitution of Northern Ireland*, 100.

112. Section 12.

113. Buckland, *Factory of Grievances*, 43–44.

114. Birrell and Murie, *Policy and Government*, 27.

115. Calvert, *Constitutional Law*, 50.

116. Ibid., 288.

117. Hadfield, *Constitution of Northern Ireland*, 86.

118. Buckland, *Factory of Grievances*, 225–26. Proportional representation had been introduced into Irish local government elections in 1919. Quekett, *Constitution of Northern Ireland*, 1:15.

119. Buckland, *Factory of Grievances*, 208–9.

120. Ibid., 272.

121. Ibid., 267–75.

122. Draft letter by Hugh Kennedy, 9 August 1922, Kennedy MSS. P4/180, University College, Dublin.

123. Churchill to William Cosgrave, telegram, 11 September 1922, Kennedy MSS. P4/181, University College, Dublin.

124. Patrick Buckland, *A History of Northern Ireland* (Dublin: Gill and Macmillan, 1981), 90–91; Birrell and Murie, *Policy and Government*, 235–39.

125. Ibid., 237–38.

126. See Birrell and Murie, *Policy and Government*, 164–65, 214–15; Buckland, *Factory of Grievances*, 20–22, 206–20, 237–45; and John Whyte, "How Much Discrimination Was There under the Unionist Regime, 1921–1968?," in Tom Gallagher and James O'Connell, eds., *Contemporary Irish Studies* (Manchester, England: Manchester University Press, 1983), 1–35.

127. Ivor Jennings, *The Law and the Constitution* (London: University of London Press, 1959), 157; cited in Birrell and Murie, *Policy and Government*, 9.

128. Calvert, *Constitutional Law*, 96–98.

129. Ibid., 98–99.

130. Ibid., 96.

131. Hadfield, *Constitution of Northern Ireland*, 104.

132. Buckland, *Factory of Grievances*, 26.

133. Calvert, *Constitutional Law*, 88–90.

134. Paul Canning, *British Policy towards Ireland, 1921–1941* (Oxford: Clarendon Press, 1985), 72–73.

135. John A. Oliver, "The Stormont Administration, 1921–72," *Contemporary Record* 5, no. 1 (1991): 71–104.

136. Calvert, *Constitutional Law*, 93–94; Birrell and Murie, *Policy and Government*, 14.

137. Wallace, *Northern Ireland*, 167.

138. Ibid., 39.

139. Ibid.

140. Buckland, *History of Northern Ireland*, 138–39; Wallace, *Northern Ireland*, 169–71.

141. Birrell and Murie, *Policy and Government*, 14–15; Wallace, *Northern Ireland*, 168–69.

142. Hadfield, *Constitution of Northern Ireland*, 100–101; Cunningham, *British Government Policy*, 45–46; Buckland, *History of Northern Ireland*, 157.

143. Great Britain, *Northern Ireland Constitutional Proposals*, Cmnd. 5259, March 1973; cited in Hadfield, *Constitution of Northern Ireland*, 119n.

144. Birrell and Murie, *Policy and Government*, 47.

145. Lawrence, *Government of Northern Ireland*, 14.

146. Quoted in Birrell and Murie, *Policy and Government*, 268.

## Chapter 6. Constitutional Postscript

1. Great Britain, *Northern Ireland Constitutional Proposals*, Cmnd. 5259, 21; quoted in Hadfield, *Constitution of Northern Ireland*, 103.

2. John McGarry and Brendan O'Leary, "Conclusion: Northern Ireland's Options: A Framework and Analysis," in John McGarry and Brendan O'Leary, eds., *The Future of Northern Ireland* (Oxford: Clarendon Press, 1990), 269.

3. See, for example, Arendt Lijphart, *Democracy in Plural Societies* (New Haven, Conn.: Yale University Press, 1977).

4. Hadfield, *Constitution of Northern Ireland*, 119n.

5. Ibid., 106.

6. Ibid., 104–10.

7. Cunningham, *British Government Policy*, 53–54.

8. Hadfield, *Constitution of Northern Ireland*, 100–117; Garret FitzGerald, *All in a Life: Garret FitzGerald, An Autobiography* (Dublin: Gill and Macmillan, 1991), 196–224.

9. Buckland, *History of Northern Ireland*, 169.

10. Cunningham, *British Government Policy*, 56.

11. Buckland, *History of Northern Ireland*, 169–72; Hadfield, *Constitution of Northern Ireland*, 116–17; Cunningham, *British Government Policy*, 90–92.

12. Paul R. Maguire, "Parliament and the Direct Rule of Northern Ireland," *Irish Jurist*, n.s., 10 (1975): 81–92; Hadfield, *Constitution of Northern Ireland*, 132–34.

13. Ibid., 255; *Irish Political Studies* 8 (1993): 175–78.

14. McGuire, "Parliament and Direct Rule," 86.

15. Ibid., 82.

16. Hadfield, *Constitution of Northern Ireland*, 129.

17. Ibid., 128; Cunningham, *British Government Policy*, 98.

18. Hadfield, *Constitution of Northern Ireland*, 130.

19. Cunningham, *British Government Policy*, 101.

20. Hadfield, *Constitution of Northern Ireland*, 151–77; Cunningham, *British Government Policy*, 146–50.

21. See Hadfield, *Constitution of Northern Ireland*, 156–68; Peter Smyth, "The Northern Ireland Assembly: A New Exposition of Democracy," *Administration* 36 (1989): 91–126.

22. The agreement is printed in Hadfield, *Constitution of Northern Ireland*, 261–68, and in McGarry and O'Leary, eds., *Future of Northern Ireland*, 304–10. For an extensive discussion of the negotiations, see FitzGerald, *All in a Life*, 494–575.

23. FitzGerald, *All in a Life*, 462–93.

24. Article 1.

25. Article 2.

26. Article 4(a).

27. *Irish Times*, 25 April 1991.

28. *Irish Times*, 7 July 1992.

29. See, for example, FitzGerald, *All in a Life*, 376–78, 500–501.

30. *Irish Times*, 6, 7, 8 July 1992.

31. Great Britain, *Parliamentary Debates*, 5th series, vol. 922, 13 December 1976, cols. 1044–45.

32. FitzGerald, *All in a Life*, 288.

33. *New York Times*, 22 September 1992.

34. Statement by the Secretary of State for Northern Ireland, Sir Patrick Mayhew, in the House of Commons, 11 November 1992. British Information Services, New York, 12 November 1992.

35. Great Britain, *Royal Commission on the Constitution, 1969–1973*, Cmnd. 5460, 477.

36. In Scotland 52 percent of the voters approved devolution, but that result fell below the requirement in the act that 40 percent of the electorate must vote yes. In Wales only 20 percent of those who voted supported devolution.

37. Balfour, *Nationality and Home Rule*, 19.

38. Great Britain, *Royal Commission on the Constitution, 1969–1973*, 1973, Cmnd. 5460, 385.

39. Butler and Sloman, *British Political Facts*, 210.

40. Great Britain, *Parliamentary Debates*, vol. 939, 14 November 1977, col. 85.

41. Ibid., cols. 121–22.

42. Ibid., col. 87.

43. *Irish Times*, 3 July 1987, 8.

44. Hadfield, *Constitution of Northern Ireland*, 255, reported in 1988 that the Northern Ireland Committee had not sat since 1985.

45. Hugh Roberts, "Sound Stupidity: The British Party System and the Northern Ireland Question," in McGarry and O'Leary, ed., *Future of Northern Ireland*, 116.

46. Rick Wilford, "The 1992 Westminster Election in Northern Ireland," *Irish Political Studies* 7 (1992): 105–10.

## Chapter 7. Dáil Éireann Constitution

1. Curran, *Birth of the Irish Free State*, 23.

2. J. L. McCracken, *Representative Government in Ireland: A Study of Dáil Éireann, 1919–1948* (London: Oxford University Press, 1958), 22.

3. See Brian Farrell, "The Legislation of a 'Revolutionary' Assembly: Dáil Decrees, 1919–1922," *Irish Jurist*, n.s., 10 (1975): 112–27.

4. McCracken, *Representative Government*, 23–29.

5. Maire Comerford, *The First Dáil: January 21, 1919* (Dublin: Joe Clarke, 1969), 12.

6. F. S. L. Lyons, *Ireland since the Famine* (London: Weidenfeld and Nicolson, 1971), 261.

7. McCracken, *Representative Government*, 30–34.

8. Ibid., 23.

9. Brian Farrell, *The Founding of Dáil Éireann* (Dublin: Gill and Macmillan, 1971), 51.

10. Eamon de Valera and Arthur Griffith, both still in prison, and George Plunkett.

11. The Declaration of Independence and the Democratic Program are reproduced in Curtis and McDowell, *Irish Historical Documents*, 318–20.

12. Dorothy Macardle, *The Irish Republic* (New York: Farrar, Straus and Giroux, 1965), 284.

13. See Ward, *Ireland and Anglo-American Relations*, 214–36.

14. Dáil Éireann, *Private Sessions of the Second Dáil*, 328; Macardle, *Irish Republic*, 503.

15. McBride, *Greening of Dublin Castle*, 267.

16. McCracken, *Representative Government*, 35.

17. Ronan Fanning, *The Irish Department of Finance, 1922–1958* (Dublin: Institute of Public Administration, 1978), 13–29; McCracken, *Representative Government*, 26.

18. Basil Chubb, *The Government and Politics of Ireland*, 3d ed. (London and New York: Longman, 1992), 29. Also see McBride, *Greening of Dublin Castle*, 262–64, 276–77; McCracken, *Representative Government*, 27.

19. Ibid., 44–45.

20. Hugh Kennedy memorandum on Irish constitutional development, 1800–1923, 23 May 1923, in Kennedy MSS. P4/847, University College, Dublin.

21. Farrell, *Founding of Dáil Éireann*, 61–63. The drafting committee members were George Gavan Duffy, James O'Mara, Seán T. O'Kelly, E. J. Duggan, P. Béaslaoí, and Eoin MacNeill.

22. The constitution is printed in Farrell, *Founding of Dáil Éireann*, 86–87; also see McCracken, *Representative Government*, 25–26.

23. Ward, "Exporting the British Constitutions," *passim*.

24. Farrell, *Founding of Dáil Éireann*, 70–74.

25. Macardle, *Irish Republic*, 276.

26. Dáil Éireann, *Minutes of Proceedings, 1919–1921*, vol. 2, 10 January 1922, col. 399.

27. Hugh Kennedy memorandum on Irish constitutional development, 1800–1922, 23 May 1923, in Kennedy MSS. P4/847, University College, Dublin.

28. Brendan Sexton, *Ireland and the Crown, 1922–1936* (Dublin: Irish Academic Press, 1989), 26.

29. Farrell, *Founding of Dáil Éireann*, 68–69.

30. See, for example, numerous committee reports in the George Gavan Duffy Papers, MSS. 15439, National Library, Dublin.

31. Farrell, *Founding of Dáil Éireann*, 69.

32. Duffy Papers, MSS. 15439, National Library, Dublin.

33. Farrell, *Founding of Dáil Éireann*, 69–70.

34. Brian Farrell discusses Dáil procedure in "The Legislation of a 'Revolutionary' Assembly," *passim*; also see his *Founding of Dáil Éireann*, 68, and Duffy MSS. 15440(3), National Library, Dublin.

35. Farrell, *Founding of Dáil Éireann*, 70; Duffy Papers, MSS. 15439.

36. McCracken, *Representative Government*, 25–26; Duffy Papers, MSS. 15440(3), National Library, Dublin.

37. Farrell, *Founding of Dáil Éireann*, 68.

38. Ibid., xviii.

39. Fair, *British Interparty Conferences*, 260.

40. Curran, *Birth of the Irish Free State*, 71.

41. Ibid., 73.

42. Ibid.

43. For a discussion of the negotiating positions, see Curran, *Birth of the Irish Free State*, 64–98; and Mansergh, *Unresolved Question*, 177–89.

44. De Valera to Joseph McGarrity, 7 December 1921, quoted by Curran, in *Birth of the Irish Free State*, 76.

45. Ibid., 77–78; Mansergh, *Unresolved Question*, 203.

46. Curran, *Birth of the Irish Free State*, 230.

47. Mansergh, *Unresolved Question*, 219–39.

48. Canning, *British Policy towards Ireland*, 8.

49. Maurice Moynihan, ed., *Speeches and Statements by Eamon de Valera, 1919–1973* (Dublin: Gill and Macmillan, 1980), 90–91.

50. Curran, *British Policy towards Ireland*, 141–42.

51. Lyons, *Ireland since the Famine*, 442.

52. Dáil Éireann, *Minutes of Proceedings, 1919–1921*, vol. 2, 7 January 1922, p. 344.

53. Curran, *Birth of the Irish Free State*, 155.

54. Canning, *British Policy towards Ireland*, 10.

55. The treaty is reprinted in many books. See, for example, Curran, *Birth of the Irish Free State*, 284–88; Macardle, *Irish Republic*, 953–58; and Curtis and McDowell, *Irish Historical Documents*, 322–27.

56. Dáil Éireann, *Minutes of Proceedings*, vol. 2, 9 January 1922, p. 349.

57. Dáil Éireann, *Minutes of Proceedings, 1919–1921*, vol. 2, 10 January 1922, pp. 410–11; Curran, *Birth of the Irish Free State*, 153–58.

58. Ibid., 158–60; Fanning, *Irish Department of Finance*, 54.

59. Ibid., 54–55.

## Chapter 8. *Irish Free State Constitution*

1. For detailed descriptions of the drafting of the constitution, see Curran, *Birth of the Irish Free State*, 200–218; and D. H. Akenson and J. F. Fallin, "The Irish Civil War and the Drafting of the Irish Free State Constitution," in three parts, *Éire-Ireland* 5, no. 1 (1970): 10–26; 5, no. 2 (1970): 42–93; and 5, no. 4 (1970): 28–70 (hereafter referred to as Akenson and Fallin, "Irish Civil War," 5, no. 1; 5, no. 2; or 5, no. 4). Also see Brian Farrell, "The Drafting of the Irish Free State Constitution," in four parts, *Irish Jurist*, n.s., 5, pt. 1 (1970): 115–40; n.s., 5, pt. 2 (1970): 343–56; n.s., 6, pt. 1 (1971): 111–35; and n.s., 6, pt. 2 (1971): 345–59 (hereafter referred to as Farrell, "Drafting of the Irish Free State Constitution," 5, pt. 1; 5, pt. 2; 6, pt. 1; or 6, pt. 2).

2. Akenson and Fallin, 5, no. 1, 12–20; O'Sullivan, *The Irish Free State and Its Senate* (London: Faber and Faber, 1940), 69–70.

3. Farrell, "Drafting of the Irish Free State Constitution," 6, pt. 1, 114–35; contains Drafts B and C. Akenson and Fallin, "Irish Civil War," 5, no. 2, 57–93; contains drafts A and B.

4. Brian Farrell, "From First Dáil through Irish Free State," in Brian Farrell, ed., *De Valera's Constitution and Ours* (Dublin: Gill and Macmillan, 1988), 20.

5. Emmet Larkin, "The Irish Political Tradition," in Hachey and McCaffrey, eds., *Perspectives on Irish Nationalism*, 101.

6. Dail Éireann, *Debates*, vol. 1, 18 September 1922, col. 479.

7. Mansergh, *Commonwealth Experience*, 1:24; D. W. Harkness, *The Restless Dominion: The Irish Free State and the British Commonwealth of Nations, 1921–31* (New York: New York University Press, 1970), 3–4.

8. David Harkness, "Britain and the Independence of the Dominions: The 1921 Crossroads," in T. W. Moody, ed., *Nationality and the Pursuit of National Independence* (Belfast: Appletree Press, 1978), 149.

9. Minutes of a meeting of United Kingdom and Irish representatives, 29 May 1922, file S8955A, National Archives, Dublin.

10. Curran, *Birth of the Irish Free State*, 82–83.

11. Memorandum on the first draft of an Irish Free State constitution, 29 May 1922, CAB 43/3, pp. 192–93, Public Records Office, London.

12. Sexton, *Ireland and the Crown*, 81–85.

13. Arthur Berriedale Keith, ed., *Speeches and Documents on the British Dominions, 1918–1931* (London: Oxford University Press, 1932), 83–84.

14. Keith, *Speeches and Documents*, 84.

15. Harkness, *Restless Dominion*, 16.

16. Minutes of meeting, 24 January 1922, file S8952, National Archives, Dublin; Kennedy MSS. P4/299 (1–4), University College, Dublin.

17. Farrell, "Drafting the Free State Constitution," 5, pt. 1, 121.

18. Copy enclosed in Michael Collins to James Douglas, 20 January 1922, file S.8952, National Archives, Dublin. Farrell prints the whole document, from a copy in the James Douglas Papers, as having been shown to Collins rather than emanating from him, but the National Archives copy shows it to have been drafted by Collins with the help of an unnamed solicitor. See Farrell, "Drafting the Free State Constitution," 5, pt. 1, 122–24.

19. Tim Pat Coogan, *Michael Collins* (London: Hutchinson, 1990), 311. Also see Akenson and Fallin, "Irish Civil War," 5, no. 4, 21–23, 30.

20. The articles were republished in Darrell Figgis, *The Irish Constitution* (Dublin: Mellifont Press, 1922); see pp. 7–10.

21. The draft is reproduced in Akenson and Fallin, "Irish Civil War," 5, no. 4, 41–53, and in Farrell, "Drafting the Free State Constitution," 6, pt. 2, 357–59.

22. Minutes of a meeting of Irish and United Kingdom delegates, 27 May 1922, file S8955A, National Archives, Dublin.

23. Figgis memorandum, n.d., Kennedy MSS. P4/320, University College, Dublin.

24. Curran, *Birth of the Irish Free State*, 204–16.

25. Minute of a meeting between United Kingdom and Irish delegates, 27 May 1922, file S8955A, National Archives, Dublin.

26. Memorandum, 29 May 1922, CAB 43/3, p. 191, Public Records Office, London.

27. Canning, *British Policy towards Ireland*, 41.

28. Figgis, *Irish Constitution*, 10.

29. Kennedy memorandum, 30 May 1922, Kennedy MSS. P4/1252, University College, Dublin.

30. Curran, *Birth of the Irish Free State*, 208–9.

31. For the pact and its implications, see Curran, *Birth of the Irish Free State*, 186–95, and Akenson and Fallin, "Irish Civil War," 5, no. 4, 34–40.

32. Document No. 2 was de Valera's proposed alternative version to the Anglo-Irish Treaty; see Curran, *Birth of the Irish Free State*, 289.

33. Ibid., 118–19.

34. Akenson and Fallin, "Irish Civil War," 5, no. 4, 36–38.

35. Kennedy to Collins, copy, 21 May 1922, Kennedy MSS. P4/236, University College, Dublin.

36. Curran, *Birth of the Irish Free State*, 190–92.

37. Ibid., 195.

38. Canning, *British Policy towards Ireland*, 15–16.

39. Curran, *Birth of the Irish Free State*, 209–17.

40. Ibid., 220–21.

41. O'Sullivan, *Irish Free State and Its Senate*, 62–63.

42. Dail Éireann, *Debates*, vol. 1, 18 September 1922, cols. 497–99.

43. Ibid., cols. 531–34.

44. Ibid., cols. 354–87.

45. Curran, *Birth of the Irish Free State*, 261–63.

46. Canning, *British Policy towards Ireland*, 45.

47. O'Sullivan, *Irish Free State and Its Senate*, 66.

48. Curran, *Birth of the Irish Free State*, 230–31.

49. O'Sullivan, *Irish Free State and Its Senate*, 52.

50. Ibid., 57.

51. Saorstat Éireann, *Constitution of the Free State of Ireland* (Dublin: Stationery

Office, n.d.). It is also printed as an appendix in Kohn, *Constitution of the Irish Free State*.

52. Lloyd George to Griffith, 13 December 1921, published in the London *Times*, 20 December 1921.

53. Sexton, *Ireland and the Crown*, 86; Harkness, *Restless Dominion*, 22.

54. Kohn, *Constitution of the Irish Free State*, 50–51.

55. Minutes of meeting of 29 May 1922, CAB 43/1, p. 68, Public Records Office, London.

56. Minutes of meeting of 9 June 1922, CAB 43/1. See also minutes of meeting of 10 October 1922, CAB 43/2, pp. 110ff., Public Records Office, London.

57. Dáil Éireann, *Debates*, vol. 1, 5 October 1922, col. 1260.

58. Article 37.

59. Article 28.

60. Article 53.

61. John McColgan, *British Policy and the Irish Administration, 1920–22* (London: George Allen and Unwin, 1983), 119.

62. Article 24.

63. Article 81.

64. Article 27.

65. Article 28.

66. Government brief, n.d., on Constitution (Amendment No. 3) Act, 1937, file S4469/4, National Archives, Dublin.

67. Article 24.

68. Akenson and Fallin, "Irish Civil War," 5, no. 1, 25–26; Minutes of Constitution Committee, 24 January 1922, Kennedy MSS. P4/299, University College, Dublin.

69. Midleton to Figgis, copy in Figgis to Collins, 19 May 1922, file S8954A, National Archives, Dublin.

70. O'Sullivan, *Irish Free State and Its Senate*, 78–81.

71. Article 31.

72. Article 32.

73. Article 33.

74. O'Sullivan, *Irish Free State and Its Senate*, 80–81.

75. The Provisional government accepted a British request that the President should consult with Chambers of Commerce, the Colleges of Physicians and Surgeons, Benchers of Kings Inn and the Incorporated Law Society, and the Corporations of Dublin and Cork before making his nominations; see minutes of meeting of 13 June 1922, Kennedy MSS. P4/366 (i), University College, Dublin.

76. O'Sullivan, *Irish Free State and Its Senate*, 84.

77. Ibid., 116–17.

78. Lyons, *Parnell*, 468.

79. O'Sullivan, *Irish Free State and Its Senate*, 95.

80. Figgis, *Irish Constitution*, 60.

81. Kohn, *Constitution of the Irish Free State*, 195.

82. Figgis memo, n.d., Kennedy MSS. P4/320, University College, Dublin.

83. Figgis to Kennedy, 16 March 1922, Kennedy MSS. P4/309(1), University College, Dublin.

84. Figgis to Collins, comment on draft document 15, n.d., Kennedy MSS. P4/320, and Figgis to Collins, 7 March 1922, Kennedy MSS. P4/339, University College, Dublin.

85. Harkness, *Restless Dominion*, 28.
86. Article 66.
87. Dáil Éireann, *Debates*, vol. 1, 20 September 1922, col. 481.

## Chapter 9. Irish Free State

1. J. G. Swift MacNeill, *Studies in the Constitution of the Irish Free State* (Dublin: Talbot, 1925), xi.
2. Kohn, *Constitution of the Irish Free State*, 80.
3. Article 55.
4. David Gwynn Morgan, *Constitutional Law of Ireland*, 2d ed. (Blackrock, County Dublin: Round Hall Press, 1990), 70.
5. Article 52.
6. The Commission on the Second House, 1936, file S8642/2, National Archives, Dublin.
7. Seanad Éireann, *Debates*, vol. 1, 14 June 1923. See also discussion of Seanad and money bills in file S5687, National Archives, Dublin.
8. The Provisional government originally proposed a 180-day period of delay, but this was extended to 270 days at the request of the Southern unionists.
9. Figgis, *Irish Constitution*, 30.
10. Amendment No. 13. O'Sullivan, *Irish Free State and Its Senate*, 87–88.
11. Ibid., 148.
12. Articles 32 and 82.
13. See discussion in chapter 10.
14. Article 32.
15. O'Sullivan, *Irish Free State and Its Senate*, 208.
16. McCracken, *Representative Government*, 137–38.
17. O'Sullivan, *Irish Free State and Its Senate*, 205.
18. Ibid., 202–3.
19. Ibid., 121.
20. Ibid., 122.
21. Ibid., 145. All the bills amended by the Senate are listed on 606–19.
22. Ibid., 131–32.
23. Ibid., 519–24.
24. Curran, *Birth of the Irish Free State*, 188. See also the Anti-Treaty Committee report, 11 May 1922, file 15440(1), in the G. Gavan Duffy Papers, National Library, Dublin.
25. Maurice Manning, *Irish Political Parties: An Introduction* (Dublin: Gill and Macmillan, 1972), 9–18.
26. Ibid., 34–43; Thomas Garvin, *The Evolution of Irish Nationalist Politics* (Dublin: Gill and Macmillan, 1981), 154; Michael Gallagher, *Political Parties in the Republic of Ireland* (Manchester, England: Manchester University Press, 1985), 10–12.
27. R. K. Carty, *Party and Parish Pump: Electoral Politics in Ireland* (Atlantic Highlands, N.J.: Humanities Press, 1981), 85.
28. Ibid., 91–92
29. Gallagher, *Political Parties*, 135–36.
30. See, for example, Warner Moss, *Political Parties in the Irish Free State* (New York: Columbia University Press, 1933); E. Rumpf and A. C. Hepburn, *Nationalism and Socialism in Twentieth Century Ireland* (Liverpool, England: Liverpool University Press, 1977); Garvin, *Evolution of Irish Nationalist Politics*; and Jeffrey

Prager, *Building Democracy in Ireland: Political Order and Cultural Integration in a Newly Independent Nation* (Cambridge: Cambridge University Press, 1986).

31. Garvin, *Evolution of Irish Nationalist Politics*, 135.

32. Carty, *Party and Parish Pump*, 97.

33. Ibid., 97.

34. Chubb, *Government and Politics of Ireland*, 172–73.

35. Ronan Fanning, *"The Four Leaved Shamrock": Electoral Politics and the National Imagination in Independent Ireland*, The 25th O'Donnell Lecture (Dublin: National University of Ireland, 1983), 3–8.

36. Carty, *Party and Parish Pump*, 89–90.

37. O'Sullivan, *Irish Free State and Its Senate*, 5.

38. Carty, *Party and Parish Pump*, 98–100.

39. McCracken, *Representative Government*, 71; Chubb, *Government and Politics of Ireland*, 134.

40. Moss, *Political Parties*, 23.

41. See Gallagher, *Political Parties*, 159, and McCracken, *Representative Government*, 103–5.

42. Memorandum by Ernest Blythe, 13 April 1926, Ernest Blythe Papers, P24/211 (79–85), University College, Dublin.

43. Patrick Fay, "The Amendments to the Constitution Committee, 1926," *Administration* 26, no. 3 (1978): 345–46.

44. McCracken, *Political Parties*, 120–21.

45. Minutes of the Provisional government, 11 August and 26 August 1922, file S.7871A, National Archives, Dublin.

46. Minutes of the Provisional government, 28 April 1924, file S.7871A, National Archives, Dublin.

47. Fanning, *Irish Department of Finance*, 113.

48. Ibid., 575; also see 101–5.

49. Notes by Hugh Kennedy, n.d., Kennedy MSS. P4/361(1), University College, Dublin.

50. Dáil Éireann, *Standing Orders*, 1923.

51. McCracken, *Political Parties*, 129–30.

52. See, for example, Fanning, *Irish Department of Finance*, 111, 201–2, 231.

53. Article 53.

54. Fay, "Amendments to the Constitution Committee," 335.

55. Brian Farrell, *Chairman or Chief? The Role of the Taoiseach in Irish Government* (Dublin: Gill and Macmillan, 1971), 5.

56. Ibid., 2–3.

57. Ibid., 20–21.

58. Dáil Éireann, *Debates*, vol. 1, 12 October 1922, col. 1618.

59. Kohn, *Constitution of the Irish Free State*, 51.

60. See discussion in chapter 8.

61. Memorandum on the Governor-General and the Assent, 30 January 1936, file S8577, National Archives, Dublin; Sexton, *Ireland and the Crown*, 93–94.

62. Mary MacMillan, "Legislative Authority, Sovereignty, Legitimacy and Political Development: The Constitutional Basis of the Irish Free State," 2 vols. (Ph.D. diss., University College, Dublin, 1986), 2:177–81.

63. McCracken, *Political Parties*, 157, 119–20; Sexton, *Ireland and the Crown*, 90–92.

64. Kohn, *Constitution of the Irish Free State*, 214.

65. Farrell, ed., *De Valera's Constitution and Ours*, 29–30.

66. O'Sullivan, *Irish Free State and Its Senate*, 339.

67. See Ward, "Exporting the British Constitution," 15–23.

68. External ministers are considered in Ward, "Challenging the British Constitution," *passim*.

69. Dáil Éireann, *Debates*, vol. 1, 5 October 1922, cols. 1242–43.

70. Farrell, "Drafting the Free State Constitution," 5, pt. 1, 131.

71. Dáil Éireann, *Debates*, vol. 1, 12 October 1922, col. 1590.

72. Dáil Éireann, *Debates*, vol. 1, 5 October 1922, col. 1245.

73. Dáil Éireann, *Debates*, vol. 1, 20 September 1922, col. 487.

74. See Dáil Éireann, *Debates*, vol. 5, 10 September 1923, cols. 51–65.

75. Dáil Éireann, *Debates*, vol. 1, 5 October 1922, col. 1245.

76. Article 55.

77. See, for example, Dáil Éireann, *Debates*, vol. 1, 5 October 1922, cols. 1275–78; and vol. 1, 6 October 1922, cols. 1300–1304, 1311–13.

78. Gallagher, *Political Parties*, 157; Farrell, *Chairman or Chief*, 88–89; Kohn, *Constitution of the Irish Free State*, 281.

79. Dáil Éireann, *Debates*, vol. 1, 6 October 1922, col. 1305.

80. Dáil Éireann, *Debates*, vol. 1, 20 September 1922, col. 485.

81. Dáil Éireann, *Debates*, vol. 1, 6 October 1922, cols. 1307–8.

82. Dáil Éireann, *Debates*, vol. 1, 5 October 1922, col. 1246.

83. Dáil Éireann, *Debates*, vol. 1, 20 September 1922, col. 487.

84. Memo by Kennedy, Douglas, and France, 13 April 1922, Kennedy MSS. P4/339, and memo, n.d., by Kennedy, Kennedy MSS. P4/307, University College, Dublin. Kennedy later retreated from this interpretation. See Kennedy to Collins, copy, 21 May 1922, Kennedy MSS. P4/236, University College, Dublin.

85. See discussion in chapter 8.

86. Kennedy memo, n.d., Kennedy MSS. P4/307, University College, Dublin.

87. Article by Alfred O'Rahilly in the *Standard*, 25 May 1951; see file S8959, National Archives, Dublin.

88. MacNeill, *Studies in the Constitution*, xviii.

## Chapter 10. Amending the Constitution

1. McBride, *Greening of Dublin Castle*, 303.

2. O'Halpin, *Decline of the Union* 212.

3. Harkness, *Restless Dominion*, 13.

4. Mansergh, *Unsolved Question*, 269–71.

5. Harkness, *Restless Dominion*, 26.

6. Ibid., 67–72.

7. Ibid., 60.

8. Ibid., 36.

9. Ibid., 57–62.

10. Ibid., 63–67, 136–37.

11. Ibid., 70.

12. Ibid., 140–41.

13. Ibid., 141–42; Arthur Berriedale Keith, *The Dominions as Sovereign States* (London: Macmillan, 1938), 59.

14. Harkness, *Restless Dominion*, 229–39.

15. Keith, *Speeches and Documents*, xxii–xxiii, 149–52.

16. Harkness, *Restless Dominion*, 98. Harkness covers the 1926 Imperial Conference at length on pp. 80–134.

17. Keith, *Dominions as Sovereign States*, 64–65.

18. Harkness, *Restless Dominion*, 149–72.

19. Mansergh, *Commonwealth Experience*, 31.

20. Harkness, *Restless Dominion*, 173–228.

21. Ibid., 240–48.

22. Ibid., 243.

23. The discussion of the Amendments to the Constitution Committee is taken from Patrick Fay, "The Amendments to the Constitution Committee, 1926," *Administration* 26, no. 3 (1978): 349; Kohn, *Constitution of the Irish Free State*, 256–57; files S.2696 and S.4650 in the National Archives, Dublin; and "Constitution Committee," Ernest Blythe Papers, P24/211 (1–112), University College, Dublin.

24. "Constitution of 1922," file S.8953, National Archives, Dublin.

25. Figgis, *Irish Constitution*, 39.

26. Ibid., 41.

27. Dáil Éireann, *Debates*, vol. 1, 5 October 1922, col. 1267.

28. Dáil Éireann, *Debates*, vol. 1, 6 October 1922, col. 1294.

29. Dáil Éireann, *Debates*, vol. 5, 20 September 1923, col. 45.

30. Ibid., col. 49.

31. Ibid., cols. 45–46.

32. Ibid., col. 48.

33. Macardle, *Irish Republic*, 982.

34. Dáil Éireann, *Debates*, vol. 5, 10 October 1923, cols. 194, 202.

35. Ibid., col. 193.

36. Ibid., cols. 193–94.

37. Ibid., col. 197.

38. Memorandum from the Department of Finance, n.d., Ernest Blythe Papers, P24/211 (1–6), University College, Dublin.

39. Denis R. Gwynn, *The Irish Free State, 1922–1927* (London: Macmillan, 1928), 45, 135–37; Ronan Fanning, *Independent Ireland* (Dublin: Helicon, 1983), 101. Walsh left the government and joined Fianna Fáil in 1927.

40. Fay, "Amendments to the Constitution Committee," 334. This had actually been suggested by the government during the Dáil debate on the provisions for the executive in the constitution in September 1923, but it was not pressed at that time; see Dáil Éireann, *Debates*, vol. 1, 19 October 1922, col. 1749.

41. Constitution (Amendment No. 5) Act, 1927, file S.4469/5, National Archives, Dublin; Dáil Éireann, *Debates*, vol. 17 , 16 November 1926, cols. 419–28.

42. Kohn, *Constitution of the Irish Free State*, 271.

43. Fay, "Amendments to the Constitution Committee," 335.

44. Gwynn, *Irish Free State*, 214–15.

45. Roderick O'Hanlon, "A Constitution for a Free People," *Administration* 15, no. 2 (1967): 85–101.

46. O'Sullivan, *Irish Free State and Its Senate*, 234.

47. Ibid., 232.

48. "Amendments to the Constitution," S.4469/6, National Archives, Dublin.

49. Fay, "Amendments to the Constitution Committee," 338–40.

50. O'Sullivan, *Irish Free State and Its Senate*, 277.

51. Fay, "Amendments to the Constitution Committee," 348.

52. Amendments to the Constitution Committee Report, 6 May 1925, Ernest Blythe Papers, P24/211 (111), p. 11, University College, Dublin.

53. Fay, "Amendments to the Constitution Committee," 342–44.

54. Ibid., 336; Lyons, *Ireland since the Famine*, 472.

55. Kohn, *Constitution of the Irish Free State*, 199–200, 242–43; Lyons, *Ireland since the Famine*, 472; Earl of Longford and Thomas P. O'Neill, *Eamon de Valera* (London: Hutchinson, 1970), 205–6; O'Sullivan, *Irish Free State and Its Senate*, 228–30; McCracken, *Representative Government*, 60–61.

56. Fay, "Amendments to the Constitution Committee," 341; O'Sullivan, *Irish Free State and Its Senate*, 232–36.

57. Andrew E. Malone, "Party Government in the Irish Free State," *Political Science Quarterly* 44, no. 3 (1929): 376.

58. Moynihan, *Speeches and Statements*, 150; O'Sullivan, *Irish Free State and Its Senate*, 214–17.

59. Gwynn, *Irish Free State*, 50.

60. Frank Munger, *The Legitimacy of Opposition: The Change of Government in Ireland in 1932* (Beverly Hills, Calif.: Sage, 1975), 22.

61. Gwynn, *Irish Free State*, 193.

62. O'Sullivan, *Irish Free State and Its Senate*, 220.

63. Munger, *Legitimacy of Opposition*, 54.

64. Fanning, *Irish Department of Finance*, 282–307; Canning, *British Policy towards Ireland*, 127–38.

65. Harkness, *Restless Dominion*, 29.

66. Longford and O'Neill, *Eamon de Valera*, 289.

67. Keith, *Speeches and Documents*, 460.

68. Ibid., 462.

69. Harkness, *Restless Dominion*, 239–40.

70. Moynihan, *Speeches and Statements*, 196–202; O'Sullivan, *Irish Free State and Its Senate*, 206; Kohn, *Constitution of the Irish Free State*, 215–19.

71. O'Sullivan, *Irish Free State and Its Senate*, 308–9.

72. Arthur Berriedale Keith, ed., *Letters on Imperial Relations and International Law, 1916–1935* (London: Oxford University Press, 1935), 128.

73. O'Sullivan, *Irish Free State and Its Senate*, 312.

74. Ibid., 325.

75. Kohn, *Constitution of the Irish Free State*, 373–83.

76. O'Sullivan, *Irish Free State and Its Senate*, 462–63.

77. Sexton, *Ireland and the Crown*, 122–23.

78. Farrell, "Drafting the Free State Constitution," 5, pt. 1.

79. Sexton, *Ireland and the Crown*, 124–30.

80. Ibid., 131–34.

81. Kennedy to de Valera, 6 October 1932, Hugh Kennedy Papers, P4/1258, University College, Dublin; Sexton, *Ireland and the Crown*, 135–36, 142–45.

82. Ibid., 139–41.

83. Ibid., 151–57.

84. Dáil Éireann, *Debates*, vol. 48, 14 July 1933, cols. 2752–54.

85. Dáil Éireann, *Debates*, vol. 53, 20 June 1934, col. 807.

86. O'Sullivan, *Irish Free State and Its Senate*, 325; Sexton, *Ireland and the Crown*, 158.

87. Lyons, *Ireland since the Famine*, 513–14.

88. O'Sullivan, *Irish Free State and Its Senate*, 478–85.

89. Memorandum by Michael McDunphy, 22 December 1936, file 1086, de Valera MSS, Franciscan Archives, Killiney, Co. Dublin, and file S7810, National Archives, Dublin.

90. Sexton, *Ireland and the Crown*, 166–67.

91. Ibid., 164; Longford and O'Neill, *Eamon de Valera*, 291–93; Deirdre McMahon, *Republicans and Imperialists: Anglo-Irish Relations in the 1930s* (New Haven, Conn.: Yale University Press, 1984), 198–200.

92. Dáil Éireann, *Debates*, vol. 64, 11 December 1936, col. 1280.

93. Ibid., col. 1295.

94. Draft of "Foreign Relations Bill, 1936" by John J. Hearne, 6 September 1936, file 1029/4, de Valera MSS, Franciscan Archives, Killiney, Co. Dublin.

95. Dáil Éireann, *Debates*, vol. 64, 11 December 1936, col. 1232.

96. John O'Brien, "Ireland's Departure from the Commonwealth," *Round Table* 306 (1988): 188.

97. Canning, *British Policy towards Ireland*, 70–71.

98. Dáil Éireann, *Debates*, vol. 1, 10 October 1922, col. 1404.

99. Transcription of shorthand notes of Judicial Committee of the Privy Council session, 25 July 1923, Kennedy MSS. P4/515; Kennedy to President Cosgrave, 30 July 1923, Kennedy MSS. P4/516, University College, Dublin.

100. Kohn, *Constitution of the Irish Free State*, 357–63.

101. Harkness, *Restless Dominion*, 114, 204.

102. Ibid., 204.

103. Keith, ed., *Letters on Imperial Relations and International Law*, 137; Lyons, *Ireland since the Famine*, 510–12.

104. McMahon, *Republicans and Imperialists*, 158; O'Sullivan, *Irish Free State and Its Senate*, 462–63.

105. McMahon, *Republicans and Imperialists*, 1.

106. Canning, *British Policy towards Ireland*, 128, 152.

107. Great Britain, *Parliamentary Debates*, vol. 281, no. 140, 14 November 1933, vol. 281, no. 140, cols. 727–30; McMahon, *Republicans and Imperialists*, 130.

108. Keith, *Speeches and Documents*, 92.

109. McMahon, *Republicans and Imperialists*, 43.

110. Ibid., 186.

111. Ibid., 172–77; Canning, *British Policy towards Ireland*, 145–46, 174.

112. McMahon, *Republicans and Imperialists*, 206–7.

113. Canning, *British Policy towards Ireland*, 170.

114. Dáil Éireann, *Debates*, vol. 51, 18 April 1934, cols. 1869–70.

115. O'Sullivan, *Irish Free State and Its Senate*, 514–17.

116. Ibid., 429.

117. Ibid., 317.

118. Ibid., 466.

119. Ibid., 349–53.

120. Ibid., 347.

121. Ibid., 516.

122. Ibid., 362.

123. Dáil Éireann, *Debates*, vol. 51, 22 March 1934, col. 1461.

124. Dáil Éireann, *Debates*, vol. 51, 18 April 1934, cols. 1828–29.

125. Ibid., col. 1830.

126. O'Sullivan, *Irish Free State and Its Senate*, 378.

127. Ibid., 379.
128. Ibid., 366–67.
129. Ibid., 455–61.
130. Ibid., 469.
131. Ibid., 353.
132. Michael Rohan, "University Representation, 1918–1938," *Administration* 29, no. 3 (1981–82): 260–85.
133. O'Sullivan, *Irish Free State and Its Senate*, 413–17.

## Chapter 11. The 1937 Constitution

1. Report of Saorstát Éireann Constitution Committee, 3 July 1934, file 1047/1–2, de Valera MSS, Franciscan Archives, Killiney, Co. Dublin, and file S.2979, National Archives, Dublin.
2. Hearne to de Valera, 18 May 1935, file 1029/6, de Valera MSS, Franciscan Archives, Killiney, Co. Dublin.
3. For the drafting of the constitution, see Dermot Keogh, "The Irish Constitutional Revolution: An Analysis of the Making of the Constitution," in Frank Litton, ed., *The Constitution of Ireland, 1937–1987* (Dublin: Institute of Public Administration, 1988), 4–85; Brian Kennedy, "John Hearne and the Irish Constitution," *Éire-Ireland* 25, no. 2 (Summer 1989): 121–27; and Ronan Fanning, "Mr. de Valera Drafts a Constitution," in Farrell, ed., *De Valera's Constitution and Ours*, 33–45.
4. Keogh, "Irish Constitutional Revolution," 68.
5. Dáil Éireann, *Debates*, vol. 67, 11 May 1937, col. 83.
6. Lyons, *Ireland since the Famine*, 534–35.
7. Longford and O'Neill, *Eamon de Valera*, 294.
8. Republic of Ireland, *Report of the Committee on the Constitution* (Dublin: Stationery Office, 1967), 7.
9. John Kelly, T.D., "The Constitution: Law and Manifesto," in Litton, ed., *Constitution of Ireland*, 209.
10. Morgan, *Constitutional Law*, 31–32.
11. See files S.11580, 11769, 11770, 11777A, 11780, 11782, 11784, 11786, 11787, 11791, 11792, National Archives, Dublin.
12. Article 30.
13. Morgan, *Constitutional Law*, 59–60.
14. Neill Collins and Frank McCann, *Irish Politics Today* (Manchester, England: Manchester University Press, 1989), 52.
15. *Report of the Committee on the Constitution*, 7.
16. Dáil Éireann, *Debates*, vol. 67, 26 May 1937, cols. 1071–80, 1084–95.
17. Coakley, "Constituency Boundary Revision," 291–328.
18. Dáil Éireann, *Debates*, vol. 67, 11 May 1937, col. 56.
19. Dáil Éireann, *Debates*, vol. 51, 18 April 1934, col. 1830.
20. Dáil Éireann, *Debates*, vol. 62, 28 May 1936, col. 1199.
21. Draft heads of a constitution, 17 May 1935, file 1029/6, de Valera MSS, Franciscan Archives, Killiney, Co. Dublin.
22. See drafts, n.d., file 1029/2, and 20 August 1936, file 1029/3/1, de Valera MSS, Franciscan Archives, Killiney, Co. Dublin.
23. In 1952 the Seanad sent a bill back to the Dáil with amendments after 152 days. The Dáil accepted the amendments. The Attorney General, Ó Dálaigh, argued

that the 90-day limit was designed to limit the Seanad's power to delay bills and should not be construed to deny the Dáil the right to consider amendments at any time; see file S.11786, National Archives, Dublin.

24. Summary of proposals, n.d., Commission on the Second House, 1936, file S.8642/2, National Archives, Dublin; Fay, "Amendments to the Constitution Committee," 338–39.

25. File S.8642/8, National Archives, Dublin. The reports were published as Saorstát Éireann, *Report of the Second House of the Oireachtas Commission* (Dublin: Stationery Office, 1936).

26. Kennedy report, 28 September 1936, in Kennedy to de Valera, 30 September 1936, file S.8642/8, National Archives, Dublin.

27. Commission report enclosed in Kennedy to de Valera, 30 September 1936, file S.8642/8, National Archives, Dublin.

28. Minority report enclosed in Kennedy to de Valera, 30 September 1936, file S.8642/8, National Archives, Dublin.

29. Dáil Éireann, *Debates*, vol. 48, 20 June 1933, col. 784.

30. De Valera speech to Fianna Fáil Ard-Fheis, 3 November 1936, file S.13365, National Archives, Dublin.

31. Dáil Éireann, *Debates*, vol. 67, 1 June 1937, col. 1472.

32. Lee, *Ireland: 1912–1985*, 271–72.

33. Ibid., 271.

34. Commission report enclosed in Kennedy to de Valera, 30 September 1936, file S.8642/8, National Archives, Dublin.

35. See discussion in chapter 5.

36. Dáil Éireann, *Debates*, vol. 98, 11 October 1945, cols. 273–85.

37. Sean Dooney and John O'Toole, *Irish Government Today* (Dublin: Gill and Macmillan, 1992), 63–64.

38. John Colgan, "Local Elections: Behind the Results," *Administration* 39, no. 4 (1992): 373.

39. Article 34.3.

40. Article 26.

41. Dáil Éireann, *Debates*, vol. 67, 25 May 1937, col. 1065.

42. Explanatory memorandum in Hearne to de Valera, 18 May 1935, file 1029/6, de Valera MSS, Franciscan Archives, Killiney, Co. Dublin.

43. See discussion in chapter 10.

44. Copy of MacDonald to Irish High Commissioner, 3 April 1937, file S.10463, National Archives, Dublin.

45. Canning, *British Policy towards Ireland*, 174.

46. Copy of statement by the British government, 30 December 1937, file 1043, de Valera MSS, Franciscan Archives, Killiney, Co. Dublin.

47. McMahon, *Republicans and Imperialists*, 243–44.

48. Ibid., 173; Joseph T. Carroll, *Ireland in the War Years* (New York: Crane, Russak, 1975), 26.

49. McMahon, *Republicans and Imperialists*, 280, 294–95; Canning, *British Policy towards Ireland*, 176–219.

50. Carroll, *Ireland in the War Years*, 26.

51. Ibid., 30–31.

52. Ibid., 19.

53. Ibid.

54. Mansergh, *Unresolved Question*, 311–12.

55. Carroll, *Ireland in the War Years*, 31.
56. Ibid., 42–44.
57. Ibid., 78–94.
58. Ibid., 39–59, 111–13; Mansergh, *Unresolved Question*, 312.
59. Carroll, *Ireland in the War Years*, 177–78.
60. Mansergh, *Unresolved Question*, 318.
61. Ibid., 334.
62. Fanning, *Independent Ireland*, 172–76; O'Brien, "Ireland's Departure from the Commonwealth," 179–94.
63. Mansergh, *Unresolved Question*, 336.
64. O'Brien, "Ireland's Departure from the Commonwealth," 186–91.
65. FitzGerald, *All in a Life*, 611.
66. Cunningham, *British Government Policy*, 14.
67. See John Whyte, *Church and State in Modern Ireland, 1923–79* (Dublin: Gill and Macmillan, 1989); Dermot Keogh, "The Irish Constitutional Revolution: An Analysis of the Making of the Constitution," in Litton, ed., *Constitution of Ireland*, 4–84; Frank Litton, "Church, State and Society," in Farrell, ed., *De Valera's Constitution and Ours*, 103–22; and Enda McDonagh, "Philosophical–Theological Reflections on the Constitution," in Litton, ed., *Constitution of Ireland*, 192–205.
68. Lee, *Ireland: 1912–1985*, 271.
69. Collins and McCann, *Irish Politics Today*, 76.
70. Sunniva McDonagh, ed., *The Attorney General v. X and Others* (Dublin: Incorporated Council of Law Reporting for Ireland, 1992), *passim*.
71. *Irish Times*, 24 November 1992.
72. *Sunday Independent* (Dublin), 29 November 1992.

## Chapter 12. The 1937 Constitution/Responsible Government

1. Article 15.2.1°.
2. See below, section entitled "A Week Head of State."
3. Chubb, *Government and Politics of Ireland*, 169.
4. See Alan J. Ward, "The Irish Constitution and the Political Crisis of 1989," *Parliamentary Affairs* 43, no. 3 (1990): 366–70.
5. R. M. Punnett, *British Government and Politics*, 5th ed. (Waveland Heights, Ill.: Waveland, 1988), 67.
6. Anthony King et al., *Britain at the Polls* (Chatham, N.J.: Chatham House, 1992), 171–73.
7. Gallagher, *Political Parties*, 156; *Sunday Tribune* (Dublin), 18 June 1989.
8. Republic of Ireland, *Report of the Informal Committee on the Constitution, December 1967* (Dublin: Stationery Office, 1967), 25–26.
9. Alan J. Ward, "Parliamentary Procedures and the Machinery of Government in Ireland," *Irish University Review* 4 (1974): 239–41; Longford and O'Neill, *Eamon de Valera*, 445–46; Lee, *Ireland: 1912–1985*, 330–31.
10. Michael Gallagher, "Does Ireland Need a New Electoral System?," *Irish Political Studies* 2 (1987): 27–48.
11. FitzGerald, *All in a Life*, 308–9; Chubb, *Government and Politics of Ireland*, 159–60.
12. *Irish Times*, 13 July 1989.
13. *Irish Times*, 30 June 1989.

14. See Ward, "Irish Constitution," 366–79.

15. *Sunday Tribune* (Dublin), 29 November 1992.

16. *Irish Times*, 12 December 1992.

17. *Sunday Tribune* (Dublin), 29 November 1992.

18. *Irish Times*, 10 December 1992.

19. *Irish Times*, 23 November 1992.

20. *Irish Times*, 20 November 1992.

21. FitzGerald, *All in a Life*, 641.

22. See discussion in chapter 13.

23. London *Times*, 24 January, 6 and 12 February 1992.

24. *Irish Times*, 6 November 1992.

25. Michael Marsh and Richard Sinnott, "How the Voters Decided," in Michael Gallagher and Richard Sinnott, eds., *How Ireland Voted, 1989* (Galway: Centre for the Study of Irish Elections, 1990), 117.

26. Ibid., 117.

27. Ibid., 125.

28. Article 28.4.1°.

29. Article 13.1.

30. Articles 28.7.1° and 28.7.8°.

31. Article 35.4.1°.

32. Article 28.3.3°.

33. Article 21.

34. Article 23.

35. Article 24.

36. Morgan, *Constitutional Law*, 96; McCracken, *Representative Government*, 151–52.

37. Article 18.8.

38. Dáil Éireann, *Debates*, vol. 98, no. 1, 10 October 1945, col. 285.

39. Ted Nealon, *Nealon's Guide: 26th Dáil and Seanad Election '89* (Dublin: Platform Press, 1989), 166.

40. Morgan, *Constitutional Law*, 90.

41. Seanad Éireann, *Debates*, vol. 130, no. 3, 30 October 1991, col. 237.

42. Morgan, *Constitutional Law*, 90.

43. Ibid., 123.

44. Ibid., 91, 273.

45. Dooney and O'Toole, *Irish Government Today*, 52, 65.

46. Chubb, *Government and Politics of Ireland*, 189n, 198; Raymond Smith, *Garrett the Enigma: Dr. Garrett FitzGerald* (Dublin: Aherlow, 1985), 122–23, 378–79; FitzGerald, *All in a Life*, 363.

47. Lee, *Ireland: 1912–1985*, 274–75.

48. Dáil Éireann, *Debates*, vol. 98, no. 1, 10 October 1945, cols. 273–85.

49. FitzGerald, *All in a Life*, 60.

50. *Report of the Informal Committee on the Constitution, December 1967*, 30.

51. Ibid., 31.

52. Ibid., 29.

53. Ibid., 32.

54. Fine Gael, *How the Dáil and the Seanad Can Provide Better Laws, Wiser Spending, Speedier Redress of Injustice* (Dublin: Fine Gael, 1990), 12.

55. Ibid., 12.

56. Morgan, *Constitutional Law*, 273.

57. *Irish Times*, 7 August 1992; Dooney and O'Toole, *Irish Government Today*, 68–69.

58. Morgan, *Constitutional Law*, 83.

59. FitzGerald, *All in a Life*, 632.

60. Morgan, *Constitutional Law*, 84.

61. Ibid., 85.

62. Conor Cruise O'Brien, *States of Ireland* (New York: Pantheon, 1972), 212–13; Gallagher, *Political Parties*, 20.

63. Dáil Éireann, *Debates*, vol. 402, no. 3, 31 October 1990, cols. 831–34; *Washington Post*, 10 November 1990.

64. Morgan, *Constitutional Law*, 186–87.

65. Lee, *Ireland: 1912–1985*, 272.

66. Cited in *Report of the Informal Committee on the Constitution, December 1967*, 128.

67. Dáil Éireann, *Debates*, vol. 98, no. 1, 10 October 1945, col. 125.

68. Ibid., col. 252.

69. Article 12.4.2°.

70. Janet Egleson Dunleavy and Gareth Dunleavy, *Douglas Hyde: A Maker of Modern Ireland* (Berkeley and Los Angeles: University of California Press, 1991), 364–91.

71. Morgan, *Constitutional Law*, 52–53.

72. See Morgan, *Constitutional Law*, 52–53.

73. *Irish Times*, 16 October 1990.

74. See Brian Farrell, "Ireland: The Irish Cabinet System: More British than the British Themselves," in J. Blondel and F. Müller-Rommel, eds., *Cabinets in Western Europe* (London: Macmillan, 1988), 33–46.

75. FitzGerald, *All in a Life*, 310.

76. Dooney and O'Toole, *Irish Government Today*, 4–5.

77. Article 17.2.

78. Article 28.4.3°.

79. Article 35.1 as qualified by Article 13.9.

80. Article 12.9.

81. Article 13.7.2° and 13.7.3°.

82. Article 24.1.

83. Article 29.4.1°.

84. Article 28.3.1° and 28.3.2°.

85. Morgan, *Constitutional Law*, 61.

86. T. J. Barrington, *The Irish Administrative System* (Dublin: Institute of Public Administration, 1980), 31.

87. Chubb, *Government and Politics of Ireland*, 187.

88. See discussion in chapter 10.

89. Morgan, *Constitutional Law*, 73.

90. *Irish Times*, 8 July, 22 August, 23 November 1992.

91. Dooney and O'Toole, *Irish Government Today*, 120.

92. Morgan, *Constitutional Law*, 136–39.

93. Barrington, *Irish Administrative System*, 35–36.

94. Morgan, *Constitutional Law*, 85–86.

95. Ibid., 117.

96. Collins and McCann, *Irish Politics Today*, 59.

97. Morgan, *Constitutional Law*, 138.

98. Dáil Éireann, *Debates*, vol. 339, 27 January 1983, col. 523.

99. Morgan, *Constitutional Law*, 102–3; Brian Farrell, "Odd Man Out? The Role of Ministers in the Irish Political System" (Unpublished paper, Department of Politics, University College, Dublin), 5.

100. Dooney and O'Toole, *Irish Government Today*, 59–60.

101. Ibid., 152–55, 280–81.

102. Audrey M. Arkins, "Legislative and Executive Relations in the Republic of Ireland," *West European Politics* 13 (1990): 90–102.

103. Dooney and O'Toole, *Irish Government Today*, 52.

104. Richard Humphreys, "Legislative Obstruction: How to Do It," *Administration* 39, no. 1 (1991): 55–70.

105. Ibid., 85–86.

106. Basil Chubb, "'Going about Persecuting Civil Servants': The Role of the Irish Parliamentary Representative," *Political Studies* 11, no. 3 (1963): 272–86.

107. Lee Komito, "Voters, Politicians and Clientalism: A Dublin Survey," *Administration* 37, no. 2 (1989): 174.

108. Ibid., 184.

109. Collins and McCann, *Irish Politics Today*, 48, 61.

110. Dáil Éireann, *Debates*, vol. 339, 2 February 1983, col. 945.

111. Valerie Kelly, "Focus on Clients: A Reappraisal of the Effectiveness of TDs' Interventions," *Administration* 35 (1987): 130–51.

112. Chubb, *Government and Politics of Ireland*, 204.

113. Ibid., 178–79.

114. FitzGerald, *All in a Life*, 425–26.

115. Ibid., 309. See also Chubb, *Government and Politics of Ireland*, 195–96.

116. *Irish Times*, 27 April 1991.

117. *Irish Times*, 22 March 1991.

118. *Irish Times*, 30 June, 4 July 1992.

119. Draft Article 21.9, n.d, file 1977/2, de Valera MSS, Franciscan Archives, Killiney, Co. Dublin.

120. See Dáil Éireann, *Debates*, vol. 67, 11 May 1937, col. 29.

121. Dáil Éireann, *Debates*, vol. 67, 26 May 1937, col. 1169.

122. See file S.9799A, National Archives, Dublin.

123. Articles 28.10 and 28.11.1°.

124. Article 13.1.2°.

125. Article 28.10.

126. Fay, "Amendments to the Constitution Committee," 335.

127. Article 28.9.4°.

128. Dáil Éireann, *Debates*, vol. 67, 26 May 1937, cols. 1177–78.

129. Ibid., cols. 1186–87.

130. Ibid., col. 1188.

131. See discussion in chapter 13.

132. See discussion in chapter 9.

133. Fay, "Amendments to the Constitution Committee," 342.

134. See discussion in chapter 13.

135. Morgan, *Constitutional Law*, 55–56; Dooney and O'Toole, *Irish Government Today*, 11–18.

136. Chubb, *Government and Politics of Ireland*, 105.

137. Morgan, *Constitutional Law*, 86–87; *Irish Times*, 11 November 1991.

138. Michael Gallagher, "The President, the People and the Constitution," in Farrell, ed., *De Valera's Constitution and Ours*, 75.

139. Article 28.5.2°.

140. *Irish Times*, 9 November 1990.

141. Chubb, *Government and Politics of Ireland*, 183.

142. *Irish Times*, 8 July 1992.

143. Dáil Éireann, *Debates*, vol. 67, 28 May 1937, col. 1277.

144. Article 30.2.

145. Article 33.

146. Morgan, *Constitutional Law*, 46.

147. Article 35.1.

148. See Dáil Éireann, *Debates*, vol. 67, 25 May 1937, col. 1008.

149. Ibid., cols. 1030–32.

150. Ibid., col. 52.

151. Dáil Éireann, *Debates*, vol. 67, 28 May 1937, col. 1243.

152. Dáil Éireann, *Debates*, vol. 67, 11 May 1937, col. 50.

153. Ibid., col. 51.

154. Article 13.2.3°.

155. Article 24.1.

156. Article 22.2.

157. Article 27.1.4°.

158. Article 26.1.1°.

159. Article 31.3.

160. Article 13.2.2°.

161. Dooney and O'Toole, *Irish Government Today*, 98; Morgan, *Constitutional Law*, 28.

162. Ibid., 49; Dooney and O'Toole, *Irish Government Today*, 103–4.

163. Smith, *Garrett*, 289–304; FitzGerald, *All in a Life*, 315–17; Basil Chubb, *A Source Book of Irish Government* (Dublin: Institute of Public Administration, 1964), 51–55.

164. Memoranda by M. Dunphy, 10 May 1944 and 1 May 1945, file S.15805, National Archives, Dublin.

165. Smith, *Garrett*, 30.

166. Ibid., 24.

167. Ibid., 22; FitzGerald, *All in a Life*, 398.

168. Smith, "When Haughey Hoped to Assume Power—Without an Election," in *Garrett*, 22–33.

169. *Irish Times*, 20 October 1990.

170. *Irish Times*, 23 October 1990.

171. Dáil Éireann, *Debates*, vol. 402, 24 October 1990, col. 318.

172. Dáil Éireann, *Debates*, vol. 402, 31 October 1990, col. 574.

173. *Irish Times*, 23 October 1990.

174. *Irish Times*, 24 October 1990.

175. *Irish Times*, 26 October 1990.

176. *Irish Times*, 26 October 1990, and *Sunday Independent*, 10 February 1991.

177. Dáil Éireann, *Debates*, vol. 402, 31 October 1990, cols. 831–34.

178. *Irish Times*, 24 October 1990.

179. *Irish Times*, 26 October 1990.

180. *Irish Times*, 24 October 1990.

181. Ibid.

182. Dáil Éireann, *Debates*, vol. 67, 26 May 1937, col. 1212.

183. *Irish Times*, 3 July 1989.

184. Ronan Fanning, "The FG Leader Who Stepped Down to Form a Government," *Irish Times*, 28 June 1989.

185. Dáil Éireann, *Report of the Informal Committee on the Constitution* (Dublin: Stationery Office, 1967), 11–13.

186. FitzGerald, *All in a Life*, 644–45.

187. Alfred O'Rahilly, *Thoughts on the Constitution* (Dublin: Browne and Nolan, n.d.), 32.

188. *Report of the Committee on the Constitution*, 8.

189. *Irish Times*, 10 November 1990.

## Chapter 13. Concentration of Power

1. Bagehot, *English Constitution*, 67–68.

2. Ibid., 158.

3. Morgan, *Constitutional Law*, 64.

4. Bagehot, *English Constitution*, 158–59.

5. Ibid., 150.

6. Ibid., 158.

7. Ibid., 161.

8. Brian Farrell, "The Constitution and the Institutions of Government," in Litton, ed., *Constitution of Ireland*, 168–69.

9. Chubb, *Government and Politics of Ireland*, 262–86; Collins and McCann, *Irish Politics Today*, 79–91; Dooney and O'Toole, *Irish Government Today*, 136–44.

10. Barrington, *Irish Administrative System*, 40.

11. Ibid., 47.

12. Chubb, *Government and Politics of Ireland*, 265.

13. Donal de Buitleir, "Local Finance in Ireland—The Options," *Administration* 39, no. 4 (1992): 295–99.

14. Humphreys, "Legislative Obstruction," 59.

15. Dooney and O'Toole, *Irish Government Today*, 9.

16. Chubb, *Government and Politics of Ireland*, 244–61; Dooney and O'Toole, *Irish Government Today*, 152–73.

17. Chubb, *Government and Politics of Ireland*, 270.

18. Dooney and O'Toole, *Irish Government Today*, 155–56.

19. Fine Gael, *Reform of the Dáil* (Dublin: Fine Gael, 1980), 9.

20. Dooney and O'Toole, *Irish Government Today*, 169–70.

21. Chubb, *Government and Politics of Ireland*, 246, 324–25.

22. David Kennedy, "Privatisation—An Irish Solution?," *Administration* 39, no. 3 (1991): 199.

23. Ibid., 199–209.

24. Ira Sharkansky, *Wither the State? Politics and Public Enterprise in Three Countries* (Chatham, N.J.: Chatham House Publishers, 1979), xi.

25. Lee, *Ireland: 1945–1970*, 19–21.

26. *Irish Times*, 5 January 1991.

27. *Irish Times*, 23 January 1991.

28. Seanad Éireann, *Debates*, vol. 130, no. 3, 30 October 1991, col. 233.

29. *Irish Times*, 20 February 1991.

30. Peter Sutherland, "Twin Perspectives: An Attorney-General Views Political and European Dimensions," in Farrell, ed., *De Valera's Constitution and Ours*, 176.

31. For a discussion of the drafting of these sections, see Dermot Keogh, "The Irish Constitutional Revolution: An Analysis of the Making of the Constitution," in Litton, ed., *Constitution of Ireland*, 4–84.

32. Anthony Coughlin, "The Constitution and Social Policy," in Litton, ed., *Constitution of Ireland*, 144.

33. James Casey, "Changing the Constitution: Amendment and Judicial Review," in Farrell, ed., *De Valera's Constitution and Ours*, 156–61; Chubb, *Government and Politics of Ireland*, 49.

34. Sutherland, "Twin Perspectives," 180–81.

35. Keogh, "Irish Constitutional Revolution," 73–74.

36. Justice Brian Walsh, "The Constitution: A View from the Bench," in Farrell, ed., *De Valera's Constitution and Ours*, 195. See also Brian Walsh, "The Constitution and Constitutional Rights," in Litton, ed., *Constitution of Ireland*, 86–109.

37. See Yvonne Scannell, "The Constitution and the Role of Women," and John Kelly, T.D., "Fundamental Rights in the Constitution," in Farrell, *De Valera's Constitution and Ours*, 123–36, and 168–72.

38. Scannell, "Constitution and the Role of Women," 132.

39. Morgan, *Constitutional Law*, 78–79.

40. Joseph F. Zimmerman, "The Office of Ombudsman in Ireland," *Administration* 37 (1989): 259–60.

41. Morgan, *Constitutional Law*, 103.

42. Ibid., 14; FitzGerald, *All in a Life*, 609.

43. Zimmerman, "Office of Ombudsman in Ireland," 260–63.

44. Ibid., 269–70.

45. Farrell, *Founding of Dáil Éireann*, 68–70.

46. McCracken, *Representative Government*, 167.

47. Morgan, *Constitutional Law*, 100.

48. Ibid., 145–46.

49. John Smyth, *The Houses of the Oireachtas*, 3d ed. (Dublin: Institute of Public Administration, 1973), 50–51; Dáil Éireann, *Debates*, vol. 237, 20 November 1968, cols. 756–811.

50. FitzGerald, *All in a Life*, 74.

51. Barry Desmond, T.D., "The House of the Oireachtas—A Plea for Reform," *Administration* 23 (1975): 425.

52. Ibid., 437–39.

53. Barrington, *Irish Administrative System*, 64.

54. Ibid., 217; Audrey M. Arkins, "Legislative and Executive Relations in the Republic of Ireland," *West European Politics* 13 (1990): 93–94.

55. Dáil Éireann, *Debates*, vol. 339, 27 January 1983, col. 650.

56. Fine Gael, *Reform of the Dáil*, 3.

57. Dooney and O'Toole, *Irish Government Today*, 69. Senators shared one assistant per three members.

58. FitzGerald, *All in a Life*, 387–88.

59. Dáil Éireann, *Debates*, vol. 339, 26 January 1983, col. 419.

60. Dáil Éireann, *Debates*, vol. 339, 8 February 1983, col. 1277, and vol. 343, 21 June 1983, cols. 2362ff.

61. Dáil Éireann, *Debates*, vol. 339, 26 January 1983, cols. 432–33.

62. Dáil Éireann, *Debates*, vol. 343, 21 June 1983, col. 2379.

63. Dáil Éireann, *Debates*, vol. 339, 2 February 1983, cols. 913–15.

64. Dáil Éireann, *Debates*, vol. 342, 21 June 1983, col. 2407.

65. Ibid., col. 2380.

66. For an evaluation of the committees, see Joseph Zimmerman, "An Oireachtas Innovation: Backbench Committees," *Administration* 36 (1988): 265–87.

67. Audrey M. Arkins, "The Committees of the 24th Oireachtas," *Irish Political Studies* 3 (1988): 91–97.

68. Morgan, *Constitutional Law*, 146.

69. Zimmerman, "An Oireachtas Innovation."

70. Morgan, *Constitutional Law*, 273.

71. Arkins, "Committees of the 24th Oireachtas," 91–97.

72. Ibid., 94.

73. Audrey M. Arkins, "Giving Real Power to the Oireachtas Committee System," *Irish Times*, 26 June 1989.

74. Morgan, *Constitutional Law*, 274–75, 279.

75. Arkins, "Giving Real Power to the Oireachtas Committee System," 2.

76. Fine Gael, *How the Dáil and Seanad Can Provide Better Laws*.

77. *Irish Times*, 11 February 1991.

78. Seanad Éireann, *Debates*, vol. 130, 30 October 1991, cols. 232–52.

79. Ibid., col. 373.

80. Dáil Éireann, *Debates*, vol. 339, 27 January 1983, col. 563.

81. *Irish Times*, 19 October 1991.

82. See, for example, interview in the *Irish Times*, 16 October 1990.

83. FitzGerald, *All in a Life*, 254; Chubb, *Government and Politics of Ireland*, 200.

84. *Irish Times*, 4 October 1990.

85. *Irish Times*, 16 October 1990.

86. *Irish Times*, 12 October 1990.

87. *Irish Times*, 27 September 1990.

88. *Irish Times*, 10 November 1990.

89. *Irish Times*, 8 and 16 October 1990.

90. *Irish Times*, 8 October 1990.

91. David Gwynn Morgan, "A Reformist President Faces Official—and Less Overt—Obstacles," *Irish Times*, 3 October 1990.

92. *Irish Times*, 20 October 1990.

93. *Irish Times*, 15 October 1990.

94. *Irish Times*, 17 October 1990.

95. *Irish Times*, 8 October 1990.

96. Dáil Éireann, *Debates*, vol. 402, 24 October 1990, col. 323.

97. Ibid., cols. 323–33.

98. Ibid., col. 337.

99. Ibid., col. 338.

100. Ibid., col. 341.

101. Ibid., col. 336.

102. *Irish Times*, 1 November 1990.

103. *Irish Times*, 19 April 1991.

104. President de Valera addressed a joint session of Dáil and Senate in the Mansion House on the fiftieth anniversary of the first Dáil Éireann in 1969.

105. *Irish Times*, 21 February 1991.

106. *Irish Times*, 8 July 1992.

107. Melanie Phillips, "The Dignity of Royal Labour," *Guardian Weekly*, 23 August 1992.

108. Brian Farrell, "Ireland: The Irish Cabinet System: More British than the British Themselves," in Blondel and Müller-Rommel, eds., *Cabinets in Western Europe*, 44.

109. Punnett, *British Government and Politics*, 261–64.

110. Morgan, *Constitutional Law*, 144.

111. Chubb, *Government and Politics of Ireland*, 229.

# Bibliography

## Books

Bagehot, Walter. *The English Constitution*. Edited by R. H. Crossman. Ithaca, N.Y.: Cornell University Press, 1963.

Balfour, Arthur. *Nationality and Home Rule*. London: Longmans Green, 1914.

Barrington, T. J. *The Irish Administrative System*. Dublin: Institute of Public Administration, 1980.

Bartlett, Thomas. *The Fall and Rise of the Irish Nation*. Dublin: Gill and Macmillan, 1992.

Barton, Brian. *Brookeborough: The Making of a Prime Minister*. Belfast: Institute of Irish Studies, Queen's University, 1988.

Bew, Paul. *C. S. Parnell*. Dublin: Gill and Macmillan, 1980.

Birrell, Derek, and Alan Murie. *Policy and Government in Northern Ireland: Lessons of Devolution*. Dublin: Gill and Macmillian, 1980.

Blake, Robert. *Unrepentant Tory*. New York: St. Martin's Press, 1956.

Blondel, J., and F. Müller-Rommel, eds. *Cabinets in Western Europe*. London: Macmillan, 1988.

Bogdanor, Vernon. *Devolution*. Oxford: Oxford University Press, 1979.

Bolton, G. C. *The Passing of the Act of Union*. Oxford: Oxford University Press, 1966.

Boyce, D. George. *Nationalism in Ireland*. Baltimore: Johns Hopkins University Press, 1982.

Brynn, Edward. *Crown and Castle: British Rule in Ireland, 1800–1830*. Dublin: O'Brien Press, 1978.

Buckland, Patrick. *The Factory of Grievances: Devolved Government in Northern Ireland, 1921–1939*. Dublin: Gill and Macmillan, 1979.

———. *A History of Northern Ireland*. Dublin: Gill and Macmillan, 1981.

———. *Irish Unionism 1: The Anglo-Irish and the New Ireland, 1885 to 1922*. Dublin: Gill and Macmillan, 1972.

———. *Irish Unionism 2: Ulster Unionism and the Origins of Northern Ireland, 1886–1922*. Dublin: Gill and Macmillan, 1973.

Butler, David, and Anne Sloman. *British Political Facts, 1900–1979*. New York: St. Martin's Press, 1980.

Calvert, Harry. *Constitutional Law in Northern Ireland: A Study in Regional Government*. London: Stevens/Northern Ireland Legal Quarterly, 1968.

Canning, Paul. *British Policy towards Ireland, 1921–1941*. Oxford: Clarendon Press, 1985.

Carroll, Joseph. *Ireland in the War Years*. New York: Crane, Russak, 1975.

Carty, R. K. *Party and Parish Pump: Electoral Politics in Ireland*. Atlantic Highlands, N.J.: Humanities Press, 1981.

Chubb, Basil. *The Government and Politics of Ireland*. 3d ed. London and New York: Longman, 1992.

———. *A Source Book of Irish Government*. Dublin: Institute of Public Administration, 1964.

Cohan, Al. *The Irish Political Élite*. Dublin: Gill and Macmillan, 1972.

Collins, Neill, and Frank McCann. *Irish Politics Today*. Manchester, England: Manchester University Press, 1989.

Comerford, Maire. *The First Dáil: January 21, 1919*. Dublin: Joe Clarke, 1969.

Cunningham, Michael J. *British Government Policy in Northern Ireland, 1969–1989*. Manchester, England: Manchester University Press, 1991.

Curran, Joseph. *The Birth of the Irish Free State, 1921–1923*. University: University of Alabama Press, 1980.

Curtis, Edmund, and R. B. McDowell. *Irish Historical Documents, 1172–1922*. London: Methuen, 1968. (Originally published in 1943.)

Cusack, M. F. *The Speeches and Public Letters of the Liberator*. Dublin: McGlashan and Gill, 1875.

Dangerfield, George. *The Damnable Question: A Study of Anglo-Irish Relations*. Boston: Little, Brown, 1976.

Davis, Richard. *The Young Ireland Movement*. Dublin: Gill and Macmillan, 1987.

Dicey, A. V. *A Leap in the Dark*. London: John Murray, 1893.

———. *Lectures Introductory to the Study of the Law of the Constitution*. London: Macmillan, 1885.

Dooney, Sean, and John O'Toole. *Irish Government Today*. Dublin: Gill and Macmillan, 1992.

Doyle, David Noel. *Ireland, Irishmen and Revolutionary America*. Dublin: Mercier, 1981.

Dunleavy, Janet Egleson, and Gareth Dunleavy. *Douglas Hyde: A Maker of Modern Ireland*. Berkeley and Los Angeles: University of California Press, 1991.

Elliott, Marianne. *Wolfe Tone: Prophet of Independence*. New Haven, Conn.: Yale University Press, 1989.

Fair, John. *British Interparty Conferences: A Study of the Procedure of Conciliation in British Politics, 1867–1921*. Oxford: Clarendon Press, 1980.

Fanning, Ronan. *"The Four Leaved Shamrock": Electoral Politics and the National Imagination in Independent Ireland*. The 25th O'Donnell Lecture. Dublin: National University of Ireland, 1983.

———. *Independent Ireland*. Dublin: Helicon, 1983.

———. *The Irish Department of Finance, 1922–1958*. Dublin: Institute of Public Administration, 1978.

Farrell, Brian. *Chairman or Chief? The Role of the Taoiseach in Irish Government*. Dublin: Gill and Macmillan, 1971.

———, ed. *De Valera's Constitution and Ours*. Dublin: Gill and Macmillan, 1988.

———. *The Founding of Dáil Éireann*. Dublin: Gill and Macmillan, 1971.

———, ed. *The Irish Parliamentary Tradition*. Dublin: Gill and Macmillan, 1973.

———. *Seán Lemass*. Dublin: Gill and Macmillan, 1983.

Farrell, Michael. *The Orange State.* 2d ed. London: Pluto, 1980.

Figgis, Darrell. *The Irish Constitution.* Dublin: Mellifont Press, 1922.

FitzGerald, Garret. *All in a Life: Garret FitzGerald, An Autobiography.* Dublin: Gill and Macmillan, 1991.

Fitzpatrick, W. J., ed. *Correspondence of Daniel O'Connell.* 2 vols. London: John Murray, 1988.

Foster, R. F. *Modern Ireland, 1600–1972.* London: Allen Lane/Penguin, 1988.

Gailey, Andrew. *Ireland and the Death of Kindness: The Experience of Constructive Unionism, 1890–1905.* Cork: Cork University Press, 1987.

Gallagher, Michael. *Political Parties in the Republic of Ireland.* Manchester, England: Manchester University Press, 1985.

Gallagher, Michael, and Richard Sinnott. *How Ireland Voted, 1989.* Galway: Center for the Study of Irish Elections, University College, Galway, 1990.

Gallagher, Tom, and James O'Connell, eds. *Contemporary Irish Studies.* Manchester, England: Manchester University Press, 1983.

Garvin, J. L. *The Life of Joseph Chamberlain.* London: Macmillan, 1932.

Garvin, Thomas. *The Evolution of Irish Nationalist Politics.* Dublin: Gill and Macmillan, 1981.

———. *The Irish Senate.* Dublin: Institute of Public Administration, 1969.

Gwynn, Denis R. *The Irish Free State, 1922–1927.* London: Macmillan, 1928.

———. *The Life of John Redmond.* London: G. Harrap, 1932.

Gwynn, Stephen. *Henry Grattan and His Times.* Westport, Conn.: Greenwood Press, 1971. (Originally published in 1939.)

Hachey, Thomas E. *Britain and Irish Separatism: From the Fenians to the Free State, 1867–1922.* Chicago: Rand McNally, 1977.

Hachey, Thomas E., and Lawrence J. McCaffrey, eds. *Perspectives on Irish Nationalism.* Lexington: University Press of Kentucky, 1989.

Hadfield, Brigid. *The Constitution of Northern Ireland.* Belfast: SLS Legal Publications, 1989.

Hammond, J. C. *Gladstone and the Irish Nation.* London: Frank Cass, 1964. (Originally published in 1938.)

Harkness, D. H. *The Restless Dominion: The Irish Free State and the British Commonwealth of Nations, 1921–31.* New York: New York University Press, 1970.

Harlow, Vincent T. *The Founding of the Second British Empire, 1763–1793.* 2 vols. London: Longmans, 1952.

Hoppen, K. Theodore. *Elections, Politics, and Society in Ireland, 1832–1885.* Oxford: Clarendon Press, 1984.

Jackson, Alvin. *The Ulster Party: Irish Unionism in the House of Commons, 1884–1911.* Oxford: Clarendon Press, 1989.

Jalland, Patricia. *The Liberals and Ireland: The Ulster Question in British Politics to 1914.* New York: St. Martin's Press, 1980.

Jenkins, Brian. *Era of Emancipation: British Government of Ireland, 1812–1830.* Montreal: McGill-Queen's University Press, 1988.

Jenkins, Roy. *Asquith.* New York: Chilmark, 1964.

Johnston, Edith. *Great Britain and Ireland, 1760–1800.* London: Oliver and Boyd, 1963.

———. *Ireland in the Eighteenth Century.* Dublin: Gill and Macmillan, 1974.

Kee, Robert. *The Green Flag.* New York: Delacorte, 1972.

Keith, Arthur Berriedale. *The Dominions as Sovereign States*. London: Macmillan, 1938.

———, ed. *Letters on Imperial Relations and International Law, 1916–1931*. London: Oxford University Press, 1935.

———, ed. *Speeches and Documents on the British Dominions, 1918–1931*. London: Oxford University Press, 1932.

Kendle, John. *Ireland and the Federal Solution: The Debates over the United Kingdom Constitution, 1870–1921*. Montreal: McGill-Queen's University Press, 1989.

Kohn, Leo. *The Constitution of the Irish Free State*. London: Allen and Unwin, 1932.

Larabee, Leonard W. *Royal Government in America: A Study of the British Colonial System before 1783*. New Haven, Conn.: Yale University Press, 1930.

Lawrence, R. J. *The Government of Northern Ireland: Public Finance and Public Services, 1921–1964*. Oxford: Clarendon Press, 1965.

Lecky, W. E. H. *A History of Ireland in the Eighteenth Century*. Abridged by L. P. Curtis, Jr. Chicago: University of Chicago Press, 1972.

Lee, J. J. *Ireland: 1912–1985*. Cambridge: Cambridge University Press, 1989.

Lefevre, G. Shaw. *Peel and O'Connell*. London: Kegan Paul, Trench, 1887.

Lijphart, Arendt. *Democracy in Plural Societies*. New Haven, Conn.: Yale University Press, 1977.

Litton, Frank, ed. *The Constitution of Ireland, 1937–1987*. Dublin: Institute of Public Administration, 1988.

Longford, Earl of, and Thomas P. O'Neill. *Eamon de Valera*. London: Hutchinson, 1970.

Loughlin, James. *Gladstone, Home Rule, and the Ulster Question, 1882–93*. Atlantic Highlands, N.J.: Humanities Press International, 1987.

Lyons, F. S. L. *Charles Stewart Parnell*. London: Collins, 1977.

———. *Ireland since the Famine*. London: Weidenfeld and Nicolson, 1971.

McBride, Lawrence W. *The Greening of Dublin Castle*. Washington, D.C.: The Catholic University of America Press, 1991.

McCaffrey, Lawrence J. *Daniel O'Connell and the Repeal Year*. Lexington: University Press of Kentucky, 1966.

———. *Irish Federation in the 1870s: A Study in Conservative Nationalism*. Philadelphia: American Philosophical Society, 1962.

McCardle, Dorothy. *The Irish Republic*. New York: Farrar, Straus and Giroux, 1965. (Originally published in 1937.)

McColgan, John. *British Policy and the Irish Administration, 1920–22*. London: George Allen and Unwin, 1983.

McCracken, J. L. *Representative Government in Ireland: A Study of Dáil Éireann, 1919–1948*. London: Oxford University Press, 1958.

Macdonagh, Michael. *The Life of Daniel O'Connell*. London: Cassell, 1903.

MacDonagh, Oliver. *The Emancipist: Daniel O'Connell, 1830–1847*. London: Weidenfeld and Nicolson, 1989.

———. *Ireland*. Englewood Cliffs, N.J.: Prentice-Hall, 1968.

McDowell, R. B. *Ireland in the Age of Imperialism and Revolution, 1760–1801*. Oxford: Clarendon Press, 1979.

———. *The Irish Administration, 1801–1914*. London: Routledge and Kegan Paul, 1964.

———. *The Irish Convention, 1917–1918.* London: Routledge and Kegan Paul, 1970.

———. *Irish Public Opinion, 1750–1800.* London: Faber and Faber, 1964.

McGarry, John, and Brendan O'Leary, eds. *The Future of Northern Ireland.* Oxford: Clarendon Press, 1990.

Macintyre, Angus. *The Liberator: Daniel O'Connell and the Irish Party, 1830–1847.* London: Hamish Hamilton, 1965.

McKenzie, Robert. *British Political Parties.* London: Mercury, 1964.

Mackintosh, John. *The British Cabinet.* 2d ed. London: Methuen, 1968.

McMahon, Deirdre. *Republicans and Imperialists: Anglo-Irish Relations in the 1930s.* New Haven, Conn.: Yale University Press, 1984.

MacNeill, J. G. Swift. *Studies in the Constitution of the Irish Free State.* Dublin: Talbot, 1925.

Magnus, Philip. *Gladstone.* London: John Murray, 1954.

Malcomson, A. P. W. *John Foster: The Politics of the Anglo-Irish Ascendancy.* Oxford: Oxford University Press, 1978.

Manning, Maurice. *Irish Political Parties: An Introduction.* Dublin: Gill and Macmillan, 1972.

Mansergh, Nicholas. *The Commonwealth Experience.* 2 vols., 2d ed. London: Macmillan, 1932.

———. *The Irish Question, 1841–1921.* 3d ed. London: George Allen and Unwin, 1975.

———. *The Unresolved Question: The Anglo-Irish Settlement and Its Undoing, 1912–1972.* New Haven, Conn.: Yale University Press, 1991.

Marsh, Michael, and Richard Sinnott, eds. *How Ireland Voted, 1989.* Galway: Centre for the Study of Irish Elections, 1990.

Martin, F. X., ed. *Leaders and Men of the Easter Rising: Dublin 1916.* Ithaca, N.Y.: Cornell University Press, 1967.

Moody, T. W., ed. *Nationality and the Pursuit of National Independence.* Belfast: Appletree Press, 1978.

Morgan, David Gwynn. *Constitutional Law of Ireland.* 2d ed. Blackrock, County Dublin: Round Hall, 1990.

Moss, Warner. *Political Parties in the Irish Free State.* New York: Columbia University Press, 1933.

Moynihan, Maurice, ed. *Speeches and Statements by Eamon de Valera, 1919–1973.* Dublin: Gill and Macmillan, 1980.

Munger, Frank. *The Legitimacy of Opposition: The Change of Government in Ireland in 1932.* Beverly Hills, Calif.: Sage, 1975.

Murphy, John A. *Ireland in the Twentieth Century.* Dublin: Gill and Macmillan, 1975.

Nicolson, Harold. *King George V: His Life and Reign.* New York: Doubleday, 1953.

Nowlan, Kevin. *The Politics of Repeal: A Study in the Relations between Great Britain and Ireland, 1841–1850.* London: Routledge and Kegan Paul, 1965.

Nowlan, Kevin, and Maurice R. O'Connell, eds. *Daniel O'Connell: Portrait of a Radical.* Dublin: Appletree, 1984.

O'Brien, Conor Cruise. *States of Ireland.* New York: Pantheon, 1972.

O'Brien, Gerard. *Anglo-Irish Politics in the Age of Grattan and Pitt.* Dublin: Irish Academic Press, 1987.

O'Connell, Maurice R., ed. *The Correspondence of Daniel O'Connell.* 8 vols. Dublin: Blackwater, 1972–74.

———. *Irish Politics and Social Conflict in the Age of the American Revolution.* Philadelphia: University of Pennsylvania Press, 1965.

O'Day, Alan. *Parnell and the First Home Rule Episode.* Dublin: Gill and Macmillan, 1986.

O'Ferrall, Fergus. *Catholic Emancipation: Daniel O'Connell and the Birth of Irish Democracy, 1820–1830.* Dublin: Gill and Macmillan, 1985.

O'Halpin, Eunan. *The Decline of the Union: British Government in Ireland, 1892–1920.* Syracuse, N.Y.: Syracuse University Press, 1987.

O'Neill, Terence. *Ulster at the Crossroads.* London: Faber and Faber, 1969.

O'Sullivan, Donal. *The Irish Free State and Its Senate.* London: Faber and Faber, 1940.

Porter, J. G. V. *Ireland.* London: Ridgeway, 1844.

Prager, Jeffrey. *Building Democracy in Ireland: Political Order and Cultural Integration in a Newly Independent Nation.* Cambridge: Cambridge University Press, 1986.

Precursor Association. *Five Reports of the Committee of the Precursor Association.* Dublin: Richard Grace, 1839.

Punnett, R. M. *British Government and Politics.* 5th ed. Waveland Heights, Ill.: Waveland, 1988.

Quekett, Sir Arthur. *The Constitution of Northern Ireland.* 3 vols. Belfast: His Majesty's Stationery Office, 1928, 1933, 1946.

Rumpf, E., and A. C. Hepburn. *Nationalism and Socialism in Twentieth Century Ireland.* Liverpool, England: Liverpool University Press, 1977.

Sexton, Brendan. *Ireland and the Crown, 1922–1936.* Dublin: Irish Academic Press, 1989.

Shannon, Catherine. *Arthur J. Balfour and Ireland, 1874–1922.* Washington, D.C.: The Catholic University of America Press, 1988.

Sharkansky, Ira. *Wither the State? Politics and Public Enterprise in Three Countries.* Chatham, N.J.: Chatham House, 1979.

Shipkey, Robert Carl. *Robert Peel's Irish Policy, 1812–1846.* New York: Garland, 1987.

Smith, Raymond. *Garrett the Enigma: Dr. Garrett FitzGerald.* Dublin: Aherlow, 1985.

Smyth, John. *The Houses of the Oireachtas.* 3d ed. Dublin: Institute of Public Administration, 1973.

Thornley, David. *Isaac Butt and Home Rule.* London: Macgibbon and Kee, 1964.

Trench, Charles Chevenix. *The Great Dan: A Biography of Daniel O'Connell.* London: Jonathan Cape, 1984.

Valiulis, Maryann Gialanella. *Portrait of a Revolutionary: General Richard Mulcahy and the Founding of the Irish Free State.* Lexington: University Press of Kentucky, 1992.

Vincent, John. *Gladstone and Ireland.* London: British Academy/Oxford University Press, 1977.

Wade, E. C. S., and G. Godfrey Phillips. *Constitutional and Administrative Law.* 9th ed. London: Longman, 1977.

Wallace, Martin. *Northern Ireland: Fifty Years of Self-Government.* New York: Barnes and Noble, 1971.

Ward, Alan J. *The Easter Rising: Revolution and Irish Nationalism*. Arlington Heights, Ill.: Harlan Davidson, 1980.

———. *Ireland and Anglo-American Relations: 1899–1921*. London: Weidenfeld and Nicolson/London School of Economics, 1969.

Ward, John Manning. *Colonial Self-Government: The British Experience, 1759–1856*. London: Macmillan, 1976.

Whyte, John. *The Independent Irish Party*. London: Oxford University Press, 1958.

## Dissertation

MacMillan, Mary. "Legislative Authority, Sovereignty, Legitimacy and Political Development: The Constitutional Basis of the Irish Free State." Ph.D. diss., University College, Dublin, 1986.

## Articles

Akenson, D. H., and J. F. Fallin. "The Irish Civil War and the Drafting of the Irish Free State Constitution." *Éire-Ireland* 5, no. 1 (1970): 10–26; 5, no. 2 (1970): 42–93; 5, no. 4 (1970): 28–70.

Arkins, Audrey M. "The Committees of the 24th Oireachtas." *Irish Political Studies* 3 (1988): 91–97.

———. "Legislative and Executive Relations in the Republic of Ireland." *West European Politics* 13 (1990): 90–102.

Coakley, John. "Constituency Boundary Revision and Seat Re-Distribution in the Irish Parliamentary Tradition." *Administration* 28, no. 3 (1980): 291–328.

Colgan, John. "Local Elections: Behind the Results." *Administration* 39, no. 4 (1992): 370–75.

de Buitleir, Donal. "Local Finance in Ireland—The Options." *Administration* 39, no. 4 (1992): 295–309.

Desmond, Barry. "The Houses of the Oireachtas—A Plea for Reform." *Administration* 23 (1975): 423–44.

Dunne, John. "The Politics of Institutional Reform in Ireland: Lessons of the 1982–87 Government." *Irish Political Studies* 4 (1989): 1–20.

Farrell, Brian. "The Drafting of the Irish Free State Constitution." *Irish Jurist*, n.s., 5, pt. 1 (1970): 115–40; n.s., 5, pt. 2 (1970): 343–56; n.s., 6, pt. 1 (1971): 111–35; n.s., 6, pt. 2 (1971): 345–59.

———. "The Legislation of a 'Revolutionary' Assembly: Dáil Decrees, 1919–1922." *Irish Jurist*, n.s., 10 (1975): 112–27.

Fay, Patrick. "The Amendments to the Constitution Committee, 1926." *Administration* 26, no. 3 (1978): 331–51.

Gallagher, Michael. "Does Ireland Need a New Electoral System?" *Irish Political Studies* 2 (1987): 27–48.

———. "The Presidency of the Republic of Ireland: Implications of the Donegan Affair." *Parliamentary Affairs* 30, no. 1 (Winter 1977): 373–84.

Howard, C. H. D., ed. "Documents Relating to the Irish 'Central Board' Scheme, 1884–1885." *Irish Historical Studies* 8 (1952–53): 237–63.

———. "Joseph Chamberlain, Parnell and the Irish 'Central Board' Scheme, 1884–1885." *Irish Historical Studies* 8 (1952–53): 324–61.

Humphreys, Richard F. "Legislative Obstruction: How to Do It." *Administration* 39, no. 1 (1991): 55–70.

Jalland, Patricia. "Irish Home Rule Finance: A Neglected Dimension of the Irish Question." *Irish Historical Studies* 23, no. 91 (1983): 233–53.

Kelly, Valerie. "Focus on Clients: A Reappraisal of the Effectiveness of TDs Interventions." *Administration* 35 (1987): 130–51.

Kennedy, Brian. "John Hearne and the Irish Constitution." *Éire-Ireland* 25, no. 2 (Summer 1989): 121–27.

Kennedy, David. "Privatisation—An Irish Solution?" *Administration* 39, no. 3 (1991): 199–209.

Kennedy, Denis. "The Irish Whigs and the Regency Crisis in Ireland, 1788–1789." *Éire-Ireland* 18, no. 3 (Fall 1983): 54–70.

Komito, Lee. "Voters, Politicians and Clientalism: A Dublin Survey." *Administration* 37, no. 2 (1989): 171–91.

Lyne, Thomas. "The Progressive Democrats, 1985–87." *Irish Political Studies* 2 (1987): 107–14.

Maguire, Paul. "Parliament and the Direct Rule of Northern Ireland." *Irish Jurist*, n.s., 10 (1975): 81–92.

Malone, Andrew E. "Party Government in the Irish Free State." *Political Science Quarterly* 44, no. 3 (1929): 363–78.

O'Brien, John. "Ireland's Departure from the Commonwealth." *Round Table* 306 (1988): 179–94.

O'Halpin, Eunan. "The Civil Service and the Political System." *Administration* 38, no. 4 (1991): 283–302.

O'Hanlon, Roderick. "A Constitution for a Free People." *Administration* 15, no. 2 (1967): 85–101.

Oliver, John A. "The Stormont Administration, 1921–72." *Contemporary Record* 5, no. 1 (1991): 71–104.

Rohan, Michael. "University Representation, 1918–1938." *Administration* 29, no. 3 (1981–82): 260–85.

Smyth, Peter. "The Northern Ireland Assembly: A New Exposition of Democracy." *Administration* 36 (1989): 91–126.

Ward, Alan J. "Challenging the British Constitution: The Irish Free State and the External Minister." *Parliamentary History* 9, pt. 1 (1990): 116–28.

———. "Exporting the British Constitution: Responsible Government in New Zealand, Canada, Australia and Ireland." *Journal of Commonwealth and Comparative Politics* 25, no. 1 (1987): 3–25.

———. "Frewen's Anglo-American Campaign for Federalism." *Irish Historical Studies* 15, no. 59 (1967): 256–75.

———. "The Irish Constitution and the Political Crisis of 1989." *Parliamentary Affairs* 43, no. 3 (1990): 366–79.

———. "Lloyd George and the 1918 Irish Conscription Crisis." *Historical Journal* 17, pt. 1 (1974): 107–29.

———. "Models of Government and Anglo-Irish Relations." *Albion* 20, no. 1 (Spring 1988): 19–42.

———. "Parliamentary Procedures and the Machinery of Government in Ireland." *Irish University Review* 4 (1974): 222–43.

Ward, John Manning. "The Responsible Government Question in Victoria, South

Australia and Tasmania, 1861–1856." *Journal of the Royal Australian Historical Society* 63, pt. 4 (1978): 221–47.

Wilford, Rick. "The 1992 Westminster Election in Northern Ireland." *Irish Political Studies* 7 (1992): 105–10.

Zimmerman, Joseph F. "The Office of Ombudsman in Ireland." *Administration* 37, no. 3 (1989): 258–72.

———. "An Oireachtas Innovation: Backbench Committees." *Administration* 36, no. 3 (1988): 265–87.

## *Manuscripts*

Blythe, Ernest. Papers. University College, Dublin.

de Valera, Eamon. Papers. Franciscan Archives, Killiney, County Dublin.

Duffy, George Gavan. Papers. National Library, Dublin.

Gladstone, William Ewart. Papers. British Library, London.

Kennedy, Hugh. Papers. University College, Dublin.

Parnell, Charles Stewart. Papers. National Library, Dublin.

British Cabinet Papers, 1919–22. Public Records Office, London.

Miscellaneous Irish State Papers, 1922–45. National Archives, Dublin.

# Index

*The Irish Constitutional Tradition: Responsible Government and Modern Ireland, 1782–1992* was composed in 10/13 Sabon by World Composition Services, Inc., Sterling, Virginia; printed on 60-pound Glatfelter Supple Opaque Recycled paper and bound by Thomson-Shore, Inc., Dexter, Michigan; and designed and produced by Kachergis Book Design, Pittsboro, North Carolina.